Seafood Supply Chains

This book provides a historical and analytical account of changes in the seafood supply chain in Britain from the mid-twentieth century to the present, looking at the impact of various types of governance.

The governance of marine fisheries has been a contested issue for decades with increasing anxieties about overfishing. In tandem, the rise of aquaculture, fish and shellfish farming, has driven another set of environmental concerns. In the food system, there have been scandals about safety failures and about fraud. At the same time, governments issue advice urging people to eat fish for its health benefits. In the context of these problems and contradictions, how have governments, the food industry and ordinary consumers responded? The author shows how different types of governance and regulation have been used to seek seafood sustainability and food safety and to communicate nutritional messages to the public and with what effects. The book also presents a new model for understanding food chains which combines governance and power approaches with an emphasis on understanding the interests served and the resulting balance of public and private benefits. This shows that the role of state regulation should have greater emphasis in governance and agri-food analysis and that theories about supply chain functioning, including the part played by major retailers and civil society, should be modified by a more nuanced understanding of the role of standards and certification systems.

Although much of the focus is on the UK and Europe, this book provides key lessons internationally for the governance of seafood and other agri-food supply chains. The book will be of interest to students of food policy and those working in the seafood industry or studying for connected qualifications, and more widely to readers with an interest in seafood issues and problems.

Miriam Greenwood has held a number of research and senior management posts in the National Health Service (UK). She has an MSc in the Sociology of Health and Sickness from South Bank University, UK, and a PhD in Food Policy from City, University of London, UK.

Routledge Studies in Food, Society and the Environment

For further details please visit the series page on the Routledge website: www.routledge.com/books/series/RSFSE/

Seafood Supply Chains
Governance, Power and Regulation

Miriam Greenwood

LONDON AND NEW YORK

First published 2019
by Routledge
2 Park Square, Milton Park, Abingdon, Oxon OX14 4RN

and by Routledge
52 Vanderbilt Avenue, New York, NY 10017

First issued in paperback 2020

Routledge is an imprint of the Taylor & Francis Group, an informa business

British Library Cataloguing-in-Publication Data
A catalogue record for this book is available from the British Library

Library of Congress Cataloging-in-Publication Data
Names: Greenwood, Miriam, author.
Title: Seafood supply chains : governance, power and regulation /
Miriam Greenwood.
Description: New York, NY : Routledge, 2019. | Includes
bibliographical references and index.
Identifiers: LCCN 2018045799 | ISBN 9781138063167 (hardback)
Subjects: LCSH: Seafood industry–Government policy–Great Britain. |
Fisheries–Government policy–Great Britain. | Business logistics.
Classification: LCC HD9461.6 .G74 2019 | DDC 338.3/720941–dc23
LC record available at https://lccn.loc.gov/2018045799

ISBN 13: 978-0-367-66217-2 (pbk)
ISBN 13: 978-1-138-06316-7 (hbk)

Typeset in Bembo
by Wearset Ltd, Boldon, Tyne and Wear

Contents

Figures

Tables

Preface and acknowledgements

There are so many special things about seafood, fish, which have drawn me to research the subject over the last 16 years: the astounding growth of aquaculture all around the world, dramatic changes affecting fisheries – near-disasters of overfishing but also recoveries – the variety of what is available, its health benefits. There also the questions about the food system as a whole – what are the systems and institutions that make it possible for us to have safe food? Who runs it and how much does the public benefit? Can we rely on them to ensure sustainable supplies of safe and healthy seafood into the future? These are some of the questions I have tried to address in this book.

In doing the research for it, I have been lucky to have met so many people in the industry who are passionate as well as knowledgeable about seafood and who have shared with me their deep and sometimes idiosyncratic thoughts and given me so many insights. I am also very thankful for the resources of the organisation Seafish and the help of individuals working in it with so many of my queries.

I am been very fortunate in having had the research support of two exceptional supervisors, Professor David Barling and Professor Tim Lang, who have made it possible for me to develop some initially inchoate ideas into a fully developed work.

Finally to the person who has most kept me going with his unstinted support, my partner George Barratt – immense appreciation and gratitude.

Acronyms

ASC	Aquaculture Stewardship Council
BRC	British Retail Consortium
BSE	Bovine Spongiform Encephalopathy
CCRF	Code of Conduct for Responsible Fisheries
Cefas	Centre for Environment, Fisheries and Aquaculture Science
CFP	Common Fisheries Policy
CIWF	Compassion in World Farming
CoGPSFA	Code of Good Practice for Scottish Finfish Aquaculture
COMA	Committee on Medical Aspects of Food Policy/ Committee on the Medical Aspects of Food and Nutrition Policy
COT	Committee on Toxicity
DAERA	Department of Agriculture, Environment and Rural Affairs (Northern Ireland)
DEFRA (Defra)	Department for Environment, Food and Rural Affairs (UK)
EC	European Communities *or* European Commission
ECPAFP	European Convention for the Protection of Animals Kept for Farming Purposes
E. coli	*Escherichia Coli* O157
EEC	European Economic Community
EEZ	Exclusive Economic Zone
EFF	European Fisheries Fund
EFSA	European Food Safety Authority
EHO	Environmental Health Officer
EJF	Environmental Justice Foundation
EMFF	European Maritime and Fisheries Fund
EU	European Union
EUMOFA	EU Market Observatory for Fishery & Aquaculture Products
EUREPGAP	Euro Retailer Group for Good Agricultural Practices

FAD	Fish aggregating device – objects used to attract certain species including tuna.
FAO	Food and Agriculture Organisation of the United Nations
FAWC	Farm Animal Welfare Council *or* Farm Animal Welfare Committee
FIFG	Financial Instrument for Fisheries Guidance
FIFO	Fish In:Fish Out (feed conversion ratio)
FQA	Fixed Quota Allocation
FSA	Food Standards Agency
FSS	Food Standards Scotland
FTE	Full-Time Equivalent
GAA	Global Aquaculture Alliance
GAP	Good Agricultural Practice
GCC	Global Commodity Chain
GDA	Guideline Daily Amount
GG/GLOBALG.A.P.	Global Good Agricultural Practices
GPN	Global Production Network
GSI	Global Salmon Initiative
GVC	Global Value Chain
HACCP	Hazard Analysis of Critical Control Points
HMRC	Her Majesty's Revenue and Customs
ICES	International Council for the Exploration of the Sea
IFCA	Inshore Fisheries and Conservation Authorities
IFG	Inshore Fisheries Group
ISO	International Organisation for Standardisation
ITQ	Individual Transferable Quota
IUU	Illegal, Unreported and Unregulated (fishing)
IVMS	Inshore Vessel Monitoring System
MAFF	Ministry of Agriculture, Fisheries and Food
MAP	Modified Atmosphere Packaging
MCS	Marine Conservation Society
MCZ	Marine Conservation Zone
MMO	Marine Management Organisation
MPA	Marine Protected Area
MSC	Marine Stewardship Council
MSY	Maximum Sustainable Yield
NACNE	National Advisory Committee on Nutrition Education
NFFF	National Federation of Fish Friers
NFFO	National Federation of Fishermen's Organisations
NGO	Non-Governmental Organisation
NPM	New Public Management
NUFTA	New Under Ten Fishermen's Association
OIE	Office International des Epizooties (World Organisation for Animal Health)

PHE	Public Health England
PO	Producers' Organisation
QIM	Quality Index Method
RAC	Regional Advisory Council
RFMO	Regional Fishery Management Organisation
RFS	Responsible Fishing Scheme
RIFG	Regional Inshore Fisheries Group
RO	Regulating Order
ROF	Regulating our Futures (FSA strategy)
RSPCA	Royal Society for the Prevention of Cruelty to Animals
RUMA	Responsible Use of Medicines in Agriculture Alliance
SACN	Scientific Advisory Committee on Nutrition
SAGB	Shellfish Association of Great Britain
SALSA	Safe and Local Supplier Approval
Seafish	Sea Fish Industry Authority
SFF	Scottish Fishermen's Federation
SFP	Sustainable Fisheries Partnership
SI	Statutory Instrument
SME	Small & Medium-Sized Enterprises
SRA	Sustainable Restaurant Association
SR(NI)	Statutory Rule, Northern Ireland
SSC	Sustainable Seafood Coalition
SSGO	Scottish Salmon Growers Association
SSI	Scottish Statutory Instrument
SSPO	Scottish Salmon Producers' Organisation
STECF	Scientific, Technical and Economic Committee for Fisheries
TAC	Total Allowable Catch (quota)
TCE	Transaction Cost Economics
UNCLOS	United Nations Convention on the Law of the Sea
VHP	Veterinary Health Plan
WFA	White Fish Authority
WHO	World Health Organisation
WTO	World Trade Organisation
WWF	World Wide Fund for Nature

Foreword

Tim Lang

It is surprising, given that the planet is largely sea, how little attention has been given by academics to how societies manage and mismanage the seas. What! I hear you say. Does he not know that there have been agreements on sea borders for decades? Of course. But these emerged in the nineteenth century to resolve conflicts over offshore and fishing ground ownership after centuries of ad hoc treaties and use of naval and imperial power. This step towards a semblance of rational sea management was part of that great awakening in the West that some problems cross borders – disease, for example – and that naked power is not the only or best way to manage matters of mutual interest and potential conflict.

In West Europe, for instance, the North Seas Convention was signed in 1888 setting shore rights at three miles. And, after two dreadful world wars, in the new spirit of international co-operation, this was revised in 1963 at the London Convention pushing it out to 12 miles, among other conclusions. It was the UK which triggered this revision process by denouncing the 1888 convention to which it had been a party. The resulting London Convention, as is known, transmogrified into the European Union's Common Fisheries Policy (CFP), a slow, crabby policy framework, if ever there was. And then, just when the CFP was at last beginning to address some fundamental problems such as over-fishing, crazy quotas and market distortion, in 2016 the UK again denounced what it had been party to by stating it would leave both the CFP *and* the predecessor London Convention. The UK was once more denouncing what it had helped set up! This was not so much in a fit of rational politics or desire for sustainability governance but more as expression of the nationalistic (and even imperial) politics which had re-emerged the name of leaving the EU, the so-called Brexit process.

A kind of 'territorial' sea governance is thus both old and evolving, which needs cool analysis and evaluation, such as is provided in this book. To be fair, marine scientists have done great work in gently but persistently delivering data on the state of the seas. Yet we have lacked the exploration of the intricate governance of the kind which this book explores. So I welcome this thoughtful and detailed book. It is not a global overview but a pioneering and fascinating policy analysis of one country's seafood governance. As such it both contributes to and builds on the new thinking about governance, a word which crept into academic and policy-makers' discourse in recent years.

This term governance in the book's title has emerged for good reason. It indicates not just what decision-makers do but how and why. It has crept into daily policy use partly in recognition of the fact that governments are no longer the sole or main source of government. Numerous studies of the food system, for example, have shown how the nation state's control (and potential to control) over food has been tamed or narrowed, even as there are pressures for it to expand its remit. Late twentieth century neoliberalism and the Washington Consensus made virtues of rolling back the state, even as grounds for action grew on matters such as climate, pollution, ecosystems and health. As a result, while states became reluctant to act, other forms of governance took their place. Commercial and even civil society governance became more apparent.

For years, lone voices arguing that seafood policy was in need of overhaul were fobbed off. It's too complex. Too many interests. Not high enough public profile. And then celebrity chefs or TV programmes could run high profile TV campaigns and suddenly previously resistant power blocs changed: ridiculous fish discard policies were revised; retailers fell over themselves to assure consumers they only used 'sustainably sourced' fish; and most recently, moral panics about profligate plastics pollution swept the globe. Not before time, it should be noted; the so-called efficient modern food system is entirely reliant on plastics. Cutting plastic bags is symbolically good but peripheral when set against the normality of only 14% being recycled, 40% ending in landfill and the rest dumped in ecosystems, much ending in the seas.

By the early twenty-first century, we thus could see everywhere parallel and often inadequate systems of governance operating in the same policy space: state, commerce and civil society – sometimes in combination, as happened when Unilever (then a big fish oil company) spawned the Marine Stewardship Council as an arms-length governance mechanism. It's this kind of new framework governance that Dr Greenwood's book explores. Her book studies the UK, one small but rich country off the continent of Europe but one with a particularly complex history of the seas, marine power and sealife. We need more such studies, and urgently, as the annual reports on the state of the seas from bodies such as the UN's Food and Agriculture Organisation or conservation bodies such as WWF constantly remind us.

That fish and seafood are hugely important economically, nutritionally and environmentally is well known. Some developing countries are far more dependent on seafood for protein and livelihoods than the UK. Indeed, fishing is tiny within the UK's food economy. In 2018 it employed only 9,000 people working in 3,932 enterprises (i.e. tiny firms) and yielded only £0.788 billion in gross value-added (GVA) out of the food economy's total of over £120 billion GVA. But symbolically, fishing matters in UK policy discourse. It has great emotive power. British people are conscious of being an island nation. Tiny it may be but fishing was a disproportional feature in Britain's anxieties about membership of the European Union.

Global pressures are impinging on old forms of sea governance. That is clear. But what to do about them? Consumer pressures in rich societies continue to send giant fishing fleets into waters they historically rarely entered once the previous imperial regimes had declined. And today, climate change is altering ecosystems. Technical and engineering developments mean seafood can be vacuumed or trawled on a previously impossible scale. Pollution – chemicals, plastic – alters the delicate state of what Charles Darwin memorably called the 'web of life'. To this already messy mix is added the consistent advice from public health nutritionists to eat significant amounts of seafood. Eat two portions of fish a week, of which one should be oily, UK official advice says. Now that it tempered by 'nudging' consumers to eat only sustainable fish. But what is that? In short, seafood exhibits a bundle of policy contradictions.

'We are where we are' is a sound rule in policy analysis. Whatever direction decision-makers wish to pursue, they – and the public interest as well as the seas – will always benefit from a good understanding of realities. This book sets out fascinating insights into one country's seafood governance. I salute and welcome it for that. I also know, too, that we need more books like this, and a crescendo of articulate expression of where sane, rational seafood governance should be heading.

1 Governance and its seafood objectives

Introduction: why governance matters for seafood

We experience the food system on a day-to-day basis as predominantly economic, producing through a series of physical and economic processes and delivering to us as consumers for the most part via simple transactions in a store, a takeaway or a restaurant. But in the background, there is a whole other level of decision-making involved which is considered in this book under the heading of governance. Governance is about establishing and ensuring the standards not only of the end products that fetch up on our plates but about all of the processes which got them there. What are these rules, who decides them and most importantly who benefits from them? To what extent are they in the public interest? This book examines such questions by focusing on one type of food, fish or more generally seafood, an important constituent of our diet.

It is also particularly fascinating because with all the tremendous changes in food systems from the middle of the twentieth century into the first decades of the twenty-first nowhere has there been such an extensive transformation as in the supply chain for seafood. Added to revolutionising impacts of massive developments in food processing and storage, in logistics, retailing and foodservice shared with the rest of the food system are radical changes in its two production systems, fishing and farming, that have resulted in a thorough makeover of what seafood is presented to British consumers and how it has become available.

The rules, the governance systems examined in this book, are intended to achieve specific requirements. Three have been selected as particularly important and therefore have been taken as the focal points of the investigation. The first is nutrition, then there are the linked topics of food safety, quality and authenticity and third there is the quest for sustainability.

Seafood, a term that covers both fish and shellfish, is recognised as a vital source of protein and contributor of other nutrients. Although not the most important source of protein in the British diet, it nevertheless has a long-established place within the nation's food choices. Recent years have seen greatly increased recognition of fish as a particularly healthy food and regular consumption is urged in national nutritional guidelines. This means the need both for adequate supply to be available and for people to recognise its benefits and actually include seafood in their regular eating patterns.

Food that is safe, of high quality and authentic in the sense that what is presented is what it says on the label, is a general expectation but cannot be taken for granted as successive food scandals have shown. A series of problems over the late 1980s and into the 1990s, most notably over Bovine Spongiform Encephalopathy (BSE), broke the trust of the public and while they led to important reforms for better food safety, recent problems such as the horsemeat debacle of 2013 and the contaminated eggs recall of 2017 illustrate the continuation of significant risks in the food system. Seafood too has had problems of food safety and food authenticity which remain important issues for its supply chain.

The third of the three big requirements is about the need to produce seafood sustainably. Longstanding problems of overfishing and relatively new but complex issues round aquaculture, beg questions about how supplies of seafood can be secured on an ongoing basis without irreparable environmental damage.

In order to consider how governance rules do or do not successfully address these three major issues, nutrition plus consumption, food safety and quality and achieving sustainable supply, it is necessary to understand where power lies in relation to the food system. While there are broad structural changes in play, local and historical factors are equally relevant to how specific systems develop so this enquiry concentrates on how governance rules deriving from particular sources of power have affected the seafood supply chain in one country, Britain, and over a specific period from the mid-twentieth century into the first two decades of the twenty-first.

There are two main sources of governance in relation to the food system: one is the state and its connected agencies, the other consists of larger companies in the private sector occupying certain positions which allow them to exercise some control within supply chains. A third potential source is civil society, particularly in the form of NGOs (non-governmental organisations), certain of which have become influential in recent years. The state in a democracy is expected to act in the public interest; whether it does so can be judged in relation to particular issues. NGOs too base their claim to support on the grounds that they are acting in the public interest including such broad concerns as environmental conservation and human rights. Private food businesses as well as narrower commercial objectives are fulfilling fundamentally important public needs and may (or may not) also seek to do so in a way that is consistent with broader principles.

Power can take many forms ranging from absolute control, through varying types of dominance, to modulated forms of influence. Power means access to resources and, particularly for states, ability to control institutions. Other actors such as pressure groups have much less access to resources but can still deploy other forms of influence. In whatever sphere, it is of course individuals within them who make decisions and choose whether or how to exercise power at their disposal, so the way power is used cannot be pre-determined and is open to change.

As there are two main sources of power in relation to the food system, the state and certain food companies, two matching streams of theory are used as guides for making sense of the particular part of the food system being investigated. The former aims to explain how the exercise of power in states has been changing and why, the latter how the food system has been changing and how power has been exercised within it. Conversely, the seafood story can be a test of their validity.

Before discussing this theory, it is necessary to clarify what is meant by governance and how the concept is used in various fields of enquiry. Governance is a concept that has been employed and elaborated in a variety of ways and many different sub-types have been identified including global governance, intra-company corporate governance, participatory governance and good governance in the public sector (Mayntz 2003; Pattberg 2007; Van Kersbergen & Van Waarden 2004). Broadly, in political science writings, it signifies a less hierarchical form of state government, with a focus on sharing and devolution of power mechanisms which may be contrasted with the related concept of regulation as in: 'The shaping of the conduct of others through network forms of organization involving a wide range of non-state actors but also government, mainly through exchange and negotiation rather than through traditional state-led regulation' (Ponte, Gibbon & Vestergaard 2011, p. 1). In economics, governance refers to supply chain co-ordination within the private sector in which control is exerted by some parties upon others as expressed in this definition: 'We use the term to express that some firms in the chain set and/or enforce the parameters under which others in the chain operate. A chain without governance would just be a string of market relations' (Humphrey & Schmitz 2001, p. 20).

It is a peculiarity that the same concept is used to indicate reduced control in relation to states but more control in commercial relations. However, both approaches to governance are relevant to understanding the seafood supply chain. Hence, in relation to the sea and fisheries, definitions have encompassed both political and economic concepts as put here: 'The term "governance" is used to refer to the framework of social and economic systems and legal and political structures through which the ocean is managed' (Allison 2001, p. 934).

Varying perspectives on the notion of governance have been employed in different disciplines and fields of investigation including political science, economics, management, marketing and development studies. The range of conceptual approaches and the aspects of the seafood chain to which they apply are summarised in Table 1.1.

In some of these analyses, 'governance' and the related term 'regulation' have been used with overlapping meanings, even interchangeably. Both relate to ways of influencing, sometimes controlling, how economic and technological systems

Table 1.1 Conceptual approaches to governance relevant to food supply chains

Public/private decision-making	Discipline/field	Theoretical focus	Main issues	Relevance to seafood
Public	Political science	Role of state	Types of governance Regulation/deregulation/re-regulation	Regulation of primary production and food safety
Private	Economics	Transaction cost economics	Information asymmetry, asset specificity Types of co-ordination including hierarchy, contracts	Relationship between firms in supply chains
	Management	Power analysis	Power-based relationships	Relationship between firms in supply chains
	Management	Supply chain management	Relationships/collaboration Power	Relationship between firms in supply chains
	Marketing	Transaction cost and organisation theory	Relationships/collaboration Power	Relationship between firms in supply chains
	Agri-food studies/ Development studies/ Geography	Commodity systems Commodity chains Global commodity chains Global value chain	Industrialisation of agriculture and food production Power Transnational corporations Industrialised/developing country relationships	Industrialisation of capture fishing Aquaculture as industrialised development Global sourcing
Private and public plus civil society with overlapping objectives	Economics Agri-food studies	Governance through standards and audit systems	Relations between public and private governance Role of civil society	Impact of public/private/civil society Relationship between firms in supply chains

Source: author.

work but in this book, regulation refers to the public realm of government action, that is legislation and related systems of rules, while governance, the broader notion, additionally covers private rule setting and various other modes of influence which may also be exercised by business and civil society actors. Thus governance as used here can also refer to public regulation but the reverse does not apply.

The role of the state and food

There has been a strong strand of analysis that argues that the role of the national state has generally weakened because of two levels of change. On one side there has been the development of the supra-state European Union (EU) and its predecessors and of global governance mechanisms. At the same time internally more functions have been delegated to other agencies and networks or regionally devolved. This was seen as involving a change from a command-and-control, hierarchical style of governing to one involving an emphasis on participation in decision-making by a wider group of social actors (Bache & Flinders 2004; Bartolini 2011; Bevir & Rhodes 2003). The process, sometimes termed 'agencification', whereby functions shift from direct political control to a large number of quasi-autonomous bodies, has been described in detail for the UK (Flinders 2008). The changes were captured in powerful metaphors: the 'hollowing-out of the state' and the state 'steering, not rowing' (Barling 2008; Rhodes 1996).

The new 'governance paradigm' did not only seek to explain, it also had normative elements as having a more participatory and democratic character which would also be more efficient. In tandem, the New Public Management (NPM) model for public governance with an emphasis on public services was definitely normative, urging an emphasis on efficiency to be achieved through market mechanisms. A further New Public Governance approach then aimed to integrate the advantage of the NPM's emphasis on service delivery and outcomes with pluralist decision-making in a complex world (Osborne 2006; Peters 2011). The NPM was philosophically related to and overlapped in time (the late 1970s onwards) with the 'public choice' (or 'rational choice') stream of thought which focused on government failures, characterising state regulation as inherently heavy-handed, reflecting special interests and inefficient (Balleisen & Moss 2010; Butler 2012).

Such views were not limited to academia but enacted in the real world where in the UK there were large-scale privatisations of once state-managed industries and services as well as other forms of delegation of government activity. Successive governments linked reform of public services to the introduction of market mechanisms and regulation became connected in much public discourse with unnecessary and oppressive bureaucracy. Sufficient time has now elapsed for the impact of NPM in practice to be assessed and the judgement has been that it has not achieved much either by improving services or reducing costs (Hood & Dixon 2015) but in some political thought anti-regulation rhetoric persists along with a belief that the role of the state should be reduced.

In parallel to the accounts of reducing states, others asserted that the state has remained the key channel for pursuing collective interests and viewed the greater sharing of power with others, sometimes called multi-level governance, as a means of strengthening its efficacy (Bell & Hindmoor 2009; Peters & Pierre 2001). Further, the need to guard a public interest in relation to essential services such as water, energy and communications, which were being privatised, led to the establishment of a series of regulators over these industries. General regulation of the private sector was also pursued by the establishment of competition authorities and via legislation over general company duties including the requirement for corporate social responsibility to be exercised. The end result has been characterised as re-regulation or the establishment of what is termed either a regulatory or post-regulatory state (Jordana & Levi-Faur 2004; Scott 2004; Yeung 2010). Some more recent academic work on governance has reasserted the centrality of the state (Capano, Howlett & Ramesh 2015). Particularly relevant for the subjects covered in this book there has been a vigorous defence of the need for regulation (Stiglitz 2010).

Against this background of varying ideas and reservations about what the role of the state is and should be, its activity in relation to food in Britain since the mid-twentieth century can be outlined. During the post-World War II period, a time when Keynesian economics and the welfare state were accepted, the key role of the state was not disputed and government action regarding food was taken for granted. Both the UK and the then European Economic Community were motivated by a productionist ethos to avoid the food shortages recently experienced in the conflict period. Incentives to promote both agriculture and fishing were introduced. Later, when these activities had become too successful and in the case of agriculture had produced some embarrassing surpluses, support was moderated and quota systems introduced in some certain areas of agriculture. Fishing quotas were also put into place but for different reasons as will be detailed later. More recently, food security has receded in importance while sustainability has been recognised as a major food issue though no British governments has yet produced a policy to achieve it.

Where there has, by contrast, been ongoing regulatory effort is over food safety, with legislation in every decade of the second half of the twentieth century.[1] The *Food Safety Act 1990* is generally considered to be a milestone among these interventions because it introduced the concept of 'due diligence', which made agents in various parts of food chains exercise governance functions in relation to their suppliers to ensure that they themselves could meet legally required standards. Because of the requirement for private sector companies to take on such governance responsibilities, this legislation has sometimes been seen as the state delegating its responsibilities. However, at the time it was definitely considered to be strengthening official regulation with its new enforcement capabilities, removal of Crown immunities[2] from many state-managed premises and increased power for codes of practice to be issued; an additional £30 million was allocated to local authority grants to pay for the extra work expected which clearly indicates the intention for state action to increase.

The extra work was about the monitoring needed for the new legislation to be effective, mainly carried out by local authority environmental health officers (EHOs). As with regulatory enforcement in general there is a range of measures they can take, starting with advice, persuasion and education and only extending to more severe action in cases of the worst infractions (Ayres & Braithwaite 1992). The culture of EHOs in the UK has long been one of using support and negotiation, with prosecutions pursued only as a last resort and research has shown such an approach is more effective than an emphasis on deterrence and penalties (Fairman & Yapp 2005; Hutter 2011). Thus, characterising state regulation as only 'command-and-control' was always misleading.

Despite the new legislation, the following decade saw a series of food scandals, most but not all, occurring not at the level EHOs operate but elsewhere in the food chain. The eventual British state response (after a change of government) was institutional reform; food responsibilities were hived off from the then Ministry of Agriculture, Fisheries and Food into a new Food Standards Agency (FSA) with a remit focused on the interests of consumers. The establishment of the FSA in 2000 reasserted the need for public oversight of food safety while at the same time exemplifying the trend for delegation to semi-independent agencies. Further regulation took place at the European level with the major 2002 General Food Regulation which had requirements for traceability, labelling and the precautionary Hazard Analysis of Critical Control Points (HACCP) system for managing risk. The HACCP system had begun in the private sector but through regulation was over time to be generalised throughout the food system. A further significant area of European legislation was the 2006 Nutrition and Health Claims Made on Food Regulation. All of this increased regulation was important for the seafood chain as will be discussed in later chapters.

Supply chain governance theories

In parallel to the regulatory developments in the world of politics, there were governance changes in the private world of business. As indicated in Table 1.2, the main formal theoretical approaches to understanding them have been transaction cost economics (TCE) and commodity chain and value chain analysis but marketing and organisation theory as well as management writings have also contributed insights. The changes in food supply chains over the last 60 years and how they have been understood through these organising narratives are explored in Chapter 2.

TCE is the branch of neo-institutional economics which aims to explain institutions on the basis of neo-liberal economic theory and is particularly associated with the work of Oliver Williamson, building on earlier insights from RH Coase. It starts with the assumption that in a perfect market of many buyers and many sellers there would simply be individual transactions governed by price and the supply chain would then consist of successive spot transactions through which goods and services would pass from producers to final consumers. However, because of the costs of transactions and various aspects of buyer and seller behaviour more formal arrangements are needed resulting in various forms of contract or vertical integration. These are conceptualised as modes of governance. The theory proposes that a firm will vertically integrate if the costs of internal administration are less than the costs of using the open market but that intermediate forms of governance, termed hybrids, might be selected under appropriate circumstances. The TCE concepts of *bounded rationality*, *uncertainty* and *information asymmetry*, relating to differential knowledge between the two parties, the resulting scope for one party's potential *opportunism* or *moral hazard* risk-taking and the *asset specificity* of financial or human investment have been found valuable in other explanatory approaches (Coase 1937; Williamson 1985, 1987).

The TCE framework has been criticised for its assumptions about markets and organisations unrelated to how the social world actually functions. In practice economic transactions are embedded in social relations and long-term, trust-based associations in business have been common so are not necessarily a sign of change being made for cost-saving or any other reason (Granovetter 1985; Gummesson 1999). However, TCE provided a starting point which proved very useful to researchers grappling with contemporary change in supply chains with little theory available to explain this.

That power is involved in the inter-firm or intra-firm connections said to constitute governance arrangements was specifically denied in the original TCE framework with some limited exceptions (Williamson 1995). However, a parallel strand of American marketing theory in the 1970s and 1980s produced analyses of supply chain relationships in which power was seen as a key factor.[3] These generally did not deal with food chains but their ideas were picked up or echoed by British researchers from the 1990s who were seeking to explain the consequences of the then-recent growth and concentration of supermarkets in the UK. These accounts described the impact of the concentrated buying power being exerted by these multiples on their suppliers (Collins 2001; Dobson, Waterson & Chu 1998; Howe 1998). How power was exercised was argued to depend on the relative bargaining strength of each party in particular contexts, different for example between a large supermarket chain and a company manufacturing for that retailer's own-label lines compared to that same supermarket dealing with a manufacturer of nationally recognised major brands, or depending on whether there are a small or large number of alternative suppliers for a particular item (Bowlby & Foord 1995; Hogarth-Scott & Parkinson 1993; Ogbonna & Wilkinson 1998).

A more rigorous development of power-focused analysis was carried out by Andrew Cox and his collaborators, using the TCE concepts of bounded rationality and uncertainty but taking issue with that approach by asserting the significance of power relations. In this work four possible descriptions of the relations between any two parties are put forward based on the utility and scarcity of the resource each controls; these are dominant buyer, dominant supplier, independence or interdependence, but a given company could be in a different category in its upstream (supplier) compared to its downstream (customer) relations. Case studies showed that the companies defined as more powerful were likely to be much more successful financially, taking a relatively large share of the gains produced by the chain as a whole (Cox et al. 2002; Cox & Chicksand 2007). This body of work, it should be noted, is not only analytic but oriented to management support with the idea that a realistic understanding of the individual company's position will best enable those within it to formulate successful strategies. There has also been broader recognition of the power that is exerted by large food companies including retailers (Clapp & Fuchs 2009; Sodano 2006).

Contrasting with power analysis, another strand of work concentrated on collaboration. Here, though generally the term is not explicitly used, governance is directed at managing the whole supply chain in such a way that all participants benefit. In this context, supermarkets' power can be seen as helpfully integrative and their need for partners who can deliver consistent quality may be emphasised (Bowlby & Foord 1995; Dawson & Shaw 1989; Mazé 200). The co-operative approach is echoed by relational marketing literature in which longer-term bonds are contrasted with and sometimes said to be replacing more adversarial single transactions, in part because this way of doing business is better suited to meeting more individualised customer requirements (Buttle 2012; Gummesson 1999).

Collaboration is not only analysed but often has been urged and to develop it in an example of mixed governance, a large UK government grant was given to the Food Chain Centre. The Centre was established in 2002 in response to the recommendation of the official Curry Commission which had examined policy issues for food and farming.[4] The Food Chain Centre, as had been recommended by the Commission, was hosted by the Institute of Grocery Distribution, a body representing the retail industry and involving major supermarkets. Many of the projects were based on the idea of bringing lean techniques to the food industry to improve flow and minimise waste, thereby reducing costs; several concluded that significant savings could be made by more collaborative working (Boys 2007; Duffy 2002; Duffy & Fearne 2004; Food Chain Centre 2007). In this normatively-oriented management literature, the issue of relative benefits to be obtained by different chain participants tended to be ignored, an omission corrected by the power analysts discussed in a previous paragraph.

The question of much greater profits going to supermarkets than achieved by their suppliers had already become a public issue in the early 1980s when the first competition authority report on the subject was published. This took the view that the situation was acceptable if consumers still benefited from lower prices and providing no illegal price-fixing was taking place. However, public disquiet continued and there were further investigations in the 2000s resulting in a voluntary Code of Practice for dealings between supermarkets and their suppliers and subsequently, when that was seen to be ineffective, the establishment of the Groceries Code Adjudicator from 2013.[5] Thus, the state's governance role in relation to the supermarkets has included both support for the retail industry as when it funded the Food Chain Centre and acting as an umpire over relationships with suppliers in the work of the competition authorities and when legislating for the Adjudicator role.

Returning to theorisation about private governance, commodity-based thinking which developed from different disciplinary bases including political economy and rural sociology has provided some of the most comprehensive accounts of food, or rather agri-food, chains to use the terminology preferred. They can be grouped under two headings, commodity systems and (global) commodity chains. 'Commodity systems' is a broad term covering various mainly American studies of processes connected with the industrialisation of agriculture, often involving vertical integration in which certain companies, some transnational, were key movers. As with management approaches to supply chains discussed earlier, the terminology of governance was not in use but it is quite clear in each account which parties are dominant and able to determine the operative rules using various mechanisms such as contracts and the ownership and control of inputs like genetics and feed (Friedland 2001; Heffernan & Constance 1994; Watts 2004).

The similar sounding 'commodity chain' approach, which morphed into the 'global commodity chain' (GCC) and then the 'global value chain' (GVC) emerged from theorising about the world capitalist economy and much of its focus has been about how richer countries relate to less industrialised, poorer ones but in this literature is analysed in terms of relationships between private companies (Gibbon, Bair & Ponte 2008). A key concept in the GCC is that of a buyer-driven chain, with its demonstration of governance mechanisms used to lead and co-ordinate globally-organised industries (Gereffi 2005). This showed how control was effective without the hierarchical integration posited by the transaction cost model, but the latter had provided the concept of governance which had been absent in earlier commodity studies. When this thinking was applied to food, leading supermarkets were readily seen as the chain leaders who could dominate suppliers wherever in the world they were based.

What are these mechanisms of control? In summary, they are systems of standards covering quality and food safety requirements which are enforced by audits. The basic transactional ability to withdraw custom remains as a final sanction but the standards and audit regimes will generally ensure that desired products are delivered. The audits need to be seen as objective so carried out neither by the buyer nor the supplier but by third parties, namely specialist audit and certification companies. The various theoretical threads outlined in this section increasingly overlapped as they took these widespread systems into account.

So, the next question is about the basis for the standards. They do not emerge in a vacuum, simply connected with the buyer's business. Rather they are connected with and take fully into account the rules set through governmental regulation within which that business operates. This indicates the inter-relationship of private and public forms of governance. In the UK, the 'due diligence' obligation in the 1990 *Food Safety Act* gave a huge impetus to supermarkets' use of standards and audit schemes as a means of satisfying this requirement and in any case quality assurance provides various internal advantages to companies such as preventing costly failures and maintaining brand value (Henson & Northen 1998).

A further significant development of the standards approach came in the 1990s when campaigning NGOs switched from just aiming pressure at governments to working on private companies. Sometimes this meant hostile action but in other cases it took the form of persuasion, including promotion of fair trade and other ethical certification schemes. In so doing NGOs too became agents in an extended form of private governance (Hyatt & Johnson 2016; Pattberg 2007). The result was that standards in addition to covering food safety and quality might now also include broader objectives such as environmental protection and fair labour conditions. NGOs have become increasingly involved in the governance of supply chains for environmental and social sustainability (Bush et al. 2015).

Private governance is all about relationships between parties in the supply chain and most approaches recognise power disparities in these relationships, with governance mechanisms directed by the more dominant. Whether considering regulation or governance in its various meanings the issue is about not just the existence of power but about how it is used. Governments have the power and also legitimacy to make and enforce binding laws. Other governance actors have a range of options which extend from the raw economic power of powerful corporations over small suppliers to the influence of civil society actors affecting reputations by campaigning. But while governments and organisations have power over resources and institutions, how it is used is not pre-determined. Choices and decisions have been made which produced the systems we now have and by the same token, these could be different in the future. This book aims to clarify the way both public regulation and private governance have developed in relation to the seafood chain and to consider their impacts.

Agents of governance for the seafood chain in Britain

The enactment of governance in the seafood chain involves a considerable range of organisations working at different levels. The roles they play will be detailed in the following chapters but here they are introduced, listed in Table 1.2 with their key responsibilities. The table is divided into several sections, starting with various types of public authority, going on to some combination public-private organisations, then the private level and finally civil society.

Table 1.2 Levels of governance andactors affecting the seafood industry

Level/group	Key actors	Field of action
Global governance	UN and agencies particularly Food & Agriculture Organisation (FAO) and WHO Regional fisheries management organisations	United Nations Convention on the Law of the Sea (UNCLOS); FAO guidelines on fisheries, food safety and related issues Management of fishery resources in international waters/straddling species
	World Trade Organisation	Facilitating/regulating global trade
Supra-state governance	European Union	Common Fisheries Policy (CFP) Single market – food hygiene and consumer protection regulation
National governance	British Government	Economic policy Influencing and implementing CFP; national fisheries and aquaculture policy, enforcement Food safety policy and legislation Nutritional advice
Governance relating to fisheries, aquaculture and environment devolved/delegated to public bodies	Devolved administrations	Policy and implementation for fishing, aquaculture, environment
	Inshore Fisheries and Conservation Authorities/ Regional Inshore Fisheries Groups/Inshore Fishery Groups	Implementation and management of local fisheries and aquaculture regulation in England/Scotland/Wales
	Marine Management Organisation/ Marine Scotland	Implementation of fisheries and fish farm licensing and fishing quota systems; enforcement of fisheries regulation
	Centre for Environment, Fisheries & Aquaculture/ Marine Scotland	Data collection and research
	Animal and Plant Health Agency	Controlling fish/shellfish disease and protecting public
	Fish Health Inspectorates	Maintaining aquatic animal health

	Veterinary Medicines Directorate	Authorising and monitoring veterinary medicines and usage
	Local authority planning departments	Aquaculture planning permissions
	Crown Estate	Authorising aquaculture leases
	Environment agencies	Implementing environmental legislation; aquaculture licensing and water quality
Governance relating to food safety devolved/delegated to public bodies	Food Standards Agency/Food Standards Scotland	Food safety policy and implementation
	Local authority environmental health and trading standards departments	Food safety local implementation
	Port Health Authorities	Border health controls
Governance relating to labour delegated to a public body	Gangmasters Licensing Authority	Preventing worker exploitation
Mixed public–private governance	Sea Fish Industry Authority (Seafish)	Seafood industry development
	Producer Organisations	Implementation of CFP: quota allocation and market management
Private-led governance	Seafood companies, foodservice companies and retailers	Transactions which maintain seafood supply and ensure appropriate standards Corporate social responsibility
	Certification organisations and companies	Managing certification schemes
	Trade organisations	Representing interests of fishermen, farmers, processors, retailers
Civil society governance	Environmental NGOs and other civil movements	Formulating and campaigning for environmental goals relating to the seas.

Source: author.

At the top of the table is the supra-state level, the global dimension and the European Union. During the period being considered, international rule-making under the auspices of the United Nations (UN) became increasingly significant in relation to oceans, fish and fishing as well as to other issues relevant to the seafood supply chain such as food hygiene practices and labour standards. In addition, there are multi-country regional fisheries management organisations (RFMOs) under UN auspices. A separate international body, the World Trade Organisation (WTO), has also had an important impact on the seafood chain. Thus there is a global dimension to seafood governance.

When the UK joined the then European Economic Community in 1973 it entered a wider polity that came to be increasingly influential in relation to the seafood supply chain, the major impacts being first in relation to the Common Fisheries Policy (CFP), particularly after this became an active management tool from 1983, and second the Single Market which came into force in 1993, requiring level playing fields to be established and bringing a raft of food safety regulations. There have also been impacts in relation to EU legislation for environmental protection and marine planning. Britain's decision to leave the EU in March 2019 of course means that European legislation will no longer apply directly after this date. However, the need to share fisheries management and the likely conditions of any trade agreement to be negotiated suggest that much of it will remain relevant to the UK.

At the national UK level there are currently various bodies with a potential governance impact on the seafood chain. With the exception of national external relations, responsibility for fisheries, aquaculture, the environment and food safety, areas critical to various aspects of the seafood supply chain, were devolved to the Scottish, Welsh and Northern Ireland governments/administrations in 1999. There are four bodies dealing with the environment: the Environment Agency in England, Natural Resources Wales, the Northern Ireland Environment Agency and the Scottish Environment Protection Agency. Managing fisheries and aquaculture was from the mid-2000s delegated away from direct central government departmental management and for England now rests with the Marine Management Organisation and elsewhere with the devolved administrations. A dedicated agency, the Centre for Environment, Fisheries & Aquaculture deals with data and research for England and Wales; Marine Scotland performs similar functions but is part of the Scottish Government and the arrangement is similar for Northern Ireland. Fish Health Inspectorates for England and Wales and in the devolved Scottish and Northern Irish administrations have specific responsibilities in relation to the health of fish and shellfish. Aquaculture is covered by different bodies variously dealing with licensing, leases and planning permissions, with water quality and with animal health.

For local coastal management, England has ten Inshore Fisheries and Conservation Authorities (ICFAs) which replaced Sea Fisheries Committees in 2011 and have wider responsibilities than their predecessors. Regional Inshore Fisheries Groups (RIFGs) have a similar but more limited role in Scotland (these were Inshore Fisheries Groups (IFGs) between 2009 to 2016). There were Inshore Fishery Groups in Wales but at the time of writing they were inoperative. In Northern Ireland, inshore fisheries are managed directly by the devolved administration.

Food safety is overseen by Food Standards Scotland (FSS) and by the Food Standards Agency (FSA) for England, Northern Ireland and Wales with implementation the responsibility of environmental health departments of local authorities in relation to premises in their areas and of port health authorities for ensuring that neither unsafe foods nor organisms risky to animal health enter the country. When first established in 2000, the FSA was also given responsibility for nutrition and issued dietary advice but in 2010 this was taken back into central government except in Scotland and Northern Ireland.

To add to these various governmental bodies there are further entities which have mixed government and private sector characteristics. The Sea Fish Industry Authority, generally known as Seafish, is a quango responsible to Parliament but with a remit to support the seafood industry which is obliged to pay for its functioning through a levy. Producer Organisations (POs) on the other hand are fishing industry bodies but established as part of the EU Common Organisation of the Markets and have a legislated role in implementing the Common Fisheries Policy. Their role after Britain leaves the EU is yet to be clarified.

Beyond these mainly state-based organisations, there is a constant background of private sector governance incorporated into daily transactional interchange and the movement of goods. Trade organisations play a part in maintaining industry norms as well as advocating for commercial interests. In recent years much private sector governance has been exercised through a considerable number of certification schemes overseen by mixed stakeholder bodies and certification companies. Finally, civil society, mainly in the form of environmental NGOs, has an influencing role especially in relation to sustainability.

The diverse and highly complex contemporary picture just outlined and summarised in Table 1.2 can be contrasted with the very different situation at our starting point, around 1950. Then there was very limited fisheries management which was exercised either centrally or for England and Wales locally by the Sea Fisheries Committees which had been established late in the nineteenth century. Some efforts towards introducing an international element to managing fisheries had taken place, but these had a limited impact on fishing practice at the time. There were two predecessors to Seafish in existence, the White Fish Authority from 1951 and the Herring Industry Board dating back to the 1930s, but POs were to come later with European Economic Community membership. Aquaculture had not yet started in the UK so did not need to be regulated. Beyond the state, neither private certification schemes nor NGO campaigning had started in relation to seafood.

Thus both governance and regulation have increased considerably in the intervening period. Much of the increase is related to securing two of our key seafood objectives, sustainability and food safety. The questions are about why and how things have developed to get to the current situation and what was happening in the seafood chain along the way.

Book outline

This book is based on a research project considering the whole seafood supply chain. It involved interviewing a range of people in the seafood industry, attending trade conferences and visits to salmon and trout farming facilities and to seafood processing plants. The desk part of the research included the compilation of a database of seafood companies which then provided the sampling frame for selecting which ones to contact for interviews; these were chosen with an emphasis on those in the middle of the chain concerned with processing and distribution in four regions: Scotland and three English zones: Central/South, East/North East and South West. The research is detailed in the resulting thesis (Greenwood 2015).

This chapter has reviewed the development of regulation and other forms of governance affecting food companies and Table 1.2 has listed the resulting governance actors impacting on the seafood chain. This book aims to show how these various agents, and the many developments in the public and private sectors, as well as from civil society, have been responsible for changes within it and with what effects. Chapter 2 continues with an overview of how concepts of private governance as set out in the theoretical approaches outlined above were used to explain changes in food chains that were occurring from the middle of the twentieth century. The following chapters follow a supply chain logic starting with production. Chapter 3 examines the impact of governance interventions on the primary production of seafood by both fishing and farming and the pursuit of sustainability. In Chapter 4, the processing and distribution part of the chain and the pursuit of seafood safety and quality is the subject. With Chapter 5, we come to nutrition messages and other influences on consumption while Chapter 6 shows how at the end of the chain retail and foodservice concerns have impacted consumption of seafood while themselves being the object of certain governance efforts (foodservice referring to provision outside the home). Finally, the concluding chapter reviews the impacts of governance in the seafood chain, considers how they would be affected by Britain leaving the European Union and reflects on the implications for theorising governance in the food system generally.

Notes

1 Legislation connected with food protection in the second half of the twentieth century: the *Food and Drugs Act 1955*, the 'Food Hygiene Regulations 1955', the 'Food Hygiene (Scotland) Regulations 1959', the 'Food Hygiene (Markets, Stalls and Delivery Vehicles) Regulations 1959', the 'Food Hygiene (General) Regulations 1970', the *Food Act 1984* (for England and Wales), the *Food Act (Scotland)*

1985, the *Food Safety Act 1990* and the *Food Standards Act 1999* plus other associated regulations.

2 Crown immunities indicate that the Crown, in practice the state, is not constrained by statute unless expressly stated to be so; this meant, for example, that until immunity was lifted in 1986, the NHS was not bound by food hygiene regulation.

3 The marketing channel studies contain descriptive observations on such issues as exercised versus non-exercised and coercive versus non-coercive types of power and on factors conducive to conflict or its avoidance (El-Ansary & Stern 1972; Hunt & Nevin 1974; Lusch & Brown 1982).

4 This was the report produced by the Policy Commission on the Future of Farming and Food, in 2002, *Farming and Food: A Sustainable Future*, issued by the Cabinet Office.

5 Competition Authority reports relating to supermarkets: Monopolies and Mergers Commission, 1981, *Discounts to Retailers*, London, HMSO; Office of Fair Trading, 1985, *Competition and Retailing*, London, OFT; Competition Commission, 2000, *Report on the Supply of Groceries from the Multiple Stores in the United Kingdom*, Norwich, Stationery Office, Cmnd 4842; Competition Commission, 2003, *Safeway plc and Asda Group limited (owned by Wal-Mart Stores Inc); Wm Morrison Supermarkets plc; J Sainsbury plc; and Tesco plc: A Report on the Mergers in Contemplation*, London, Competition Commission; Competition Commission, 2008, *The Supply of Groceries in the UK Market Investigation*, London, Competition Commission.

References

Allison E 2001, 'Big laws, small catches: global ocean governance and the fisheries crisis', *Journal of International Development*, vol. 13, no. 7, pp. 933–950.

Ayres I & Braithwaite J 1992, *Responsive Regulation: Transcending the Deregulation Debate* Oxford University Press, New York.

Bache I & Flinders M 2004, 'Multi-level governance and the study of the British state', *Public Policy and Administration*, vol. 19, no. 1, pp. 31–51.

Balleisen EJ & Moss DA 2010, 'Introduction', in *Government and Markets: Toward A New Theory of Regulation*, Balleisen EJ & Moss DA, eds., Cambridge University Press, Cambridge.

Barling D 2008, 'Governing and governance in the agri-food sector and traceability', in *Ethical Traceability and Communicating Food*, Coff C, ed., Springer, Dordrecht.

Bartolini S 2011, 'New modes of European governance: an introduction', in *New Modes of Governance in Europe: Governing in the Shadow Of Hierarchy*, Héritier A & Rhodes M, eds., Palgrave Macmillan, Basingstoke & New York.

Bell S & Hindmoor A 2009, *Rethinking Governance: The Centrality of the State in Modern Society* Cambridge University Press, Port Melbourne.

Bevir M & Rhodes RAW 2003, *Interpreting British Governance* Routledge, London & New York.

Bowlby S & Foord J 1995, 'Relational contracting between UK retailers and manufacturers', *International Review of Retail, Distribution and Consumer Research*, vol. 5, no. 3, pp. 333–360.

Boys J 2007, *Review of Food Chain Initiatives*, Department for Environment Food and Rural Affairs, London.

Bush SR, Oosterveer P, Bailey M & Mol APJ 2015, 'Sustainability governance of chains and networks: a review and future outlook', *Journal of Cleaner Production*, vol. 107, no. 16, November, pp. 8–19.

Butler E 2012, *Public Choice: A Primer*, Institute of Economic Affairs, London.

Buttle F 2012, 'Relationship marketing', in *Relationship Marketing: Theory and Practice*, Buttle F, ed., Paul Chapman Publishing, London.

Capano G, Howlett M & Ramesh M 2015, 'Bringing governments back in: governance and governing in comparative policy analysis', *Journal of Comparative Policy Analysis*, vol. 17, no. 4, pp. 311–321.

Clapp J & Fuchs D 2009, 'Agrifood corporations, global governance and sustainability: a framework for analysis', in *Corporate Power in Global Agrifood Governance*, Clapp J & Fuchs D, eds., The MIT Press, Cambridge MA & London.

Coase R 1937, 'The nature of the firm', *Economics*, vol. 4, November, pp. 386–405.

Collins A 2001, *An Investigation into Retailers' Margin Related Bargaining Power*, National University of Ireland, Cork, Discussion Paper No 34.

Cox A & Chicksand D 2007, 'Are win-wins feasible? Power relationships in agri-food supply chains and markets', in *Supermarkets and Agri-food Supply Chains: Transformations in the Production and Consumption of Foods*, Burch D & Lawrence G, eds., Edward Elgar, Cheltenham.

Cox A, Ireland P, Lonsdale C, Sanderson J & Watson G 2002, *Supply Chains, Markets and Power: Mapping Buyer and Supplier Regimes* Routledge, London.

Dawson J & Shaw SA 1989, 'Horizontal competition in retailing and the structure of manufacturer-retailer relationships', in *Retail and Marketing Channels: Economic and Marketing Perspectives on Producer-Distributor Relationships*, Pellegrini L & Reddy SK, eds., Routledge, London & New York.

Dobson P, Waterson M & Chu A 1998, *The Welfare Consequences of the Exercise of Buyer Power*, Office of Fair Trading, London, Research Paper 16.

Duffy R 2002, *The Impact of Supply Chain Partnerships on Supplier Performance: A Study of the UK Fresh Produce Industry, Briefing Note No 2*, Centre for Food Chain Research, Imperial College, London.

Duffy R & Fearne A 2004, 'Partnerships and alliances in the UK supermarket supply networks', in *Food Supply Chain Management*, Bourlakis MA & Weightman PWH, eds., Blackwell Publishing, Oxford.

El-Ansary AI & Stern LW 1972, 'Power measurement in the distribution channel', *Journal of Marketing Research*, vol. 9, no. 1, pp. 47–52.

Fairman R & Yapp C 2005, 'Enforced self-regulation, prescription and conceptions of compliance with small businesses: the impact of enforcement', *Law & Policy*, vol. 27, no. 4, pp. 491–519.

Flinders M 2008, *Delegated Governance and the British State: Walking without Order* Oxford University Press, Oxford.

Food Chain Centre 2007, *Completion Report 2007* www.foodchaincentre.com, accessed 3 January 2018.

Friedland W 2001, 'Reprise on systems methodology', *International Journal of Sociology of Agriculture and Food*, vol. 9, no. 1, pp. 82–103.

Gereffi G 2005, 'The global economy: organization, governance and development', in *Handbook of Economic Sociology*, 2nd edn, Smelser N & Swedberg R, eds., Princeton University Press, Princeton NJ.

Gibbon P, Bair J & Ponte S 2008, 'Governing global value chains: an introduction', *Economy and Society*, vol. 37, no. 3, pp. 315–338.

Granovetter M 1985, 'Economic action and social structure: the problem of embeddedness', *American Journal of Sociology*, vol. 91, no. 3, pp. 481–510.

Greenwood M 2015, *Governance and Change in the British Seafood Supply Chain 1950 to 2013*, Thesis submitted for the degree of Doctor of Philosophy, City University London.

Gummesson E 1999, *Total Relationship Marketing: Rethinking Marketing Management from 4Ps to 30Rs*, Butterworth-Heinemann, Oxford.

Heffernan W & Constance DH 1994, 'Transnational corporations and the globalisation of the food system', in *From Columbus To Conagra: The Globalization of Agriculture and Food*, Bonnano A, ed., University Press of Kansas, Kansas.

Henson S & Northen J 1998, 'Economic determinants of food safety controls in the supply of retailer own-branded products in the United Kingdom', *Agribusiness*, vol. 14, no. 2, pp. 113–126.

Hogarth-Scott S & Parkinson ST 1993, 'Retailer-supplier relationships in the food channel', *International Journal of Retail and Distribution Management*, vol. 21, no. 8, pp. 11–18.

Hood C & Dixon R 2015, *A Government that Worked Better and Cost Less?: Evaluating Three Decades of Reform and Change in UK Central Government* Oxford University Press, Oxford.

Howe WS 1998, 'Vertical market relations in the UK grocery trade: analysis and government policy', *International Journal of Retail and Distribution Management*, vol. 26, no. 6, pp. 212–224.

Humphrey J & Schmitz H 2001, 'Governance in global value chains', *IDS Bulletin*, vol. 32, no. 3, pp. 19–29.

Hunt SD & Nevin JR 1974, 'Power in a channel of distribution', *Journal of Marketing Research*, vol. 11, no. 2, pp. 186–193.

Hutter BM 2011, *Managing Food Safety and Hygiene: Governance and Regulation as Risk Management*, Edward Elgar, Cheltenham.

Hyatt DG & Johnson JL 2016, 'Expanding boundaries: non-governmental organizations as supply chain members', *Elementa: Science of the Anthropocene*, vol. 4, no. 2, March, p. 4:000093.

Jordana J & Levi-Faur D 2004, 'The politics of regulation in the age of governance', in *The Politics of Regulation: Institutions and Regulatory Reforms for the Age of Governance*, Jordana J & Levi-Faur D, eds., Edward Elgar, Cheltenham & Northampton MA.

Lusch RF & Brown JR 1982, 'A modified model of power in the marketing channel', *Journal of Marketing Research*, vol. 19, no. 3/4, pp. 312–323.

Mayntz R 2003, 'New challenges to governance theory', in *Governance as Social and Political Communication*, Bang HP, ed., Manchester University Press, Manchester & New York.

Mazé A 200, '"Retailers" branding strategies: Contract design, organisational change and learning', *Chain and Network Science*, vol. 2, no. 1, pp. 33–45.

Ogbonna E & Wilkinson B 1998, 'Power relations in the UK grocery supply chain: developments in the 1990s', *Journal of Retailing and Consumer Services*, vol. 5, no. 2, pp. 77–86.

Osborne SP 2006, 'The New Public Governance?', *Public Management Review*, vol. 8, no. 3, pp. 377–387.

Pattberg PH 2007, *Private Institutions and Global Governance* Edward Elgar, Cheltenham & Northampton MA.

Peters BG 2011, 'Steering, rowing, drifting, or sinking? Changing patterns of governance', *Urban Research & Practice*, vol. 4, no. 1, pp. 5–12.

Peters BG & Pierre J 2001, 'Developments in intergovernmental relations: towards multi-level governance', *Policy & Politics*, vol. 29, no. 2, pp. 131–135.

Ponte S, Gibbon P & Vestergaard J 2011, 'Governing through standards: an introduction', in *Governing through Standards: Origins, Drivers and Limitations*, Ponte S, Gibbon P & Vestergaard J, eds., Palgrave Macmillan, Basingstoke & New York.

Rhodes R 1996, 'The new governance: governing without government', *Political Studies*, vol. 44, no. 4, pp. 652–667.

Scott C 2004, 'Regulation in the age of governance: the rise of the post-regulatory state', in *Politics of Regulation: Institutions and Regulatory Reforms for the Age of Governance*, Jordana J & Levi-Faur D, eds., Edward Elgar, Cheltenham & Northampton MA.

Sodano V 2006, 'A power-based approach to the analysis of the food system', in *International Agri-Food Chains and Networks: Management and Organization*, Bijman J, ed., Wageningen Academic Publishers, Wageningen.

Stiglitz JE 2010, 'Government failure vs market failure: principles of regulation', in *Government and Markets: Towards A New Theory of Regulation*, Balleisen EJ & Moss DA, eds., Cambridge University Press, Cambridge.

Van Kersbergen K & Van Waarden F 2004, '"Governance" as a bridge between disciplines: cross-disciplinary inspiration regarding shifts in governance and problems of governability, accountability and legitimacy', *European Journal of Political Research*, vol. 43, no. 2, pp. 143–171.

Watts M 2004, 'Are hogs like chickens? Enclosure and mechanization in two "white meat" filières', in *Geographies of Commodity Chains*, Hughes A & Reimer S, eds., Routledge, London & New York.

Williamson OE 1985, *The Economic Institutions of Capitalism* Free Press, New York.

Williamson OE 1987, 'Transaction cost economics: the comparative contracting perspective', *Journal of Economic Behavior and Organization*, vol. 8, no. 4, pp. 617–625.

Williamson OE 1995, 'Hierarchies, markets and power in the economy: an economic perspective', *Industrial and Corporate Change*, vol. 4, no. 1, pp. 21–49.

Yeung K 2010, 'The regulatory state', in *The Oxford Handbook of Regulation*, Baldwin R, Cave M & Lodge M, eds., Oxford University Press, Oxford.

2 Governance and change in food chains

Introduction

In this chapter, major changes in supply chains for food that took place in the last quarter of the twentieth century and the governance systems at work in them are outlined along with the ways different analysts have characterised what has been happening, with an emphasis on fresh foods. While much has been written about changes in the UK food system, little of it deals with fish. Although three dozen studies bearing on all, or most often part, of a seafood chain were found, just one was about Britain. That is not to say there is a lack of material which relates to seafood in the UK; indeed, such information has been vital for the present enquiry. There are many studies of particular aspects and a wealth of statistics which is mainly designed for usefulness to the seafood industry and policymakers in which fishing and fisheries have received most attention, the rest of the seafood chain much less. Thus there is much material of interest but it does not generally investigate the governance forces influencing change in the British chain, the motivating question for this study.

The term 'supply chain' is a minimal way to describe the pathway from 'fish to fork' or 'net to plate'. But while the process is much more convoluted than evoked by the idea of a linear chain, the concept has correctly been called a 'powerful metaphor' which 'simplifies a complex reality' (Cox 1999, p. 211). Food theorists have used various other images such as 'commodity chain', 'value chain', 'commodity network' and 'global production network'. These aim to indicate complexities such the commodification which emphasises trade and profit-making rather than simply food production and also the involvement of a broader range of participants in the production and distribution nexus. Such wider factors in the seafood chain will certainly be considered in this book, but the terminology of 'supply chain' is used as the simplest way of referring to the systems whereby raw material is produced and by various routes becomes food to be eaten.

The UK seafood chain transformation

The supply chain for seafood at around 1950, the starting point for the analysis, was a simple one which differs from the present in many respects. First, the species consumed by British people then were limited; as far as fresh fish was concerned, they almost entirely comprised cod, haddock and herring. Salmon whether fresh or smoked was a luxury except for the canned version; tinned tuna and sardines were also available. Oysters too were a luxury and shellfish generally was mainly available in coastal towns. Second, with the exception of the tinned options, the fish available in the early period was mainly the catch brought by the British fishing fleet. The third point is that in the early period there was no farmed seafood in the mix; the development of aquaculture was to come in subsequent decades. The fourth distinction is about presentation; frozen fish was not yet available, and the trade was mainly in whole fish. If processed, this mainly meant smoking to produce traditional foods like kippers and bloaters although there were also proprietary brands of fish paste. The fifth difference is about the logistical systems: in the past landings were sold at auction to wholesalers and a considerable proportion sent on to the then great urban inland wholesale markets. The supply, whether from these inland markets or direct from port wholesalers, went on to fishmongers to be sold in shops, stalls or mobile vans, or to the foodservice (using a later term) sector of caterers, restaurants and fish and chip shops.

By contrast, a huge range is now available, summarised under 14 categories in Table 2.1. It features a large variety of species of fish and shellfish which may be from capture (wild) or farmed sources, obtained from many parts of the world and presented in many formats including chilled (fresh), frozen, smoked and with choices of constantly evolving ready meals.

A few of the categories in Table 2.1 may include distinctive distribution paths such as frozen-at-sea whitefish fillets geared to the fish and chip trade or special processing formats like langoustines (*Nephrops norvegicus*) turned into scampi. But most are part of the broad offer provided to retail and foodservice customers or available for the kind of processing in which diverse ingredients such as Scottish farmed salmon, wild haddock from Icelandic waters and farmed warm-water prawns from South Asia might be combined into a fish pie ready meal. The groupings therefore partly show the complexity of sourcing and supply routes, partly some specific features of British seafood consumption preferences (scampi, fish and chips) and partly the flexibility by which many species can be regarded as alternative ingredients from the globally sourced cornucopia. Tinned fish, continuing to be imported and sold through retail outlets seems to have been the least changing element but the species, sourcing and presentation may all have altered and certainly now offer far more choice.

A schematic picture of the current British supply chain which delivers this impressive array of seafood is shown in Figure 2.1. It starts on the left with diverse sources of supply both domestically produced and imported. A range

Table 2.1 Types of seafood currently available in Britain

Species based categories	Producing country/region	Formats/processing	Consumer routes
Capture (wild)			
Whitefish – cod and haddock	Iceland, Norway, Russia	Frozen-at-sea	Fish and chip shops; other foodservice
Mixed – includes whitefish, lemon/Dover sole, monkfish, plaice, sea bass	Britain, Iceland, Norway, Russia	Chilled; frozen; smoked; ready meals	Fishmongers; online; foodservice; some major retailers
Pelagics – herring, mackerel	Britain, Norway	Chilled; smoked; cured; pâté	Major retailers; fishmongers; some foodservice
Preserved – anchovy, mackerel, sardines, salmon, tuna	Global sourcing	Canned	Retail, all types
Cold water prawns	Norway, Greenland, Canada	Chilled; frozen; cooked; sandwiches	Major retailers; fishmongers; foodservice
Langoustines	Britain	Scampi	Foodservice, retail
Other shellfish (includes crabs, lobster, scallops)	Britain	Live; chilled; cooked	Fishmongers; major retailers; foodservice
High value – includes tuna, grouper, kingfish, salmon	Global sourcing	Chilled	Major retailers; selected foodservice
Farmed			
Salmon	Britain, Norway, Chile	Chilled; frozen; smoked; ready meals; sandwiches	Fishmongers; retailers; foodservice
Trout	Britain	Chilled; ready meals	Retail; foodservice
Mediterranean – sea bass, sea bream	Greece, France, Turkey	Chilled; ready meals	Major retailers; foodservice
Warm water prawns	South East Asia, Latin America	Chilled; cooked; ready meals	Retailers; foodservice
Mussels, scallops and oysters	Britain & EU	Live; chilled; cooked	Major retailers; fishmongers; foodservice
Tropical – pangasius and tilapia	Global sourcing	Chilled	Major retailers

Source: author.

Note
Any type sold as chilled may have been previously frozen.

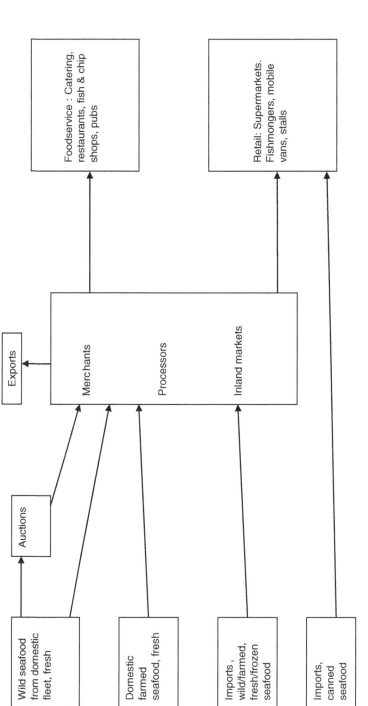

Figure 2.1 The twenty–first century chain for seafood.

of merchants and processors manipulate the raw material to a greater or lesser extent and then send it as fresh or frozen seafood or in various processed forms, including ready meals and other convenience food, to either the food service or retail sectors, the latter consisting of supermarkets and fishmongers, some still sometimes operating from stalls or mobile vans.

Behind this chain outline, there have been major logistical and distribution changes. There is still a very British active fishing fleet which supplies some of the whitefish staples, cod and haddock, but most are now imported while the greater part of its catch is sold abroad. Hence the well-established paradox about the current seafood position in Britain that 'The UK imports what we eat and exports what we catch' (Rutherford 2009) which was not the case in the past. Now, although auctions do still operate, the greater part of the seafood supply goes to major retail and foodservice companies via large processing and distribution companies who get their supplies of raw material direct, much of it imported. One further difference which is not represented on either the supply chain diagram Figure 2.1 or in Table 2.1 but which is nevertheless very important is that food hygiene standards in handling fresh fish were low in the past but have now greatly improved as will be explained in a later chapter.

Thus the change from the 1950 situation to the present has been immense. Much has been the result of technological developments such as the mastery of aquaculture and freezing fish technology or the product of general economic forces such as those giving impetus to the rise of supermarkets but a lot too can be attributed to governance factors. These are first examined in relation to food chains generally and particularly those dealing with fresh produce, in particular, to see what light they throw on the forces of change. Studies relating to seafood are then considered, looking for any identification of governance forces in them. Drawing from this review, a model is put forward of how governance forces have changed the way the British seafood chain operates to guide the detailed examination in the following chapters.

Governance in food chains

Those studying the US agriculture system in the latter part of the twentieth century were struck by changes in supply chains leading to more vertical co-ordination. Parties along the chain instead of just conducting individual transactions were becoming more closely linked in some fashion. Similar trends were then detected in other countries. Depending on use of transaction cost economics (TCE), various management approaches or commodity systems/ chains theories these changes were interpreted in somewhat different ways.

The TCE analysts mainly explained increasing vertical co-ordination and use of non-market mechanisms as motivated by reducing transaction costs such as for negotiating and monitoring individual contracts. Studies referring to this framework cover food chains in several countries including beef from Scotland (Hobbs 1996), grains and poultry production in the US (Hobbs &

Young 2000; Vukina 2001), lamb in Canada (Stanford et al. 1999), fruit from Brazil (Cavalho, Loader & Hallam 2000) and potatoes grown in Egypt for the British market (Loader 1997). Traceability systems in various European meat chains were seen to be reducing information transaction costs (Buhr 2003). But these studies were limited by not including actual costs due to their non-availability and by the fact that the key TCE concepts as listed in Chapter 1 – *bounded rationality, information asymmetry, opportunism* and *asset specificity* – turned out to be difficult to operationalise and measure. They also had difficulty in pinning down causal factors in relation to governance. So, although TCE thinking introduced the notion of governance in supply chains along with other useful concepts, the work carried out under its umbrella did not in practice get very far in explaining changes in food chains.

From different perspectives, some empirical British studies saw change as coming about from the competitive needs of the major supermarkets rather than in terms of a wider theoretical framework. This included a positive approach to the strategies advocated by the Food Chain Centre reported in the previous chapter as exemplified by one title, *Making Lean Supply Work in the Food Industry* (Simons et al. 2004). There were some relatively upbeat findings about collaboration in red meat chains, such as more partnerships between producers, abattoirs and supermarkets during the 1990s and productivity improvements achieved in meat processing (Fearne 1998; Simons & Zokaei 2005). Apart from lean strategy promotion, studies were finding closer collaboration being developed in food chains generally, starting in the 1990s. The impetus was seen to be coming mainly from supermarkets seeking to manage the whole supply chain to achieve quality standards for competitive advantage as well as to meet the 1990 *Food Safety Act* requirements with IT and logistics developments also relevant (Duffy & Fearne 2004; Fearne & Hughes 1999; Leat & Revoredo-Giha 2013). However, there was occasional recognition of power disparities and the possibility of conflicts within these partnerships (Wilson 1996).

This last issue of disparities and their implications was at the centre of the work of power regime theorists, Andrew Cox and his collaborators. Food has featured in three of their analyses, all applying to Britain: forecourt outlets, the industrial sugar chain and supply chains for fresh meat.

With the first of these, a special type of convenience store in petrol filling stations, relationships relevant to typical purchases of confectionary, snacks and soft drinks were analysed. They showed that each dyadic relationship in the chain had a different power structure and a different pattern of financial returns. For example, the retailer was deemed to be in a stronger position than the customer because of convenience aspects and impulse buying so could charge higher prices. The forecourt retailer was in an independent relationship with the supplying distributor because there was sufficient competition for each to be able to find alternative suppliers or retail customers. But the distributor was weaker than the manufacturer of branded goods who was therefore able to impose relatively high prices. Relationships between manufacturers and suppliers of raw materials were analysed in a similar way. In the industrial sugar chain, the analysis showed that while power was not a feature of all the dyadic relationships the sugar processors had most, making margins of about 25% and that the farmers also did well, both being protected by regulatory arrangements at the time (the then EU sugar regime); the supermarkets had some power in relation to the food and drink manufacturers but less so than with other products (Cox et al. 2002).

The power regime investigation of lean techniques in meat chains cast doubts on the assumption that collaborative working for better efficiency and less waste would enable all participants to benefit from the resulting competitive advantage. For beef and lamb variable demand and supply situations, the advantage to producers of an export market and uneven and only partial concentration of processing and distribution functions militated against co-operation. The pig chain by contrast was characterised by more intensive farming, greater concentration and considerable vertical integration and did use lean practices but the benefits were not shared throughout the chain; the supermarkets gained and others in the chain saw their returns decline. The analysts concluded that in circumstances where collaboration was not feasible or not profitable, a short-term opportunistic approach might be the rational choice. As with the industrial sugar and forecourt chains, each dyad in each chain was classified as being about buyer or supplier dominance, interdependence or independence and where information was available supported by figures for the differential returns made by different participants (Cox, Chicksand & Palmer 2007). These three food chain examples show the usefulness of the power regime analysis for understanding the particularities and dynamics of individual supply chains, lessons useful in considering the seafood chain.

In the US the commodity systems analyses of food chains focused on a different force for vertical co-ordination in the agriculture system from the middle of the chain as retailer concentration and power were slower to develop. Both chicken and pork production were being transformed by large integrator-processors who controlled farming production by means of contracts which might specify inputs and production methods as well as the outputs expected. Another model of co-ordination involved major grain companies expanding into meat-packing and processing while also controlling feed. The accounts here covered similar ground to some of the TCE work but were more critical and emphasised two major aspects of the changes. First, they represented industrialisation of livestock farming; this involved altering animals' genetics and controlling their feed and living conditions so that they would reach marketable size in a short time-scale and produce higher proportions of chicken breast or lean pork meat than in their natural state to accord with consumer preferences. Second, these accounts called attention to the power aspects of the new arrangements as exerted by the integrator-processors who were their main commercial beneficiaries (Heffernan & Constance 1994; Page 1997; Watts 2004). Outside the US, a commodity system analysis of chicken production in Australia indicated a system more like that in Britain where major retailers were the most powerful actors and led the restructuring of the supply chain (Dixon 2002). In a Britain-focused study, the northern Europe tomato growing chain for the UK was also noted as controlled by supermarkets (Harvey, Quilley & Beynon 2002).

In relation to food, the (global) commodity chain framework has been particularly evident in analyses of vegetables grown in East and Southern Africa for the British market, applying a buyer-driven governance framework. Various studies have shown how leading supermarkets in the UK have imposed their standards on the whole production process, favouring large farms and large export companies to better control their risks and expecting their suppliers to bear additional costs associated with their adoption of ethical standards such as worker benefits (Dolan & Humphrey 2000; Friedberg 2003). However, when applied to pineapple exported to the EU and US from two countries, Côte d'Ivoire and at a later period Costa Rica, the chains were not defined as buyer-driven because it was the fruit companies not the retailers who were responsible for key decisions, changing to a different commercial variety and shifting much production from Africa to Central America (Vagneron, Faure & Loeillet 2013).

This brief overview of changes in food supply chains as described from various theoretical viewpoints has provided some options to test in relation to the British seafood chain, the dominant one being moves towards vertical integration of chains and in Britain, supermarket power and leadership. The question to be addressed next is how far seafood chains have followed similar trajectories.

Governance factors in seafood chains

Thirty-six studies were found which dealt with at least some part of a seafood chain. As well as varying theoretical starting points (or none) they cover a large variety of species, methods of production, geographical area and power arrangements. The studies are listed in Table 2.2 in various sections according to what the key governance factor seemed to be: long-term traditional market relationships, vertical integration, processor/merchant-driven, buyer-driven, state governance and mixed leadership with a residual category where no governance factor was indicated. One of these studies has a theoretical framework not mentioned previously, filière; this refers to a French tradition of mainly tropical commodity chain analysis.

Considering the range of factors and the time span of the studies from the mid-1980s to the mid-2010s only a few generalisations about them are possible. TCE was only used in the earliest period and has been superseded, mainly by forms of commodity analysis, but some studies are simply within a management framework. The four analyses that found processor–merchant driven chains were all of the fisheries in East Africa so there may be cultural factors at work. Most but not all of the aquaculture chains involved vertical co-ordination or were buyer-driven in some form. Some analysts emphasised the influence of richer countries' buyers and NGOs over production in the global South. It is interesting that state forms of governance were indicated in four of the studies as this did not seem to feature in the general food chain accounts discussed in the previous section. A few of these references are worth considering in a bit more detail either because of possible theoretical implications or because they can be related to the British seafood chain in some way.

The power regime methodology has not been used in relation to seafood but an FAO study, while not mentioning power explicitly, indicates asymmetries through information about profit differentials. Thus the comparison of two white fillet chains found that retailers obtained 61% of the value of Tanzanian Nile perch but only a 37% share of Icelandic cod while in contrasting pelagic chains retail achieved 75% for Moroccan anchovy but only 38% for Danish herring. The developing country producers clearly received a much lower share in each case though the differentials were attributed in part to the fact that they carried out less processing (Gudmundsson, Asche & Nielsen 2006).

An analysis of the British chain covering three key species found a complicated picture. For chilled (fresh) cod, supermarkets took 67% of added value, processors only a third, but in foodservice nearly all the value could be taken by upmarket restaurants with little going to processors or distributors; by contrast, the added value of fish fingers was shared equally between processors and supermarkets. Fish and chip shops took two-thirds of the value of fresh or frozen haddock, the processor the next largest share and the vessel least but if fresh haddock was added to a fish pie the added value went mainly to the supermarket and primary processor, the boat getting the next share and the secondary processor least. Finally there was a contrast between two forms of langoustines: as frozen coated scampi two-fifths went to the secondary processor, most of the rest being shared between retail and vessel, but when the same animal was exported live nearly half was taken by the restaurant and a quarter by the boat, the rest being shared between exporters and importers (Sandberg et al. 2004). No overall patterns were discerned by looking at these three sub-chains and no governance factors were discussed.

In an analysis of the chain for frozen cod from Norway into the UK, there was a more straightforward finding that processors were squeezed between supply difficulties on the one hand and the purchasing power of retailers and food service companies on the other so that a high proportion had been failing to make a profit; the study also noted stable relationships between processors and retail/catering with higher levels of trust compared to those between processor and fishermen and in the latter some trend to vertical integration, albeit limited by legal restrictions on the ownership of vessels (Grunert et al. 2004). An account of the Icelandic cod chain (relevant to Britain to which so much is exported) was managerial in nature, producing recommendations for greater efficiency (Hameri & Pálsson 2003).

Table 2.2 Governance and power relations identified in seafood supply and commodity chain studies

Reference	Country of production	Production type	Theoretical framework	Governance/power relations
Long-term traditional market relationships				
Acheson 1985	US	Fishery – lobster	Transaction Cost Economics	Long-term relationships between fishers and buyers
Bush & Oosterveer 2007	Vietnam	Aquaculture – prawn	Commodity networks	Market relationships embedded socially
Marks 2012	US	Fishery – prawn	Commodity chain	Long-term relationships between fishers and buyers but under strain
Wilson 1980	US	Fisheries	Transaction cost economics	Long-term relationships between fishers and buyers
Vertical integration				
Campling 2012	France and Spain	Fishery – tuna	Commodity chain/political economy	Varying degrees of vertical integration applying to different companies
Dawson 2003	US	3 fisheries (South Atlantic wreckfish, Pacific halibut/sablefish, North Pacific pollock)	Transaction cost economics	Vertical integration more likely where asset specificity whether fisher and/or processor capital
Gallick 1984	US	Fishery – tuna	Transaction cost economics	Fisher-processor vertical integration
Goss et al. 2000	Thailand	Aquaculture	Commodity systems	Vertical integration
Grunert et al. 2004	Norway	Fishery – frozen cod	Value chain analysis	Trend to vertical integration fishers-processors; long-term relationships processors and retail/foodservice with latter more powerful
Skladany & Harris 1995	Global	Aquaculture	Commodity systems	Considerable vertical integration

Reference	Country of production	Production type	Theoretical framework	Governance/power relations
Processor/merchant-driven				
Gibbon 1997a	Tanzania	Fishery – Nile perch	Commodity chain	Processors control chain, international market controls prices
Gibbon 1997c	Tanzania	Fishery – *dagaain* (silver cyprinid)	Filière	Wholesaler cartel control
Henson et al. 2000	East Africa	Fishery – Nile perch	Management	Traders/processors over fishers; EU over processors
Schuurhuizen et al. 2006	Kenya	Fishery – Nile perch	Management	Buying agents over fishers; international traders not directly involved in chain
Buyer-driven				
Barton & Fløysand 2010	Chile	Aquaculture – salmon	Political ecology	Increased influence of buyers and NGOs + more state governance
Belton et al. 2011	Bangladesh and Vietnam	Aquaculture – pangasius	Global Value Chain	Driven by retailers and NGOs in North
Guillotreau & Le Grel 2001	Europe	Salmon and whitefish	Value chain analysis	Increasing vertical integration led by supermarkets
Hatanaka 2009	Indonesia	Aquaculture – prawns	Standards (organic certification)	Northern NGOs/consumers over Southern NGOs and farmers
Mansfield 2003	US and Thailand	Fisheries (3) – whitefish for surimi (fish paste)	Relationship between nature and social processes	Different end markets determine different constructions of quality in each chain
Phyne & Mansilla 2003 Islam 2008	Chile Bangladesh	Aquaculture – salmon Aquaculture – prawns	Commodity chain Commodity chain	Buyer-driven Driven by buyers, NGOs and state regulation
Tran et al. 2013	Vietnam	Aquaculture – prawns	Global Value Chain	Buyer-driven from processor level upstream but production not governed

continued

Table 2.2 Continued

Reference	Country of production	Production type	Theoretical framework	Governance/power relations
State governance				
Bush & Oosterveer 2007	Thailand	Aquaculture – prawns	Commodity networks	State regulation over nitrofuran problem
Kambewa et al. 2006	East Africa	Fishery – Nile perch	Management	Increased government action to deal with EU food safety concerns
Ponte 2007	Uganda	Fishery – Nile perch	Standards	Increased government action with private sector to deal with EU food safety concerns
Vandergeest et al. 1999	Thailand	Aquaculture – prawns	Political ecology	Increased government regulation in certain areas
Mixed leadership/other				
Belton et al. 2009	Thailand	Aquaculture – tilapia	Sustainability (certification)	Large-scale and export-oriented companies favoured
Bonanno & Constance 1996	US	Fishery – tuna	Political economy	Processors changed from 1970s vertical integration to 1980s spot-market purchasing Government regulation for 'dolphin-friendly' tuna changed supply sourcing
Gibbon 1997b	Tanzania	Fishery – prawns	Commodity chain	2 chains, export-led and artisanal; tied relationships within each but neither driven
Miller 2014	Western and Central Pacific Ocean	Fishery – tuna	Global Production Network	Supra-state bodies (Parties to the Nauru Agreement and EU) and NGOs

Reference	Country of production	Production type	Theoretical framework	Governance/power relations
Peterson et al. 2000	Australia	Fisheries (prawn, abalone, general & tuna) & prawn aquaculture	Management	3 chains led by exporters, 1 by major wholesalers, 1 by fishers
Thorpe & Bennett 2004	East Africa	Fishery – Nile perch	Chain management	Hybrid: neither producer nor buyer-driven; increased government action with private sector to deal EU food safety concerns
Wilkinson 2006	Global	All types	Global Value Chain	Driven by various powerful companies including producers, retailers, foodservice
Governance factors not discussed				
Eltholth et al. 2015	Egypt	Aquaculture – tilapia	Management	Not discussed
Hameri & Pálsson 2003	Iceland	Fisheries – cod	Management	Not discussed
Gudmundsson et al. 2006	Various	Fisheries	Value chain analysis	Not discussed
Sandberg et al. 2004	Various	Fisheries	Value chain analysis	Not discussed

Source: author's interpretation of these references.

Note
Bush & Oosterveer 2007 has two entries in this table, in the 'Long-term traditional market relationships' and the 'State governance' sections because the article dealt with two different case studies, in Vietnam and Thailand respectively.

A Europe-wide value chain analysis for seafood noted that the salmon one in Britain showed some vertical integration in a trend to formal contracts between aquaculture producers and supermarkets. In both the salmon and whitefish chains, retailers were seen as putting pressure on the middle of the chain, resulting in fewer small processors and less fish sold at auction (Guillotreau & Le Grel 2001).

A political economy variant of commodity chain-led analysis analysed the French and Spanish industrialised tuna fleets which largely produce canned fish for European markets. There have been varying degrees of vertical co-ordination involving different companies in the sector, including processing firms integrating upstream and a fishing enterprise integrating downstream with a manufacturer. In addition, considerable rationalisation has taken place, associated with the development of ever-larger vessels chasing depleted resources in the successive 'commodity frontiers' of new fishing grounds (Campling 2012).

The varied structures identified in these studies do not present an obvious framework for understanding the UK seafood supply chain. They do not agree about what are the key governance factors which clearly varied, nor with few exceptions indicate which parts of seafood chains gain most and least. None covers a complete 'net to plate' picture in a developed or indeed any country. Neither does any of them deal with the consumption part of the chain. So before the outline structure for the investigation of the British situation is put forward, the next section considers ways that governance of food consumption can be conceptualised.

Governing food consumption

Governance in relation to food consumption does not mean the same kind of power exercised by either the state or by companies in supply chains as considered so far; rather it is about many forms of influence, some explicit, others disguised in forms that can be seen as manipulation or seduction. Both governments and the food industry do affect consumption but manage this more subtly by decisions affecting what is available and the prices at which different items are sold.

Britain has long had policies to keep food prices low including agriculture subsidies, most recently through the EU's Common Agricultural Policy. The UK's wider economic policies have supported the global widening of trade which has included food since the establishment of the WTO, enlarging the options available. More directly, the state has since World War II required certain foods to be fortified. By establishing rules about food production and standards, public regulation structures choices (Flynn, Harrison & Marsden 1998; Foster & Lunn 2007).

The food industry including primary production, with a greater or lesser impact from state policies, determines availability and pricing. Agricultural decisions have led to leaner meat and different varieties of fruit and vegetables being offered. Increasing supply while reducing prices can increase demand as has occurred with farmed salmon and cheap chicken and pork (Ritson & Hutchins 1995; Rivera-Ferre 2009). Processing developments and refrigeration have enlarged the range of foods and the general availability of nutritional benefits, but, with more processing, there has been a deleterious impact on some intakes such as high levels of salt and sugar (Duff 1999). The major retailers have a huge influence on consumption through decisions on what to stock, the location of stores, targeted promotions and the use made of loyalty cards; they respond to consumers but also shape demand (Dawson 1995, 2013; Wrigley 1998). Advertising is an aspect of supermarket layout and display while also extensively used by brand manufacturers and retailers in various forms of media to influence purchasing.

More focused are two strands of explicit messages designed to affect food consumption. One is about doing good to oneself and others in the household by using food to improve health. The other is potentially about doing good in the world by making ethical choices. Health messages about individual benefits are a province of public pronouncements but also a field of action for industry. Messages about doing good in the world such as by choosing on the basis of better environmental impacts, animal welfare or labour conditions, generally originate from civil society but then involve private delivery arrangements although some claims may be publicly regulated. Both health and ethics in food consumption are areas of contestation, given formulations by public authorities and/or civil society on the one hand and potential profits to be made by commercial interests on the other and both are relevant to seafood consumption.

Nutritional advice from the government, though a feature of World War II controlled food policy did not continue after it for some time. It tentatively re-emerged as some very broad guidelines in a 1978 Department of Health and Social Security paper, *Eating for Health*; these were general statements without precise targets such as 'to eat less salt might be beneficial'. A much bigger impact on the public was made by the 1983 National Advisory Committee on Nutrition Education (NACNE) report which for the first time addressed to the public specific objectives for lower consumption of fats, sugar and salt. However, behind the scenes, from the early 1960s, there has been an expert body providing advice to the government on diet and nutrition, first the Committee on Medical Aspects of Food Policy (COMA), subsequently the Scientific Advisory Committee on Nutrition (SACN). It was SACN that formulated the recommended nutrient intakes used for the NACNE publication[1] (Foster & Lunn 2007; NACNE 1983; Smith 1998).

When initially established in 2000 the remit of the FSA (Food Standards Agency) included nutrition and it gave dietary advice to the public. However, the 2010–2015 Coalition Government removed this nutrition responsibility and returned it to the Department of Health. The issue of responsibilities for nutritional guidelines will be shown to be significant in relation to seafood. The removal of some FSA responsibilities by the government in 2010 has been criticised in several reviews (Elliott 2013; House of Commons EFRA Committee 2013; National Audit Office 2013) and the erosion of its role has been described as 'alarming' (Hutter 2011, p. 151). Although this change did not involve a transfer of a public role to others but was rather a case of reverse delegation, it can be seen as an example of action to weaken state regulation, illustrating continuing contestation over governance of the food system. Indeed, this very struggle over the role of the FSA was presciently outlined before the agency had even started work:

> Some sections of industry do not want to see a strong interventionist agency, and if there is to be one, want it restricted to safe territory like microbiological safety rather than entering into 'danger zones' such as nutrition and the ethics of genetic engineering.
>
> (Lang 1999, p. 175)

The opposition of the food industry to a nutrition remit for the FSA was made clear in evidence given to a Parliamentary Select Committee at the time when legislation to establish the FSA was being discussed; the rationale given was a need to concentrate on food safety but there is no necessary contradiction between this and the nutritional role so the obvious inference is that the motive was avoidance of governance intervention in the food industry.[2] This desire was unsuccessful when the FSA was established but achieved some years later with a change of government.

Food advice for consumers has been contested by others putting forward their own versions or it may be used or misused for commercial purposes. In the former category, the Institute of Grocery Distribution produced guideline daily amounts (GDAs) of nutrients for population groups and these have been widely used in packaging information. The existence of the GDA system in parallel to public nutritional guidelines has been a potential source of confusion to the public especially as the quantities can easily be read as advice to consume certain levels of fats, sugar and salt rather than these being upper limits which should not be exceeded.

Commercial health claims about specific items of food are widespread. This includes 'functional foods' in which certain nutrients have been added or increased so that specific claims about them can be made and a range of supplements. The trend has been criticised as 'nutritionism', the engineering of highly processed items based on nutritional elements abstracted from ordinary foods, thus contradicting much public nutritional advice on the benefits of minimally processed fruits and vegetables (Scrinis 2008). Nutritionist thinking is relevant to fish as will be seen in Chapter 5.

How consumers actually respond to the multitude of public and commercial messages about healthy food is complex. Psychological and emotional factors influencing food choices interrelate with physiological mechanisms (Leng et al. 2016). Food and meal patterns have symbolic and communicative as well as physical aspects and are affected by social factors including class, gender, life course changes and belief systems all of which interact with nutritional advice and cut across its usually individualistic assumptions (Bourdieu 1984; Devine 2005; Dibsdall, Lambert & Frewer 2002; Douglas 2003; Maddock, Leek & Foxall 1999; Parraga 1990). In this context, food recommendations can be seen as externally imposed, restrictive and unacceptable as vividly demonstrated on British television in 2005 by the mothers protesting about healthy food changes introduced by celebrity chef Jamie Oliver at their children's school (Bisogni et al. 2012; O'Key & Hugh-Jones 2010).

Regardless of attitudes, there may be various practical barriers that limit access to healthy food, some linked to low incomes which affect transport options as well as affordability, others characteristic of local areas with more limited retail or takeaway food choices. A concerning trend for healthier foods to cost more than those with a poorer impact on health has been documented (Jones et al. 2014). Such issues show the limitations of the personal information approach to nutrition, indicating that attention should be paid to policies relevant to structural disadvantage and more generally to the operation of the food system (Caraher et al. 1998; Caraher & Coveney 2004; Lang & Caraher 1998). At the same time, the effectiveness of nutritional advice has been questioned. Although some changes have taken place over the last 60 years which do accord with nutritional advice, notably to lower fat meat and dairy products, obesity has become a major problem in the period since nutrition guidelines were first issued (Anderson, Milburn & Lean 1995; Foster & Lunn 2007).

In this context, recent nudge thinking emanating from behavioural economics has suggested other ways that consumption may be governed. The idea is to steer people to make healthier choices without feeling a sense of compulsion by means of 'choice architecture'. Interventions have included smaller portion sizes and moving unhealthier foods further away and healthier ones closer in choice situations. Reviews of such experiments (some conducted before nudge terminology came into play) have concluded that they can influence food choices in positive directions and some consider that they may be a useful public health tool (Arno & Thomas 2016; Bucher et al. 2016; Lycett et al. 2017). However, there was usually no follow-up to see if there was any effect on longer-term behaviour and most interventions were conducted in out of home settings so not a guide to what might take place domestically.

Some nudge thinkers envisage more wide-ranging measures which might include legal compulsion for a range of health and environmentally beneficial objectives (Reisch & Sunstein 2016). These shade into more interventionist governance moves which have taken place outside nudge thinking. Control of advertising unhealthy food to children is one such area with codes of practice on the subject produced under the aegis of regulator the Advertising Standards Authority. The FSA when it still had nutritional responsibilities led a campaign to reduce salt consumption, working with food manufacturers to reformulate accordingly. A further step has been taken with fiscal measures, such as the UK sugar tax and minimum pricing of alcohol in Scotland which both started in 2018.

Turning to ethical food consumption, the governance tools are certification schemes intended to establish and maintain better than normal commercial standards in relation to labour conditions and remuneration (fair trade) or better environmental outcomes (organics and individual schemes related to particular products such as palm oil and soy and also including fish). Such schemes, as noted in Chapter 1, are part of the standards and audit systems which have become a feature of governance in food chains. How far consumers are willing to pay more to support such standards and what persuades them to do so is a complex question and connected with various social factors. Motivations may be moral or something more like a lifestyle choice while the additional costs are a barrier (Boström & Klintman 2009; Gribben & Gitsham 2007; Zwart 1999). Research questioning consumers in six European countries including Britain over four labels/topics (fair trade, Rainforest Alliance, carbon footprint and animal welfare) concluded that sustainability labels did not play a significant role in the food choices made by consumers (Grunert, Hieke & Wills 2014). While choosing organic foods has been considered one of the most useful contributions the consumer can make to a more sustainable system, (Thøgersen 2010) for most British purchasers health and food safety constitute the main incentive (Baker et al. 2004; Padel & Foster 2005).[3] Unlike the case with other certification schemes, organic standards are regulated and organic production obtains conversion subsidies while the certifying bodies remain private.[4]

While health and ethical objectives provide a positive impetus, there is also a negative one namely risk avoidance. The background is the increased separation of consumers from the reality of food production and their sense of decreasing influence over it (Shaw 1999), the foreground periodically occupied by food scares and scandals.

In making choices, the traditional methods of assessment open to consumers, namely search based on visible attributes and experience, are felt to be decreasingly useful guides when the processes involved in getting food to the supermarket are complex and little understood by most people. Hence a further type, credence attributes, have become much more important, so that whether seeking safety, taste, health or ethical production the purchaser relies both on the provider of food and the information supplied by that provider. This has highlighted the issue of trust, the obverse of risk concerns. So a key aspect of the governance of consumption is over the mechanisms which attempt to convey trustworthiness: brands, labelling and assurance schemes. Here, the information needs of consumers come together with the requirement of the food industry for verifiable standards.

Labelling is one route for providing consumers with confidence in the food they buy. Under its original remit, the FSA carried out work on how this could be most helpful to the public. Food labelling regulation had started in 1946 and after revisions in 1953 and 1970 became more extensive in the

1980s and 1990s when European Directives were incorporated (Turner 2007). However, there was still dissatisfaction over the adequacy of information on food labels. The FSA, using research carried out in 2006 which had indicated that a high/medium/low-level colour icon would be most helpful to consumers, started to promote a 'traffic light' design. After years of disputation over this proposal from sections of the food industry, in 2013 the government announced an accord for a voluntary traffic light coded 'reference intake' labelling scheme, voluntary but with the agreement of all the major retailers and of some food manufacturing companies. While the public agency achieved the traffic light logo, reference intake being another term for the GDA concept put forward by the industry, the agreement marked a considerable concession to the business viewpoint, underscored by its voluntary nature. Despite this, some major manufacturers of soft drinks, snacks and confectionary declined to participate. A few years later certain of those same companies put forward a proposal to roll out a traffic light system based on the reference intake concept through all the countries of the EU but with a crucial difference: instead of presenting nutritional information as percentages it would be based on portion size. The proposal was immediately criticised by consumer bodies because portions could be manipulated to give the appearance of a less unhealthy profile.[5] The level of contestation over labelling indicates its importance as a governance mechanism.

Companies use various approaches to build a basis for trust and this is the essence of branding. Specific food product brands have long been familiar and more recently company branding has also become established particularly for the supermarket chains. Standards and audits as well as being a means of governing their supply chains can also be a means of achieving public trust and legitimacy especially when connected to ethical objectives. While regulation in the form of the 2006 *Companies Act* includes a requirement for corporate social responsibility policies, positive engagement can be beneficial for businesses. By adopting environmental and ethical standards and engaging with the NGOs that promote them, food companies can self-present as guardians of values, a useful aspect of marketing strategy and positioning (Hatanaka, Bain & Busch 2005). This may provide an additional motive for supermarkets stocking fair trade and other ethical ranges and for emphasising domestic sourcing of various foods.

In this section, various types of governance have been shown to be in operation in relation to consumption but functioning in a less direct way than is the case within supply chains and not raising the same issues of power. There is an inherent recognition of the need for persuasion: consumers cannot be compelled to adopt any particular dietary plan. The situation is well recognised in the statement of one official report: 'Precise targets might be misunderstood as biologically optimal, but targets are usually a compromise between biological advantage and social, cultural or economic acceptability' (Committee on Medical Aspects of Food Policy 1994, p. 5). This is a negotiating stance albeit in an indirect way, indicating a need to find middle ground between scientifically advisable goals and what is believed to be tolerable to consumers at large. Similarly, health or ethical claims made by food producers aim to persuade and have varying impacts. In addition to the negotiation between the state and consumers and between food companies and consumers, governance of consumption is also marked by a tension between state and food industry in pursuing interests which sometimes overlap and sometimes are at odds, leading to contestation over the governance of consumption.

Governance of the seafood chain in Britain – a model

The modes of governance that have been highlighted in this and the previous chapter are state and supra-state regulation, private governance through supply chain relationships, more formal means of private governance exerted though standards schemes, sometimes with civil society involvement and direct and indirect ways of exerting influence on consumers. They involve different ways of exerting power, whether the state's legitimising expression of public interest as well as its potential use of coercive powers, the relative market power of different parties in supply chains and the arguable force of consumer (potentially withheld) buying power.

Equally important is the question of what interests are actually served by different modes of governance in food systems. All in fact serve both business and public interests to different degrees in different situations. Private food businesses work to a profit-seeking imperative but also fulfil socially essential functions and serve the public interest equally with their own in relation to key objectives like hygiene. They may well provide healthy and safe food in a socially and environmentally responsible way at reasonable prices – but cannot always be relied upon so to do. Hence there is the necessity for state regulation and enforcement. State action, however, may also be promotional and facilitative to the food and seafood industries or may at times be most concerned with mediating a balance between different interests that bear on the food system. Finally, the civil society organisations which have had an impact on the food system all act in the name of a public interest ethical objectives but those who have chosen to collaborate with business are connected to an extent to the interests of those companies. Therefore, in considering modes of governance in play for the seafood supply chain it will be relevant to ask in each case whose interests are served.

From the overview of studies examining changes in food chains reviewed in this chapter, not all which were carried out in accordance with a theoretical scheme, it can be concluded that the TCE approach has been superseded by various forms of commodity chain analysis and that for the British situation it is essential to examine the role of the major retailers. The power regime schema though not adopted beyond the particular group of collaborators who worked with it was seen to have useful explanatory capabilities. When seafood chains were examined no particular framework was dominant which is not surprising given the range of different situations they encompassed.

Therefore, the conceptual framework adopted for examining the seafood supply chain serving UK consumers is a modified form of commodity systems analysis, selected as providing a comprehensive structure which includes both consumption and the role of the state at least in some formulations. However, there are two important modifications. The first is the emphasis on governance, which although it started with TCE owes much to the global commodity chain (GCC) and global value chain (GVC) approaches, the second is the incorporation of insights from the power regime framework. But unlike the most common usage of GCC and GVC analysis, in this study governance does not highlight relations between buyers in richer and suppliers in less industrialised countries but concentrates on the nature of supply chain ties within a single developed country. Also, while following a commodity systems approach this research is not inclusive of all its possible elements and in particular does not extend to labour processes nor discuss in detail scientific and technological inputs into production; these are clearly important but limits to this study had to be drawn.

In the framework, seafood companies are seen to experience or exert governance impacts in relation to their transactions with supply chain partners (sometimes adversaries) while the conduct of their business generally may be affected by governance exerted externally by state regulation, the actions of various state and private actors, by consumers and sometimes by others including civil society organisations; different forms and extent of power are involved in these various relationships. Figure 2.2 illustrates the two levels.

In Figure 2.2, supply chain relationships indicated by two-way arrows are the locus of the various types of private governance reviewed in this chapter; this is where the mechanisms of the power model and/or the buyer-driven control of the GCC and GVC potentially take place, possibly involving standards regimes. Externally to the supply chain, the various actors introduced in Chapter 1 who may have an impact upon it are shown (of course a greatly simplified representation since these in reality also impact on each other). The model is consistent with the perspectives of commodity systems and to some extent with GCC/GVC analyses. This book examines the nature and impact of governance both inside seafood supply chains and as exerted by external forces on the seafood supply chain as a whole. While there is no means of obtaining historical data relating to the former aspect, it aims to cover changes in external governance forces over the period covered by the study.

Governance in relation to consumers takes a different form, a matter more of influence than direct power. Its sources are shown schematically in Figure 2.3.

On top is the food provisioning system which by virtue of what it makes available has a powerful direct impact on consumption; to this is added the influence of advertising, which may include health claims. It should be noted here that agents in the food provision box are subject to the same governance factors as shown for seafood companies in Figure 2.2 though with differential

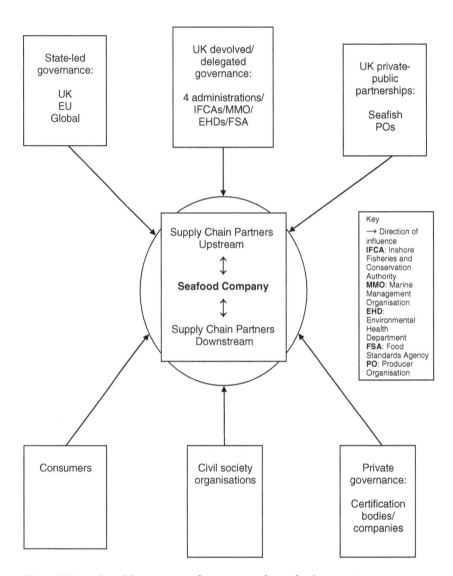

Figure 2.2 Levels and key sources of governance for seafood companies.

impacts. However, this is not a unidirectional process and the two-way arrow here takes into account the impact exerted on provisioners by purchase decisions. At the other end, various actors aim to affect consumption, involving such means as the official promulgation of nutritional guidelines, the maintenance of consumer-facing certification systems and the urging of various types of ethical purchasing. The way all these factors play out in relation to seafood consumption is explored in Chapters 5 and 6.

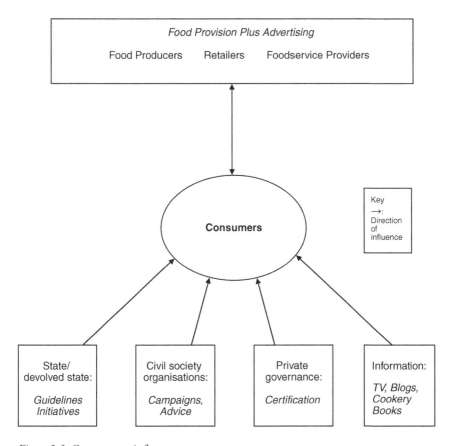

Figure 2.3 Governance influences on consumers.

In what follows, the impacts of different types of external governance are examined in a historical context describing the development of the seafood situation in the period starting in the mid-twentieth century. In Chapter 3, it is in relation to the seafood supply situation and how this has evolved, external factors having been of high importance. Chapter 4 turns the spotlight on the safety and quality of seafood and here governance factors within as well as upon the supply chain are examined. Seafood consumption governance factors are considered in Chapter 5 and governance impacts on retail and foodservice actors in Chapter 6.

Notes

1 The Committee on Medical Aspects of Food Policy (COMA) ran from 1963 to 1998, was reconstituted as the Committee on the Medical Aspects of Food and Nutrition Policy 1998 to 2000 when it was replaced by the Scientific Advisory

Committee on Nutrition (SACN) which continues. NACNE, unlike COMA and SACN was not directly associated with the government but formed, initially as the Joint Advisory Committee on Nutrition Education, by the British Nutrition Foundation and the Health Education Council so represented a combination of private and public action. The work of SACN can now be accessed at www.gov. uk/government/groups/scientific-advisory-committee-on-nutrition.

2 See Minutes of Evidence given by John Wood and Derrick Kilsby of the Food and Drink Federation and memoranda submitted by the British Retail Consortium and by J Sainsbury plc in (House of Commons Agriculture Committee 1998).

3 Whether or not organic foods are indeed healthier or safer than conventional products is a highly disputed question (Crinnion 2010; Dangour et al. 2009; Heaton 2001; Magkos, Arvaniti & Zampelas 2006; Smith-Spangler et al. 2012; Soil Association & Sustain 2001; Williamson 2007) and it is significant that nonetheless, with some negative reporting and with little advertising, contrasting with the energetic marketing of functional foods, that positive views about the health and food safety advantages of organics have become established.

4 UK regulation of the organic sector started in 1993 to put into effect EU Regulation (EEC) No 2092/91 On organic production of agricultural products and indications referring thereto on agricultural products and foodstuffs. It was overseen by quangos, initially the United Kingdom Register of Organic Food Standards, replaced in 2003 by the Advisory Committee on Organic Standards, on behalf of the competent authority, DEFRA; however, this was closed by the Coalition Government in 2010 and there has been no replacement. Subsidies for organic production started with the UK Organic Aid Scheme in 1994; in 2017 they are an element of the Countryside Stewardship scheme. As of March 2017 there were nine approved UK control bodies (certifiers).

5 While food companies Nestlé UK and PepsiCo UK did participate in the 2013 scheme, Coca-Cola, Dairy Crest, Kellogg, Mondelēz (Cadbury), Unilever and United Biscuits did not (see Hall J 2013, 'Plans for new food labelling to combat UK obesity are dealt blow as Cadbury and Coca-Cola reject "traffic light" system', *Independent*, 19 June 2013). Yet in March 2017 Coca-Cola, Mondelēz and Unilever together with Nestlé and Pepsico proposed their portion-based version of the scheme to be used throughout the EU (see Michael N 2017, 'Six industry giants to launch UK-style traffic light labels in Europe', 8 March 2017, www.foodnavigator.com, accessed 14 September 2017); it is not clear whether or when this proposal will be going ahead.

References

Acheson JA 1985, 'The Maine lobster market: between market and hierarchy', *Journal of Law, Economics & Organization*, vol. 1, no. 2, pp. 385–398.

Anderson A, Milburn K & Lean M 1995, 'Food and nutrition: helping the consumer understand', in *Food Choice and the Consumer*, Marshall DW, ed., Blackie Academic & Professional, Glasgow.

Arno A & Thomas S 2016, 'The efficacy of nudge theory strategies in influencing adult dietary behaviour: a systematic review and meta-analysis', *BMC Public Health*, vol. 16, no. 30, July, p. 676.

Baker S, Thompson KE, Engelken J & Huntley K 2004, 'Mapping the values driving organic food choice: Germany vs the UK', *European Journal of Marketing*, vol. 38, no. 8, pp. 995–1012.

Barton JR & Fløysand A 2010, 'The political ecology of Chilean salmon aquaculture, 1982–2010: a trajectory from economic development to global sustainability', *Global Environmental Change*, vol. 20, no. 4, pp. 739–752.

Belton B, Haque MM, Little DC & Smith LX 2011, 'Certifying catfish in Vietnam and Bangladesh: who will make the grade and will it matter?', *Food Policy*, vol. 36, no. 2, pp. 289–299.

Belton B, Little D & Grady K 2009, 'Is responsible aquaculture sustainable aquaculture? WWF and the eco-certification of tilapia', *Society and Natural Resources: An International Journal*, vol. 22, no. 9, pp. 840–855.

Bisogni CA, Jastran M, Seligson M & Thompson A 2012, 'How people interpret healthy eating: contributions of qualitative research', *Journal of Nutrition Education and Behavior*, vol. 44, no. 4, pp. 282–301.

Bonanno A & Constance D 1996, *Caught in the Net*, University Press of Kansas, Kansas.

Boström M & Klintman M 2009, 'The green political food consumer', *Anthropology of Food*, Special Issue, vol. 5.

Bourdieu P 1984, *Distinction: A Social Critique of the Judgement of Taste* Routledge, London.

Bucher T, Collins C, Rollo ME, McCaffrey TA, De Vlieger N, Van der Bend D, Truby H & Perez-Cueto FJA 2016, 'Nudging consumers towards healthier choices: a systematic review of positional influences on food choice', *British Journal of Nutrition*, vol. 115, no. 12, pp. 2252–2263.

Buhr BL 2003, 'Traceability and information technology in the meat supply chain: implications for firm organisation and market structure', *Journal of Food Distribution Research*, vol. 34, no. 3, pp. 13–26.

Bush SR & Oosterveer P 2007, 'The missing link: intersecting governance and trade in the space of place and the space of flows', *Sociologia Ruralis*, vol. 47, no. 4, pp. 384–399.

Campling L 2012, '"The tuna 'commodity' frontier": business strategies and environment in the industrial tuna fisheries of the Western Indian Ocean', *Journal of Agrarian Change*, vol. 12, no. 2/3, pp. 252–278.

Caraher M & Coveney J 2004, 'Public health nutrition and food policy', *Public Health Nutrition*, vol. 7, no. 5, pp. 591–598.

Caraher M, Dixon P, Lang T & Carr-Hill R 1998, 'Access to healthy food; part I. Barriers to accessing healthy foods: differentials by gender, social class, income and mode of transport', *Health Education Journal*, vol. 57, no. 3, pp. 191–201.

Cavalho JM, Loader R & Hallam D 2000, 'Governance structures of two innovative fruit chains in Brazil', in *Chain Management in Agribusiness and the Food Industries: Proceedings of the Fourth International Conference on Chain Management in Agri and Food Business*, Trienekens J & Zuurbier PJP, eds., Wageningen Pers, Wageningen.

Committee on Medical Aspects of Food Policy 1994, *Nutritional Aspects of Cardiovascular Disease*, HMSO, London, Department of Health Report on Health and Social Subjects, No. 46.

Cox A 1999, 'A research agenda for supply chain and business management thinking', *Supply Chain Management: An International Journal*, vol. 4, no. 4, pp. 209–211.

Cox A, Chicksand D & Palmer M 2007, 'Stairways to heaven or treadmills to oblivion? Creating sustainable strategies in red meat supply chains', *British Food Journal*, vol. 109, no. 9, pp. 689–720.

Cox A, Ireland P, Lonsdale C, Sanderson J & Watson G 2002, *Supply Chains, Markets and Power: Mapping Buyer and Supplier Regimes* Routledge, London.

Crinnion WJ 2010, 'Organic foods contain higher levels of certain nutrients, lower levels of pesticides, and may provide health benefits for the consumer', *Alternative Medicine Review*, vol. 15, no. 1, pp. 4–12.

Dangour AD, Dodhia SK, Hayter A, Allen E, Lock K & Uauy R 2009, 'Nutritional quality of organic foods: a systematic review', *American Journal of Clinical Nutrition*, vol. 90, pp. 680–685.

Dawson J 1995, 'Food retailing and the consumer', in *Food Choice and the Consumer*, Marshall DW, ed., Blackie Academic & Professional, Glasgow.

Dawson R 2003, *Vertical Integration in Commercial Fisheries*, Thesis submitted for the degree of Doctor of Philosophy, Virginia Polytechnic Institute and State University.

Dawson J 2013, 'Retailer activity in shaping food choice', *Food Quality and Preference*, vol. 28, no. 1, pp. 339–347.

Devine CM 2005, 'A life course perspective: understanding food choices in time, social location and history', *Journal of Nutrition Education and Behaviour*, vol. 37, no. 3, pp. 121–128.

Dibsdall LA, Lambert N & Frewer LJ 2002, 'Using interpretive phenomenology to understand the food-related experiences and beliefs of a select group of low-income UK women', *Journal of Nutrition Education and Behavior*, vol. 34, no. 6, pp. 298–309.

Dixon J 2002, *The Changing Chicken: Chooks, Cooks and Culinary Culture*, University of New South Wales, Sydney.

Dolan C & Humphrey J 2000, 'Governance and trade in fresh vegetables: the impact of UK supermarkets on the African horticulture industry', *Journal of Development Studies*, vol. 37, no. 2, pp. 147–176.

Douglas M 2003, 'Standard social uses of food: introduction', in *Food in the Social Order*, Douglas M, ed., Routledge, London & New York.

Duff J 1999, 'Setting the menu: dietary guidelines, corporate interests, and nutrition policy', in *A Sociology of Food and Nutrition: The Social Appetite*, Germov J & Williams L, eds., Oxford University Press, South Melbourne.

Duffy R & Fearne A 2004, 'Partnerships and alliances in the UK supermarket supply networks', in *Food Supply Chain Management*, Bourlakis MA & Weightman PWH, eds., Blackwell Publishing, Oxford.

Elliott C 2013, *Review into the Integrity and Assurance of Food Supply Networks: Interim Report*, HM Government Publications, London.

Eltholth M, Fornace K, Grace D, Rushton J & Häsler B 2015, 'Characterisation of production, marketing and consumption patterns of farmed tilapia in the Nile Delta of Egypt', *Food Policy*, vol. 51, February, pp. 131–143.

Fearne A 1998, 'The evolution of partnerships in the meat supply chain: insights from the British beef industry', *International Journal of Supply Management*, vol. 3, no. 4, pp. 214–231.

Fearne A & Hughes D 1999, 'Success factors in the fresh produce supply chain: insights from the UK', *International Journal of Supply Management*, vol. 4, no. 3, pp. 120–129.

Flynn A, Harrison M & Marsden T 1998, 'Regulation, rights and the structuring of food choices', in *The Nation's Diet: The Social Science of Food Choice*, Murcott A, ed., Longman, London & New York.

Foster R & Lunn J 2007, *40th Anniversary Briefing Paper: Food Availability and Our Changing Diet*, British Nutrition Foundation, London.

Friedberg S 2003, 'Cleaning up down south: supermarkets, ethical trade and African horticulture', *Social and Cultural Geography*, vol. 4, no. 1, pp. 27–43.

Gallick EC 1984, *Exclusive Dealing and Vertical Integration: The Efficiency of Contracts in the Tuna Industry*, Federal Trade Commission, Washington DC, Federal Trade Commission Bureau of Economic Staff Report.

Gibbon P 1997a, *Of Saviours and Punks: The Political Economy of the Nile Perch Marketing Chain*, Centre for Development Research, Copenhagen, Working Papers on Globalisation and Economic Restructuring in Africa, 97.3.

Gibbon P 1997b, 'Prawns and piranhas: the political economy of a Tanzanian private sector marketing chain', *Journal of Peasant Studies*, vol. 25, no. 1, pp. 1–86.

Gibbon P 1997c, *The Poor Relation: A Political Economy of the Marketing Chain for Dagaa in Tanzania*, Centre for Development Research, Copenhagen, Working Papers on Globalisation and Economic Restructuring in Africa, 97.2.

Goss J, Burch D & Rickson RE 2000, 'Agri-food restructuring and Third World transnationals: Thailand, the CP Group and the global shrimp industry', *World Development*, vol. 28, no. 3, pp. 513–530.

Gribben C & Gitsham M 2007, *Food Labelling: Understanding Consumer Attitudes and Behaviour*, Ashridge Business School, Ashridge.

Grunert KG, Fruensgaard Jeppesen L, Risom Jespersen K, Sonne A-M, Hansen K, Trondsen T & Young JA 2004, *Four Cases on Market Orientation of Value Chains in Agribusiness and Fisheries*, Aarhus School of Business, University of Aarhus, Aarhus, MAPP Working Paper No. 83–2004.

Grunert KG, Hieke S & Wills J 2014, 'Sustainability labels on food products: consumer motivation, understanding and use', *Food Policy*, vol. 44, pp. 177–189.

Gudmundsson E, Asche F & Nielsen M 2006, *Revenue Distribution through the Revenue Chain*, Food and Agriculture Organisation, Rome.

Guillotreau P & Le Grel L 2001, *Analysis of the European Value Chain for Aquatic Products*, SALMAR, European Commission, Brussels.

Hameri A-P & Pálsson J 2003, 'Supply chain management in the fishing industry: the case of Iceland', *International Journal of Logistics: Research and Applications*, vol. 6, no. 3, pp. 137–149.

Harvey M, Quilley S & Beynon H 2002, *Exploring The Tomato: Transformations in Nature, Economy and Society*, Edward Elgar, Cheltenham.

Hatanaka M 2009, 'Certification, partnership, and morality in an organic shrimp network: rethinking transnational alternative agrifood networks', *World Development*, vol. 38, no. 5, pp. 706–716.

Hatanaka M, Bain C & Busch L 2005, 'Third-party certification in the global agri-food system', *Food Policy*, vol. 30, no. 3, pp. 354–369.

Heaton S 2001, *Organic Farming, Food Quality and Human Health: A Review of the Evidence*, Soil Association, Bristol.

Heffernan W & Constance DH 1994, 'Transnational corporations and the globalisation of the food system', in *From Columbus To Conagra: The Globalization of Agriculture and Food*, Bonnano A, ed., University Press of Kansas, Kansas.

Henson S, Brouder A-M & Mitullah W 2000, 'Food safety requirements and food exports from developing countries: the case of fish exports from Kenya to the European Union', *American Journal of Agricultural Economics*, vol. 82, no. 5, pp. 1159–1169.

Hobbs JE 1996, 'A transaction cost approach to supply chain management', *Supply Chain Management: An International Journal*, vol. 1, no. 2, pp. 15–27.

Hobbs JE & Young ML 2000, 'Closer vertical co-ordination in agri-food supply chains: a conceptual framework and some preliminary evidence', *Supply Chain Management: An International Journal*, vol. 5, no. 3, pp. 131–142.

House of Commons Agriculture Committee 1998, *Food Safety*, The Stationery Office, London, Fourth Report of Session 1997–1998, HC331-I.

House of Commons Environment Food and Rural Affairs Committee 2013, *Food Contamination*, The Stationery Office, London, Fifth Report of Session 2013–2014.

Hutter BM 2011, *Managing Food Safety and Hygiene: Governance and Regulation as Risk Management* Edward Elgar, Cheltenham.

Islam MS 2008, 'From pond to plate: towards a twin-driven commodity chain in Bangladesh shrimp aquaculture', *Food Policy*, vol. 33, no. 3, pp. 209–223.

Jones NRV, Conklin AI, Suhrcke M & Monsivais P 2014, 'The growing price gap between more and less healthy foods: analysis of a novel longitudinal UK dataset', *PLOS ONE*, vol. 9, no. 10, p. e109343.

Kambewa E, Ingenbleek P, Van Tilburg A & Van der Lans I 2006, 'Improving quality and ecological sustainability of natural resources in international supply chains: The role of market-based incentives', in *International Agri-Food Chains and Networks: Management and Organization*, Bijman J, ed., Wageningen Academic Publishers, Wageningen.

Lang T 1999, 'The complexities of globalization: the UK as a case study of tensions within the food system and the challenge to food policy', *Agriculture and Human Values*, vol. 16, no. 2, pp. 169–185.

Lang T & Caraher M 1998, 'Access to healthy foods: part II. Food poverty and shopping deserts: what are the implications for health promotion policy and practice?', *Health Education Journal*, vol. 57, no. 3, pp. 201–211.

Leat P & Revoredo-Giha C 2013, 'Risk and resilience in agri-food supply chains: the case of the Asda PorkLink supply chain in Scotland', *Supply Chain Management: An International Journal*, vol. 18, no. 2, pp. 219–231.

Leng G, Adan RAH, Belot M, Brunstrom JM, de Graaf K, Dickson SL, Hare T, Maier S, Menzies J, Preissl H, Reisch LA, Rogers PR & Smeets PAM 2016, 'The determinants of food choice', in *Proceedings of the Nutrition Society*, University College Dublin, Dublin, Paper presented at Nutrition Society Summer Meeting, 11–14 July 2016.

Loader R 1997, 'Assessing transaction costs to describe supply chain relationships in agri-food systems', *Supply Chain Management: An International Journal*, vol. 2, no. 1, pp. 23–35.

Lycett K, Miller A, Knox A, Dunn S, Kerr JA, Sung V & Wake M 2017, ' "Nudge" interventions for improving children's dietary behaviors in the home: a systematic review', *Obesity Medicine*, vol. 7, September, pp. 21–33.

Maddock S, Leek S & Foxall G 1999, 'Healthy eating or chips with everything?', *Nutrition and Food Science*, vol. 99, no. 6, pp. 270–277.

Magkos F, Arvaniti F & Zampelas A 2006, 'Organic food: buying more safety or just peace of mind? A critical review of the literature', *Critical Reviews in Food Science and Nutrition*, vol. 46, no. 1, pp. 23–56.

Mansfield B 2003, 'Fish, factory trawlers, and imitation crab: the nature of quality in the seafood industry', *Journal of Rural Studies*, vol. 19, no. 1, pp. 9–21.

Marks B 2012, 'The political economy of household commodity production in the Louisiana shrimp fishery', *Journal of Agrarian Change*, vol. 12, no. 2/3, pp. 227–251.

Miller A 2014, *Governance Innovation Networks for Sustainable Tuna*, Thesis submitted for the degree of Doctor of Philosophy, Wageningen University.

NACNE 1983, *A Discussion Paper on Proposals for Nutritional Guidelines for Health Education in Britain*, Health Education Council, London.

National Audit Office 2013, *Food Safety and Authenticity in the Processed Meat Supply Chain*, The Stationery Office, London, HC 685.

O'Key V & Hugh-Jones S 2010, '"I don't need anybody to tell me what I should be doing": a discursive analysis of maternal accounts of (mis)trust of healthy eating information', *Appetite*, vol. 54, no. 3, pp. 524–532.

Padel S & Foster C 2005, 'Exploring the gap between attitudes and behaviour: understanding why consumers buy or do not buy organic food', *British Food Journal*, vol. 107, no. 8, pp. 606–625.

Page B 1997, 'Restructuring pork production, remaking rural Iowa', in *Globalising Food: Agrarian Questions and Global Restructuring*, Goodman D & Watts M, eds., Routledge, London & New York.

Parraga I 1990, 'Determinants of food consumption', *Journal of the American Dietetic Association*, vol. 90, no. 5, pp. 661–663.

Peterson J, Cornwell F & Pearson CJ 2000, *Chain Stocktake of Some Australian Agricultural and Fishing Industries*, Bureau of Rural Sciences, Department of Agriculture, Fisheries and Forestry, Canberra.

Phyne J & Mansilla J 2003, 'Forging linkages in the commodity chain: the case of the Chilean salmon farming industry', *Sociologia Ruralis*, vol. 43, no. 2, pp. 108–127.

Ponte S 2007, 'Bans, tests and alchemy: food safety regulation and the Uganda fish export industry', *Agriculture and Human Values*, vol. 27, no. 2, pp. 179–193.

Reisch LA & Sunstein CR 2016, 'Do Europeans like nudges?', *Judgment and Decision Making*, vol. 11, no. 4, pp. 310–325.

Ritson C & Hutchins R 1995, 'Food choice and the demand for food', in *Food Choice and the Consumer*, Marshall DW, ed., Blackie Academic & Professional, Glasgow.

Rivera-Ferre MG 2009, 'Supply vs demand of agri-industrial meat and fish products: a chicken and egg paradigm?', *International Journal of Agriculture and Food*, vol. 16, no. 2, pp. 90–105.

Rutherford J 2009, 'Sea fish', in *Feeding Britain*, Bridge J & Johnson N, eds., The Smith Institute, London.

Sandberg MG, Gjermundsen A, Hempel E, Olafsen T, Curtis HC & Martin A 2004, *Seafood Industry Value Chain Analysis: Cod, Haddock and Nephrops*, Seafish, Edinburgh.

Schuurhuizen R, Van Tilburg A & Kambewa E 2006, 'Fish in Kenya: the Nile-perch chain', in *Agro-Food Chains and Networks for Development*, Ruben R, Slingerland M & Nijhoff H, eds., Springer, Dordrecht, pp. 155–164.

Scrinis G 2008, 'On the ideology of nutritionism', *Gastronomia*, vol. 8, no. 1, pp. 39–48.

Shaw A 1999, 'What are "they" doing to our food?: Public concerns about food in the UK', *Sociological Research Online*, vol. 4, no. 3, www.socresonline.org.uk/4-3/shaw.html.

Simons D, Samuel D, Bourlakis M & Fearne A 2004, *Making Lean Supply Work in the Food Industry*, Food Process Innovation Research Unit, Cardiff Business School, Cardiff.

Simons D & Zokaei K 2005, 'Application of lean paradigm in red meat processing', *British Food Journal*, vol. 107, no. 4, pp. 192–211.

Skladany M & Harris CK 1995, 'On global pond: international development and commodity chains in the shrimp industry', in *Food and Agrarian Orders in the World-Economy*, McMichael P, ed., Praeger, Westport CT & London.

Smith D 1998, 'The discourse of scientific knowledge of nutrition and dietary change in the twentieth century', in *The Nation's Diet: The Social Science of Food Choice*, Murcott A, ed., Longman, London & New York.

Smith-Spangler C, Brandeau ML, Hunter GE, Bavinger JC, Pearson M, Eschbach PJ, Sundaram V, Liu H, Schirmer P, Stave C, Olkin I & Bravata DM 2012, 'Are organic foods safer or healthier than conventional alternatives? A systematic review', *Annals of Internal Medicine*, vol. 157, no. 5, pp. 348–366.

Soil Association & Sustain 2001, *Organic Food and Farming, Myth and Reality – Organic vs Non-organic: the Facts*, Soil Association and Sustain, Bristol & London.

Stanford K, Hobbs JE, Gilbert M, Jones SDM, Price MA & Kerr WA 1999, 'Lamb-buying preferences of Canadian abattoirs and producer marketing groups: implications for the Canadian supply chain', *Supply Chain Management: An International Journal*, vol. 4, no. 2, pp. 86–94.

Thøgersen J 2010, 'Country differences in sustainable consumption: the case of organic food', *Journal of Macromarketing* no. 30, pp. 2–171.

Thorpe A & Bennett E 2004, 'Market-driven international fish supply chains: the case of Nile perch from Africa's Lake Victoria', *International Food and Agribusiness Management Review*, vol. 7, no. 4, pp. 40–57.

Tran N, Bailey C, Wilson N & Phillips M 2013, 'Governance of global value chains in response to food safety and certification standards: the case of shrimp from Vietnam', *World Development*, vol. 45, May, pp. 325–336.

Turner A 2007, 'The development of food labelling regulations in the UK', *Nutrition Bulletin*, vol. 32, no. 2, pp. 161–167.

Vagneron I, Faure G, & Loeillet D 2013, 'Is there a pilot in the chain? Identifying the key drivers of change in the fresh pineapple sector', *Food Policy*, vol. 34, no. 5, pp. 437–446.

Vandergeest P, Flaherty M & Miller P 1999, 'A political ecology of shrimp aquaculture in Thailand', *Rural Sociology*, vol. 64, no. 4, pp. 573–596.

Vukina T 2001, 'Vertical integration and contracting in the US poultry sector', *Journal of Food Distribution Research*, vol. 52, no. 2, pp. 29–38.

Watts M 2004, 'Are hogs like chickens? Enclosure and mechanization in two "white meat" filières', in *Geographies of Commodity Chains*, Hughes A & Reimer S, eds., Routledge, London & New York.

Wilkinson J 2006, 'Fish: a global value chain driven onto the rocks', *Sociologia Ruralis*, vol. 46, no. 2, pp. 139–153.

Williamson CS 2007, 'Is organic food better for our health?', *Nutrition Bulletin*, vol. 32, no. 2, pp. 104–108.

Wilson JA 1980, 'Adaptation to uncertainty and small numbers exchange: the New England fresh fish market', *The Bell Journal of Economics*, vol. 11, no. 2, pp. 491–504.

Wilson N 1996, 'The supply chains of perishable products in Northern Europe', *British Food Journal*, vol. 98, no. 6, pp. 9–15.

Wrigley N 1998, 'How British retailers have shaped food choice', in *The Nation's Diet: The Social Science of Food Choice*, Murcott A, ed., Longman, London & New York.

Zwart H 1999, 'A short history of food ethics', *Journal of Agricultural and Environmental Ethics*, vol. 12, no. 2, pp. 113–126.

3   Achieving sustainable supply

Changes in supply from fishing

Following fishing disruption during World War II and some exceptional catches immediately after it, British fishing production had returned to something like the pre-war situation by the 1950s and 1960s. Although there had been changes in capture methods, catch composition and ports, the size of whitefish catches were similar at the end of the 1950s to the position 25 years previously (Taylor 1960). In the mid-1950s, the UK fishing industry was one of the six largest global producers in terms of catch (FAO 1956).

The success of the fleet was not due to economic factors alone: the British state took a significant promotional role in the post-World War II period, an aspect of the productionist approach to food generally followed by the Western European erstwhile combatants. The British fishing fleet was substantially modernised with state support organised via the delegated body the White Fish Authority, established by the *Sea Fish Industry Act 1951*. Its mandate to reorganise, develop and regulate included the provision of grants and loans for fishing boats and equipment as well as for quayside requirements, fish processing plants and specialised transport. A substantial programme of vessel modernisation was underway by the end of the 1950s; in addition, prices were subsidised by additional payments related to catches (Coull 1996; Foreman 1989). A similar role during the post-war period was carried out by the Herring Industry Board (established at an earlier stage in 1935) using grants and loans to support fleet modernisation and providing a subsidised minimum price scheme (Reid 1998). State promotion of the fishing industry through such mechanisms in fact had a long history going back to the Fishery Board set up in 1809 (Coull 1996).

The UK's fleet's operations then ranged over three broad fishing grounds: the distant water fishery (including Icelandic waters and the Barents Sea), the near and middle water fishery including the North Sea and finally the inshore fishery of smaller boats around the coasts (White Fish Authority 1959). During the 1960s, UK boats landed between 843,000 and 954,000 tonnes of fish per annum, a range indicating considerable variation but all the same accounting for between 83% and 86% in each year of the total available for domestic consumption. A high proportion of this catch, never less than three-quarters and sometimes reaching 85%, consisted of demersal species (those living close to the bottom of the sea), predominantly cod and haddock, the whitefish well-established by then as the dominant preference of British consumers.

However, a marked change occurred in subsequent years in the relative share of landings by UK vessels compared to imports in the key demersal (whitefish) category. This is illustrated in Table 3.1 giving the five-year interval picture for the years between 1960 and 2015 of seafood landed in British ports. The high proportion coming from UK vessels shown in the last column continued through most of the 1970s but began to change at the end of the decade. The transformed situation meant that in 1980 the contribution from domestic production, hitherto consistently over 80%, was down to 64%. The share continued to decline in the following period so that by the end of the 1990s less than half of the seafood eaten in Britain came from UK vessels. In 2010 just 24% of the whitefish going into the supply chain was landed by British boats and in 2015 it was similar at 27%. Thus, over these decades, the situation had been transformed from predominantly domestic production to a reliance on imports for these key species.

Other transformations occurred at different times as experienced by those involved in the seafood industry. One interviewee who had worked in it for 20 years (so talking about the early 1990s) recalled:

> When I was in my teens to my twenties, sort of thing, the fish market down here, one end to the other shots, each boat's landing is a shot. You had them laid out side by side and you basically just walked up and down and took note, mental note, the ones you wanted or thought better quality.... Now there is none of that at all. You went from, say 100 to 1,000 boxes, maybe twice a week on this market to something like 20 or 30, huge difference, huge.
>
> (Managing director, small company 6)

Another could refer to a decade earlier:

> The biggest change without doubt is the changes to the catching side, the supply of fish to the UK market. Thirty years ago there was as much fish as you wanted on this market on a daily basis, it was a thriving industry and lots and lots of big processors processing fresh fish on a daily basis. Today there's probably none, not big ones.
>
> (Managing director, large company)

The reasons for the change in supply were not to do with a diminution of the British fishing industry as Table 3.2 giving fleet information shows (although the definitional bases of the figures have changed over the period so that they are not exactly comparable over time, the series indicates the broad picture).

Table 3.1 Landings and demersal imports for selected years from 1948 to 2015 by UK vessels into the UK

Year	Total landings	Demersal landings	Demersal imports	Demersal landings + imports	Demersal landings % of total demersal
1948	1,097	783	184	967	81
1960	843	693	116	809	86
1965	926	799	172	971	82
1970	975	731	158	889	82
1975	869	579	111	690	84
1980	759	384	217	601	64
1985	762	402	339	741	54
1990	662	311	433	744	42
1995	726	372	406	778	48
2000	440	203	452	655	31
2005	475	141	587	728	19
2010	411	115	356	470	24
2015	416	118	328	446	27

Source: figures extracted by author from Sea Fisheries Statistical Tables and UK Sea Fisheries Statistics as follows: Total Supplies Table (1967); Balance Sheet Tables (1980, 1985, 1990, 1991–1992, 1995, 1999–2000 and 2005) and Landings and Imports Tables (2010 & 2015) issued successively by the Ministry of Agriculture, Fisheries and Food, DEFRA and the Marine Management Organisation.

Notes

Over the years, definitions of categories and content of the tables have changed so that figures in different years may not be strictly comparable. but they are still valid for examining the trend over time.

The Sea Fisheries Statistical Tables generally provide a series for the most recent years, but the figures for any one year in successive publications may not be identical; where different ones have been noted, those published at a later date have been selected on the assumption that these are corrected ones.

Landings are into UK by UK vessels.

Figures are in 000 tonnes; those sourced from older publications have been converted from cwt.

Table 3.2 UK fishing fleet for selected years from 1950 to 2016

Year	Number vessels	Gross (registered) tonnage	Power (kW)
1950	7,192	134,790	NA
1960	7,883	NA	NA
1965	8,130	NA	NA
1970	5,923	NA	NA
1975	6,686	NA	NA
1980	6,895	179,557	NA
1985	7,920	121,656	NA
1990	11,189	206,591	NA
1995	9174	206,580	NA
2000	7,818	262,406	980,636
2005	6,716	217,617	876,479
2010	6,477	207,424	826,668
2015	6,187	187,371	769,532
2016	6,191	185,734	765,810

Source: figures extracted by author from Sea Fisheries Statistical Tables and UK Sea Fisheries Statistics. The 1960 number of vessels is for England, Scotland and Wales only. For the earlier years gross tonnage is not available and power information has only been provided for the more recent period.

Notes
NA: Not available.
Pre-1990 vessel numbers refer to active vessels, from then onwards to the registered fleet.
There are no tonnage figures for the years 1960, 1965, 1970 and 1975. For 1950, 1980, 1985, 1990 and 1995 the figures seem to be for registered tonnage. Finally, from 2000 onwards, gross tonnage based on the International Tonnage Convention measurement has been used in the official statistics.
So, neither vessel number nor tonnage figures are exactly comparable across the series, but the table presents a general picture within the limitations of data available.

The number of vessels actually went up during the 1980s. The high spike in 1990 is probably due to one of the definition changes, here from counting active vessels to the more inclusive measure of registered ones. In subsequent years, boat numbers decreased, but the gross tonnage has remained at a high level indicating fewer vessels each with greater catching capacity. In 2016, based on gross tonnage, the UK fishing fleet was the second largest in the EU and fourth in size based on its power capacity.

The fishing industry as a whole continues to be very successful and its landings in 2016 in both British ports and abroad had a value of £936 million. The type of seafood caught has changed over the years and the corollary of the lower whitefish landings is that now more than half the volume is made up of pelagic (mid-water dwelling) species, particularly herring and mackerel. A fifth consists of shellfish, mainly langoustines (*nephrops norvegicus*) but also scallops, oysters and squid. Much of the pelagic catches and the shellfish is exported. Hence, returning to Table 3.1 the first column shows a decline in landings into the UK from 2000 but total landings both into British ports and abroad have been much higher; thus, in 2015 while domestic landings were 416,000 tonnes, the total including landings abroad was 708,000 tonnes (Richardson 2016, 2017).

Fishery regulation and the issue of sustainability

International changes

There have been two broad governance reasons for the transformation of the products of British fishing over the decades. The first is to do with supra-national regulation, fishing being affected by rules instituted at both global and European levels. The second reason, intertwined with the first, has been the need for conservation measures to deal with the effects of overfishing. A further reason for the large declines in fish quantities going through local markets is connected with changes in the logistics of the seafood supply chain which made local markets a great deal less important and reoriented much of the system to directly supplying supermarkets and the foodservice industry; this is discussed in Chapter 4.

International regulation of sea fisheries involving Britain had been initiated back in the nineteenth century with an 1839 Anglo-French accord relating to the English Channel and later the 1882 six-country North Sea Convention which established the principle of three-mile territorial waters (Oddy 1971; Steinberg 2001). A shared scientific basis for management started with the inauguration of the International Council for the Exploration of the Sea (ICES) in 1902, the UK being one of the eight founding members. The 1937 agreement on an International Convention for the Regulation of the Meshes of Fishing Nets and the Size Limits of Fish was stalled by World War II but was renewed subsequently in the 1946 Convention with the same title. This was superseded by the 1959 North East Atlantic Fisheries Convention and this in turn by North East Atlantic Fisheries Commission (NEAFC) headquartered in London which continues (Bjørndal 2009; Halliday & Pinhorn 1996). In the European Fisheries Convention (known as the London Convention) of 1964, in force from 1966, 13 countries including Britain agreed that each state would have exclusive jurisdiction over fishing in the six-mile band from its coasts but that in the six to 12-mile band there would be fishing access for countries whose vessels had been fishing there in the reference period 1953 to 1962, with the coastal state having the right to establish rules in the area. Thus, already at this point, there had been longstanding recognition first of the need for rules about shared access to fishing waters and second of the principle of taking conservation measures to protect fish stocks, albeit the latter having little practical impact at the time.

These diplomatic developments had not altered the way that the British fishing industry operated but change was to come with the advent of the 'Cod Wars'. They started when Iceland declared a 12-mile territorial zone in 1958, followed by 50 miles in 1972 and finally 200 miles in 1975, each step vehemently protested by Britain but eventually accepted (Foreman 1989; Kurlansky 1999).

Compared to the six miles of exclusive jurisdiction in the London Convention, the Icelandic approach was far more radical. But it proved to be part of a series of international developments which eventually resulted in such claims being recognised globally in the United Nations Convention on the Law of the Sea (UNCLOS), concluded in 1982 and fully into effect in 1994 which laid down the rights and duties of national states in relation to the use of the seas. Those responsibilities include conservation of the 'living resources' under their charge and co-operation with other states that share those resources. Under this treaty, nearly all of the world's coastal countries eventually declared Exclusive Economic Zones (EEZs) of 200 nautical miles from their coasts. The UK itself did so in the *Fishery Limits Act 1976*.[1]

With the EEZ principle in the ascendant, the British distant water fleet lost its access to what had been its largest source of whitefish and its problems were exacerbated by hefty increases in fuel costs in the mid-1970s resulting from OPEC (Organization of the Petroleum Exporting Countries) oil price rises (Robinson 1998). The number of vessels was drastically reduced, fishing effort being redeployed. A traumatic change for the fishing and processing industries resulted and the impact on British fish supply was sharp. Direct landings of cod were greatly reduced and imports increased. The east coast ports of Hull and Grimsby where the main whitefish landings had taken place managed to maintain their seafood processing plants but now they depended on imports from the 'Nordic countries', that is Iceland, Norway, the Faroes and Greenland. The fish was coming to a large extent from the same marine sources, but now it was a foreign not domestically produced supply (Symes 1985a, 1985b, 1991; Symes & Haughton 1987). This dependence has continued (Garrett et al. 2010).

The Common Fisheries Policy

Concurrently with these developments, governance of fishing was affected by Britain becoming a member of the European Economic Community (EEC) in 1973. This meant also becoming a partner in the Common Fisheries Policy (CFP) so that the UK's 200 mile EEZ became part of European Community waters. The only exception has been the 12-mile zone where member states retained exclusion rights while historic fishing rights in the six to 12-mile band continued, thus continuing the principles established in the London Convention. Originally intended to be a short-term transitional measure this derogation from equal access has been retained in every successive round of CFP reforms.

In the collective memory of British fishing communities, the impact of Iceland's Cod War successes and the implications of general EEZ recognition has become amalgamated with the experience of the CFP. They overlapped in time and while the CFP continued to be a very live issue in the following years, the Cod Wars and the significance of UNCLOS faded into the background. Hence problems experienced by the fishing industry were all attributed to Europe and the terms on which the UK entered the EEC. As colourfully put by one wholesaler during an interview but reflecting widespread sentiment in the industry that fishing was given low priority in the negotiations, the problem was that the Prime Minister responsible for negotiating Britain's accession:

> … didn't like fishermen because he was a yachtie.[2] He didn't. He sold the fishing industry out to creep up to France & Germany 'cos they missed the opportunity years before.
>
> (Managing director, small company 1)

However, contrary to widespread views in the fishing industry that there was a sell-out of its interests in 1973 when Britain entered the EEC, Britain was then still in cod war mode, less interested in its potential EEZ than in maintaining access for its distant waters fleet. The UK had not then declared its 200-mile zone; this only took place with the 1976 Act already mentioned. The country could hardly have asserted rights to its EEZ at the same time as arguing that Iceland should not do likewise.

A key motive for Iceland's position was concern about overfishing. This factor came into the equation more and more forcefully in the years following Britain's entry into European arrangements. It turned attention to the issue of sustainability of the fish stocks on which the fishing industry relied and in time this became the focus of the CFP. Growing recognition went hand in hand with the development of active fisheries management which had not been practised previously.

However, this was not how the CFP started. Initially, the key principles agreed in 1970 were equal access to other member states' waters and a common market in the outputs of the fishing industry; this agreement was reached as Britain's EEC accession negotiations were about to begin, that is before the UK could participate in these initial decisions. It has been seen as deliberate policymaking to present Britain and other applicant countries possessing major fishing industries with a *fait accompli* (Lequesne 2004). But subsequent resolutions took place after Britain's 1973 entry starting with the 1976 Hague Declarations and resulting legislation which dealt with extending jurisdictions to the 200-mile level and laid down initial principles for fisheries policy and so were agreed by the UK government of the day.[3] Up to this point, it could be considered that the objectives behind the CFP were more about European unity than effective fisheries management (Crean 2000).

A significant step came with the 1983 regulation which made fisheries management a key function of the CFP.[4] It recognised that overfishing of key species was occurring so that rationing of fishing opportunities, formally called 'total allowable catches' (TACs) but generally referred to as quotas, should be established, in theory for the species under most pressure, in reality for those most commercially important (Peñas Lado 2016). Their distribution was to be based on the principle of 'relative stability' under which member states' shares would echo their catch records over 1973–1978. The share-out based on relative stability has been criticised but the decision to use historical fishing patterns as the basis for quota allocation was fair and reasonable at the time. No alternative method was available so this had been an underlying principle of the 1964 London Convention and internally the UK was to use the same approach in its initial quota allocations to individual fishers/vessels. Britain's relative stability share included extra elements to compensate for lost access to Icelandic waters due to the then-new EEZ system and to take account of the special needs of coastal communities highly dependent on fishing so it was a favourable arrangement under the circumstances. The problem has been that relative stability was based on a fishing period taken too soon after the changes to reflect all the adjustments that fishers were to make in the new EEZ-defined world but it became set in stone, not revised in subsequent years to reflect changes in either fishing practices or fish movements.

While relative stability was to determine national shares of quota, the actual amount to be divided up each year was to be based on scientific advice which now became an important governance factor in relation to fisheries (Halliday & Pinhorn 1996). The operation of the CFP in practice was to show that such advice was often not accepted, certainly not fully, but it has been the touchstone of what ought to be done in the interests of sustainability. The scientific contribution though subject to criticisms on the grounds of inadequate knowledge, not least from fishers, could at least be seen as disinterested, unlike politicians' decisions about quotas. Credibility has been enhanced when scientific assessments are publicly available, as on the International Council for the Exploration of the Sea (ICES) website, again unlike the negotiations over quotas. The 1983 CFP regulation included the establishment of a Scientific and Technical Committee for Fisheries under the aegis of the European Commission to provide it with scientific advice. With an expanded brief it became the Scientific, Technical and Economic Committee for Fisheries (STECF) in the next, 1992 CFP revision. For the northern seas within the CFP's remit ICES has been the authoritative source of scientific assessments and recommendations.

Another key aspect of the CFP, introduced in 1983, was financial support which at the start was part of agricultural funding.[5] Following the first CFP review, a dedicated fund was established, the Financial Instrument for Fisheries which ran over 1994–2006. It was replaced by the European Fisheries Fund 2007–2013 and most recently by the European Maritime and Fisheries Fund 2014–2020.

The CFP and quotas in particular unsurprisingly became a focus of contestation. Much concentrated on the annual December fixing of quotas for the following year by fisheries ministers of EU member states. They naturally received representations from fishing interests, in Britain from the National Federation of Fishermen's Organisations (NFFO), formed in 1977 specifically to influence the process that resulted in the 1983 CFP regime[6] and from the

Scottish Fishermen's Federation (SFF), founded earlier in 1973. Frequently the allocations made by these politicians were considerably more generous than what was advocated by scientists, although at the same time they could be bitterly disappointing to fishers.

Stepping back from this beginning of systematic fisheries management affecting the European industry the circumstances which made it necessary must be understood. Overfishing in European waters including by British fishers had been known for decades before the CFP came into existence and was the long-term result of the development of industrialised fishing from the late nineteenth century onwards (Graham 1943; Lee 1992; Roberts 2007). A study of demersal landings from England and Wales-registered trawlers going back to 1889 found that considerable stock collapse had happened before the 1983 start of CFP management (Thurstan, Brockington & Roberts 2010). In the twentieth century inter-war period British fishing yields from the North Sea gradually declined because of fishing pressures (FAO 1956). The British herring fishery had to be closed from 1977 to 1983 because of overfishing (Reid 1998; Smith 2011). However, the seriousness of decline had long been masked by technological developments such as steam engines which enabled more powerful vessels with bigger nets to travel further into more difficult seas and obtain large catches by exploiting previously little-touched stocks. The development of large vessels by British and other European fleets targeting Icelandic waters and the Barents Sea expanded greatly during the 1930s (Roberts 2007). Eventually, concern about the resulting pressures on these stocks led Iceland to start territorialising its waters and eventually, after the Cod Wars and the widespread adoption of EEZs, British distant water fishing operations had to end. As a result, since the relevant species had already been overfished in the North Sea, most of the supply of whitefish for domestic consumption had to be imported.

Despite these developments, a situation of ongoing stock decline was not widely recognised by fishers at the time of the inception of the CFP or for many succeeding years. They were accustomed to major fish movements in response to natural causes, reacting to low catches in any one area by going elsewhere, and they felt that their knowledge was a better basis than the scientific data for making judgements about the situation. The thinking is encapsulated by an interviewee statement reflecting the contrast between fisher knowledge and formal scientific methodology based on sampling a survey area:

> We get scientists come and hire a boat for a day, a fishing boat. They'll get on the co-ordinates, the boat will go out and fish there and they pull the net up, nothing in it, the sea's empty, that's your proof. But if that same scientist were just to go in a boat for a day's fishing, the fishermen would go over here and get the fish, plenty of fish. So they're only doing their job, they know there's no fish there. Whereas the fishermen know there's no fish there so they wouldnae go there.
>
> (Managing director, small company 6)

The impact of CFP management on the unaccustomed fishing industry was hard and provoked opposition. In addition to representations from the NFFO and SFF, there was more radical activity with the goal of complete exit from the CFP first by Save Britain's Fish in the early 1990s for about a decade and then in the mid-2000s by the dual campaign the United Fishing Industry Alliance and Cod Crusaders, all these groups being based in Scotland.[7]

More insidiously, 'black fishing' excess to quota was widespread (Lequesne 2004; McDiarmid 1990). A survey in one region found that only 20% of fishermen said they never landed illegally (Cabinet Office 2004), and the illegitimate trade was so well-developed that it was known that non-traceable cod could be purchased at a 20% discount.[8] A sophisticated scam that was eventually prosecuted involved 17 pelagic boats and three Scottish land-based processors who maintained secret conveyor belts and weighing devices; it is estimated to have laundered fish worth £100 million between 2002 and 2005 (Smith 2015). Some interviews carried out for this project indicated that a certain amount of illegal fishing was still taking place in the late 2000s. In one area, it was described as 'substantially reduced' (Manager, trade organisation 1). In another, a regular black fish sales arrangement was described to the author off the record. While there were obvious financial incentives for these activities they could also be seen as marking some fishers' underlying sense of entitlement and their lack of trust in the fisheries management system.

What was experienced as top-down and inflexible rule-making, contrasting with the unpredictability of fish behaviour and the complexity of decision-making needed to fish, could result in fishery management lacking legitimacy in the views of those expected to implement it (Abernethy 2010). Further, the CFP restrictions might create considerable difficulties for those trying to make a living from fishing:

> If you spoke to a fisherman you would absolutely and unequivocally get the view that they are over-regulated and it is very difficult for them because fundamentally their ability to fish is severely restricted and their capacity to fish continues to grow. There's always going to be a tension there. And these are generally one-man businesses, owning their own boats, and so it's really going directly to the heart of their livelihoods.
>
> (Director, large company)

There were mixed feelings among those working in the seafood industry about the CFP, ranging from acceptance of its necessity to scornful rejection:

> I don't have a lot of issues with quota management, it's one of the bulwarks against over-exploitation to be quite honest with you.
>
> (Managing director, small company 1)

> You've got the Common Fisheries Policy which has failed on every front, every objective set for the Common Fisheries Policy has failed, it's

failed socially, it's failed on economic grounds, it's failed on conservation grounds. It annoys the life out of me that we go around the world telling people how to manage fisheries and we are the worst managers of our fisheries that exist in the world.

(Trade organisation representative 3)

The sceptical view seemed justified because in the period following the establishment of the CFP the deterioration of European fish stocks continued apace. In the North Sea overfished stocks rose from 10% in 1970 to nearly half the total in 2000 (Roberts 2007) and a decade later for assessed stocks in all Europe's seas it was a shocking 75% (Schacht et al. 2012). While the CFP was not the cause of the ongoing decline it had egregiously failed to halt it. Criticisms of the CFP came from all sides, from environmentalists and scientists as well as the fishing industry. Various reasons for the failure were given, the chief being politicians' disregard for scientific advice in making allocations, the overcapacity of fleets in relation to fish availability, inappropriate subsidies and poor enforcement of quota limits (Boude, Boncoeur & Bailly 2001; Brown 2006; Froese & Quaas 2012; Khalilian et al. 2010). The science underlying quota recommendations was criticised especially as considerable black fishing distorted the validity of landings data used (Daw & Gray 2005).

There were periodic attempts to improve the CFP system and deal with shortcomings identified. A ten-year review period had been built into the 1983 CFP regulation and this resulted in a revision in 1992, its advances being the requirement for fishing licence systems to be established and the added option of restricting fishing effort, for example limiting days at sea.[9] A much stronger and more comprehensive attempt to reform the system came from the following review and resulting 2002 regulation. It adopted a more precautionary, ecosystem approach with significant innovations in three areas: multi-annual management plans would at least partially overcome the limitations of the annual quota bargaining process with stronger recovery plans mandated for the most damaged stocks; member states were required to reduce the capacity of fishing fleets to match the level of fish available and vessel modernisation subsidies were to be phased out; and third enforcement of the rules was to be tightened (Lutchman, Van den Bossche & Zino 2008). In addition, Regional Advisory Councils (RACs) representing fishers and other stakeholders such as environmental NGOs were introduced in response to criticisms of over-centralised decision-making.[10] In relation to the enforcement of CFP rules which has been identified as an area of weakness by the European Court of Auditors, the Community Fisheries Control Agency was established in 2006 to co-ordinate member states' activity and a comprehensive Control Regulation passed (Peñas Lado 2016).[11]

The new measures were gradually put into effect but towards the end of the decade there seemed to be scant signs of improvement as far as fish stocks were concerned and some concluded simply that the 2002 CFP reform had failed (House of Lords European Union Committee 2008). The Commission started the next ten-year review process early with a Green Paper containing its own hard-hitting critique of the situation (European Commission 2009). A significant problem highlighted was that quotas were resulting in the scandal of discards, an unintended consequence, partly because fishers sought to maximise the value of their limited quotas by eliminating smaller, less profitable parts of the catch and fish with little commercial value (termed 'high-grading') but often because species excess to quota had to be removed from nets containing a mixture of fish. This was upsetting to people in the seafood industry: 'I feel really passionately about discards, chucking away perfectly good fish' as the managing director of one company said. Along with the general problem of overfishing it was of course also particularly shocking to environmentalists and environmental NGOs (non-governmental organisations) who were to intensify their efforts into this review, partly because the European Parliament now had greater powers and could be more effective as a channel of democratic representations.[12] For the first time, there was a public campaign connected with a CFP review under the name Fish Fight, focusing on discards, which has been credited with influencing the resulting reforms.[13]

Produced after a particularly lengthy review process, the 2013 CFP regulation continued 2002 policies such as multi-annual plans and fleet overcapacity measures and added two ambitious new targets and associated rules. The first was to achieve maximum sustainable yield (MSY which is the largest catch that can be taken from a stock over an indefinite period without impairing its ability to reproduce itself) by 2015 for most stocks or by 2020 at the latest. The second was the radical innovation of a landing obligation for quota species, radical because the rules would now control what is actually caught instead of what is landed onshore, with the intention that after the phasing-in period, by the end of 2018, there should be a general end to discards (albeit with some specified exceptions). The obligation includes the requirement for catch smaller than the defined reference size for the species concerned to be landed but it may not be used for human consumption (Hedley, Catchpole & Ribeiro Santos 2015). Another aspect of the new regulation was strengthened stakeholder participation: the RACs, renamed Advisory Councils, were expanded in number and given greater influence within CFP processes.[14]

On the seas, meanwhile, something of a transformation was occurring. Evidence began to emerge of real improvements in the northern European waters. The European Commission published information in 2012 showing that in the previous ten years the share of Atlantic stocks fished within safe biological limits rose from 29% to 56% and that quotas set above sustainable levels had gone down from 46% in 2003 to 11%.[15] In 2017 (based on 2015 data), it reported that 39 of 66 stocks in the NE Atlantic were exploited at MSY level that is 59%; in the NE Atlantic 68% stocks were classified as within safe biological limits compared to just 35% in 2003.[16] While the situation has remained problematic in the Mediterranean and Black Seas, academic assessments concur that significant improvements have taken place elsewhere in EU waters (Cardinale et al. 2013; Fernandes & Cook 2013). These improvements began before the 2013 regulation was passed so it was the 2002 CFP reform that started the upward process of stock restoration but it had taken time for the various measures to be put into effect, for some trial and error learning as with designing multi-annual management plans, and then for the changes to have an impact.

It had been a very long journey before fisheries management under the CFP began to work. Many aspects had to change before this happened: its objectives, mechanisms and enforcement tools all had to be greatly strengthened. Above all, two things were needed: political willingness to put arrangements in place which could put long-term interests over short-term pressures and fishers' and fishing industry support for fisheries management.[17]

The positive developments do not mean that the battle for sustainable fishing in EU waters has been won by any means. First, there are the practical difficulties of putting aspects of the 2013 CFP reform into operation, particularly the landing obligation (discard ban) which was expected to cause particular problems for those working small-scale fisheries (Villasante et al. 2018). In mixed fisheries catching fish additional to the target species is unavoidable which can lead to the 'choke' problem. This occurs when a vessel has exhausted its quota for one species and therefore becomes unable to fish for species for which it does have unused quota, the latter usually being its main target. This may not just reduce the profitability of certain fisheries but could render them unviable (Poseidon Aquatic Management 2013). A key part of the solution is much greater selectivity in fishing including further development of gears to reduce taking unwanted and undersize fish and choices about location and timing of fishing, all of which can affect what ends up in the nets. The British fishing industry has foreseen that such measures will be insufficient and looks to other ways out such as increasing quota for the potential choke species (taking into account the former level of discards) and/or extended use of the exceptions and flexibilities in the regulation. This is likely to feed pressures for quota uplift. The discard ban has been put into operation in stages from 2015 to 2018, and it will take some time for its full implications to be demonstrated.

Second, political actions continue to be less than wholeheartedly consistent with the CFP's sustainability objectives, presumably in response to representations from national fishing industries. An analysis of ministerial quota decisions over the period 2010 to 2017 showed that well over half the TACs set were at levels that exceeded scientific advice while concurrently the trend for overfishing to decline has stalled since 2012 (Borges 2018; Salomon, Markus & Dross 2014). The UK has been identified as one of the four worst offenders in seeking and obtaining quota in excess of scientifically advised levels (Carpenter 2018). Another indication is the weakening of the North Sea Multi-Annual Plan to facilitate the achievement of CFP targets in these complex mixed demersal fisheries. In its original form as approved by the European Parliament it was welcomed by environmental NGOs but after changes following some political haggling, they criticised it for allowing some overfishing.[18] Thus the work of making the CFP a tool for sustainability continues.

UK governance of fishing

While CFP policies are set at European level, member states have always been able to decide how to implement them. They have determined how to distribute their national quotas, what policies should apply within their 12-mile zones, the way enforcement is carried out and how their shares of CFP funds will be distributed.

Quota distribution

In Britain, fish Producer Organisations (POs) have been made central to the share-out of fishing quotas, not necessarily the case elsewhere in the EU (Kleinjans & Carpenter 2017; Symes & Phillipson 1999). POs were mandated early on in the development of the CFP as part of arrangements for a common market in fishery products so as to carry out marketing functions and administer the EU's seafood minimum pricing scheme under government supervision.[19] In the UK, quota management has become the main function of the fishery POs rather than the activities connected with marketing set out in the original European regulation (Marine Scotland 2012). The British POs (there were 24 in 2016) not only manage quotas on behalf of their members, they also have an enforcement role, penalising infringements with quota deductions independently of the role of the public agencies (National Audit Office 2003). POs therefore 'are not public bodies but they inhabit a strange quasi-public world' (Appleby 2013, p. 5); it is all the stranger when three of them in 2016 consisted of a single (different) fishing company.[20]

Not all fishers or rather vessel licensees are members of POs; just over a third of the larger vessels are out of them in what official terminology calls the 'non-sector' as are most of the smaller boats (defined as under ten metres long), also described as the inshore fleet. These obtain allocations from the 'pool' of remaining quota not passed to the POs. Since 2012, the UK national quota allocation is divided between the relevant devolved agencies for England, Northern Ireland, Scotland and Wales on the basis of a Concordat and they in turn allocate to POs and within the pool.[21]

The distribution of quota between the different parts of the industry, which it should be emphasised is entirely under UK control, has been the subject of criticism over the very small share going to the under 10-metre boats, amounting to just 6% of the UK quota and 4% of the England share. Greater recognition of this issue has come with the formation in 2006 of the New Under Ten Fishermen's Association (NUTFA) to represent these interests and the environmental NGO Greenpeace began campaigning support for these smaller boats with a relatively low environmental impact and which are important providers of jobs in coastal communities. The sector does not depend on quota: fishers may get much, some even all, of their income from catching species, especially shellfish, that are not subject to the rationing of fishing opportunities. That situation, however, is forced by lack of quota and a greater share should be allocated to this part of the fleet for overall balance and viability.

Government recognition of the issue came in a 2012 announcement that following a consultation process, some underutilised quota from the England PO share would be transferred to the English inshore small boat fleet. Although only a small amount of quota was involved the decision was challenged by the UK Association of Fish Producer Organisations in a judicial review also involving NUFTA and Greenpeace. The government position and plan was upheld and the judgement included the resonant phrase 'no-one can own the fish of the sea'.[22] A couple of years later, Greenpeace challenged the government in another judicial review. It argued that the CFP regulation requiring fishing opportunities to be allocated on environmental, social and economic criteria meant that more should go to the lower impact inshore fleet sector but the claim failed because of the discretion allowed to member states on how the criteria should be balanced.[23] A significant subsequent development has been the creation of a Coastal PO for small-scale fishers to represent this sector including lobbying for a fairer share of quota.

If no-one can own the fish of the sea can the right to fish them be owned nevertheless? The right to fish is embodied in fishing licences and quota allocations. When the 1983 CFP introduced TACs, the British licensing system was extended to all over ten-metre fishing vessels that targeted them; previously only the largest boats had to be licensed. From 1993, with the reformed CFP, licensing was extended to the smaller vessels. Initially, licences were issued freely but in subsequent years various restrictions on the granting of licences and their transferability between vessels were introduced from time to time because of concerns about excess capacity and resulting pressure on fish stocks. From the late 1990s no new licences have been issued.

The quota system started with allocations to licensed vessels; trading was allowed to give flexibility to the scheme. These quotas are shares in the national pot while the pot itself has been decided annually by EU fisheries ministers or more recently for certain stocks via multi-annual plans. POs have discretion over internal methods of actual quota allocation to their members. Quota shares were initially based on vessel landings over the previous three years but this method was perceived to incentivise either overfishing or artificial inflation of records, so in 1999 there was a change to fixed quota allocations (FQAs) calculated from a reference period in the mid-1990s; this meant that quota holders had more certainty regardless of actual catches. By this time, dating from 1995, the landings records were connected to licences rather than vessels making licences more valuable. In 2002 there was a change which permitted FQAs to be transacted separately from vessels in defined situations, a further step in making the right to fish an article of trade.

Official guidance and ministerial pronouncements have emphasised that FQAs do not constitute a property right and that legal ownership rests with the state.[24] At the same time, fishing licences and FQAs have become valuable assets which are traded at high levels and can be used as security for bank loans meaning that the right to fish is being bought and sold. The right to fish is a public resource deriving from national entitlement over territorial waters but as a result of the various decisions over the management of quota allocation and fishing licences which have been outlined it has been semi-privatised in the UK and this has happened without public or Parliamentary debate.

One result of the tradability of quota is that much of the UK's share is held by non-British European companies, sometimes called 'quota-hopping'. The UK government did attempt to protect British ownership legislatively but lost its case in the European Court of Justice in a judgement based on the right of establishment provisions of the Single Market which in this respect over-ruled the relative stability aspect of the CFP. The UK then established certain requirements intended to benefit the domestic economy through what is called the 'Economic Link' but this has had limited effect.[25] The upshot is that semi-privatisation has allowed the effective reduction of the national quota from the viewpoint of the British fishing industry and the loss of related economic benefits. It has been estimated that 40% of the UK quota is held by non-British companies and there are British POs which consist almost entirely of foreign-owned vessels (Le Gallic, Mardle & Metz 2017).[26]

Two contrasting views have been put forward on how the UK system of fishing rights could develop. The first is by adopting a model such as an Individual Transferable Quota (ITQ) scheme in which the right to fish does become owned and fully tradable and the allocation of quota is left to market mechanisms; this would be a fully privatised system. Such an arrangement is argued to facilitate the reduction of excess fleet capacity (because less profitable vessels would have their quota bought out) so resulting in a more efficient industry. It is also advocated as favourable to conservation because fishers have an incentive to ensure the long-term benefits of a resource they own. ITQ systems applied in several countries have been shown to result in capacity rationalisation and stock recovery as well as achieving greater profitability for the fishing industry (Hatcher et al. 2002; Iudicello, Weber & Wieland 1999). However, there may also be negative effects with quota holders not necessarily being active fishers, difficulty for new entrants because of the cost of quota and over-concentration of power and wealth in the fishing industry (Bradshaw 2004; Hersoug 2018; Pantzar 2016). Some of these problems have indeed already occurred with the British FQA system (Cardwell & Gear 2013).

From a different point of view, the right to fish is a public asset and it should not be simply given away for free. Instead, as with other Crown Estate resources, there should be a market valuation and appropriate rents charged to benefit the public purse (Appleby, van der Werf & Williams 2016). What has happened instead is that the valuable right to fish was gifted to a particular cohort of fishers who happened to be active in the period when quota shares were allocated, without any public recompense being required. An ITQ approach could include imposing some kind of fee or tax on quota holders (Cunningham et al. 2010) but a public asset model and franchise leasing would provide more direct recompense.

Other fishing governance policies in the UK

Funds associated with the CFP were initially focused on fishing fleet modernisation but as sustainability became more of a focus and excess capacity increasingly recognised as a driver of overfishing there was an increasing shift to capacity reduction, particularly after the 2002 reforms (Brown 2006). That meant decommissioning programmes to put boats out of action. But, funding for this purpose has not necessarily been used effectively and can be useless or even counterproductive if resulting in a smaller number of more powerful boats with collectively the same or greater power and therefore catching ability.

In Britain an early 1983–1986 decommissioning scheme was slated in a Parliamentary review as excessively expensive in relation to what it achieved. The next one, which ran from 1993 to 1997, was considered successful when its first stage, which cost £36 million, was formally evaluated because a sizeable number of owners did apply for the scheme and decommission their boats and the payments were below assessed commercial values. But the vessels concerned were generally older ones and the owner's motive often was about funding a replacement while the specific reduction targets for fleet segments were not met (Nautilus Consultants 1997). Subsequent schemes ran in 2001–2002, 2003, 2007 and 2008–2009. Motives are illustrated in relation to one Scottish scheme in which the objectives were officially stated to be reducing the size of the fleet and conserving North Sea stocks but according to an industry representative it was more about improving profitability: 'We will still be catching the same amount of fish albeit with fewer vessels'.[27] The impact of the series of schemes was eventually reflected in significant capacity reduction. Between 2000 and 2016 the number of boats declined by a fifth, as did power capacity while in terms of gross tonnage the fall was somewhat greater, indicating a trend to greater power for a given size of vessel. Some later schemes were targeted at removing specific capacity in line with recovery plans such as for cod and sole (Richardson 2017). The UK decommissioning programmes along with similar ones by other countries has been judged to have made a worthwhile contribution to the revival of specific fisheries.[28]

Decommissioning offered carrots but the stick of enforcement has also been necessary for achieving fishery management objectives. The main responsibility lies with the Sea Fisheries Inspectorates which exercise responsibilities on both land and on sea. Fisheries Monitoring Centres analyse data from the vessel monitoring system which all fishing boat above a certain size are required to have fitted.[29] Catches are checked onboard, at landing sites and at the premises of processors to ensure that records are accurate and that landings conform with quota allocations. The supply chain also became part of the enforcement system with the significant innovation of requiring registration of fish buyers and sellers; this made auctions and first line purchasers of catches responsible for taking only legally caught fish (discussed in more detail in Chapter 4). Infractions of fishing rules are pursued in the courts and convictions include a small number of sensationally large cases like the pelagic scam mentioned previously but many more for offences such as failing to keep full records, misreporting catches or fishing in closed areas and they all incur fines. Such convictions are important; a survey of UK fishers showed that the probability of violating quotas was inversely related to a low perceived risk of detection and low level of fines imposed (Hatcher et al. 2000). Thus it is a matter of concern from the viewpoint of fisheries management that there was a reduction in fishery protection vessel capacity from April 2013 which resulted in sharp decreases of both boat boardings and of convictions for quota infractions.[30]

As already noted, EU member states retain sole control over the six-mile coastal band of territorial seas. Within Britain, management is delegated to Inshore Fisheries and Conservation Authorities (IFCAs) in England and to Regional Inshore Fisheries Groups (RIFGs) in Scotland; in Northern Ireland and Wales responsibility lies with the devolved administration/government.[31] Most of what is fished in these inshore waters, often predominantly shellfish, is outside the quota system (langoustines being the only shellfish governed by the CFP) and management is the responsibility of the local bodies. There may be a range of management measures in place such as minimum landing sizes (brown crab, cockles, scallops), local prohibitions on taking berried, that is egg-bearing, crabs and lobsters, gear restrictions (such as on certain scallop dredges), vessel licensing and bed closures (Bannister 2006). The local bodies need to act in conjunction with local stakeholders and take into account their competing demands such as for tourism and recreational angling in addition to their environmental objectives. IFCAs however have the authority to make by-laws and also have enforcement capabilities so can prosecute infractions.

Within the inshore waters arrangements, shellfish has its own legislative regime under the *Sea Fisheries (Shellfish) Act 1967*. It includes 'Regulating Orders', a sort of franchise which for a defined period gives the holder the ability to exercise a certain control over a shellfishery, effectively private governance over the right to fish. It should be used to improve management by controlling access through a licensing arrangement and setting conditions or restrictions by which the fishery operates and is granted by Marine Scotland or by DEFRA for England and Wales; (the 1967 Act did not include Northern Ireland). The shellfish fishing sector remains relatively less regulated to an extent that is found problematic within the industry. The NFFO established a Shellfish Committee and became active in pressing for more action, not only at local (IFCA) level but national legislative action to limit the high volume crab fleet because of concerns that sustainability is threatened by excessive capacity.[32]

Despite the frustration over lack of action on this particular issue, more broadly the state in Britain has over the years provided various facilitative and supportive services for the fishing industry. In the mid-twentieth century there were fisheries departments in the Ministry of Agriculture, Fisheries and Food (MAFF) and in the Scottish Office. Support for fishery management objectives from the current bodies, the Centre for Environment, Fisheries and Aquaculture Science (Cefas), the Marine Management Organisation (MMO) and Marine Scotland has included tests of selective trawls and catch quota schemes, directed to reducing discards, and the Scottish Conservation Credits Scheme aimed at more sustainable fishing practices. Trials have been useful in demonstrating before the landing obligation became mandatory that reduction of discards to a very low level could be successful but also flagged up a considerable number of practical problems that would need attention (Carter 2014; Catchpole et al. 2014; Marine Management Organisation 2013).[33] More broadly, the government funded nearly 100 projects via the Fisheries Science Partnership between Cefas and the NFFO fisher representative organisation between 2003/2004 and 2011/2012. Responding to proposals from the fishing industry, they included stock assessments in specified zones, catch composition studies, gear change assessments and studies of the survivability of certain discard species. As well as the delivery of useful information through combining fisher knowledge with scientific methods, this joint work has led to greatly improved mutual understanding and co-operation between fishers and scientists (Armstrong et al. 2013).

A particularly significant contribution was made by the Aberdeen-based Torry Research Station, originally situated within the government Department of Scientific and Industrial Research. The Torry role in relation to research on freezing fish at sea can be considered an example of the 'entrepreneurial state' when public agencies progress technological developments that the private sector considers too risky (Mazzucato 2018). The research station pursued ways of achieving freezing at sea over a long period from 1929 onwards when the fishing industry was too risk-averse to follow suit, not without reason as various experiments in Britain and other countries failed to achieve solutions with long-term commercial viability. Eventually, only in the post-World War II period a couple of UK companies did engage in such experimental development and then an experimental freezer-trawler was converted under Torry supervision and using freezers developed by Torry (with a commercial partner) in a joint venture funded by the government, White Fish Authority and vessel owners in 1955. After this another couple of companies, each receiving Torry expert support undertook freezing at sea in the early 1960s. British freezer factory ships did finally take off in the early 1970s to enjoy a brief heyday before the advance of EEZs meant that they could no longer fish distant waters as already explained and so they lost their rationale (Waterman 1987).[34] Other innovatory Torry work is included in Chapter 4.

Further support to the fishing industry and indeed the whole seafood sector is supplied by the Sea Fish Industry Authority, generally known as Seafish. Established by a legislative Act and formally required to present an annual report to Parliament but funded by an industry levy, the organisation is positioned at the cusp of the public-private interface.[35] Seafish advises and assists the industry in various ways and promotes it externally. In relation to fishing, it initiated and continues to support the Responsible Fishing Scheme (discussed in Chapter 4) and its activities include safety at sea training. The usefulness of Seafish to the seafood industry was tested when one company challenged its right to levy funds based on imports, arguing that the system had been designed in relation to domestic landings. While the resulting court case was in train from 2009 to 2011, the disputed part of the levy was suspended, reducing the organisation's activities considerably and its continued existence was in doubt. However, the Supreme Court finally found in favour of Seafish. It then emerged that a government-commissioned review on the future of the agency had been completed but kept under wraps while the case proceeded, which turned out to be a critical report recommending significant reforms (Cleasby 2010). Seafish subsequently carried out a consultation with its stakeholders and, having received sufficient support to continue, restructured and developed a new work programme with strong industry involvement.

Although these various state bodies have supported the seafood industry in various ways, the UK government of the day has rarely taken a particular interest in it. One major exception was the production of the Cabinet Office report *Net Benefits: A Sustainable and Profitable Future for UK Fishing*, which put forward a set of recommendations, some of which came to fruition in subsequent years (Cabinet Office 2004). The DEFRA-commissioned Fishing for the Markets project 2010–2012 was geared to increasing use of less familiar seafood species in order to reduce discards at a time when public recognition of the problem was growing but before the CFP had been reformed to radically reduce it (DEFRA 2012).[36] The Department also funded work by Cefas to identify which underutilised species could be safely promoted without the risk of too much fishing pressure (Catchpole 2011). Fishing issues are set to become more politically prominent in the coming years as a result of Brexit with participation in the CFP being replaced by British policies (discussed further in the final chapter).

While the emphasis so far has been on EU and UK state action, civil society input by environmental NGOs should also be noted. Greenpeace campaigning in favour of a higher quota share for small fishing boats has been recorded in this section while the previous one included the Fish Fight campaign to change the CFP in order to end discards. The World Wide Fund for Nature (WWF) contributed to pressure for reform of the CFP particularly in relation to subsidies for vessel modernisation and overcapacity with some hard-hitting reports (Coffey 2006; MacGarvin & Jones 2000). Another NGO organisation campaigning for sustainable fishing and environmental protection is the Blue Marine Foundation which has projects in various parts of the world including Britain. Open Seas concentrates on campaigning to protect the seabed and environment around the Scottish coast from damaging fishing activities.[37] These activities have primarily been about putting pressure on state agencies. In the next section we see what happened when an NGO got involved in an activity aimed at changing practice within the fishing industry.

A new governance tool for fishing: certification

So far, this chapter has considered fisheries management and the impetus for securing sustainable supply in terms of various forms of state and supra-state regulation but at the end of the twentieth century, an additional form of governance became relevant. As explained in Chapter 1, systems of standards, enforced by audits, had come to be the dominant means of control by more powerful companies in supply chains, including food chains. When certain NGOs started to focus their attention on private companies in the 1990s, they began using this system to achieve ethical and environmental objectives. Such thinking reached the world of fishing initially with the development of an eco-labelling scheme for 'dolphin-friendly' tuna in the US but with much broader impact when the Marine Stewardship Council (MSC) was founded in 1997, jointly by a large food corporation, Unilever (then owner of the seafood manufacturer Birds Eye) and an environmental organisation, WWF (the World Wide Fund for Nature).

The motivations for establishing the MSC were a perceived failure of state governance to deal with what WWF characterised in a campaign as 'endangered seas' and which from Unilever's point of view was a risk to the future supply of fish (Flower & Heap 2000; Howes 2008). In short, state regulation did not at the time seem able to deal with overfishing and the new factors expected from an eco-certification scheme were the market and consumer choice (Oosterveer 2005; Parkes et al. 2009).

Critical responses to the establishment of the MSC attacked the governance aspects of the scheme. Some Nordic governments objected to a non-state body intervening in this way, seeing the MSC as 'an attempt to create a private transnational management regime beyond national jurisdiction' (Gulbrandsen 2009, p. 656). It was viewed as deliberately bypassing states to appeal directly to consumers, pre-empting what should be the role of each government to secure a broad national benefit (Steinberg 1999) and in relation to less industrialised countries embodying a neo-liberal approach in the interests of the richer Northern ones (O'Riordan 1996).

At this point, there was already a global governance response to the widespread concern over over-exploitation of fisheries in the form of the *Code of Conduct for Responsible Fisheries* (CCRF), produced in 1995 by the Food and Agriculture Organisation of the United Nations (FAO). It laid down principles for conservation, set out the obligations of states and other parties and outlined a framework for fisheries management. Concerns about the role of the MSC expressed in the FAO's Committee on Fisheries spurred the organisation to produce its own eco-labelling guidelines for both marine and inland fisheries (FAO 2009; FAO 2011a; Willmann, Cochrane & Emerson 2008) and subsequently an evaluation schema for assessing eco-labelling programmes (FAO 2011c). These developments were intended to counter the position of eco-labelling schemes standing completely outside any state governance framework (Gulbrandsen 2009; Washington & Ababouch 2011). The FAO's wider work for fisheries conservation has included guidelines for reducing discards and facilitating an international agreement on what states with ports should do to counter illegal fishing.[38] The limitation of all this activity is over implementation which rests on individual states in relation to their territorial waters and with the supra-national Regional Fishery Bodies (RFBs) and Regional Fisheries Management Organisations (RFMOs) for the rest of the high seas. These as consensus organisations have to move at the pace of the slowest and most reluctant member states and have had variable impacts (Garcia & Rosenberg 2010). Nevertheless, while the *Code of Conduct* and other FAO guidelines are voluntary and do not have legal force in the same way as the UNCLOS, they have been characterised in an FAO review as 'soft law' which has impacted on policy goals for fisheries (Sainsbury 2010). In its 20-year look back on the CCRF, the FAO noted a large number of improvements that accord with its guidance (FAO 2016).

The MSC for its part has explicitly aimed to make its scheme consistent with FAO guidance, initially on the basis of the CCRF, and subsequently amending it when the eco-labelling guidelines appeared (Auld 2007; Gulbrandsen 2009). In addition, the FAO documents have been used by other organisations as benchmarks against which to assess the MSC and other seafood-related schemes meaning all of them are expected to use the standards they set (Parkes et al. 2009). 'All of them' because the MSC was joined by other certification schemes relating to seafood but it has maintained a pre-eminent place in regard to capture fish.[39]

The MSC scheme, working to three overarching principles or goals – sustainable fish stocks, minimising environmental impacts and effective management – has established a set of standards which fisheries must reach to be certified, standards which are formulated with the participation of a range of stakeholders and which are periodically revised. The standards are translated into performance indicators against which fisheries are assessed by third-party certifiers. The performance indicators show how requirements are tied to existing fisheries management arrangements. Evidence of 'harvest control rules' in the indicator associated with sustainable fish stocks includes the kind of measures we have seen used in the CFP such as quotas and effort limits; the first requirement of the effective management principle is that a fishery management system is in place. Indeed the organisation acknowledges that 'we do indeed need states to ensure management arrangements are in place'.[40] Far from being an alternative to state and supra-state regulation, the MSC and similar schemes are complementary to state-led fisheries management, not in competition with it (Washington & Ababouch 2011). What they add is a commercial incentive for those in the fishing industry to ensure that the management arrangements work. The strength of the incentive is down to the impact of certification on supply chains and consumers.

The limitations of the MSC were illustrated when it was involved in the mackerel quota dispute between the EU and Norway on one side and the Faroes and Iceland on the other which started in 2009. The latter two countries claimed larger shares on the grounds that more fish were now spending time in their waters. When no agreement was reached each party unilaterally set its own share meaning that the total was excessive and led to overfishing. Consequently, MSC certification was suspended for a period. Some parties urged the MSC to sanction Iceland and the Faroes by withdrawing accreditations which it declined to do, reportedly saying it had to remain impartial. Here an attempt was made to use certification as a weapon in an inter-state quarrel which in reality could only be resolved by states. More recently the EU has come to an agreement with the Faroes but not with Iceland and certain certifications have been restored.

At the end of 2016 there were nearly 300 MSC-certified fisheries, 12% of the global total. Although one of the first three certifications in 2000 was English and the fifth one in the following year Welsh (the small Thames Blackwater herring and the Burry Inlet cockle fisheries respectively), the initial reaction of the UK fishing industry was generally unenthusiastic (MacMullen 1998). This changed over time and by 2017 Scottish certified fisheries covered specific haddock, saithe, herring and mackerel stocks as well as various shellfish species, there were Northern Ireland certified herring and mackerel fisheries and more fisheries in the pipeline undergoing the assessment process.[41] The seafood marketed from certified fisheries does not necessarily produce a financial premium at first sale, though extra value may emerge further downstream in the supply chain; its benefits for fishers are rather in maintaining and increasing market share as the demand for sustainable products grows (Nimmo & Capell 2014).

Undertaking certification is much more challenging for the small inshore fisheries which may be data-deficient and lack developed management arrangements for non-quota species. To assist them the Seafish-led Project Inshore identified and supported fisheries in England which could be successful in the MSC process and gave advice on how management gaps in other fisheries might be addressed.[42] A similar project is progressing in Wales led by the Welsh Fishermen's Association.[43] Thus a concerted effort has been underway to get British fisheries certified or at least with strengthened management arrangements. This has been industry driven in Scotland, Northern Ireland and Wales while for England the combination public-private organisation Seafish has taken the lead and the local Inshore Fisheries and Conservation Authorities are involved in implementation.

From the viewpoint of supply for domestic consumption, it is equally relevant to consider how far major imports come from certified sources.

Whitefish comes mainly from the Iceland and Norwegian fisheries which are generally acknowledged to be well-managed and which have achieved MSC certification for cod and haddock in Icelandic waters and the Barents Sea.[44] Capture Pacific salmon may be from certified Alaska fisheries. Much of the cold-water prawn supply is from MSC-certified Canadian fisheries. So, towards the end of the second decade of the twenty-first century, a considerable proportion of the seafood from capture sources in the British supply chain is likely to be from fisheries that have been certified as sustainably managed. But there are gaps, a major one being tuna; there are MSC-certified tuna fisheries but it is unclear what proportion of imports they supply.

Despite the extent of certification efforts, views about the MSC in the British seafood industry can be mixed:

> I'm not saying I'm against it, because I think you have to have something, but I don't think it's the panacea that it purports to be, I think there's a lot of problems with it. But having said that of course we do have to have something.
>
> (Trade organisation representative 1)

> Personally I believe it should be, these things should be policed properly and you shouldn't need a thing like MSC to be involved in it. It's another body taking money out of the system and shouldn't be there.
>
> (Director, medium-large company)

The questions implied by the first of these comments are indeed pertinent. What are the problems with the MSC and how much of a panacea is it for the problem of overfishing? Eco-labelling schemes generally face a certain quandary: standards if high denote better practice but need to be achievable by enough producers to get the output necessary for a market presence as without this there cannot be an impact in the market or an incentive for certification. Hence it is not surprising that some have considered the MSC's standards to be too low. The MSC's counter view is that engaged fisheries make improvements during the assessment process and also after certification since this may carry conditions requiring further action. Another key issue is that certifiers are the clients of the fisheries they assess, having tendered for the work, so there is potential for conflicts of interest to occur, affecting ratings (Kalfagianni & Pattberg 2013; Ward 2008). In comparisons of fishery eco-labelling schemes the MSC has scored well (James Sullivan Consulting 2012) but the crunch issue is whether the MSC has had an impact on the sustainability of fish stocks and their ecosystems. Here, there is considerable disagreement with both positive assessments and scepticism and even controversy on whether the MSC has certified overfished stocks (Agnew et al. 2013; Cambridge et al. 2011; Froese & Proelss 2012; Gulbrandsen 2010; Opitz et al. 2016). An overall judgement based on these varied evaluations is that the scheme has achieved some improvements but not so far made a significant ecological impact.

Governance of aquaculture production

Turning to the second source of supply, fish and shellfish farming took off during the last decades of the twentieth century in many parts of the world. Previously it was limited to the freshwater rearing of a small number of species but from the 1970s technical advances gave full control of the reproduction and rearing of many species used for human consumption. For Britain, this meant an expansion of home-produced supply options, primarily Scottish salmon but also trout, a range of shellfish species and small quantities of other finfish. New import options also became available.

In Scotland, salmon production (of Atlantic salmon, *salmo salar*) increased from modest quantities of less than 1,000 tonnes per annum in the 1970s to 32,000 tonnes in 1990, 129,000 tonnes in 2000, 154,000 in 2010 and 163,000 in 2016.[45] About half of this is exported but a sizeable amount of salmon is also imported so the amount available for domestic consumption is considerable, about 100,000 tonnes per annum excluding canned options. Production of trout, mostly rainbow, has developed in all four parts of the UK; the volume available for domestic consumption has run at around 10,000 tonnes each year from the late 1980s and around 12,000 from the late 1990s onwards; in 2016, it was 13,850. Small quantities of other finfish including cod and barramundi have also been farmed at different times without becoming established and recently some English Nile tilapia and Welsh sea bass have been available. Farmed shellfish developed later, rising from 9,000 tonnes in 1995 to 45,000 in 2010 but much of this production is for export. Mussels form the biggest share of British shellfish production: 11,000 tonnes were produced in 2000 and over 30,000 in 2010 but the volume then reduced and was somewhat below 15,000 in 2016. Pacific oysters are the next shellfish type in importance, from the early 2000s generally producing over 1,000 tonnes each year and over 2,000 in 2016.[46] From all this domestic aquaculture farmed salmon has had the biggest impact on supply. As the trade organisation Scottish Salmon Growers Association could already claim nearly three decades ago:

> Whereas Scottish salmon was a luxury, only seasonally available, and with relatively few and privileged consumers, today it is an affordable product, with continuity of supplies of fresh and smoked fish, and widely available in fishmongers, retail stores and catering establishments.
>
> (House of Commons Agriculture Committee 1990)

Governing fish farming in Britain

The starting point for state regulation of UK aquaculture was the system applied to agriculture. Although exemptions from planning control enjoyed by farmers were removed from fish farming (Howarth 1993) legislation over feed, veterinary medicines and pesticides apply to both sectors (Spreij 2005). As aquaculture developed, certain issues emerged and needed specific attention. In relation to production and the environment the two important areas are sites and animal health, discussed below; other governance topics related to aquaculture in the supply chain including slaughter are considered in Chapter 4.

The special site issue in relation to certain types of aquaculture is their use of marine waters, in Britain specifically for the post-juvenile grow-out stage of salmon (hatcheries and the rearing of the emergent alevin and the young fry and parr are land-based) and for shellfish. The state was involved in the form of the Crown Estate, as the owner in the UK of the seabed and foreshore all around the coast except in the Shetlands.[47] The Crown Estate is a semi-independent, incorporated public body, directly accountable to Parliament, which administers its extensive properties on a commercial basis for the benefit of the public purse; therefore its primary goal is to produce an income stream for the national Treasury. This is changing in Scotland where following the transfer of powers relating to the Crown Estate there to the Scottish Parliament, legislation being processed in 2018 will alter the remit from being purely commercial to also take into account broader social, economic and environmental factors and allow delegation of responsibilities to public and community bodies.[48] However, Crown Estate decisions affecting the development of aquaculture to date were made on the basis of the previous regime which also continues in place for the rest of the UK.

Salmon farmers have to obtain a lease from the Crown Estate in order to establish facilities in coastal waters (large pens and associated servicing). Before there were relevant provisions in the planning system, the granting of a lease was effectively a permission to operate. In this way, over three decades, the Crown Estate functioned as a quasi-planning authority for salmon farms. Only in the late 2000s was legislation passed in Scotland to bring marine aquaculture under local government planning control (but a Crown Estate lease is still required).[49] Other farming issues such as parasite control and fish escapes were then covered by the *Aquaculture and Fisheries (Scotland) Act 2007* and then the *Aquaculture and Fisheries (Scotland) Act 2013*. In the lead-up to the transfer of responsibility for authorising fish farms from the Crown Estate to local authorities, the Scottish Executive (subsequently the Scottish Government) introduced Locational Guidelines which included avoidance of further farming developments on certain coasts to protect wild salmon and classified other waters into three categories with different presumptions about the acceptability of further developments.[50] These guidelines, which continue to be regularly updated, have greatly restricted the ability of the salmon farming industry to expand geographically.

Control of infection and the protection of wild fish had started long before the jump in aquaculture production with the 1937 *Diseases of Fish Act*. It established strict conditions both to prevent fish disease being imported and to restrict movements in and out of inland waters where disease had been identified. The next *Diseases of Fish Act* in 1983, when fish farming was still at a modest level, extended the function of preventing the spread of disease to fish farms and introduced the power to require registration of these businesses. Registration of fish and shellfish farming concerns was then formally demanded by regulations a couple of years later which also obliged records of fish stockings and movements to be kept; a further 2002 regulation requires fish escapes to be reported.[51]

European level regulation started with the 1991 aquaculture directive with a broader agenda of ensuring that only products from healthy 'aquaculture animals' would be marketed, defining approved zones for movements, and requiring movement documents, traceability and programmes for disease outbreaks. This was replaced by updated legislation covering these topics in 2006 and each directive has been followed by various corresponding regulations for all the UK administrations.[52] The Fish Health Inspectorates in the various administrations have the role of implementing the aquatic animal health legislation. In England and Wales this includes authorising the establishment of aquaculture production businesses which elsewhere is carried out by Marine Scotland and DAERA (Northern Ireland); authorisation requires biosecurity and record-keeping arrangements to be in place. A major updating of European animal health law issued in 2016 for the first time covers aquatic animals (including invertebrates) and terrestrials in the same regulation although including separate provisions for the former category; it comes into effect in 2021 and may be expected to affect the UK post-Brexit in relation to trade in seafood products and live shellfish.[53]

Veterinary medicine legislation generally applies to aquaculture without particular provisions relating to it. The Veterinary Medicines Directorate, an executive agency of DEFRA, is responsible for implementing policies and regulation in this area which includes monitoring aquaculture premises. There are specific environmental risks associated with their use in aquaculture particularly in the case of treatments added to waters which are subsequently discharged as effluents. When medicated feed is supplied to fish some becomes deposited under the sea cages uneaten and drugs from this source or from faeces can enter the neighbouring waters or be consumed by wild creatures (Boxall et al. 2002).

Concern about disease is highly relevant because it has been a recurrent feature of salmon farming in different parts of the world. In Scotland, there were major losses over 1989–1993 due to furunculosis and sea lice and in the late 1990s, there were severe outbreaks of infectious salmon anaemia. Vaccine use has developed and currently gives protection against several diseases. Treatments against the parasitic sea lice by various therapeutic chemicals were successful for a period but eventually, resistances developed so that they have become much less effective; in the 2010s there was a severe recrudescence of the problem at a global level. Chemical treatments are still being used to check sea lice but other methods of control have been introduced or at least trialled including 'cleaner' fish (certain species which feed on the lice[54]), warm-water treatments and targeting with lasers; a combination of methods might be needed for an integrated approach to dealing with sea lice (Jackson et al. 2017).

A key ecological concern has been the impact on wild fish resulting from escapes. A number of potential risks have been raised including genetic changes resulting from interbreeding, competition for food and the transfer of pathogens (Naylor et al. 2005). A further potential concern would arise were genetically modified farmed fish to be allowed; transgenic salmon are produced and allowed for human consumption in North America but so far have been excluded from the EU.

For finfish farm planning applications whether in Scotland or elsewhere in the UK (where for land-based fish farms such as for trout the normal local authority planning system applies) environmental impact assessments are required. Various environmental conditions must be met to satisfy legislation over pollution control and coastal protection; there are also provisions under marine planning legislation and the EU Birds and Habitats Directives to be taken into account. Authorisation is required from the Environment Agency or the Scottish Environment Protection Agency (SEPA) under water regulations dealing among other matters with pollution and abstraction.[55] In addition, farmers must obtain marine licences from the MMO, Marine Scotland or DAERA for equipment at sea and moorings (which could be a danger for marine navigation) and also for discharging sea lice treatments from wellboats (these are vessels with tanks used to transport live fish). The whole consenting process with the need to deal with a number of different agencies is a complex one for aquaculture operators.[56]

The burst of Scottish regulatory activity over the aquaculture industry, beginning with the first Locational Guidelines in 1999, while partly necessitated by European environmental legislation, can be seen as an active response by the newly devolved administration to the needs and dilemmas posed by an increasingly important local industry, one to which the Westminster Parliament had failed to give legislative attention as demonstrated by the extraordinary length of time that the Crown Estate commissioners substituted for normal local authority planning processes. Regulation was also a response to perceived problems with salmon farming which were receiving growing publicity.

Starting at the end of the 1980s, environmental organisations published a series of reports critical of salmon farming. They highlighted issues such as fouling of the seabed with both unconsumed feed and waste products, the wider contamination from chemicals used for treatment and the impact on wild salmon of both sea lice infestation and the many large-scale escapes that had occurred (Berry & Davison 2001; Friends of the Earth Scotland 1988; Ross 1997; Staniford 2002). Angling organisations were particularly concerned about the genetic impact of escapes on wild salmon and about sea lice which, though present in the wild, has greatly proliferated, causing a much greater problem than was previously the case. On the welfare front, there were criticisms of high stocking densities, stress-inducing grading procedures, starvation before slaughter and slaughter methods (Lymbery 2002). Regular attack bulletins were issued in the name of the Salmon Farm Protest Group (active from 2002 to 2007) and negative press stories appeared (Greenwood 2003).

The industry responded positively by establishing private-led governance. Salmon farmers have successively organised themselves as the Scottish Salmon Growers Association (SSGO – 1982 to 2000), succeeded by Scottish Quality Salmon and from 2006 by the Scottish Salmon Producers' Organisation (SSPO). These organisations emphasised standard setting and positioning for premium markets (discussed more fully in Chapter 4) but also dealt with environmental and sustainability issues. The *Code of Good Practice for Scottish Finfish Aquaculture* (CoGPSFA) has been in operation since 2006 through various revisions, the most recent dated 2015, and covers salmon, trout and other farmed finfish. It includes extremely detailed prescriptions on all aspects of farming, co-operation in disease control and measures to protect the environment. There is third-party auditing of compliance. The CoGPSFA was originally produced in response to a recommendation in the Scottish Executive's 2003 Strategic Framework for Scottish Aquaculture but it is owned by the industry with the adherence of most Scottish producers.[57]

Trout producers who have their own British Trout Association have developed a standards scheme on similar lines. The Scottish Quality Trout scheme functioned from 1993 to the early 2000s but was then superseded by Quality Trout UK which from 2000 has operated an assurance scheme with third-party auditing for the main species, rainbow trout, including environmental and welfare criteria.[58] The scheme is linked to and benchmarked against CoGPSFA.

The salmon producers' organisation took a more unusual governance step when it started a programme for neighbouring farms to synchronise their sea lice treatments. Eventually, this led to the establishment of voluntary area management agreements co-ordinating fallowing and harvesting to deal with competing interests arising from the exploitation of the coastal marine resource. This example of private-led governance with public as well as commercial benefits involves a striking willingness by companies to yield significant freedom of action. What this means in practice was explained on a salmon farm visit in 2009:

> In this area, probably the largest in the country … where we are at the moment, it means that we have one synchronously farmed generation, whether it's [named companies] or anyone else farming in that area. It means that we talk to each other, exchange sea lice information, decide on what the fallowed areas should be, every two years whole areas free of any farmed fish. That's quite a good model and these same principles across the west coast are basically underway. It means that we have to have strategies for escapes, escape prevention, recapture strategies and that

document will go with the Area Management Group so you talk, this is our strategy, what do you guys think? You'd have fishery trust or fishery board folk and there is an exchange there of sea lice information on what the sea lice burden is on the farms for these area management areas. So this is really important in terms of … actually heading off some conflicts between farming and wild aspects.

(Production manager, large aquaculture company)

The single fish generation and fallowing are techniques for breaking a disease or parasite cycle (Costello et al. 2001). A few years after the visit took place, the *Aquaculture and Fisheries (Scotland) Act 2013* made such local management agreements a statutory requirement but the industry deserves the credit of having started this form of co-operation.

At a broader level, the Global Salmon Initiative (GSI) was formed in 2012 claiming to cover 70% of the world's production. Its producer members have committed to environmental, social and economic sustainability, to achieve Aquaculture Stewardship Council certification (described later in this chapter) and to publishing full information on relevant indicators including such contentious topics as escapes and parasite transfer. Thus, information on the GSI website includes sea lice counts, antibiotic use and escapes on an annual basis from 2013 for individual companies. Scotland has two major salmon companies in this organisation but others which had signed up initially left some time later.[59]

Despite regulatory and industry efforts, environmental problems connected with salmon farming in Scotland persist. Sea lice with their potential to damage wild salmon populations continue to proliferate, the chemical treatments for sea lice already mentioned and other medicines have the potential to harm other organisms, organic waste can accumulate and damage benthic animals while fish escapes average 146,000 each year (Tett et al. 2018). Active critical campaigning continues especially from Salmon and Trout Conservation Scotland and the Global Alliance Against Industrial Aquaculture.

A tool used to assess the environmental performance of marine finfish aquaculture globally by producing a combined score for ten indicators gave the UK/Scotland 72 out of 100 for its Atlantic salmon, the third highest (best) of the countries included in the analysis (Volpe et al. 2010). In the species comparisons, Atlantic salmon also came out comparatively well as the third best of the 20 assessed with a 70 rating. These scores, which present a snapshot based on information available when the calculations were produced and so will vary over time, may be relatively good but fall well short of the notional 100 which would represent zero environmental impact. In addition, scale is crucial to environmental impact so the report also presents cumulative scores and here Atlantic salmon comes out poorly with the third lowest (worst) score because its farming is so extensive.[60] Defenders of salmon farming point out that it is more efficient than capture fishing in usage of marine resources considering the fish consumed in the wild and also more efficient than pig and chicken farming in producing proteins plus other nutrients and argue that many of the problems experienced in the early years have been ameliorated although it is conceded that this is not the case for sealice and escapes (Shepherd & Little 2014). For environmentally concerned opponents the problems have not been ameliorated nearly enough.

The biggest environmental issue in relation to salmon and indeed much other farmed finfish has been over the sustainability of its feed which partly consists of fish oil and/or fishmeal made from wild 'forage fish'; these are small pelagic species including anchovies, capelin, menhaden and sardines which feed on plankton and are eaten by larger fish further up the sea food chain as well as by seabirds and marine mammals. The issues have been over the sustainability of the fisheries which supply this raw material, the ecological impacts for other creatures in the food web of removing huge quantities of it, whether such fish would be more useful if directly used as food and the ratio of feed fish to the resulting fish for human consumption that is actually produced by farming (Allsopp, Santillo & Dorey 2013).

The last of these points has often been discussed in terms of feed conversion figures, sometimes labelled 'Fish In: Fish Out' (FIFO) ratios. When the former is higher than the latter, aquaculture is seen to be resulting in a net loss of fish. The overall situation in relation to this issue is very complex with FIFO varying hugely according to species and production methods. A well-known review based on a global survey carried out in 2006 stated the overall figure to be 0.70 meaning a net gain, noting several species that did produce such a net gain, clearly contributing large volumes to the world average. However, certain other species most consumed in richer countries, salmonids, marine fish and crustaceans, had much higher ratios and were produced at a net fish loss. But the review also noted that over the previous decade the ratios had reduced considerably and anticipated a further downward trend in the use of fish oil and fishmeal in feed (Tacon & Metian 2008). Later reviews have examined future feed needs to maintain global aquaculture production (Tacon & Metian 2015) and what policies will be necessary to keep demand within the ecological boundaries of forage fish availability (Froehlich et al. 2018) emphasising the need for pre-emptive action to be taken.

Closer to home and important to both the production and consumption parts of the UK seafood supply chain, conversion figures for salmon have often been highlighted in debates. As a species at the top of the sea life food chain, salmon require a relatively high proportion of wild fish converted to fish oil and fishmeal in feed to output produced compared to other farmed species. The conversion figure of 4.9: (that is kilograms of wild fish to produce one of salmon) in the above-mentioned 2008 Tacon and Metian article has been widely quoted. The basis of this calculation has been criticised and recent much lower figures down to 2.2:1 and 1.4:1 (Jackson 2009; Shepherd 2012) have been produced; certainly reduced marine inputs within feeds over time were anticipated and the 2008 conversion figure is out of date.[61]

The sustainability of the 'reduction' or 'industrial' fisheries providing much of the raw material for fishmeal and fish oil is clearly a key aspect of ensuring aquaculture feed for the future. A 2017 partial overview produced by the Sustainable Fisheries Partnership (SFP) concluded that high volumes were sourced from reasonably well-managed stocks in South American, European and West African waters; a quarter of the fisheries examined were MSC-certified or undergoing full assessment. However, the overview excluded what it recognised as poorly-documented and managed Asian fisheries which produce nearly half the global fishmeal resource (Veiga, Martin & Lee-Harwood 2017).[62] It is therefore likely that the marine ingredients fed to European-reared finfish coming into the UK food chain came from relatively sustainable fisheries, while the reverse is more probable in relation to farmed fish from South and South East Asia.

A key reason for lower conversion figures and therefore higher net fish food gain is that because of sustainability concerns or (more probably) to reduce costs, a continuing global process of substitution for marine ingredients in feed has taken place. From 69% during the 1990s the fishmeal/oil segment had gone down to 31% by the mid-2010s.[63] Instead, plant ingredients are used and more recently also terrestrial animal proteins and there is ongoing research into the potential contribution of algae, worms and insects (Rust et al. 2010). In addition, there has been increased use of fish processing by-products formerly considered as waste in manufacturing fish oil and fishmeal.

A major contribution to the substitution of terrestrial for marine feed ingredients was made by the EU programme Aquamax, a collaboration involving not only several European countries including the UK but also China and India as well as private companies. The project developed new feeds, tested them on key species for European and global aquaculture including salmon, sea bream and carp, checked the safety and nutritional constituents of the fish produced and trialled them for consumer acceptability (European Commission 2012).[64] This can be regarded as another example of the 'entrepreneurial state' providing resources and the organising structure for innovation (Mazzucato 2018).

All of this has moderated use of wild fish while at the same time the growth of global aquaculture increases demand pressure, future sustainability depending on the fisheries concerned being managed well (Naylor et al. 2009; Shepherd, Monroig & Tocher 2015; Tacon, Hasan & Metian 2011). The strategy of reducing marine ingredients in salmon feed results in lower omega-3 oils in the end product and has been questioned on human health grounds (Byelashov & Griffin 2014). However, this can be at least partially offset by using diets higher in marine ingredients during the finishing period prior to slaughter. (The significance of certain fish as sources of omega-3 is discussed in Chapter 5.) In the sustainability calculus, that of the farmed plants contributing vegetable oils to fish feed, particularly soy, also needs to be taken into account.

An alternative approach to ameliorating the impacts is found in organic aquaculture (Ötles, Ozden & Ötles 2013). Organic standards are relatively more stringent than those for farming generally along a range of factors such as lower stocking densities, feed specifications, the use of veterinary medicines and handling procedures. The later 2000s saw the introduction of European regulation of organic aquaculture setting out detailed rules for production as well as labelling stipulations; prior to this organic aquaculture was governed by private standards or national specifications. There are two UK aquaculture certifiers, the Organic Food Federation and the Soil Association.[65] Organic production of salmon and trout constitutes a very low percentage of the aquaculture scene, less than 2% of the UK total in 2015 (EUMOFA 2017).

Governing shellfish farming in Britain

Farmed shellfish in Britain means mainly bivalve molluscs, that is mussels, oysters and scallops; of crustaceans only a small quantity of lobster and a tiny number of white-clawed crayfish have been produced in recent years. Bivalve molluscs are cultivated by the seed being collected and arranged in some way within marine waters. Some seed is produced in hatcheries but much is collected wild. Methods include mussels on ropes, which may be suspended from rafts, or laid directly on the seabed in shallow waters, oysters in sacks placed on trestles, in baskets or on trays and scallops in nets or in trays suspended from ropes. The molluscs obtain nutrients naturally within the sea or coastal environment so, unlike most farmed fish, they do not need to be fed nor do they receive veterinary treatment, thus obviating most of the environmental issues which arise with marine fish farming.

Requiring use of the coastal sea, shellfish farmers need a Crown Estate lease (though some operations like mollusc hatcheries are land-based). An alternative to leasing is afforded by the *Sea Fisheries (Shellfish) Act 1967* mentioned earlier in connection with Regulating Orders (ROs) used for certain shellfisheries. This Act also provides for 'Several Orders' (SOs) which like ROs are time-limited franchises but for farming shellfish in a specified marine area rather than fishing in them. The benefit of a Several Order compared to an ordinary Crown Estate lease has been suggested as longer-term security of tenure given the length of time needed to establish a viable operation (Whiteley 2016). This may have been a key reason in the past but more recently the Crown Estate has offered 25-year leases. The advantages of an SO are rather that it gives the holder an exclusive property right over the shellfish the holder has placed in the seabed area defined in the order and that no further payments are required whereas a Crown Estate lease only gives the right to place equipment such as longlines or trestles in the area and carries an annual rent obligation.[66] SOs like ROs are issued by DEFRA for England and Wales or by Marine Scotland. The original Act specified that applicants for Regulating and Several Orders had to obtain the consent of the Crown Estate, but this was reduced in 2009 to ministers taking into account the Crown Estate's responsibilities.[67] In Northern Ireland where the 1967 Act does not apply shellfishery licences can be issued under the *Fisheries Act*

(Northern Ireland) 1966 which give similar rights to those conferred by Several Orders, authorising farming within a specified area.

Shellfish farming applications have to meet the same requirements as for finfish so must undertake environmental impact assessments, satisfy water regulations, obtain marine licences and register as aquaculture production businesses. In addition, shellfish farmers have to deal with the regulatory framework over waters where shellfish are cultivated; this is detailed in the next chapter because its purpose is food safety.

Thus shellfish farming, like fish farming, is heavily regulated. The industry also uses some private governance mechanisms. As well as the UK-wide Shellfish Association of Great Britain (SAGB) there is a separate Association of Scottish Shellfish Growers which has produced its own Code of Good Practice although there is no audit scheme associated with it. In Wales, the largest mussel company in the UK, Bangor Mussel Producers, has agreed a Code of Practice with the Countryside Council for Wales; it is directed at avoiding the importation of species non-native to the area because the farm depends on extensive imports of seed from various locations in the British Isles. In addition, there is the option of MSC certification; although the organisation does not cover aquaculture as a whole it does include what are defined as 'enhanced fisheries' involving some human intervention in the life-cycle. On this basis mussel operations have been MSC-certified in Wales (the above-mentioned company), Northern Ireland and Scotland.[68]

Unlike much finfish farming, the kind of shellfish cultivation predominantly carried out in the UK, that of bivalve molluscs, though not entirely without some effects, does not produce significant problems. It is generally considered to be sustainable and indeed is one of the forms of aquaculture which has the least environmental impact (Jacquet 2017; Wilding & Nickell 2013).

Governance and aquaculture imports: certification and beyond

Varied imports of farmed seafood into Britain have become an increasing aspect of supply as global aquaculture has developed and they raise their own governance questions. Leaving aside imported salmon as the environmental issues have already been discussed in relation to domestic production, the farmed species with the second highest level of imports into the UK are those sold as warm-water prawns amounting to 42,000 tonnes in the year 2016/2017. These are predominantly of two species, giant tiger prawns (*Penaeus monodon*) and whiteleg shrimp (*Litopenaeus vannamei*) which may be sourced from various South and South East Asian countries or certain Latin American ones. Other major aquaculture imports include sea bass and sea bream from southern European countries as well as Turkey and pangasius (also called basa or river cobbler) from Vietnam. There are potential environmental problems associated with all these species. Sea bass and sea bream, usually farmed in open net pens, raise similar issues to those noted in relation to this method with salmon such as pollution from organic nutrients and from chemicals plus escapes with their potential impact on wild fish. Vietnamese pangasius too is cultivated in open net pens in river rather than marine settings and similar problems may occur. The greatest environmental detriments have occurred in relation to prawn farming with impacts on ecologically sensitive habitats, particularly the destruction of mangrove forests, salinisation of freshwater and disease transfer from farmed to wild crustaceans. All these species, except the omnivorous pangasius, are piscivorous and need marine ingredients in their feed which raises the issue of the sustainability of fishmeal and fish oil production, already discussed.

Various forms of aquaculture certification have developed to encourage more sustainable production practices and assuage problems. One came from an organisation founded to promote agricultural good practice in European countries when EUREPGAP, subsequently renamed as GLOBALG.A.P. (GG), launched its aquaculture assurance scheme in 2004.[69] Its aquaculture standard includes criteria for all aspects of production, environmental management and fish welfare and it limits feed sourcing to approved suppliers; it has had periodic revisions, version 5 dating to 2015. The system includes a chain of custody standard and works as usual through third-party certification companies. The function has been primarily as a business standard not as an eco-label, but the scheme has acquired a consumer-facing aspect and logo, inviting purchasers to enter an identifying number from the packaging onto the organisation's website to see information about relevant accredited producers. GG is an alliance of producers and retailers, the latter including several major UK supermarket chains. Another extensively-used scheme is the US-based Global Aquaculture Alliance (GAA) which started in 1997 with its Best Aquaculture Practices programme which covers a range of issues including environmental protection, social responsibility, animal welfare and food safety. Its third-party certifications are managed by a separate Aquaculture Certification Council. There is wide membership of the GAA covering not only producers, processors and retailers of seafood products but foodservice companies and feed and equipment suppliers.[70] Other schemes include Friend of the Sea, some put forward by individual countries such as Thai Quality Shrimp and VietGap and organic certification.

Most recently they have been joined by the Aquaculture Stewardship Council (ASC) which was initiated by WWF in response, it said, to requests from 'innumerable suppliers and retailers' in 2004. None of the other schemes had achieved the pre-eminent status enjoyed by the MSC in relation to capture fisheries and their business-to-business models did not appeal directly to consumers so a gap was felt. The process started with Aquaculture Dialogues for individual species involving a wide range of stakeholders to establish standards, a much more transparent arrangement than had occurred with other schemes and the ASC was then founded in 2010 to establish eco-labelling based on these emerging standards. In contrast to the MSC, which began with a partnership between an NGO and a multinational food manufacturing company, the ASC has been entirely a civil society affair as a joint venture between WWF and another NGO, the Dutch Sustainable Trade Initiative.[71] Like the MSC the ASC is a consumer-facing model with its own logo. Again comparably to the MSC it is based on a set of core principles translated into criteria for which separate performance indicators are laid down for each species covered and there is third-party certification.[72]

The ASC started certifying in 2012 and by early 2018 about 600 farms had achieved the status and there were 1,500 suppliers with chain of custody accreditation. At this point the greatest number of certifications and also the greatest production volume certified was for Atlantic salmon and the majority of the relevant farms, well over 100, were Norwegian. In volume terms, the next largest category was pangasius, all produced in Vietnam. In terms of number of farms the second largest group was for warm-water prawns (covering both giant and whiteleg shrimp species) mainly in India, Vietnam and Ecuador.[73] Salmon, prawns and pangasius are the main species for which UK suppliers are ASC-accredited so these are indications of important sources of seafood imports into Britain though of course not all such imports are from ASC farms. While about 70 suppliers in Britain are listed as ASC certified there has so far been very little engagement with the programme by UK aquaculture producers (nor with the other two major certifications) probably because most are already involved with the well-established Scottish salmon and UK trout schemes previously discussed while mussel farmers are able to apply for MSC certification.[74] From the viewpoint of the British seafood supply chain, the general aquaculture certifications are of interest in connection with imports.

From its earliest stage, the ASC engaged collaboratively with the pre-existing general aquaculture schemes. This became formalised in a three-way Memorandum of Agreement between the ASC, GG and the GAA to work together on certain issues, including harmonising feed standards and reducing duplication for producers seeking more than one certification with joint audits. All three include environmental, animal welfare and social criteria in their standards, but it seems that GG has a greater emphasis on safety and quality while the ASC's mission is 'to transform aquaculture towards environmental and social sustainability'.[75] While the ASC was founded by two NGOs, the GAA describes itself on its website as an 'international, non-profit trade association' a description which also fits GG but the co-operation between the three testifies to the blurring of boundaries between civil society and private interests in governance systems. In another overlap the ASC salmon standard has been accepted as a goal by the producer organisation Global Salmon Initiative.[76] Hence, all three of these certifications may be regarded as examples of private governance although the extent of NGO involvement in the ASC does provide an additional legitimising claim of public interest purpose. In all of them, private and public interests overlap. There is also co-operation between the ASC and the MSC whereby the latter is sharing its traceability system so that, with a few amendments, certifiers of the Chain of Custody for the latter can be accredited to do the same for the former.

Duplication of certification schemes in relation to aquaculture is a much wider issue than the three discussed here, at least 30 having been noted, so much so that metagovenance has emerged, that is bodies setting standards for such schemes; this is intended to simplify the field though differences between them arguably just produce more choices (Samerwong, Bush & Oosterveer 2017). There is indeed contestation as to where the right to determine standards should lie, especially as schemes with international coverage such as GG and the ASC are based in the richer importing countries but applied to producers in the global South on an unequal power basis, an arrangement that has been likened to a colonial imposition (Bain & Hatanaka 2010; Vandergeest & Unno 2012).

There is too an element of global governance in relation to aquaculture eco-labelling as the FAO has issued *Technical Guidelines on Aquaculture Certification*. Like those for capture fisheries, they deal not only with direct impacts but with organisational and procedural measures and also like them in timing seem to be a response to developing certification activities (FAO 2011d). The ASC, GAA and GG all state that they follow these guidelines. Prawns (shrimp) even have their own global governance standards, produced by a consortium made up of international agencies together with WWF (FAO/NACA/UNEP/WB/WWF 2006).[77] Thus, in the same way as for marine fish eco-labelling, the FAO has exerted influence over these non-state initiatives despite the lack of formal legislation.

By contrast, the EU's own general and voluntary eco-labelling programme, the Eco-Management and Audit Scheme, which the Commission recommended to the industry in its 2002 aquaculture strategy document has been hardly taken up in the aquaculture world. The European Commission was mandated in the 2013 common market CFP reform regulation to look into the possibility of a specific Union eco-label covering fishery and aquaculture products. Accordingly, the subject has been investigated and a report produced listing three options without making a recommendation: the first was no change but using existing legislation to oversee voluntary eco-claims; the second was setting minimum requirements for sustainability claims made about seafood; and the third was establishing an EU scheme (European Commission 2016b). Since its publication, this report has languished and it is unclear whether any of the options will be pursued.[78] This suggests that there is no need for state eco-standards for aquaculture given the existing availability of private-NGO schemes.

As with capture fishing certification, the fundamental question is whether these eco-certification schemes achieve environmental benefits. A ranking exercise carried out prior to the existence of ASC certification put most organic farming standards ahead of the rest in relation to ecological impact, placing both GG and GAA well down the performance list (Volpe et al. 2011). This simply refers to potential results and the low level of organic aquaculture production means that its actual effects must be limited. The judgements made by the UK's Marine Conservation Society, producer of the *Good Fish Guide* (discussed in Chapter 5) appear to give higher sustainability ratings to ASC certified options where available compared to those with GG or GAA certification while the latter two options are clearly indicated as better choices than uncertified seafood.

In any case, it is extremely difficult to establish a basis for evaluating the impacts of eco-certification on aquaculture. Unlike the case with capture fisheries where there is one central criterion namely the state of stocks, as well as established methods for judging this as well as baseline information, for aquaculture there are multiple possible environmental objectives which will depend on the species farmed, the production regimes that apply and the particular attributes of sites, with no systematic way of characterising the starting point. Therefore, such schemes have so far been assessed on the basis of their content rather than effects. Here, the way that standards were drawn up and implemented have been seen to reflect the interests and values of richer countries' buyers, marginalising small producers, omitting the most widely farmed species namely carp and taking little account of the growing Asian market (Belton et al. 2011; Belton, Little & Grady 2009; Jonell et al. 2013; Marschke & Wilkings 2014).

With most global aquaculture production not certified in any scheme, there are deeper problems with some farmed seafood, causing difficulties along supply chains. Their complexity can be illustrated by one case which had publicity in Britain when an aspect was included in a Channel 4 *Hugh's Fish Fight* episode in 2013 (this being the programme which began the Fish Fight campaign mentioned previously in connection with the CFP anti-discards struggle). The item was about the fish content of the feed used in Thailand prawn farming which was alleged to have been fished illegally. It reportedly resulted in 40,000 tweets being sent to supermarkets about prawn production. A few months later, seven of the supermarket chains did come together in a group set up by the British Retail Consortium to deal with the feed issue which subsequently morphed into a Seafish group with a wider ethical brief.[79] In the meantime, a *Guardian* newspaper investigation had revealed a catalogue of labour abuses, indeed the use of slave labour, in the same Thai fishing fleet accused of illegal fishing and which is an integral part of the supply chain delivering farmed prawns to the UK (and US) markets.[80] There were also reports from an NGO, the Environmental Justice Foundation, about such abuses in Thailand's seafood processing and fishing industries (EJF 2013a, 2013b, 2015).

The revelations galvanised the formation of the US-based Shrimp Sustainability Supply Chain Task Force to deal with both the social and environmental issues, its membership including Thai and American seafood companies, retailers – two of them British – and NGOs WWF and the EJF (Shrimp Sustainable Task Force 2016). This has become the Seafood Task Force to acknowledge the development of a wider remit such as issues over tuna and it has pursued various streams of work: codes of conduct, trace-ability, vessel surveillance and fishery improvement programmes; the group has also planned to expand the area of operation into Vietnam (Seafood Task Force 2017).[81] Concurrently with these industry-led efforts there has been public action against Thailand: a yellow card in 2015 from the EU for failures in relation to illegal fishing and in 2014 a listing on the US State Department Trafficking in Persons Tier 3 and then Tier 2 Watch List (the two bottom ratings), each a warning that without adequate remedial action further action would be taken. Such measures communicate the need for speedy action to the government of the country concerned and certainly some of the problems identified can only be remedied by state action. Despite legal reforms and a new inspection framework, plus the Task Force efforts, abuses have continued (Human Rights Watch 2018). While Thai prawn production has been assessed as posing the highest risk of forced labour involvement, a rating of moderate to high risk has been given to prawns from Bangladesh and Indonesia and a low to moderate risk when they are sourced in India or Ecuador. Forced labour which may amount to slavery co-exists with illegal fishing and also sex trafficking to serve fishing fleets (Nakamura et al. 2018).

All of this presents problems to those in the UK seafood industry sourcing warm-water prawns and potentially other seafood. Hence the *Guardian* forced labour exposé also prompted action closer to home as the Seafish response to expressed industry concerns included the establishment of a website called Tools for Ethical Seafood Sourcing (TESS). It presents a process for socially responsible purchasing and collects together many information sources relating to forced labour risks from external sites together with profiles it has commissioned on individual countries from which Britain imports.[82]

Future supply

The outlook for the supply of seafood is a significant issue for British food security and vital to the processing industry which depends on sourcing enough of it. At the time of the research with seafood companies there was pessimism from some who were dependent on local capture fish at a period of concern about the sustainability of fisheries and related low quotas:

> The challenges ... that this and many other businesses like it face is lack of supply because you'll get to the critical stage reasonably soon, within a two to five year period where the supply will not support the infrastructure.
>
> (Partner, medium company)

> There aren't enough sustainable fisheries out there. There are more fisheries under assessment, but that doesn't guarantee supply.
>
> (Commercial manager, medium-large company)

Improved management of fisheries has now shown that stocks can recover providing controls are maintained. More cod, haddock and other popular species like plaice and sole can be caught for the home market and there is certainly sufficient herring and mackerel for domestic consumption. Much of the whitefish wanted for UK consumption is imported from well-managed Icelandic and Norwegian fisheries, assuring future supply. However, the same cannot be said for some other imports. Tuna volumes coming in are comparable to those for cod (119,000 tonnes in 2016), comprise different species from different fisheries and unless they have MSC certification may be from problematic fisheries. There is a similar situation with imports of some other species which may be from different fisheries with varying levels of sustainability and therefore varying probabilities for the reliability of future supply.

Looking ahead, there are uncertainties related to climate change. Warming of the oceans may change fish movements so that species like red mullet may become available in domestic waters but conversely those requiring colder temperatures like cod may shift further north. Another impact may come from acidification which could be damaging to shellfish, wild or farmed (Government Chief Scientific Advisor 2018)

Some in the seafood trade looked to farmed seafood to make up for shortfalls of wild and provide a positive prospect:

> Only way you're going to bridge that gap of required protein is through aquaculture.
>
> (Group director, large company)

> It's going to be farmed fish that allows people to eat fish. Wild fish is almost going to be marginalised.
>
> (Managing director, medium-large company)

There is certainly scope for expanding British farmed seafood which has been the subject of a range of planning efforts. For Scotland, the production of its aquaculture strategy has been a public undertaking (Scottish Government 2009) and nationally a document has been produced as an EU requirement (DEFRA 2015). Outside Scotland much of the initiative and activity has come from the industry or been led by Seafish, indicated by series of reports from the mid-2000s onwards (Bannister 2006; Hambrey & Evans 2016; James & Slaski 2009; SAGB 2004). One was put out as a consultation document by DEFRA (England Aquaculture Plan Consultation Group 2012) but no follow-up report was produced by the Department and it has been left to Seafish to pick up the planning lead. However, the MMO and the Welsh Government are taking forward work to identify sites appropriate for farming in the context of coastal marine planning.

The potential for aquaculture development in Britain, both on land and offshore, has been identified (Black & Hughes 2017). This could include semi-contained recirculating aquaculture systems and aquaponics (symbiotic combined aquatic animal and plant cultivation) on land which allow high levels of control of inputs and outputs and minimise unwanted environmental effects although incurring high energy use. A key barrier is that of investment in costly and new technologies, an ideal opportunity for entrepreneurial state action were the political will to be forthcoming. There are also possibilities of aquaculture offshore and for inshore waters closed-containment systems.

A recent planning exercise is a strategy for growth along the whole seafood supply chain including both fishing and aquaculture, directed to England but referring to linked work by the devolved administrations. Instigated as part of DEFRA's *25 Year Food & Farming Plan* and produced by a group of stakeholders under the aegis of Seafish, *Seafood 2040* is directed at increasing seafood consumption and adding to the value of all parts of the chain. In relation to supply it includes proposals to facilitate the growth of aquaculture in England with a focus on mussels and trout and to create demand for a wider variety of fish that is caught but can be difficult to market (Seafish 2017) but the document assumes continuing dependence on imports and recognises a potential food security challenge.

The availability of continuing supply from farming does not seem to be in doubt at present but it is not necessarily sustainably produced. In any case, the dependence on imports does carry risks. As one interviewee in the research said:

> We source a lot of products from around the world.… We'll be bidding for that product on the global market and if we can't afford to bid for it or we get outbidded for it then it will go elsewhere and then you will start to create more pressure on your domestic stocks again.
>
> (Trade organisation representative 1)

Regardless of the sustainability of particular fisheries or farming regimes, the situation where such a high proportion of Britain's seafood supply is imported (and the UK is in the world's top ten importing countries[83]) is arguably not sustainable in the longer-term. The New Economics Foundation has devised the Fish Dependence Day concept to pinpoint how much the EU relies on imports. The UK date has been at the beginning of September, which because of the aquaculture contribution is much better than the EU average in mid-July but still means relying on other producers for nearly one-third of the seafood needed in the supply chain (Owen & Carpenter 2018).

The context is that the global yield from capture fishing after peaking in the mid-1990s has plateaued or declined with 31% of fish stocks estimated as overfished, that is being taken at a biologically unsustainable level (2013 figure) while the growth of farmed fish may be slower than in the past (FAO 2016; Pauly & Zeller 2016). Aquaculture has increased the amount of fish available overall and does provide considerable volumes for domestic consumption in the main producing countries (Belton, Bush & Little 2018). However, with global population increasing and demand for fish growing, it seems anomalous that according to some calculations 12% of the world's people in the richer countries consume 30% of the total supply of seafood (Esteban & Crilly 2011; Swartz et al. 2010). To facilitate a fairer share of this important and limited resource richer countries should be increasing farmed seafood production (Tacon & Metian 2015; Thilsted et al. 2016). Therefore food security issues in relation to seafood should be given greater priority in the UK and that means a much more proactive approach to aquaculture development.

Conclusions: governance and seafood supply

This chapter has described the way sourcing of seafood for British consumption has changed in the second half of the twentieth century and explored the different governance influences in each production sector. There was a step change in the industrialisation of seafood production in two directions. The ability to exploit capture fisheries hugely expanded with more powerful vessels and technology while mastery of the reproductive and rearing needs of many species resulted in the spectacular growth of aquaculture. These were market-led economic and technological processes which initially were uncontrolled. The success of these developments then led to an intensification of regulation in order to deal with what were increasingly seen as problematic consequences. There has been state and supra-state response and activity at various levels as this chapter has recounted.

Deepening industrialisation of fishing made such great inroads on fish stocks that recognition of stock depletion became widespread and with it the realisation that state governance had to be strengthened to ensure the continuation of both the natural resource and the economic and social benefits of its exploitation. This has been the story of the development of the CFP from a mechanism to promote the fishing industry and a common market in its products to a still-evolving system for ensuring sustainability of both the resource and the industry.

In Britain, the increase in fishery regulation was accompanied by a countervailing delegationary trend first with POs managing fishing quotas and then the semi-privatisation of shares in those quotas. The devolution process localised much state activity around fishing to three regional administrations and a separate agency for England, the Marine Management Organisation (MMO).[84] There was further localisation with the establishment of IFCAs in England and the equivalent IFGs and RIFGs in Wales (initially) and Scotland.

The slowness or perceived inability of state-led fisheries management to deal with depletions of fish stocks incentivised the development of eco-labelling programmes, marking a new kind of governance. The best known MSC had an initial environmental NGO lead and continues to have the participation of a wider range of stakeholders than had previously been involved in fisheries management (subsequently wider stakeholder representation was also introduced into the CFP with the RACs). However, while eco-certification may be bringing some benefits it has been increasingly recognised that such success rests on effective fisheries management by public authorities.

While global political and economic developments produced constraints on previous sources of supply, they also created opportunities to develop new ones. The near-universal declaration of EEZs following the significant step in global governance represented by the UNCLOS agreement reduced British access to fishing grounds. However, the expansion of global trade in combination with technological and transportation developments meant new opportunities to source supply in different ways.

In parallel, in Britain the impact of the swift development of aquaculture, particularly marine farming off the Scottish coasts and social responses to its environmental impacts led to recognition of the need for regulation. This was achieved both by state measures and for the salmon and trout farming industries by additional self-governance. Such private governance, with some civil society input, has extended more widely in aquaculture industries, bringing a broader range of eco-certified seafood products into the domestic supply chain although the bulk as yet is not certified and may be produced in problematic ways.

In terms of the framework set out in Chapter 2, it is governance from sources external to the supply chain that has been considered in this chapter. The modes, agents and impacts of governance have been shown to vary between the capture and aquaculture sectors and certain specificities relating to shellfish production have been described. Figures 3.1 and 3.2 illustrate the main governance factors which have been operative over the period reviewed for the fishery and aquaculture sectors respectively, each covering both finfish and shellfish. Arrows indicate the existence and direction of governance relationships which may operate more strongly or weakly at different times. The overall situation can be described as multi-directional governance.

In addition to what is shown in Figure 3.1, to prevent it being even more complicated, some additional governance factors are not displayed. One is the impact of FAO guidelines on the MSC, another that of scientific advice on fishery management. The fact that parts of the fishing industry have actively engaged in the MSC certification programme is also not visualised. It is important to bear in mind that governance does not mean one party acting on a passive receptor, but that it usually involves interactive relationships; indeed, these have been evident in relation to the CFP, its operation being greatly affected by the attitudes and actions of fishers. Supply chain governance in the interests of sustainability has been mentioned in this chapter but has usually been indirect.

Scientific input affects fishery decisions made at global, EU and UK government levels as well as having an impact on aquaculture developments. For fishing, there is an institutional level of governance regarding scientific advice into the CFP since there is a formal requirement to act upon it; in addition, such information, being generally available, has the capacity to influence all other parties, particularly the MSC and connected certifying organisation. For

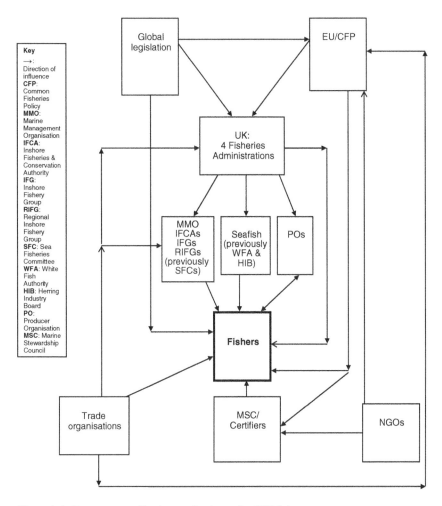

Figure 3.1 Governance affecting seafood supply: UK fishers.

aquaculture, scientific advice may impinge directly on farmers in relation to all aspects of rearing but also via impacts on decisions about sites and key regulations such as about water quality and habitats. However, scientific knowledge and advice is generated from too many sources, both public and private (in the form of consultancies), to be simply represented on these diagrams.

Figure 3.1 indicates the extent of direct impact of state and supra-state regulation on fishers. Global legislation in the form of the UNCLOS agreement had one particularly significant impact because the EEZ regime entailed the end of the British distant waters fleet. The EU through the CFP and the UK government have huge impacts through fisheries management policy and regulation, including quotas, and their enforcement but also as sources of

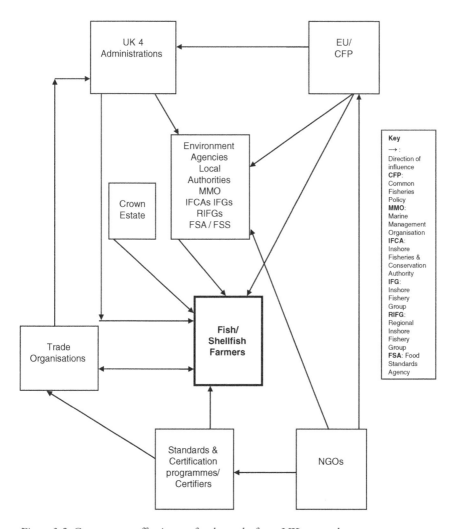

Figure 3.2 Governance affecting seafood supply from UK aquaculture.

financial assistance, having at different times emphasised vessel modernisation and vessel decommissioning. Various types of delegated state functions are named in one of the boxes below, the MMO (for England) and local management bodies. Next to it are the boxes referring to the two types of organisation previously characterised as combination public-private governance organisations, Seafish and Producer Organisations (POs).

POs with their primary role of representing the private interests of fishing operators, but at the same time constituted under European legislation, have also been allocated governmental functions in Britain in connection with fishing quota allocation so have governance arrows from both directions.

However, their separation from the state is underlined by the 2013 court case over the distribution of unused quota which the Producer Organisations' representative body brought against the government, as previously described. The devolution of the greater part of national fishing quota allocations to POs and the semi-privatisation of quota holding to individuals and companies has diluted the state's control, the more so given that a significant part of UK quota is currently held by non-British concerns, but the same court case indicated that ultimate state control is still implicit and can be asserted, while general enforcement action over CFP rules also confirms fundamental state control over fishing access rights. In the recent revision of the common market for seafood connected with CFP reforms, POs have been charged with additional responsibilities connected with the now predominant aim of sustainable fishing, arguably bringing them under greater public control and complicating still further the private-public mixture they constitute.

Seafish by contrast is a quango publicly constituted to carry out delegated state functions of promoting the seafood industry, which defines its role in terms of those industry interests, taking its lead from its main funding source, the company levy. That Seafish provides a valued service was confirmed by the support which enabled it to continue after the Cleasby review but it is subsidiary to the direct governmental functions carried out by the other bodies mentioned, that is the MMO, IFCAs (and their predecessor bodies) and POs, thus producing optional extras in the system, however beneficial they may be. There is an interesting contrast between POs and Seafish, both established by legislation, the former as industry bodies but carrying out delegated regulatory functions, the latter as a public body but devoted to industry support, effectively a public body with private functions.

Fishers, as well as being objects of governance, may exert influence on the POs and this mutual relationship also applies to their trade organisations such as the NFFO and NUFTA and to the MSC and certifiers (presumably varying with economic strength and specific individual and company interests). The trade organisations aim to influence government policy for example over the ministerial stance on quota negotiations and also the CFP directly through involvement in the Advisory Councils (ACs). Finally, certain NGOs have taken on a direct governance role through participation in the ACs and in the MSC's own governance structure as well as having impacts more generally through their campaigning and lobbying activities as has been observable in relation to CFP reform processes.

In the aquaculture diagram (Figure 3.2), mutual governance relationships are shown between farmers and both their trade organisations and relevant certification organisations, as seen with fishers. NGOs again play a role, but a lesser one, which relates to EU policy and to some certification activities. The relationship between farmers and state institutions is comparable in some respects to that with fishers in that legislation, funding (under the CFP) and broader development policy come from both the UK and European levels, but here there is no direct global governance impact. However, it differs in the greater range of delegated bodies of the British state involved in regulation, not only the MMO and local marine management bodies but also local authorities (for planning control), the environment agencies of the four administrations, and in relation to the specific water requirements for shellfish producers (detailed in Chapter 4), the food standards bodies FSA and FSS. A separate part of the state, the Crown Estate, has also had in the past exercised a form of planning control in relation to salmon farming and certain shellfish enterprises. A further difference between the two sectors is the relationship between trade organisations and certification bodies for aquaculture, reflecting the strength of privately-led governance in relation to salmon and trout farming.

As summary representations of the various relationships between social actors, the two diagrams do not model changes over time but do include some aspects that have been operative at different points in the period covered. In relation to fishing, the major global governance impact was a one-time event (the UNCLOS agreement) which had a permanent impact but became absorbed into new arrangements. By contrast, the European and UK dimensions of the CFP have been constantly shifting and adjusting, in an interaction of those exerting fishery management governance, those experiencing it and the natural world on which they are acting; the discard problem in reaction to quotas and the subsequent public and political responses make up one manifestation of these dynamics. The delegated state structures have changed such as IFCAs replacing SFCs and Seafish replacing the White Fish Authority and Herring Industry Board. Another factor is the relative newness of some of the current elements of governance in the fishing system particularly certification and the wider participation of stakeholders in the CFP through the RACs now ACs, their impact still in process of development. For aquaculture, the involvement of NGOs is even more recent, while the governance role of the Crown Estate has diminished but other elements of the system, both regulatory and self-management through standards schemes have remained fairly constant from an early stage albeit with some internal developments.

The objectives of most of the various actors engaged in the governance of seafood production are to varying degrees concerned with both the economic well-being of each sector and its sustainability, environmental and social. Only to a limited extent has the question of food security been a policy factor for the state in relation to seafood, in the immediate post-war period regarding fishing productivity and more recently with some very limited consideration of future supply.

The economic well-being of the fishing and aquaculture industries is both a private and a public interest. Sustainability and the conservation of the resource is also both a public and private interest but it has taken some time for the need for action on this front to be fully appreciated by all in the seafood industry. CFP development to an emphasis on the sustainability pole has been gradual, this being taken seriously by a majority of fishers and fishing concerns more recent still. Both at UK and EU levels, state action is often about mediating a path which can reconcile these two key aims, as seen in the most recent CFP negotiations. By contrast, the environmental NGOs and consumer-facing certifiers depend for their effectiveness on being seen to uphold a public interest in the conservation of marine ecology and the continuing sustainability of fish stocks.

Fisher support for sustainable management of fisheries is crucial to its effectiveness and there are a number of factors which would seem to account for the positive change in sentiment that has occurred in the industry. State regulation with strong enforcement has been indispensable but certification has added an inducement for compliance. In addition, the participation of fisher representatives in the CFP process is likely to have improved its credibility while involvement in the Fisheries Science Partnership has done something to increase confidence in the underlying science. Marketisation of quota has provided another form of incentive for husbanding the resource. Not least of possible reasons for a change of opinion may have been the recognition at sea that certain stocks had fallen to very low levels and that remedial steps were needed. It is likely that all these factors have been relevant.

To summarise governance in the area of supply, state and supra-state regulation has had the biggest impact in relation to the domestic fishing industry and to fisheries management for sustainability although there are also private and, in relation to certification, civil society elements. By contrast, private governance has been more important for aquaculture, particularly in relation to salmon farming, though here too there is a complex state regulation system. The public–private relationship plays out differently in other sections of the supply chain as the next chapter explores.

Notes

1 Previously the UK had established a 12-mile EEZ in the *Fishery Limits Act 1964*.
2 'Yachtie' refers to Edward Heath's reputation as a yachtsman.
3 'Regulation (EEC) No 101/76 of 19 January 1976 laying down a common structural policy for the fishing industry'.
4 'Regulation (EEC) No 170/83 Establishing a Community system for the conservation and management of fishery resources'.
5 Funding was initiated in 'Regulation (EEC) No 2908/83 of 4 October 1983 On a common measure for restructuring, modernising and developing the fishing industry and for developing aquaculture' and provided through the European Agriculture Guidance and Guarantee Fund.
6 This is explained in 'NFFO Chairman Fred Normandale' in *NFFO News*, September 2007.
7 The activities of these groups are not well documented, and the campaign websites no longer function but information was found in: Geldard I, (undated, possibly 2002) 'Save Britain's Fish: how it all began', https://groups.google.com, 'Crusaders catch lands in Brussels', 21 December 2004, www.scotsindependent. org and 'Tribute for Carol, the leading Cod Crusader', 9 November 2007, www. fishupdate.com. A petition variously reported to number 162,500 and 250,000 signatures was submitted to Brussels and Westminster and a *Fisheries Jurisdiction Bill*

to withdraw the UK from the CFP was introduced in the House of Commons by a Scottish National Party MP in 2004 as a Ten Minute Rule Bill.

8 The statement about non-traceable cod was made by Cliff Morrison, speaking as Chair of the Food and Drink Federation's Seafood Group at the Third Chatham House Update and Stakeholder meeting on 8 May 2007, sourced from www.illegal-fishing.info.

9 'Regulation (EEC) No 3760/92 establishing a community system for fisheries and aquaculture 1992'.

10 'Regulation (EC) No 2371/2002 on the conservation and sustainable exploitation of fisheries resources under the common fisheries policy 2002'.

11 'Regulation 1224/2009, establishing a community control system for ensuring compliance with the rules of the common fisheries policy'. The Community Fisheries Control Agency was later renamed as the European Fisheries Control Agency.

12 The joint letter to the then UK fisheries minister from the RSPB, Greenpeace, WWF, Ocean 2012, the Marine Conservation Society and Client Earth is at www.mcsuk.org/downloads/working_with_you/Joint_NGO_letter_to_minister.pdf, accessed 5 July 2018.

13 The Fish Fight campaign, led by celebrity chef Hugh Fearnley-Whittingstall, started in Britain on the basis of television programme and gained supporters in 11 other European countries. When the European Parliament voted in favour of a CFP reform package, including the ending of discards in February 2013, it was reported by the BBC as 'a victory for citizen power' in 'Euro MPs back large-scale fishing reform to save stocks', 6 February 2013 on the BBC website. Interviewed for a programme shown on Channel 4 on 8 August 2011, the then EU commissioner for fisheries, Maria Damanaki, said Fish Fight was 'a great power'.

14 The basic reform legislation is 'Regulation (EU) No 1380/2013 of 11 December 2013 on the Common Fisheries Policy'. The exceptions to discarding back into the sea under the landing obligation are high survivability (applying to selected species) and the '*de minimis*' exemption by which not more than 5% may be discarded where there is evidence that selectivity is very difficult or in limited cases where disproportionate costs would otherwise be incurred. There also flexibilities allowing some swapping between quotas for different species and in allowing additional quota allocation in-year. The regulation introduced the 'minimum conservation reference size' replacing the 'minimum landing size' both intended to dissuade the catching of juveniles.

15 *Fisheries and Aquaculture in Europe*, issue 57, August 2012, p. 11.

16 European Commission, 2017, *Communication on the State of Play of the Common Fisheries Policy and Consultation on the Fishing Opportunities for 2018*, European Commission, Brussels.

17 A useful view about likely fisher reaction to the 2013 CFP landing obligation which is generally relevant is that 'their acceptance of regulations is influenced by whether the implementation effects are considered fair, whether the imposed regulations are perceived as meaningful and whether there is compatibility between the regulation and the traditional fishing patterns and practices' (Hedley, Catchpole & Ribeiro Santos 2015, p. 77) though the authors do go on to also point to the importance of effective enforcement.

18 The original proposed plan is in European Commission 2016a. The reaction of environmental NGOs is in 'NGOs rail against EU's confirmed fishing plan', *Undercurrent News*, 30 May 2018.

19 'Regulation (EEC) No 3796/81 of 29 December 1981 on the common organization of the market in fishery products'.

20 The companies each forming a single PO at 2016 were Interfish with ten vessels, Klondyke with three and Lunar Group with four.

21 UK Fisheries Administrations 2012, *A Subject Specific Concordat between the Department for Environment, Food and Rural Affairs, Marine Scotland, The Welsh Government and the Department of Agriculture and Rural Development (Northern Ireland)*, London.

22 The United Kingdom Association of Fish Producer Organisations v Secretary of State for Environment, Food and Rural Affairs, [2013] EWHC 1959 (Admin), Case No: CO/4796/2012, para 112, available on www.judiciary.gov.uk.

23 The Queen (on the application of Greenpeace Limited) v The Secretary of State for Environment, Food and Rural Affairs, [2016] EWHC 55 (Admin), Case No. CO/338/2015, available at www.landmarkchambers.co.uk.

24 See the statement 'Fishermen do not, therefore, have property rights over FQA units or quota' on the webpage 'Management: administration of the UK fishing industry' at http://webarchive.nationalarchives.gov.uk. Fisheries Minister Elliot Morley stated 'the legal owner of licences and of quota remains the UK Government' when appearing before a House of Commons Select Committee (quoted in the UKAFPO v Secretary of State case).

25 The Factortame case established in 1991 that European law took priority over UK law so that the provisions of the *Merchant Shipping Act 1988* requiring fishing vessels to be 75% British-owned could not be upheld in relation to EU nationals. The Economic Link was then established to ensure benefits to the UK from its fishing quota with four criteria: at least 50% of EU quota landings to be in British ports; at least 50% of crew to be normally resident in UK coastal areas; at least 50% of operating expenditure net of wages to be spent in British coastal areas; or quota donation to the UK under-10m fleet. After a few years, a review of the Economic Link concluded that actual economic contribution is low in comparison to relevant vessel turnover and may even be zero (DEFRA 2009). Nevertheless the Scottish Government considered it worthwhile to run a consultation in 2017 on a proposal to require 55% of the Scottish share of quota landings to be in Scottish ports and to retain the option of quota to be gifted in lieu of this if not met but to drop the crew and operating expenditure requirements; the document stated an intention that this should come into force in January 2018 but at the time of writing the outcome of the consultation had not been produced and it was unclear when or whether the change would come into effect.

26 Greenpeace 2015, 'Deadly Predators', *Connect*, Spring, pp. 9–13.

27 The comment by a Scottish Fishermen's Federation representative is quoted in the BBC News report 'Fishing pay-off scheme opens', 31 August 2001.

28 The positive assessment of decommissioning in relation to North Sea cod and plaice and to demersal stocks in the Celtic Sea is given in a news item dated 16 July 2012 on the website of the National Federation of Fishermen's Associations, http://nffo.org.uk. See also Lart & Caveen 2017.

29 The principle that boats should be fitted with a device that allows them to be detected and identified by remote monitoring systems was established in the 2002 CFP reform and subsequently detailed in 'Commission Regulation (EC) No 2244/2003 of 18 December 2003' requiring Vessel Monitoring Systems to be fitted on boats 15 metres or more in length by 2005; subsequently, the requirement was extended to cover vessels 12 metres or more in length. In England, the MMO and IFCAs have been collaborating in a project to develop an inshore vessel monitoring system (IVMS) which has the potential to strengthen management of inshore fisheries and monitor marine protected areas.

30 The reduction of both boardings and convictions is detailed in Carrington D 2017, 'Admiral calls plan to police post-Brexit fishing waters "amazingly complacent"', *Guardian*, 3 July 2017.

31 IFCAs were mandated in the 2009 *Marine and Coastal Access Act*, replacing Sea Fisheries Committees which had been in place since the late nineteenth century. In Scotland, localised management started with Inshore Fisheries Groups in 2013,

replaced by the Scottish Regional Inshore Fisheries Groups in 2016. In Wales, Inshore Fisheries Groups were established but disbanded in 2016 (Terry, Lewis & Bullimore 2018).

32 The NFFO Shellfish Policy, dated September 2011, together with an update of March 2013, is on their website www.nfffo.org.uk. The capacity issues are about both the high volume fleet itself and the latent capacity of dormant and under-utilised licences in the inshore fleet. The update explicitly states that government action is needed despite the government having a 'moratorium' on new regulations on the grounds that they burden small businesses, which refers to the response given to an NFFO delegation which met DEFRA officials in 2012 as reported on 13 September 2012 by www.fishnewseu.com (accessed 13 September 2012).

33 The Centre for Environment, Fisheries and Aquaculture Science (Cefas) is an executive agency of DEFRA, the MMO is an executive non-departmental public body while Marine Scotland is part of the Scottish Government. In the catch quota schemes, fishers anticipated the landings obligation, receiving additional quota to assist them and agreeing additional onboard monitoring, achieving low discard rates; in the Scottish Conservation Credits Scheme, extra days at sea were awarded in return for observing real-time closures to protect spawning and juvenile cod plus acceptance of other restrictions.

34 The Torry Research Station began in 1929 as part of the Department of Scientific and Industrial Research, after transfers to other departments landed within MAFF in 1972 and eventually became part of the Central Sciences Laboratory.

35 Seafish was established in the *Fisheries Act 1981* to succeed both the White Fish Authority and the Herring Industry Board. The seafood industry is not unique in having a publicly constituted body acting on its behalf; the Agriculture and Horticulture Development Board is comparable and also funded by an industry levy.

36 The project produced a number of reports which were available on a dedicated website www.fishingforthemarkets.com but little direct action seems to have been taken as a result of the project and the website no longer functions.

37 The Blue Marine Foundation was established in the wake of the film about global overfishing, *The End of the Line* and particularly emphasises the establishment of marine protected areas; its website is www.bluemarinefoundation.com. Information about Open Seas is at www.openseas.org.uk.

38 See the *International Guidelines on Bycatch Management and Reduction of Discards* (FAO 2011b). The international *Agreement on Port State Measures to Prevent, Deter and Eliminate Illegal, Unreported and Unregulated Fishing* was concluded in 2009 and entered into force in 2016.

39 The term 'capture' rather than 'wild' fish is customarily used because there are certain fisheries in which there is some human intervention for example eggs or young fish produced in hatcheries are introduced into the wild meaning that their lives and reproduction are not wholly wild. The certification scheme most comparable in coverage to the MSC is Friend of the Sea but this has not been relevant to the British seafood supply chain; other than this there are national and regional ones such as the Alaska Responsible Fisheries Management, Iceland Responsible Fisheries Management Standard and Marine Eco-Label Japan.

40 The quote is from a personal communication to the author from the MSC's Communications Manager in an email dated 11 April 2014. Details of the MSC's performance indicators at February 2018 were accessed from the website https://improvements.msc.org/database/streamlining/documents/MSC_ Performance_Indicators_Explained.

41 The Scottish MSC certifications have been pursued via two organisations founded for the purpose, The Scottish Pelagic Sustainability Group and the Scottish Fisheries

Sustainable Accreditation Group (covering demersal fisheries) and also by the Shetland Shellfish Management Group which manages the inshore Shetland shellfisheries.

42 Project Inshore was a multi-agency partnership involving not just Seafish and the MSC but also the government agency MMO, the trade organisation Shellfish Association of Great Britain, merchant/processing companies, retailers and two environmental NGOs; most of these partners contributed to the funding of the project but the biggest chunk came from the CFP European Fisheries Fund (information from MSC press release 8 June 2012 headed 'English traditional coastal fisheries make plans for future generations'). In the project, all the English inshore fisheries were reviewed, selected ones were taken through the MSC pre-assessment process and a 'strategic sustainability review' was produced for each Inshore Fisheries and Conservation Authority with advice on which fisheries could be ready for the full MSC process and guidance on how management deficits might be remedied for the rest, the majority (Southall, Medley & Tully 2015). The connected Project UK Fisheries Improvements has overseen Fishery Improvement Projects on six fisheries to enable them to enter the MSC full assessment programme.

43 Information on the Welsh Fishermen's Association Pre-assessment Project has been shared in a personal communication by Mark Gray on 8 February 2018. Under the title Sustainable Fisheries for Wales Project, this is being taken forward by a Bangor University team.

44 Details of certifications for Icelandic and Norwegian fisheries are at www.msc.org. Sustainable fishing in the Barents Sea is fairly recent. In the mid-2000s, illegal fishing was widespread as revealed in investigations by Swedish journalists reported in Leigh D and Evans R 2006, 'Cod sold in hundreds of chippies linked to Russian black market', *Guardian*, 26 February 2006. Greenpeace also produced a report on this subject, *Findus, Kangamiut, Weak EU Port States and Russian Mafia: Illegal Cod Fishing in the Barents Sea Exposed*, undated but accessed on 27 February 2006 from www.greenpeace.org. However, a determined effort to deal with the problem has turned the situation around.

45 Data is from successive editions of the Scottish Fish Farms Annual Production Survey.

46 Trout and shellfish production data has been taken from Cefas publications *Trout News/Finfish News* and *Shellfish News* and the most recent years from figures produced by Cefas for Eurostat.

47 In the Shetlands, the continuation of Norse traditions extends land ownership to the low water mark and the powers given to the Shetland Islands Council under the *Shetland County Council Act 1974* enabled it to exercise local authority planning control of salmon farms at this early period. While the Crown Estate is in general the owner of the territorial seabed, exceptionally some sales have taken place as explained in *The Crown Estate Guidance Note*, available from www.the-crownestate.co.uk.

48 Powers over the revenue and management of Crown Estate resources in Scotland were transferred to the Scottish Parliament in 2017 in accordance with the *Scotland Act 2016* and in the first instance management responsibilities were assumed by an Interim Management. Permanent arrangements are set out in the Scottish Crown Estate Bill going through the Scottish Parliament in 2018.

49 These were the 'Town and Country Planning (Marine Fish Farming) (Scotland) Regulations 2007', later superseded by the 'Town and Country Planning (Marine Fish Farming) (Scotland) Regulations 2013'.

50 The criteria for the classification of waters unsuitable for further farm development are seabed impacts and nutrient loading (excess, that is unabsorbed, feed and fertiliser) from existing farms in a given area and natural heritage constraints.

Designated Special Protection Areas and Areas of Conservation under the EU's Birds and Habitats Directives also have to be taken into account.

51 These were the 'Registration of Fish Farming and Shellfish Farming Business Order 1985' and the 'Registration of Fish Farming and Shellfish Farming Businesses Amendment (Scotland) Order 2002'.

52 The '(91/67/EEC) Council Directive of 28 January 1991 concerning the animal health conditions governing the placing on the market of aquaculture animals and products' was followed by various UK 'Fish Health' and 'Diseases of Fish' regulations. 'Directive 2006/88/EC of 24 October 2006 on animal health requirements for aquaculture animals and products thereof', and on the prevention and control of certain diseases in aquatic animals (the 'EU Directive on Aquatic Animal Health') was followed by UK 'Aquatic Animals' regulations.

53 'Regulation (EU) 2016/429 of 9 March 2016 on transmissible animal diseases and amending and repealing certain acts in the area of animal health (Animal Health Law)'.

54 Wrasse is already being farmed in Scotland for use as a cleaner fish and a project is underway to fully domesticate lumpsuckers for the same purpose instead of relying on wild broodstock. See 'Wrasse farming initiative announced' 22 February 2012 and 'Lumpsucker project takes another step forward' 30 June 2016, *World Fishing*, accessed 13 February 2018.

55 Environmental assessments are required under the 'Town and Country Planning (Environmental Impact Assessment) (Scotland) Regulations 2011'. SEPA authorisation is under the 'Water Environment (Controlled Activities) (Scotland) Regulations 2011'; previously SEPA administered regulations under the 1974 *Control of Pollution Act* (as amended by the 1989 *Water Act*). The Habitats and Birds Directives were transposed into UK law in the 'Conservation (Natural Habitats, &c) Regulations 1994'.

56 A review of the consenting process has been carried out for the Scottish Government and simplifying improvements proposed so changes to the system are expected but, of course, the range of legislative requirements will still have to be met (Nimmo F et al. 2016).

57 The 2015 edition of the *Code of Good Practice for Scottish Finfish Aquaculture* is available at http://thecodeofgoodpractice.co.uk as a series of separate documents; they were accessed on 13 February 2018.

58 Information about the scheme is at www.qualitytrout.co.uk.

59 The names of companies remaining in the GSI and those that left after a short time are in Seaman T, 'Large Norway, Scottish farmers quietly exit sustainable salmon group', 5 June 2015, www.undercurrentnews.com, accessed 20 March 2018.

60 The ten indicators on which the scores were based are: use of capture fish; ecological energy; industrial energy; feed sustainability; antibiotics; antifoulants; oxygen depletion; parasiticides; escapes; pathogens.

61 Andrew Jackson and Jonathan Shepherd who produced the lower salmon conversion figures cited (in peer-reviewed journals) have both worked for IFFO The Marine Ingredients Organisation (the acronym results from its former name The Fishmeal and Fish Oil Organisation).

62 The US-based organisation Sustainable Fisheries Partnership 'fills a specific gap between industry and the marine conservation community utilising the power of the private sector to help less well-managed fisheries meet the environmental requirements of major markets' (stated on its website www.sustainablefish.org.).

63 The source of these figures is Nikolik G 2015, *The Appeal of Fishmeal: Fishmeal's Transformation from a Commodity to a High-Priced, Strategic Protein*, Rabobank, reproduced in Seafish 2016 which also contains figures showing that the UK's use of fishmeal had halved by 2008 compared to 1996.

64 The Aquamax programme 2006–2010 cost €16 million, €10.5 million of which was provided by the EU, and was co-ordinated by a Norwegian research institute.

65 The EU regulations are '(EU) No 834/2007 On organic production and labelling of organic products' and '(EC) No 710/2009 laying down detailed rules for the implementation of 'Council Regulation (EC) No 834/2007', as regards laying down detailed rules on organic aquaculture animal and seaweed production'; further changes to these regulations are under discussion and if agreed will come into force in 2021. Soil Association and Organic Food Federation aquaculture standards may be found at their respective websites, www.soilassociation.org and www.orgfoodfed.com.

66 The explanation of why a Several Order might be preferred over a Crown Estate lease was provided in a personal communication to the author by Nick Lake, Chief Executive Officer of the Association of Scottish Shellfish Growers, in an email dated 7 March 2018.

67 The change resulted from the Menai Strait legal case. Mussel farmers operating under a Several Order challenged the Crown Estate's decision to allow a marina to be built by Anglesey Council on shore areas used for mussel growing. They won their case in the High Court and subsequently, in 2009, at the Court of Appeal. This appeared at the time to be a Pyrrhic victory for shellfish farmers because the Crown Estate was thought to be blocking new Several Orders and renewals so that it could select more profitable alternatives. The solution came in the *Marine and Coastal Access Act 2009* which removed the requirement for the Crown Estate to give consent (also applying to consents from the Duchies of Cornwall and Lancaster required in the 1967 *Act*) replacing this with an obligation on ministers making these Orders to have regard to the duties and powers of the Crown Estate. There was a *quid pro* in a new provision allowing future fishery orders to be varied or revoked, albeit requiring compensation, but the change indicated a political decision to prioritise aquaculture development over maximising Crown Estate income in this instance.

68 The Association of Scottish Shellfish Growers Code of Good Practice is at http://assg.org.uk. The Bangor Mussel Producers Association Code of Good Practice for Mussel Seed Movements is at https://menaimusselemn.com. The MSC has three categories of enhanced fishery: Catch and grow fisheries, e.g. rope grown mussels based on wild spat; hatch and catch fisheries, e.g. wild capture salmon where some stocking takes place; and habitat modified fisheries, e.g. providing artificial habitats to attract and retain lobster. Information about enhanced fishery certifications is on www.msc.org.

69 EUREP-GAP stood for the Euro Retailer Group for Good Agricultural Practices, GLOBALG.A.P is Global Good Agricultural Practices; the change of name took place in 2007. Documentation connected with the EUREPGAP aquaculture scheme can still be found via the website www.eurep.org and information about the current GLOBALG.A.P scheme is at www.globalgap.org.

70 Information about the GAA is on its website www.gaaliance.org.

71 The WWF press release, which refers to innumerable requests, 'Benchmarking study: certification' is dated 14 December 2007. Despite the involvement of a development NGO, at the time the ASC proposal was announced in 2009, there were protests from a developing country perspective which expressed the view that the new body would support types of aquaculture with deleterious environmental and social impacts. See http://mangroveactionproject.org.

72 The seven ASC principles are: compliance with national and local regulation; minimising ecological impact; water conservation; responsible feed and energy use; nature conservation; better fish health; and social responsibility to workers and local communities. As with the MSC, the philosophy is that certification can be granted before all the performance indicators are met but with conditions about

achieving them within a set period. The ASC works to ten sets of standards for: abalone, bivalves, freshwater trout, pangasius, salmon, seriola + cobia, shrimp (prawns), tilapia and seaweed plus a general one for feed.

73 In addition to the countries named in the text, there were also ASC certified salmon farms in Chile and Canada with a small number from Denmark, Ireland and one in Poland. There were a small number of certified prawn/shrimp farms in other countries including Indonesia, Thailand, Belize, Honduras and Nicaragua. The information about overall numbers and volumes is from the ASC's *Certification Update: February 2018* but the details of countries concerned is from a check made in April 2018, so they are not fully comparable. All such information is available on the ASC's website, www.asc-aqua.org.

74 UK aquaculture producers certified by the ASC in early 2018 were limited to just one company producing salmon in Scotland, one Scottish mussel farm and two Jersey oyster concerns.

75 The ASC's mission statement is on its website www.asc-aqua.org.

76 See the GSI media release 'Farmed salmon industry puts sustainability before competition to meet record consumer demand', 18 March 2014 at www.global salmoninitiative.org which includes the commitment to have all member companies ASC certified by 2020.

77 The agencies in the consortium which produced the shrimp farming principles are: the Food and Agriculture Organisation of the UN, the United Nations Environment Programme, the Network of Aquaculture Centres in Asia-Pacific (an international treaty organisation), the World Bank and the WWF.

78 An enquiry in June 2018 elicited the statement that 'thus far there is no follow-up on the EU eco-label scheme for fishery and aquaculture products. The report will be debated by the European Parliament and the Council'. (Personal communication from the Europe Direct Contact Centre.)

79 The tweet campaign, retailer response and establishment of the BRC Fishmeal Working Group are reported in Ford R 2013, 'Farmed prawns cleanup underway as supermarkets tackle Fish Fight concerns', *The Grocer*, 8 July 2013, www.the grocer.co.uk. The change to the Seafish Ethics Working Group and general context is described in Welling D 2015, 'British Retail Consortium: international collaboration key to beating problems in shrimp supply chain', 21 December 2015, www.intrafish.com.

80 The *Guardian* investigation was reported in Hodal K, Kelly C and Lawrence F, 2014, 'Revealed: Asian slave labour producing prawns for supermarkets in US, UK' and Hodal K and Kelly C 2014, 'Trafficked into slavery on Thai trawlers to catch food for prawns' both on 10 June 2014.

81 The two British retailers in the Shrimp Sustainability Supply Chain Task Force in 2016 were Morrisons and Tesco; Morrisons has a place on the Board of the Seafish Task Force.

82 The webpages are at www.seafish.org/tess.

83 The UK was listed as the world's ninth largest seafood importer in 2014 (FAO 2016).

84 Delegation affecting the state structures involved in managing fisheries and aquaculture developed from the mid-2000s with functions shifted in stages from inside the Department of State (MAFF then DEFRA) to an agency within it (initially called Marine Fisheries) and subsequently for England to the quango the Marine Management Organisation (MMO). Marine Scotland was also established as a separate agency but subsequently re-incorporated into the Scottish Government.

References

Abernethy KE 2010, *Fishing for What? Understanding Fisher Decision-Making in Southwest England*, Thesis submitted for the degree of Doctor of Philosophy, University of East Anglia.

Agnew DJ, Gutiérrez NL, Stern-Pirlot A, Smith ADM, Zimmermann C & Sainsbury K 2013, 'Rebuttal to Froese and Proelss "evaluation and legal assessment of certified seafood"', *Marine Policy*, vol. 38, March, pp. 551–553.

Allsopp M, Santillo D & Dorey C 2013, 'Sustainability in aquaculture: present problems and sustainable solutions', *Ocean Yearbook*, vol. 27, pp. 291–322.

Appleby T 2013, 'Privatising fishing rights: the way to a fisheries wonderland?', *Public Law*, July, pp. 481–497.

Appleby T, van der Werf Y & Williams C 2016, *The Management of The UK's Public Fishery: A Large Squatting Claim?*, University of the West of England, Bristol.

Armstrong MJ, Payne AIL, Deas B & Catchpole TC 2013, 'Involving stakeholders in the commissioning and implementation of fishery science projects: experiences from the U.K. Fisheries Science Partnership', *Journal of Fish Biology*, vol. 83, no. 4, pp. 974–996.

Auld G 2007, *The Origins and Growth of Social and Environmental Certification Programs in the Fisheries Sector*, 11th Annual Conference of the International Society for New Institutional Economics, www.isnie.org, accessed 8 December 2011, Reykjavik, Iceland.

Bain C & Hatanaka M 2010, 'The practice of third-party certification: enhancing environmental sustainability and social justice in the global South?', in *Calculating the Social: Standards and the Reconfiguration of Governing*, Higgins V & Larner W, eds., Palgrave Macmillan, Basingstoke & New York.

Bannister C 2006, *Towards a National Development Strategy for Shellfish in England: Executive Report*, Seafish, Edinburgh.

Belton B, Bush SR & Little DC 2018, 'Not just for the wealthy: rethinking farmed fish consumption in the Global South', *Global Food Security*, vol. 16, March, pp. 85–92.

Belton B, Haque MM, Little DC & Smith LX 2011, 'Certifying catfish in Vietnam and Bangladesh: who will make the grade and will it matter?', *Food Policy*, vol. 36, no. 2, pp. 289–299.

Belton B, Little D & Grady K 2009, 'Is responsible aquaculture sustainable aquaculture? WWF and the eco-certification of tilapia', *Society and Natural Resources: An International Journal*, vol. 22, no. 9, pp. 840–855.

Berry C & Davison A 2001, *Bitter Harvest – A Call for Reform in Scottish Aquaculture*, WWF Scotland, Aberfeldy.

Bjørndal T 2009, 'Overview, roles, and performance of the North East Atlantic Fisheries Commission (NEAFC)', *Marine Policy*, vol. 33, no. 4, pp. 685–697.

Black K & Hughes A 2017, *Future of the Sea: Trends in Aquaculture*, Government Office for Science, London, Foresight Future of the Sea Evidence Review.

Borges L 2018, 'Setting of total allowable catches in the 2013 EU common fisheries policy reform: possible impacts', *Marine Policy*, vol. 91, May, pp. 97–103.

Boude J-P, Boncoeur J & Bailly D 2001, 'Regulating the access to fisheries: learning from European experiences', *Marine Policy*, vol. 25, no. 4, pp. 313–322.

Boxall ABA, Fogg L, Blackwell PA, Kay P & Pemberton EJ 2002, *Review of Veterinary Medicines in the Environment*, Environment Agency, Bristol, R&D Technical Report P6–012/8/TR.

Bradshaw M 2004, 'The market, Marx and sustainability in a fishery', *Antipode*, vol. 36, no. 1, pp. 66–85.

Brown J 2006, *Fishing Capacity Management in the EU Post 2002 CFP Reform*, Institute for European Environmental Policy, London.

Byelashov OA & Griffin ME 2014, 'Fish in, fish out: perception of sustainability and contribution to public health', *Fisheries*, vol. 39, no. 11, pp. 531–535.

Cabinet Office 2004, *Net Benefits: A Sustainable and Profitable Future for UK Fishing*, Cabinet Office, London.

Cambridge T, Martin S, Nimmo F, Grieve C, Walmsley S, Huntington T, Capell R & Agnew D 2011, *Researching the Environmental Impacts of the MSC Certification Programme*, MRAG, Poseidon and Meridian Prime, London.

Cardinale M, Dörner H, Abella A, Andersen JL, Casey J, Döring R, Kirkegaard E, Motova A, Anderson J, Simmonds EJ & Stransky C 2013, 'Rebuilding EU fish stocks and fisheries, a process under way?', *Marine Policy*, vol. 39, May, pp. 43–52.

Cardwell E & Gear R 2013, 'Transferable quotas, efficiency & crew ownership in Whalsay, Shetland', *Marine Policy*, vol. 40, pp. 160–166.

Carpenter G 2018, *Landing the Blame: Overfishing in the Atlantic 2018*, New Economics Foundation, London.

Carter C 2014, 'The transformation of Scottish fisheries: sustainable interdependence from "net to plate"', *Marine Policy*, vol. 44, pp. 131–138.

Catchpole T 2011, *Identifying Underutilised Species*, CEFAS, Weymouth.

Catchpole T, Elliott S, Peach D & Mangi S 2014, *Final Report: The English Discard Ban Trial*, Cefas, Lowestoft.

Cleasby P 2010, *Review of Seafish Report*, Quantera.

Coffey C 2006, *Fisheries Subsidies: Will the EU Turn its Back on the 2002 Reforms?*, WWF, Brussels.

Costello MJ, Grant A, Davies IM, Cecchini S, Papoutsoglou S, Quigley D & Saroglia M 2001, 'The control of chemicals used in aquaculture in Europe', *Journal of Applied Ichthyology*, vol. 17, no. 4, pp. 145–206.

Coull J 1996, *The Sea Fisheries of Scotland: A Historical Geography* John Donald Publishers, Edinburgh.

Crean K 2000, 'The influence of boundaries on the management of fisheries resources in the European Union: case studies from the UK', *Geoforum*, vol. 31, no. 3, pp. 315–328.

Cunningham S, Neiland A, Bjorndal T, Gordon D, Bezabih M, Hatcher A, McClurg T & Goodlad, J 2010, *The Potential Benefits of a Wealth-based Approach to Fisheries Management: An Assessment of the Potential Resource Rent from UK Fisheries*, IDDRA Ltd, Portsmouth, DEFRA Project MF 1210.

Daw T & Gray T 2005, 'Fisheries science and sustainability in international policy: a study of failure in the European Union's Common Fisheries Policy', *Marine Policy*, vol. 29, no. 3, pp. 189–197.

DEFRA 2009, *A Review of the Effectiveness of the Economic Link*, Department for Environment, Food and Rural Affairs, London, Vivid Economics.

DEFRA 2012, *Fishing for the Markets (Market Led Sustainability Programme): Evidence Project Final Report*, Department for Environment, Food and Rural Affairs, London.

DEFRA 2015, *United Kingdom Multiannual National Plan for the Development of Sustainable Aquaculture*, Department for Environment, Food and Rural Affairs, London.

EJF 2013a, *Sold to the Sea: Human Trafficking in Thailand's Fishing Industry*, Environmental Justice Foundation, London.

EJF 2013b, *The Hidden Cost: Human Rights Abuses in Thailand's Shrimp Industry*, Environmental Justice Foundation, London.

EJF 2015, *Thailand's Seafood Slaves: Human Trafficking, Slavery and Murder in Kantang's Fishing Industry*, Environmental Justice Foundation, London.

England Aquaculture Plan Consultation Group 2012, *Planning for Sustainable Growth in the English Aquaculture Industry*, DEFRA, London.

Esteban A & Crilly R 2011, *Fish Dependence – 2011 Update: The Increasing Reliance of the EU on Fish from Elsewhere*, Ocean 2012 and New Economics Foundation, London.

EUMOFA 2017, *EU Organic Aquaculture*, Directorate-General for Maritime Affairs and Fisheries of the European Commission, Brussels.

European Commission 2009, *Green Paper: Reform of the Common Fisheries Policy*, European Commission, Brussels, COM(2009)163.

European Commission 2012, *Investing in European Success: Developing a Bioeconomy Using Resources from Land and Sea*, 2nd edn, European Commission, Brussels.

European Commission 2016a, *Proposal for a Regulation Of The European Parliament and of the Council on Establishing a Multi-annual Plan for Demersal Stocks in the North Sea and the Fisheries Exploiting Those Stocks and Repealing Council Regulation (EC) 676/2007 and Council Regulation (EC) 1342/2008*, European Commission, Brussels, COM(2016) 493.

European Commission 2016b, *Report from the Commission to the European Parliament and the Council on Options for an EU Eco-label Scheme for Fishery and Aquaculture Products*, European Commission, Brussels, COM(2016) 263.

FAO 1956, *The State of Food and Agriculture 1956*, Food and Agriculture Organization of the United Nations, Rome.

FAO 2009, *Guidelines for the Ecolabelling of Fish and Fishery Products from Marine Capture Fisheries*, Food and Agriculture Organization of the United Nations, Rome.

FAO 2011a, *Guidelines for the Ecolabelling of Fish and Fishery Products from Inland Capture Fisheries*, Food and Agriculture Organization of the United Nations, Rome.

FAO 2011b, *International Guidelines on Bycatch Management and Reduction of Discards*, Food and Agriculture Organization of the United Nations, Rome.

FAO 2011c, *Report of the Expert Consultation to Develop an FAO Evaluation Framework to Assess the Conformity of the Public and Private Ecolabelling Schemes with the FAO Guidelines for the Ecolabelling of Fish and Fishery Products from Marine Capture Fisheries, Rome 24–26 November 2010*, Food and Agriculture Organization of the United Nations, Rome, FAO Fisheries and Aquaculture Report No 958.

FAO 2011d, *Technical Guidelines on Aquaculture Certification, Version Approved by the 29th Session of Committee on Fisheries (COFI) Held in Rome, Italy from 31 January to 04 February 2011*, Food and Agriculture Organization of the United Nations, Rome.

FAO 2016, *The State of World Fisheries and Aquaculture 2016: Contributing to Food Security and Nutrition For All*, Food and Agriculture Organization of the United Nations, Rome.

FAO/NACA/UNEP/WB/WWF 2006, *International Principles for Responsible Shrimp Farming*, Network of Aquaculture Centres in Asia-Pacific (NACA), Bangkok.

Fernandes PG & Cook RM 2013, 'Reversal of fish stock decline in the North East Atlantic', *Current Biology*, vol. 18, July.

Flower P & Heap S 2000, 'Bridging troubled waters: the Marine Stewardship Council', in *Terms for Endearment: Business, NGOs and Sustainable Development'*, Bendell J, ed., Greenleaf Publishing, Sheffield.

Foreman S 1989, *Loaves and Fishes: An Illustrated History of the Ministry of Agriculture, Fisheries and Food, 1889–1989* HMSO, London.

Friends of the Earth Scotland 1988, *The Salmon Myth*, FoE, Edinburgh.

Froehlich HE, Sand Jacobsen N, Essington TE, Clavell T & Halpern B 2018, 'Avoiding the ecological limits of forage fish for fed aquaculture', *Nature Sustainability*, vol. 1, no. 6, pp. 298–303.

Froese R & Proelss A 2012, 'Evaluation and legal assessment of certified seafood', *Marine Policy*, vol. 36, no. 6, pp. 1284–1289.

Froese R & Quaas M 2012, 'Mismanagement of the North Sea Cod by the Council of the European Union', *Ocean and Coastal Management*, vol. 70, pp. 54–58.

Garcia SM & Rosenberg AA 2010, 'Food security and marine capture fisheries: characteristics, trends, drivers and future perspectives', *Philosophical Transactions of the Royal Society*, vol. 365, pp. 2869–2880.

Garrett A, Lart B, Snowden J, Vidarsson J & Margeirsson S 2010, *Outlook for Supplies of Icelandic Cod and Haddock to the UK: Recent Events and Future Challenges for UK and Iceland Seafood Processors*, Sea Fish Industry Authority and Humber Seafood Institute, Grimsby.

Government Chief Scientific Advisor 2018, *Foresight: Future of the Sea*, Government Office for Science, London.

Graham M 1943, *The Fish Gate* Faber and Faber, London.

Greenwood M 2003, *The Dynamics of Aquaculture: Salmon and Trout Farming in Scotland 1975–2002, Unpublished MA Dissertation*, Thames Valley University.

Gulbrandsen LH 2009, 'The emergence and effectiveness of the Marine Stewardship Council', *Marine Policy*, vol. 33, no. 4, pp. 654–660.

Gulbrandsen LH 2010, *Transnational Environmental Governance: The Emergence and Effects of the Certification of Forests and Fisheries* Edward Elgar Publishing, Cheltenham.

Halliday RG & Pinhorn AT 1996, 'North Atlantic fishery management systems: a comparison of management methods and resource trends', *Journal of Northwest Atlantic Fishery Science*, Special Issue, vol. 20.

Hambrey J & Evans S 2016, *Aquaculture in England, Wales and Northern Ireland: An Analysis of the Economic Contribution and Value of the Major Sub-Sectors and the Most Important Farmed Species: Final Report to Seafish*, Sea Fish Industry Authority, Edinburgh.

Hatcher A, Jaffry S, Thébaud O & Bennett E 2000, 'Normative and social influences affecting compliance with fishery regulation', *Land Economics*, vol. 76, no. 3, pp. 448–461.

Hatcher A, Pascoe S, Banks R & Arnason R 2002, *Future Options for UK Fish Quota Management, CEMARE Report 58*, University of Portsmouth, Portsmouth.

Hedley C, Catchpole T & Ribeiro Santos A 2015, *The Landing Obligation and its Implications on the Control of Fisheries*, European Parliament, Brussels.

Hersoug B 2018, '"After all these years" – New Zealand's quota management system at the crossroads', *Marine Policy*, vol. 92, June, pp. 101–110.

House of Commons Agriculture Committee 1990, *Fish Farming in the UK, Vol 1 Report and Proceedings of the Committee*, HMSO, London, Session 1989–1990, Fourth Report.

House of Lords European Union Committee 2008, *The Progress of the Common Fisheries Policy, Volume I: Report*, The Stationery Office, London, 21st Report of Session 2007–2008.

Howarth W 1993, 'Developments in the law of aquaculture', *Proceedings of the Institute of Fisheries Management 23rd Study Course, 8–10th September*, Institute of Fisheries Management, Hull, pp. 120–131.

Howes R 2008, 'The Marine Stewardship Council programme', in *Seafood Ecolabelling: Principles and Practices*, Ward T & Phillips B, eds., Wiley-Blackwell, Chichester.

Human Rights Watch 2018, *Hidden Chains: Rights Abuses and Forced Labour in Thailand's Fishing Industry*, HRW, New York.

Iudicello S, Weber M & Wieland R 1999, *Fish, Markets and Fishermen: The Economics of Overfishing*, 2nd edn, Earthscan Publications, London.

Jackson A 2009, 'Fish in – fish out: ratios explained', *Aquaculture Europe*, vol. 34, no. 3, pp. 5–10.

Jackson D, Moberg O, Stenevik Djupevåg E, Kane F & Hareide H 2017, 'The drivers of sea lice management policies and how best to integrate them into a risk management strategy: An ecosystem approach to sea lice management', *Journal of Fish Diseases*, vol. 13, October. doi: 10.1111/jfd.12705.

Jacquet J 2017, 'Seafood in the future: bivalves are better', *Solutions*, vol. 8, no. 1, pp. 27–32.

James MA & Slaski RJ 2009, *A Strategic Review of the Potential for Aquaculture to Contribute to the Future Security of Food and Non-Food Products and Services in the UK and Specifically England, Report Commissioned by the Department for the Environment and Rural Affairs*, FRM & Epsilon Resource Management, Dunkeld.

James Sullivan Consulting 2012, *Smart Fishing Initiative: Comparison of Wild-Capture Fisheries Certification Schemes*, WWF, Gland, Switzerland.

Jonell M, Phillips M, Rönnbäck P & Troell M 2013, 'Eco-certification of farmed seafood: will it make a difference?', *AMBIO*, vol. 42, no. 6, pp. 659–674.

Kalfagianni A & Pattberg P 2013, 'Fishing in muddy waters: exploring the conditions for effective governance of fisheries and aquaculture', *Marine Policy*, vol. 38, March, pp. 124–132.

Khalilian S, Froese R, Proelss A & Requate T 2010, 'Designed for failure: a critique of the Common Fisheries Policy of the European Union', *Marine Policy*, vol. 34, no. 6, pp. 1178–1182.

Kleinjans R & Carpenter G 2017, *Who Gets to Fish? The Allocation of Fishing Opportunities to Member States*, New Economics Foundation, London.

Kurlansky M 1999, *Cod: A Biography of the Fish that Changed the World* Vintage, London.

Lart W & Caveen A 2017, *Why Has Cod Stock Recovered in the North Sea?*, Sea Fish Industry Authority, Edinburgh, Seafish Industry Guidance Note FS99_03_17.

Le Gallic B, Mardle S & Metz, S 2017, *Research for PECH Committee – Common Fisheries Policy and BREXIT – Trade and Economic Related Issues*, European Parliament, Brussels, Policy Department for Structural and Cohesion Policies.

Lee AJ 1992, *The Ministry of Agriculture, Fisheries and Food's Directorate of Fisheries Research: Its Origins and Development* Ministry of Agriculture, Fisheries and Food Directorate of Fisheries Research for England and Wales, Lowestoft.

Lequesne C 2004, *The Politics of Fisheries in the European Union* Manchester University Press, Manchester.

Lutchman I, Van den Bossche K & Zino F 2008, *Implementation of the CFP – an Evaluation of Progress Made Since 2002*, Institute for European Environmental Policy, London, JNCC Report No. 428.

Lymbery P 2002, *In Too Deep – The Welfare Of Intensively Farmed Fish*, Compassion in World Farming Trust, Petersfield.

MacGarvin M & Jones S 2000, *Choose or Lose: A Recovery Plan for Fish Stocks and the UK Fishing Industry*, WWF-UK, Godalming.

MacMullen P 1998, *A Report to the Fish Industry Forum on the Marine Stewardship Council and Related Topics*, Sea Fish Industry Authority, Edinburgh, Technical Report No CR 152.

Marine Management Organisation 2013, *Catch Quota Trials 2012: Final Report*, MMO, Newcastle-upon-Tyne.

Marine Scotland 2012, *Marine Scotland Review of Scottish Fish Producers' Organisations: Report and Recommendations*, Marine Scotland, Edinburgh.

Marschke M & Wilkings A 2014, 'Is certification a viable option for small producer fish farmers in the global south? Insights from Vietnam', *Marine Policy*, vol. 50, December, pp. 197–206.

Mazzucato M 2018, *The Entrepreneurial State: Debunking Public vs Private Sector Myths* Penguin Books, London.

McDiarmid H 1990, *Regional Study: The Fishing Industry in North East England*, Sea Fish Industry Authority, Hull, Seafish Report No 390.

Nakamura K, Bishop L, Ward T, Pramod G, Thomson DC, Tungpuchayakul P & Srakaew S 2018, 'Seeing slavery in seafood supply chains', *Science Advances*, vol. 4, no. 7, p. e1701833.

National Audit Office 2003, *Fisheries Enforcement in England*, The Stationery Office, London.

Nautilus Consultants 1997, *The Economic Evaluation of the Fishing Vessels (Decommissioning) Schemes*, Nautilus Consultants, Edinburgh.

Naylor R, Hindar K, Fleming IA, Goldburg R, Williams S, Volpe J, Whoriskey F, Eagle J, Kelso D & Mangel M 2005, 'Fugitive salmon: assessing the risks of escaped fish from net-pen aquaculture', *BioScience*, vol. 55, no. 5, pp. 427–437.

Naylor RL, Hardy RW, Bureau DP, Chiu A, Elliott M, Farrell AP, Forster I, Gatlin DM, Goldburgh RJ, Hua K & Nichols PD 2009, 'Feeding aquaculture in an era of finite resources', *PNAS*, vol. 106, no. 36.

Nimmo F & Capell R 2014, *Assessment of the Benefits of MSC Certification to a Major UK Fishery and its Supply Chain*, Poseidon Aquatic Resource Management, Edinburgh.

Nimmo F, McLaren K, Miller J & Cappell R 2016, *Independent Review of the Consenting Regime for Scottish Aquaculture*, Scottish Government, Edinburgh.

O'Riordan B 1996, 'Marine Stewardship Council: who's being seduced?', *Samudra*, July, pp. 10–11.

Oddy DJ 1971, 'The changing techniques and structure of the fishing industry', in *Fish in Britain: Trends in Supply, Distribution and Consumption During the Past Two Centuries, Occasional Paper No 2*, Barker TC & Yudkin J, eds., Department of Nutrition, Queen Elizabeth College, University of London, London.

Oosterveer P 2005, 'Global regulation of food and consumer involvement: labelling of sustainable fisheries using the Marine Stewardship Council (MSC)', in *Political Consumerism: Its Motivations, Power and Conditions in the Nordic Countries and Elsewhere, Proceedings from the 2nd International Seminar on Political Consumerism, Oslo, August 26–29 2004*, Boström M, ed., TemaNord, Copenhagen.

Opitz S, Hoffmann J, Quaas M, Matz-Lück N, Binohlan C & Froese R 2016, 'Assessment of MSC-certified fish stocks in the Northeast Atlantic', *Marine Policy*, vol. 71, pp. 10–14.

Ötles Y, Ozden O & Ötles S 2013, 'Organic fish production and the standards', *Scientiarum Polonorum Technologia Alimentaria*, vol. 9, no. 2, pp. 125–131.

Owen H & Carpenter G 2018, *Fish Dependence: 2018 Update*, New Economic Foundation, London.

Pantzar M 2016, *Total Allowable Catch (TAC), Individual Transferable Quota (ITQ) and Fishing Fee for Commercially Exploited Fish Species in Iceland*, Institute for European Environmental Policy, Brussels, www.ieep.eu.

Parkes G, Walmsley S, Cambridge T, Trumble R, Clarke S, Lamberts D, Souter D & White C 2009, *Review of Fish Sustainability Information Schemes Final Report*, MRAG, London.

Pauly D & Zeller D 2016, 'Catch reconstructions reveal that global marine fisheries catches are higher than reported and declining', *Nature Communications*, vol. 7, p. 10244.

Peñas Lado E 2016, *The Common Fisheries Policy: The Quest for Sustainability* J Wiley & Sons, Chichester.

Poseidon Aquatic Management 2013, *A Case Study Review of the Potential Economic Implications of the Proposed CFP Landings Obligation, Final Report*, Sea Fish Industry Authority, Edinburgh.

Reid C 1998, 'Managing innovation in the British herring fishery: the role of the Herring Industry Board', *Marine Policy*, vol. 22, no. 4–5, pp. 281–295.

Richardson L, ed., 2016, *UK Sea Fisheries Statistics 2015*, Marine Management Organisation, London.

Richardson L, ed., 2017, *UK Sea Fisheries Statistics 2016*, Marine Management Organisation, London.

Roberts C 2007, *The Unnatural History of the Sea* Island Press, Washington DC.

Robinson R 1998, *Trawling: The Rise and Fall of the British Trawl Fishery* University of Exeter Press, Exeter.

Ross A 1997, *Leaping in the Dark – A Review of the Environmental Impacts of Marine Salmon Farming in Scotland and Proposals for Change*, Scottish Wildlife and Countryside Link, Perth.

Rust MB, Barrows FT, Hardy RW, Lazur A, Naughten K & Silverstein J 2010, *The Future of Aquafeeds*, NOAA/USDA (National Oceanic and Atmospheric Administration/United States Department of Agriculture), Washington DC.

SAGB 2004, *Strategy for the Control and Development of the Shellfish Industry*, Shellfish Association of Great Britain, London.

Sainsbury K 2010, *Review of Ecolabelling Schemes for Fish and Fishery Products from Capture Fisheries*, Food and Agriculture Organization of the United Nations, Rome, FAO Fisheries and Aquaculture Technical Paper 533.

Salomon M, Markus T & Dross M 2014, 'Masterstroke or paper tiger: The reform of the EU's Common Fisheries Policy', *Marine Policy*, vol. 47, pp. 76–84.

Samerwong P, Bush SR & Oosterveer P 2017, 'Metagoverning aquaculture standards: a comparison of the GSSI, the ASEAN GAP, and the ISEAL', *Journal of Environment & Development*, vol. 26, no. 4, pp. 429–451.

Schacht K, McLachlan H, Hill L, Hart P & Landman J 2012, *Sorting Myth from Fact: The Truth about Europe's Common Fisheries Policy*, World Wide Fund for Nature, Brussels.

Scottish Government 2009, *A Fresh Start: The Renewed Strategic Framework for Scottish Aquaculture*, Scottish Government, Edinburgh.

Seafish 2016, *Fishmeal and Fish Oil Facts and Figures*, Sea Fish Industry Authority, Edinburgh.

Seafish 2017, *Seafood 2040: A Strategic Framework for England*, Sea Fish Industry Authority, Edinburgh.

Seafood Task Force 2017, *Fuelling the Task Force Engine and Building Foundations for Longer Term Success*, www.seafoodtaskforce.global, accessed 17 July 2018.

Shepherd CJ 2012, 'Aquaculture: are the criticisms justified? Feeding fish to fish', *World Agriculture*, vol. 3, no. 2, pp. 11–18.

Shepherd CJ & Little DC 2014, 'Aquaculture: are the criticisms justified? II – aquaculture's environmental impact and use of resources, with specific reference to farming Atlantic salmon', *World Agriculture*, vol. 4, no. 2, pp. 37–52.

Shepherd CJ, Monroig O & Tocher DR 2015, *Production of High Quality, Healthy Farmed Salmon from a Changing Raw Material Base, With Special Reference To A Sustainable Scottish Industry*, Scottish Aquaculture Research Forum (SARF), Edinburgh.

Shrimp Sustainable Task Force 2016, *How the Task Force is Leading Thailand's Seafood Supply Chain Towards a More Sustainable Pathway*, SSTF, Bangkok, Progress Report following Membership Review and Planning Meeting, August 2016, www.seafoodtaskforce.global, accessed 17 July 2018..

Smith H 2011, *The Regional Development and Management of Fisheries: the UK Case, Paper Presented at 'It's Not Just About the Fish': Social and Cultural Perspectives of Sustainable Marine Fisheries*, University of Greenwich, London, 4–5 April 2011.

Smith R 2015, 'Documenting the UK "Black Fish Scandal" as a case study of criminal entrepreneurship', *International Journal of Sociology and Social Policy*, vol. 35, no. 3/4, pp. 199–221.

Southall T, Medley P & Tully O 2015, *Project Inshore Stage 3 – Strategic Sustainability Review: A National Overview*, Accoura, Edinburgh.

Spreij M 2005, *National Aquaculture Legislation Overview. United Kingdom of Great Britain and Northern Ireland, NALO Fact Sheet*, FAO Fisheries and Aquaculture Department, Rome.

Staniford D 2002, *Sea Cage Farming: An Evaluation of Environmental and Public Health Aspects (the Five Fundamental Flaws of Sea Cage Farming)*, www.europarl.eu.int/committees/pech_home.htm, accessed 27 April 2003, Brussels, Paper presented to European Parliament's Committee on Fisheries, October 2002.

Steinberg PE 1999, *Fish or Foul: Investigating the Politics of the Marine Stewardship Council*, Paper Presented at the Conference on Marine Environmental Politics in the 21st Century, Institute for International Studies, Berkeley, California, 30 April 1999.

Steinberg PE 2001, *The Social Construction of the Ocean* Cambridge University Press, Cambridge.

Swartz W, Sumaila UR, Watson R & Pauly D 2010, 'Sourcing seafood for the three major markets: the EU, Japan and the USA', *Marine Policy*, vol. 34, no. 6, pp. 1366–1373.

Symes DG 1985a, *Fish Supplies and Processing Capacity in the United Kingdom, Part I*, Hull University and Sea Fish Industry Authority, Hull & Edinburgh, Technical Report 268.

Symes DG 1985b, *Fish Supplies and Processing Capacity in the United Kingdom, Part II*, Hull University & Sea Fish Industry Authority, Hull & Edinburgh, Technical Report 276.

Symes DG 1991, *Norfish: Imported Fish Supplies and the UK Industry*, Sea Fish Industry Authority, Edinburgh, Seafish Report 397.

Symes DG & Haughton GF 1987, 'Decline and continuity in the Humber fish industry', *Geography*, vol. 72, no. 2, pp. 241–242.

Symes DG & Phillipson J 1999, 'Co-governance in EU fisheries: the complexity and diversity of fishermen's organisations in Denmark, Spain and the UK', in *Creative*

Governance: Opportunities for Fisheries in Europe, Kooiman J, Van Vliet M & Jentoft S, eds., Ashgate, Aldershot/Brookfield/Singapore/Sydney.

Tacon AGJ, Hasan MR & Metian M 2011, *Demand and Supply of Feed Ingredients for Farmed Fish and Crustaceans: Trends And Prospects*, Food and Agriculture Organization of the United Nations, Rome, FAO Fisheries and Aquaculture Technical Paper 564.

Tacon AGJ & Metian M 2008, 'Global overview on the use of fish meal and fish oil in industrially compounded aquafeeds: Trends and future prospects', *Aquaculture*, vol. 285, no. 1–4, pp. 146–158.

Tacon AGJ & Metian M 2015, 'Feed matters: satisfying the feed demand of aquaculture', *Reviews in Fisheries Science & Aquaculture*, vol. 23, no. 1, pp. 1–10.

Taylor RA 1960, *The Economics of White Fish Distribution in Great Britain* Duckworth, London.

Terry A, Lewis K & Bullimore B 2018, *Managing the Inshore Marine Environment in the Marine and Coastal Access Era: the Welsh Experience*, University of the West of England and Aberystwyth University, Bristol & Aberystwyth.

Tett P et al. 2018, *Review of the Environmental Impacts of Salmon Farming in Scotland*, SAMS Research Services, Oban.

Thilsted SH, Thorne-Lyman A, Webb P, Bogard JR, Subasinghe R, Phillips MJ & Allison EH 2016, 'Sustaining healthy diets: the role of capture fisheries and aquaculture for improving nutrition in the post-2015 era', *Food Policy*, vol. 61, May, pp. 126–131.

Thurstan RH, Brockington S & Roberts CM 2010, 'The effects of 118 years of industrial fishing on UK bottom trawl fisheries', *Nature Communications*, vol. 1, p. 15.

Vandergeest P & Unno A 2012, 'A new extraterritoriality? Aquaculture certification, sovereignty, and empire', *Political Geography*, vol. 31, no. 6, pp. 358–367.

Veiga P, Martin D & Lee-Harwood B 2017, *Reduction Fisheries: STP Sustainability Overview 2017*, Sustainable Fisheries Partnership, Honolulu HI.

Villasante S, Pita C, Pierce GJ, Guimeráns CZ, Rodrigues JG, Antelo M, Da Rocha JM, Cutrín JG, Hastie L, Sumaila UR & Coll M 2018, 'To land or not to land: how do stakeholders perceive the zero discard policy in European small-scale fisheries?', *Marine Policy*, vol. 71, pp. 166–174.

Volpe JP, Beck M, Ethier V, Gee J & Wilson A 2010, *Global Aquaculture Performance Index*, University of Victoria, Victoria BC.

Volpe JP, Gee J, Beck M & Ethier V 2011, *How Green Is Your Eco-label? Comparing the Environmental Benefits of Marine Aquaculture Standards*, University of Victoria, Victoria BC.

Ward TJ 2008, 'Measuring the success of seafood ecolabelling', in *Seafood Ecolabelling: Principles and Practices*, Ward TJ & Phillips B, eds., Wiley-Blackwell, Chichester.

Washington S & Ababouch L 2011, *Private Standards and Certification in Fisheries and Aquaculture: Current Practice and Emerging Issues*, Food and Agriculture Organization of the United Nations, Rome.

Waterman JJ 1987, *Freezing Fish at Sea: A History* HMSO, London.

White Fish Authority 1959, *The White Fish Industry*, White Fish Authority, London.

Whiteley, R 2016, *UK Shellfish Production and Several, Regulating and Hybrid Orders: The Contribution and Value of Orders in Relation to the Sector's Past Development and Future Growth*, Seafish, Edinburgh.

Wilding TA & Nickell TD 2013, 'Changes in benthos associated with mussel (*mytilus edulis* L.) farms on the West-Coast of Scotland', *PLOS One*, vol. 8, no. 7, p. e68313. doi:10.1371/journal.pone.0068313.

Willmann R, Cochrane K & Emerson W 2008, 'FAO guidelines for ecolabelling in wild capture fisheries', in *Seafood Ecolabelling: Principles and Practices*, Ward T & Phillips B, eds., Wiley-Blackwell, Chichester.

4 Achieving seafood safety and quality

Introduction

Over the second half of the twentieth century there was a transformation of both food safety and the quality of seafood which those working in the industry personally experienced:

> In my youth, I went past many a fish shop that had brown curling stale fish in it that people would not want to eat. They used to smoke it because it could stay longer.
>
> (Managing director, small company 1)

> Obviously, the difference between 30 years ago and today, the hygiene standards, which you do have in food factories is a lot better now than it was, is a lot more regulated. I think that people understand it a lot better nowadays.
>
> (Director, medium-large company)

Documented sources support the statements about indifferent quality in the past. In the middle of the period covered by this book, fish was described as being mostly bland and tasteless, some as of extremely poor quality (Eddie 1971; Mills 1987). At an earlier time, there was a particular problem with the fish brought back by the distant water fleet which could be up to 16 days old. Large quantities were condemned as unfit for human consumption; unsurprisingly, deterioration was particularly great in the summer season (Cutting 1955; Graham 1943; Robinson 1998).

This chapter considers some of the factors relevant to defining safety and quality in seafood before tracing the governance factors involved in the positive changes that have occurred. This has been both in the production sector and in processing and distribution; together, they have produced a tremendous change for the better.

Defining quality and safety in seafood

Those working in the middle of the seafood chain as well as being responsible for safety and quality standards in their own operations need to start with raw material that conforms to those standards in the first place. Knowledge of biological processes, shared by those working in trade organisations, is one way they are equipped to assess this as shown by some interviewee explanations:

> If you buy certain fish during the spawning period, for example, it's likely to be, typically it's in a less healthy condition anyway than it would be when it's not. It's obviously a weaker animal when it's carrying the eggs. So there are certain times of the year where you know when it's the spawning season where you wouldn't tend to buy certain species.
>
> (Director, large company)

> While we want to be catching the fish [tuna] in the most sustainable methods, if you take, and handline and pole and line would be two great examples, if you take a handline fish, I've done it myself, it's a 20 minute struggle with a fish, a 50, 60 kilo fish which you're catching with something as thick as a washing line. And the lactic acid that builds up in the fish during that catching process is massive, the cellular structure, it really is a huge build up of lactic acid. So, when you catch the fish, that fish, it's worked itself up into a real frenzy, there's a lot of stress and then you then obviously kill the fish. The trick is you need to bleed it, gut it and ice it as quickly as possible after catching it and that should be within minutes. But even so, you may get some browning of the meat caused by the lactic acid around the belly.
>
> (Managing director, medium-large company)

The quality of seafood is made up from a complex amalgam of several factors. Freshness is the top requirement and most fundamental feature but, as with other foods, quality includes a range of physical and sensory qualities as well as attributes like sustainability and production conditions (Denton 2003; Whittle 1997). Lack of freshness corresponds to objective decline factors caused by microbial, oxidative and enzymic spoilage (Bayliss 1996). But, quality and freshness in fish are concepts not entities so cannot be exactly measured, rather, they need to be broken down into particular properties that are sought in relation to the species being considered such as size, colour and texture (Bremner 2002).

This indicates that quality has a relative aspect, dependent on particular purposes which are structured socially and economically as well as biologically (Mansfield 2003). One example is the difference between whole, often live, langoustines obtained by creeling (trapping) and mostly destined for export and the trawled *nephrops norvegicus* which may have claw or carapace damage but will produce appropriate quality flesh when marketed domestically as scampi. Another case in point is salmon; when obtained for smoking, the preference would be for low fat whereas for making sushi higher fat levels would be sought.

For some in the trade, quality was experiential and assessment based on experience:

> That [pollock] is absolutely fantastic quality. If you look at the gills, lovely colour, lovely eyes, lovely sheen on the fish. Thickness of the fish as well. Just says it's quality.
>
> (Managing director, small company 7)

Alternatively, formal methods of assessing properties of seafood are available. The Torry scoring system produced by the Torry Research Station sets out for individual species a range of characteristics scored up to 10, the best. Like another system, the Quality Index Method (QIM) more commonly used elsewhere in Europe, it is based on subjective judgements but made by trained assessors to produce consistency (Martinsdóttir 2002; Shewan et al. 2012). As explained by one processor:

> We assess the material on its quality in term of its appearance, its odours, its taste, we use the Torry scoring system here. We have a minimum standard for our main supplier so we're Torry scoring at 8 and above.
>
> (Technical manager, large company)

There are also a number of technologies now available to measure fish freshness using chemical, physical (such as measurements of texture and colour) or microbiological approaches (Alasalvar, Garthwaite & Öksüz 2002; Fraser & Sumar 1998). Techniques for identifying fish species and increasingly their geographical origins and whether wild or farmed are also available; these enable tests of authenticity to be carried out (Mackie 1997; Martinsohn et al. 2011).

From a safety perspective seafood carries low risk as one interviewee described with graphic detail:

> Myself and my colleague have done the advanced fish quality course. And they make you try fish that's been all the range from day 1 to day 15 and she said it was literally going yellow and green, the smell was overpowering, when you eat it it's like eating cotton wool. Fish is a very safe product from that point of view; it will look horrible and you won't want to eat it, but it still won't kill you.
>
> (Manager, trade organisation 1)

Risks are considered to be low because most types of seafood do not carry or get infected with food poisoning bacteria, seafood is generally stored at cool temperatures and usually eaten cooked in Britain (Archer, Edmonds &

George 2008). Levels of foodborne illness attributable to seafood are relatively low in the UK (Cato 1998). A study of foodborne illness carried out for the Food Standards Agency estimated that of the resulting GP consultations just 3.4% were caused by seafood while the figure for hospital admissions was 5.2%, those attributed to meat and particularly poultry being much higher (Tam, Larose & O'Brien 2014).[1]

Nevertheless, seafood is potentially a disease-carrying food, first because of the potential risk of bacterial disease, particularly the specific hazards associated with the consumption of raw molluscs, and second due to toxic syndromes including paralytic and other types of shellfish poisoning and the histamine poisoning which can be associated with scombroids such as mackerel and tuna; in addition, allergic reactions affect some people (Huss, Reilly & Ben Embarek 2000; Mavromatis & Quantick 2002; Scoging 1991). Therefore safety-enhancing practices during processing are important and action is also needed to destroy naturally-occurring parasites in fish.[2] Contaminants, however, pose different issues as they cannot be removed. In addition to those of chemical or biological origin, there is emerging awareness of the extent of microplastics and nanoplastics present in seafood as well as of the huge quantities of plastics in the oceans (EFSA Panel on Contaminants in the Food Chain (CONTAM) 2016). Issues over contaminants in aquaculture are considered later in this chapter.

When considering safety issues seafood processors need to calibrate risks in relation to specific products. How they were manufactured and whether the end purchaser would be cooking them or not will both be relevant:

> There are certain products and certain product formats that will have higher intrinsic risks than others. For example, if we're buying cooked products they would tend to carry much higher risks because the risks would be much more associated with the processing conditions in the factory wherever it is in the world.... If we buy cooked prawns, for example, cooked products carry more risks purely and simply because they're not necessarily cooked again by the consumer.
>
> (Director, large company)

Having considered the various dimensions of quality that may be desired and food safety risks to be avoided we go on to look at how quality and safety are or can be obtained first in capture, then in farmed fish.

Quality and food safety at sea

How capture fish is handled at sea is well understood as the initial key to ensuring quality:

> The biggest determinant of fish quality is the way it's handled when it comes out of the water.... When you take fish out of the water, when it

literally comes out of that water, it's in pretty good condition, it's what you do with it afterwards that determines the quality and that's really about the speed at which it's handled onboard the vessel, the conditions in which it's held, largely to do with icing and refrigeration onboard the vessel and obviously the length of time it then takes to get to the market.

(Director, large company)

As long as the boat has looked after it initially and kept it cool then we don't have any problems. All it takes is for the boat to look after it. As soon as it gets warm, no matter what I do afterwards, if the boat hasn't been looking after it initially then there's problems.

(Managing director, small company 4)

In order to keep expired fish in good condition, the most important requirement is to maintain it at a low temperature which should be at minus 1.5 to 0°C. This prevents the development of bacteria which otherwise after a few days would produce considerable contamination. The length of time fish will keep on ice varies according to species, for example, nine to 15 days for cod and haddock, but as little as two to six days for summer herring. Avoidance of rough handling is also important to prevent damage that can allow the growth of bacteria and enzymes. Packing the fish in boxes with ice rather than stacking them on open shelves in the hold has been shown to produce better results. For many whitefish species, optimal quality is obtained by bleeding and gutting as soon as possible after capture. Thus there are a number of established practices conducive to keeping seafood in good condition (Horne 1971; Huss 1995; Huss, Ababouch & Gram 2004; Whittle 1997).

Preserving the freshness of such a perishable commodity as fish has always been a concern for fishers. Vessels with various arrangements for keeping fish alive in water onboard were in use by some British vessels in the eighteenth century. Ice started to be employed in the mid-nineteenth century and had become general in the trawling fleet by the 1870s. Yet fish was often in too poor a state to be landed and would be thrown overboard. Thus discards have had a long history and certainly did not start with the CFP. Subsequently, with the development of steam trawling much longer trips became possible and the limits of keeping qualities that could be maintained using ice were frequently passed. Hence the poor quality of much that reached ports and the great quantities condemned as unfit for human consumption, in other words, discarded on land (Cutting 1955).

Technological developments in using mechanical refrigeration to supplement ice and freezing at sea eventually solved the problem of maintaining the quality of catches from distant waters (Merritt 1969). Freezer-trawlers were generally introduced from the early 1960s though the first fishing vessels to in the British fleet to freeze at sea actually functioned from the late 1920s to early 1930s but ceased for various practical reasons (Waterman 1987). By the

1960s, British trawlers could freeze either fillets or whole fish at sea and just 1% of landings were condemned, a huge reduction from the previous period (Burgess et al. 1965). As well as preventing deterioration before landing, the other quality advantages are that processing could take place on very fresh fish, reducing the occurrence of certain pathogens and other risks (Kose 2011). But, while the distant water vessels were becoming equipped to freeze, the middle water North Sea fleet continued to rely on ice, refrigeration capable of maintaining a 0° temperature only becoming widespread there in the 1980s (Engelhard 2008).

Since then, much of the supply of whitefish for the British market, caught mainly in Icelandic and Norwegian waters following the changes described in the previous chapter, consists of frozen-at-sea fillets which are generally agreed to be of high quality. As one interviewee said: 'I know that frozen-at-sea fillets are the finest fish you can buy, without question' (Managing director, large company). A trade body, the Frozen at Sea Fillets Association (FASFA) was established in 2000 to promote the product: its members comprise (mainly Nordic) fishing companies and British distributors.[3]

The development of freezer-trawlers in the distant water fleet and some years later of refrigerated holds in boats fishing the North Sea were all commercial decisions made by vessel owners and operators. There was no public action to encourage such moves whether to benefit the industry or to improve food safety and the reported view of the White Fish Authority was that quality assurance was a management responsibility in which it should not be involved (Eddie 1971).

But three decades later, with a different successor body supporting the seafood industry, there was a shift. In a new development of governance functions, the quango Seafish launched its Responsible Fishing Scheme (RFS) in 2006. Motivated by a general awareness of higher market demands, the organisation's aim was to establish quality standards for the catching sector and improve the status of its products. The standards were in four categories: care of the catch, vessel standards, crew competence and environmental awareness with much emphasis on general handling practice, hygiene and storage methods. The scheme had third-party auditing. By late 2012 there were more than 200 British vessels holding current certificates and many others engaged with the programme. Not long afterwards in 2014 Seafish undertook a thorough review of the RFS and it was relaunched in 2016 with an expanded set of standards, retaining the objectives concerned with catch handling, the vessel and the environment but with greatly strengthened requirements in relation to workers. Third-party auditing continues to be a feature of the scheme. Within the Seafish structure there is an Oversight Board for the scheme with members representing all sections of the supply chain – fishing, processing and retail – together with two NGOs. Less than two years after the relaunch there were already more than 100 vessels certified under the revised standards and between them, they accounted for over a quarter of UK boat landings.[4]

The RFS was not the only governance effort to improve catch quality. It had been preceded by the Seafood Scotland Vessel Quality and Hygiene Scheme which ran for some years from 2000.[5] A separate project aiming to raise standards of fish handling onboard, the White Fish Quality Improvement Initiative, has been operated by an independent company, Shetland Seafood Quality Control, for this specific geographical area and continues; its method is to assess the quality of landings and issue regular reports, a different approach to incentivising better handling than the usual standards schemes. Seafish has undertaken projects to provide evidence of the more profitable rewards of better handling (Curtis, Alva & Martin 2005; Curtis & Martin 2003; Seafish 2008) and has produced a series of good practice guides separately targeting demersal, *nephrops norvegicus,* pelagic and scallop fishers.[6]

These efforts to improve onboard handling have been much needed. A study carried out in the mid-1980s based on samples from ports all round Britain showed that while much of the fish was of good quality a significant amount was not, 16% being defined as Torry score 6 or less (Hill & Coutts 1986), 6 being 'the point just before off flavours and odours are detected' and 'the cut off point for sale'.[7] A decade later, an evaluation of the Seafood Scotland Vessel Quality and Hygiene Scheme found much evidence of poor as well as good quality fish being landed, the former attributed to overfilled boxes, insufficient or inadequately trained crew and the length of trips (Nautilus Consultants 2001). Another study stated that supermarket buyers did not find the quality of landings from British boats adequate although it did note that better handling and icing had improved quality (Carleton et al. 1999). The report of another project, this time covering both Scotland and Eire refers to the 'indifferent quality' of much of what their fishermen landed while significant levels of avoidable quality loss were indicated by a series of Seafish port audits (Seafish 2004, p. 8). Its onboard survey found various handling practices conducive to lower quality scores. Positive attitudes of skippers and crews and longer experience on the same boat were associated with better quality. The project concluded that lack of communication and even lack of trust within the supply chain were major factors inhibiting incentives for better quality.

The Seafish guides to good practice were not the first by any means. The earliest Torry advice for improving quality through better handling at sea was produced as far back as 1929 (Lumley, Piqué & Reay 1929). A series of Advisory Notes were published by the Torry Research Station in the 1970s covering such topics as taking care of the catch, what kind of ice to use, cleaning and the relative advantages of different methods of storage (Horne 1971). The issue has not been about lack of information but about getting practice to accord with such advice. There has been both legislation and much Seafish governance activity with such aims.

Fishing vessels were affected by European food safety regulation from the introduction of 1991 and 1992 Directives which established hygiene conditions to be maintained on vessels generally and more stringent rules for factory vessels undertaking freezing at sea and also those transporting live fish.[8] The regulatory requirements were translated by Seafish into vessel hygiene checklists, a general one and, echoing European requirements, a more stringent set of demands for factory vessels that fillet and pack fish onboard. The basic one as well as covering equipment, staff awareness and general hygiene included maintenance at the temperature of melting ice (0°C) and speedy gutting which as well as being needed for food safety are also key quality practices. The more detailed conditions for factory vessels contained an additional section on hygiene of the fish preparation area. However, only those classified as factory vessels require regulatory approval, which would be from environmental or port health authorities. These agencies do not seem to have put much inspection effort into the mass of other vessels. For these, the majority, the regulations do not seem to be enforced, particularly as far as handling practices at sea are concerned. A few years later a research project classed fish handling and storage areas of a large minority of vessels as 'medium' or 'poor' (Seafish 2004). Since that time those vessels engaged in the RFS scheme will have had an incentive to improve. However, vessel inspections seem to have remained limited.[9]

Regional organisations related to Seafish have also tried to improve standards with mixed results:

> The most important factor in determining the whole quality and shelf life of the fish is how it's treated in the first hour onboard the boat, when you catch it when it's live. How quickly you wash it, gut it, wash it and store it in ice, that then sets the tone for how long it's going to last so once we were able to explain that to the fishermen … and introduce some slush ice to make sure the temperature is controlled much quicker.… A lot of the fish merchants and fish processors give us good feedback that soft-fleshed fish like hake and megrim, which we catch quite a lot here have improved.
>
> (Manager, trade organisation 1)

Some of this effort is as basic as getting ice used onboard because despite its long history in fishing it is still not uniform practice:

> We offered the fishermen ice boxes at a discounted rate. Because … one of the things we discovered is that they don't put the fish on ice. So in these small boats, people go out 4 o'clock this morning probably and come back whenever. They catch fish and put it on deck; in this heat, the fish deteriorates immediately.… They're very insular, they're very much in their own world. They're out at sea and that's it.
>
> (Manager, trade organisation 2)

With the under ten-metre vessels fishing on short trips, and often referred to as 'day boats', some emphasised the short length of time involved in getting the product through the supply chain as the intrinsic guarantee of freshness and hence high quality without any additional measures being needed:

> None of the other ports will produce the quality of the fish you get [here] … our fleet only goes out for eight hours at a time so whatever is caught today is in London tomorrow night, so there's a very, very quick turnaround.
>
> (Director, medium company 1)

> Scottish boats, I think, are still out too long to push the quality up. But, South West England or French boats, they just run them as day boats out and back, out and back, then get a higher quality product with a higher price.
>
> (Trader, medium-large company)

In an assessment produced by the National Federation of Fishermen's Organisation under the heading 'Why do we still have a quality problem?', a number of reasons are given for this historic issue connected with the UK fishing industry. They include the lack of relationship between prices and better quality (indicating ineffective market mechanisms), longer trip lengths, problems in attracting crew and their increased workload and the lack of systems to weigh boxes on landing (Hopper et al. 2003). However, a European report a decade later struck a more positive note in stating that cod from UK vessels is of better quality than imported fish which is certainly a mark of progress (EUMOFA 2013).

The governance activity discussed so far in relation to improving quality of landed catches has been from the state through regulation and voluntary from the combo public-private organisation Seafish through its certification scheme. There is also some supply chain governance, whether specific to particular relationships or about more general involvement from downstream companies to influence what happens at the fishing stage.

One example of a specific relationship involved a processing company inviting crews from the boats from which they purchased to visit their premises and see the impact made by differences in catch quality; consistent improvements were observed as a result (Seafish 2004). Another was improving langoustine quality through a specific project which a processing company had initiated:

> The initial drive for us was quality because what we found that with the langoustine fishery if you were trawling beyond a certain length of time, the intrinsic quality would deteriorate because trapped in the nets, if there were certain locations, if, for example, we saw a significant number of berried, as we call it, langoustines then you could avoid that sort of area and obviously that impacts on quality as well [berried means egg-bearing].
>
> (Director, large company)

Such direct involvement seems to be limited to the activity of a few companies. They more usually have a general impact on production through the standards set or employed for what is purchased, as discussed in a subsequent section. However, processor and retailer involvement in the Responsible Fishing Scheme, as with Project Inshore discussed in the previous chapter, indicates an interest at least by the companies involved in these initiatives; they actively encourage, in some cases fund, efforts to improve quality in capture fisheries.

In a more diffuse way, purchasers who select better-kept fish are encouraging good practice:

> You learn the boats, you learn which boats do a good job, which boats take plenty of ice to sea, which skippers are good skippers. It just becomes experience. We buy off certain few boats.
>
> (Fish merchant, small company)

Thus market expectations can incentivise a greater onboard effort to ensure good quality. Other factors conducive to improved quality are modern, better-equipped vessels, shorter fishing trips and technological developments especially freezing at sea, though the benefits of the last of these now come to the British market mainly via imports.

An additional important issue for the fishing industry concerns its labour. A significant aspect of the relaunched Seafish Responsible Fishing Scheme is the emphasis on conditions for those employed on fishing vessels and on training and professional development. One context is a regulatory initiative, the *Modern Slavery Act 2015*, and concerns about forced labour which have extended to the British fishing fleet.[10] More broadly, there are a large number of health hazards associated with working on a fishing vessel (Watterson et al. 2008). There continues to be a large number of injuries suffered by crew on UK fishing vessels and though these have been reducing, nearly halved between 2008 and 2017 from 60 each year to 32, they are still high. This is in addition to an annual number of fatalities which have ranged between four and 13 over the same period with no definite trend (MAIB 2018). The issue has not lacked regulation and there are four agencies concerned with various aspects of safety on fishing vessels. The Marine and Coastguard Agency is responsible for safety on British fishing vessels but under a formal arrangement it is Seafish that delivers safety training which is mandatory for commercial fishers at least at basic levels. Safety during loading and unloading and general maintenance of safe conditions and equipment is under the remit of the Health and Safety Executive while it is the Marine Accident Investigation Branch that tracks and publishes details of the mishaps. Responsibilities have been broadly carried out under 1997 regulations about safety on vessels and its subsequent amendments, which gave effect to a European directive, and also general health and safety at work legislation. However, 2018 sees an overhaul of regulations in order to implement the International Labour

Organization 2007 *Work in Fishing Convention.*[11] The continuation of accidents and fatalities despite the measures taken reflects the inherent dangers of fishing as an occupation.

To summarise the position on governance for safety and quality regarding seafood caught by British boats, there is food hygiene regulation in place but apparently lax enforcement except for factory vessels and otherwise no specific rules in operation except for the RFS. This scheme provides the only functioning standards but is voluntary, so for vessels not in the schemes, practices are based on the operators' business decisions. There are limited private governance initiatives by a small number of companies which have worked closely with selected fisheries plus the more extensive work by Seafish and its linked organisations. Thus contrasting with the extensive public regulation of the activity of fishing as described in Chapter 3, much less state attention has been given to affecting the product of that activity except for the regulatory impact on factory ships. Governance for better quality has been mainly the work of the quango Seafish and associated industry-based groups together with market mechanisms. Judging by the EUMOFA report mentioned above quality has improved, presumably in response to all these influences.

Food safety and quality in farmed seafood

Food safety issues

In Chapter 3, regulation of aquaculture production in the UK was reviewed from the viewpoint of environmental protection. There is one other major production topic for shellfish farmers, the classification of waters, which has the primary purpose of protecting human health. They are categorised into Class A, B, C and Prohibited Areas, based on the level of *E. coli* (*Escherichia Coli* O157) contamination found in sampled shellfish. The products of class A waters may be directly used for human consumption but from B and C areas only after specified periods of either relaying (transfer for a period to higher quality waters) or of depuration (purification in tanks of seawater) have taken place and of course not at all from the prohibited waters. Responsibility for maintaining and improving water quality lies with the Environment Agency, the Northern Ireland Environment Agency and the Scottish Environment Protection Agency. In relation to shellfish harvesting the responsible 'competent authorities' are the Food Standards Agency (FSA) and Food Standards Scotland (FSS), but it is local authorities (environmental health departments) which carry out regular sampling from waters where shellfish are cultivated and who arrange for these to be tested in Health Protection Agency Laboratories while Cefas oversees the classification programme and carries out sanitary surveys on new production areas. Waters are also tested for phytoplankton levels and samples of shellfish taken to measure the extent of biotoxins and chemical contaminants. Temporary closures are imposed in areas where thresholds have been exceeded, meaning that harvesting is prohibited.[12]

Annual lists showing the classification of shellfish harvesting areas are published by the FSA (for England, Wales and Northern Ireland) and by FSS. For England and Wales, a long-term classification system was introduced in 2006 for established class B areas in which grading is on the basis of five years rolling data rather than being an annual event but monitoring still occurs at the same level and downgrading may take place in-year as a response to poor results. While varying over time, the general picture is that most Scottish waters are categorised as class A for at least part of the year and many have this status all year round but in the rest of the UK with few exceptions they are generally rated as B while some are as low as C. Consequently nearly all the shellfish taken in England, Northern Ireland and Wales has to be purified by relaying or depuration. Although this does not have to apply to much Scottish cultivation, industry practice there is that most mussels and much of the oyster production are in fact depurated (GVA James Barr 2014).

Purification goes back to at least the inter-war period of the twentieth century and together with relaying has long been used to render potentially polluted products consumable.[13] These methods employ the normal filter-feeding and digestive processes of bivalve molluscs by which they will self-cleanse. Depuration systems are subject to inspection and approval by local authorities (environmental health departments) with technical advice provided in the four administrations by Marine Scotland, by Cefas for England and Wales but directly by the FSA for Northern Ireland.

However, this still leaves another food safety problem affecting bivalve molluscs, particularly oysters which are often consumed uncooked. Norovirus is a major cause of gastroenteritis and though food itself (as compared with other factors like failures of hygiene in handling) causes a small proportion of its cases, shellfish looms large among them (Tam, Larose & O'Brien 2014). The water classification system plus depuration is effective in dealing with risks of *E. coli*, a bacterial infection, but it is not able to protect from noroviruses (there are several strains) for various reasons. First norovirus outbreaks in shellfish cultivation occur sporadically in response to particular events – typically when very heavy rain causes flooding which in turn impairs sewage treatment systems or during particularly cold winters – rather than being fairly constant and amenable to regular testing arrangements; second, although both *E. coli* and norovirus are linked to faecal contamination they are not necessarily found together so that the latter can be a problem even in class A waters; third, depuration as currently specified in legislation does not remove viruses from the harvested shellfish. An underlying issue is about establishing a science-based understanding of the pathogens which could be the basis for regulation since quantitative detection methods have only been available relatively recently, the virus cannot be reliably cultured in the laboratory and investigations are complicated by the variety of strains and the difficulty of distinguishing infectious from non-infectious norovirus; in addition, there is considerable under-reporting of the gastroenteritis which may be caused by these viruses so establishing its epidemiology is difficult (Campos et al. 2017;

Hassard et al. 2017; Le Guyader et al. 2006; Westrell et al. 2010). A method of removing norovirus from oysters has been devised which involves relaying in clean seawater followed by a long period of depuration at relatively high temperatures; the practicality of adopting such an approach and its effect on the quality of the end product are both unclear (Doré et al. 2010). It is also worth noting that customary light cooking of mussels does not inactivate norovirus in mussels for which using high temperatures is necessary (Flannery et al. 2014).

Hence, despite norovirus being an acknowledged public health problem and some outbreaks known to be linked to oysters, there is no European or UK regulation to deal with this pathogen in shellfish. For this to be formulated would probably require an agreed risk limitation threshold, a testing system that could be routinised and ideally a workable purification method. A preventive approach would highlight upgrades of sewage treatment works which discharge upstream of shellfish production areas as their effluents have been shown to contain norovirus and/or would exclude shellfish harvesting in defined zones round sewage discharge outlets (Aquatic Water Services Ltd 2015; Cefas 2011; Flannery et al. 2012). In the meantime, knowledge is accumulating through the FoodBorne Viruses in Europe network which was established in 1999 to monitor trends in gastroenteritis outbreaks due to noroviruses while the European Food Safety Authority (EFSA) has both issued advice and commissioned a survey to establish European prevalence of norovirus-contaminated oysters so it may be feasible to establish a control system at some point in the future which could be the basis of legislation (EFSA 2016; EFSA Panel on Biological Hazards (BIOHAZ) 2012; Lowther et al. 2012).

By contrast, feed, an area where animal and human health overlap, is thoroughly regulated. There are two key themes in European regulation governing animal feed, which are that good hygiene practices must be followed and that defined levels of contaminants must not be exceeded. The main EU regulation dealing with hygiene in feed states that aquaculture is included but without any specific provisions; it requires feed businesses to be registered and that they use the Hazard Analysis of Critical Control Points (HACCP) system in which key production points are identified and plans made for mitigating associated risks.[14] On contaminants, there have been a series of Directives defining 'undesirable substances' and setting maximum levels which may be allowed in various types of feed, again not specific to aquaculture though fish feeds are acknowledged in the more recent versions.

Some investigations have found that contaminants in fish including dioxins, polybrominated diphenyl ethers (PBDEs) and polychlorinated biphenols (PCBs) occur at higher concentrations in farmed than in wild fish. Though possibly related to contaminated sites this was thought to usually be due to the marine content of feeds resulting from pollution of the seas together with biomagnification, the increasing concentration that occurs moving up the food chain, in this case from plankton to smaller and then larger fish (Cole et al. 2009; Jacobs, Ferrario & Byrne 2002; Jacobs, Covaci &

Schepens 2002; Knowles, Farrington & Kestin 2003). Another issue is about pesticide contamination in farmed fish (Little, Milwain & Price 2008). However, EFSA examined contaminants in selected seafood species most consumed in EU countries and concluded that there was no difference between wild and farmed fish from a food safety viewpoint (EFSA 2005). Fish feed manufacturers have pursued decontamination processes, particularly dealing with dioxins and PCBs, with EFSA approval.[15] Whether due to this approach or for other reasons a later EFSA exercise reviewing dioxins and PCBs across all foods and feed in Europe saw a reversal with farmed salmon and trout being significantly less contaminated than wild-caught equivalents (EFSA 2012). The overall picture is therefore unclear or rather mixed, probably varying for different farmed species cultivated in different locations.

An important regulatory development in relation to aquaculture feed took place in 2013 when the EU allowed non-ruminant animal protein, that is derived from pigs and poultry, to be used in fish feed; previously this had been prohibited under precautionary rules which had been passed in the wake of the 1990s BSE outbreak to prevent transmissible spongiform encephalopathies.[16] In the Scottish salmon industry, the decision has been taken not to use feed containing land animal material (Shepherd, Monroig & Tocher 2015). Inclusion of protein from such sources has the potential to reduce the level of wild fish needed for feed and hence to be beneficial from the viewpoint of sustainability but may be more problematic from a consumer perspective as discussed in Chapter 5 (bearing in mind the farmed seafood other than Scottish salmon that enters the supply chain). Its safety depends on strict rules being observed during manufacture to avoid cross-contamination with ruminant proteins.

Another human health issue comes from the use of veterinary medicines in aquaculture. The previous chapter referred to environmental risks from this source especially over chemicals used to treat sea lice; from a food safety viewpoint, the questions are over veterinary residues in farmed fish and antibiotics. The former is regulated by European and UK legislation establishing maximum residue limits.[17] Merchants and processing companies which import seafood from outside the EU (with the exception of certain European countries including Iceland, Faeroes and Norway which have similar status) must comply with regulations imposing veterinary controls to ensure that incoming products conform to food safety requirements.[18]

In Britain, there is also a more informal source of governance in the non-profit organisation Responsible Use of Medicines in Agriculture Alliance which despite its name fully includes aquaculture in its work. It has produced separate guidelines for fish producers on vaccines and vaccination, on anti-parasitics and on antimicrobials.

The last of these is the cause of greatest concerns since the widespread use of antibiotics in aquaculture, as with farmed land animals, is considered a major risk factor in the development of resistances which could render these drugs ineffective for human healthcare. The route of administration in aquaculture is generally in feed which causes resistant bacteria to enter the aquatic environment and through various mechanisms the terrestrial one too while more specifically the seafood produced may itself contain antibiotic residues or resistant bacteria (Cabello 2006; Done, Venkatesan & Halden 2015; Hernández Serrano 2005; Romero, Feijoó & Navarrete 2012). It is possible to drive down antibiotic usage in aquaculture to very low levels as the huge Norwegian salmon producing industry is celebrated for achieving by means of vaccination and good husbandry.[19] Higher amounts are known to have been used in certain Asian countries which produce seafood such as warmwater prawns and pangasius which enter the UK food chain as imports; however, on the basis of a survey of veterinary medicines in four such countries, it has been noted that even the highest usage of antibiotics in Vietnamese pangasius farms was comparable to that in other livestock systems including some for salmon (Rico et al. 2013). This still means that farmed fish which have received varying amounts of antibiotics are entering the British food chain.

The EU has produced guidelines on reducing the use of antibiotics which include specific advice for aquaculturists.[20] According to the *Code of Good Practice for Scottish Finfish Aquaculture*, the salmon industry in Scotland has sharply reduced its use of antibiotics by routinising vaccination. However, there is no source of concrete data on the subject except for the two firms operating in Scotland which are part of the Global Salmon Initiative whose website provides annual figures from 2013 onwards, by company, for the number of antibiotic treatments over the entire production cycle. Antibiotics are regulated in the same way as other veterinary medicines and despite the significant public health problem of antibiotic resistance, usage is not is not officially monitored beyond the recording of sales. Rather than direct regulation, a more diffuse form of public governance is indicated by the joint Department of Health and DEFRA *UK Five Year Antimicrobial Resistance Strategy 2013 to 2018*. This includes sections on how the those involved in livestock rearing (neither aquaculture or any other sector is specified), veterinary services and even the retail part of the food chain can act to limit the resistance problem, thus urging forms of private governance to reduce the risks. EU legislation, which will come into force in 2022, to end mass prophylactic use of antibiotics in farming is in train, also applying to imports, but it is not clear what the UK approach to this will be after Brexit.

Other potential food safety problems can be reduced in aquaculture production by applying HACCP; while more difficult in small-scale, subsistence operations this is expected to be used in intensive aquaculture systems. The key control points are site selection, water (supply and treatment), feed quality and management of the grow-out stage of fish production; for each, there are potential sources of chemical and/or biological contamination which can be limited by taking precautionary measures (Joint FAO/NACA/WHO Study Group 1999).

Achieving quality in farmed seafood

From the viewpoint of ensuring quality, aquaculture has the great advantage for those upstream in the supply chain of facilitating control of all the relevant factors, allowing choices to be made about the grades to produce for particular markets. The nutritional and sensory qualities of the fish produced will depend on numerous decisions including breeding, feed type and feeding regimes, light control and the way various processes are managed (Espe 2008). The kind of influence that may be exercised over the production process was indicated by an interviewee:

> They tend to be sites you can visit, you know what the product's been consistently fed on, but you do have to check that they're using the right feeds, that the medicines they used are the correct medicines, that you've not had them use any substances.
>
> (Director, large company)

An example of the development of a premium product for a retailer customer described on a visit to a salmon farming site included the following elements: feed from sustainable sources, with lower levels of contaminants than the industry standard, such as to produce a fish that would consist of a relatively low proportion of fat overall but still provide nutritionally appropriate levels of omega-3 fatty acids (information from the account given by a production manager, large aquaculture company). Apparently exceptional as the informant said, this nevertheless illustrates the scope for upstream partners to extensively influence the production process in order to achieve desired qualities in the end product.

For both salmon and trout, the preferred degree of red to pink colouring in the flesh is a major objective, considered second only to freshness in importance to consumers. This is achieved by manipulating amounts of the caretenoid pigments astaxanthin and canthaxanthin in feeds, something which has to be carefully controlled as levels are regulated by both UK and European legislation (Davies 2008).

Better quality texture and appearance results from reduced stress at slaughter (Robb 2002). How this was achieved by one producer was described as follows:

> We've developed the system so that we chill the fish on the boat. We then have a chilling mechanism, to get the temperatures down very quickly. We have to do that for quality. If the fish is warm, it will go into rigor sooner. So the key criterion for us is to have as low-stress fish as possible. We measure the stress levels of the fish, we measure the PH of the fish every day. We have a database. We understand when something's right and when something's wrong. [*The reference to chilling on the boat indicates a well-boat with a tank in which live fish are transported and then*

> pumped into the slaughter facility so that they are not out of water until shortly
> before death.]

(Processing manager, large aquaculture company)

Other handling practices at and subsequent to slaughter are also important for quality. Bleeding salmon improves colour and taste by removing iron and avoids oxidation if frozen. As with all seafood chains, chilling and the maintenance of the fish at low temperatures by using ice is vital (Willoughby 1999).

Going beyond the sensory aspects, fish welfare may be considered as an attribute of quality as well as an ethical issue. Welfare may be understood in three ways: in terms of biological functioning, by defining a natural life including surroundings and with consideration for affective states which though hard to access in relation to fish are known to include fear and pain (Balcombe 2016; EFSA 2009; Lund & Mejdell 2006). As a researcher has emphasised, our knowledge that fish have the capacity to suffer means an obligation to care for their welfare (Braithwaite 2010). Whether invertebrates (such as mussels or squid) can experience pain is a scientifically evolving question and welfare considerations in aquaculture have so far been applied just to finfish.

Various indicators of welfare have been suggested including feed intake, growth, health and minimisation of injuries (Damsgård 2008). From a more critical perspective, aquaculture inherently involves damaging and stressful procedures including invasive techniques to remove eggs and milt (sperm), human handling, artificial lighting and pre-slaughter starvation; these may cause a number of fish health problems, although some conditions can be ameliorated and improvements in the most recent period have been acknowledged (Compassion in World Farming 2009; Stevenson 2007). There is disagreement about the importance of stocking density as an indicator of welfare (appropriate levels are affected by species and various other factors such as age and social interaction) but agreement about the fundamental significance of good water quality. Thus, there is a partial scientific knowledge base for possible governance but it lags far behind what is available in relation to terrestrial animals. At the same time the issue is very much more complex because of the number of species farmed and greater constraints to understanding what fish experience.

The first public intervention in Britain in relation to the welfare of farmed fish came in a report by the then Farm Animal Welfare Council, an independent body giving advice to the government, which produced a detailed set of recommendations for the rearing of salmon and trout; no subsequent action was taken to make any of them compulsory but they stood as authoritative guidance (Farm Animal Welfare Council 1996).[21] Not long afterwards fish were placed within the general ambit of state regulation for the welfare of farmed animals when these were defined in the 1998 EU directive on the subject as including all vertebrates. The subsequent UK *Animal Welfare Act 2006* and *Animal Health and Welfare (Scotland) Act 2006* followed this definition and in addition allowed for a possible extension to invertebrates, subject to scientific advice on whether they can experience suffering, so potentially could cover shellfish. However, the provisions in these pieces of legislation are very general, simply that needs should be met and unnecessary suffering not caused, so without any directions that relate to the specific issues that occur in aquaculture.[22]

Meanwhile, other efforts to establish welfare standards for farmed fish were proceeding. Under the European Convention for the Protection of Animals Kept for Farming Purposes (ECPAKFP), a set of Recommendation Concerning Farmed Fish was produced in 2005 with suggested rules. The European Food Safety Authority published a series of scientific opinions including a general one recognising fish sentience (EFSA 2009) and papers on welfare considerations in relation to the most important farmed species in the EU. At a global level the World Organisation for Animal Health (OIE)[23] has produced its Aquatic Animal Health Code in successive editions starting in 1995, the twentieth dated 2017; its intention has primarily been to facilitate international trade but it includes a section on the welfare of farmed fish which is particularly important as these are standards which are accepted within the WTO Sanitary and Phytosanitary Measures Agreement. In the UK, the successor entity the Farm Animal Welfare Committee (FAWC) returned to the issue of farmed fish welfare in a new assessment (Farm Animal Welfare Committee 2014a).[24] Reviewing legal protection for the welfare of fish its report noted that this was less than generally offered to terrestrial farmed animals as follow-up regulations to the above two welfare Acts exclude fish and went on to recommend that there should be specific fish welfare legislation as well as a more active approach to enforcement of existing requirements. No action seems to have been taken on these recommendations.

As fish are known to experience pain, this should be minimised pre-slaughter by stunning, preferably using the electricity method as others such as carbon dioxide take too long to produce unconsciousness (Damsgård 2008; Tinarwo 2006). The FAWC has also produced a specific report on this subject with a number of recommendations for humane treatment including stunning prior to killing (Farm Animal Welfare Committee 2014b). In reality, one source has concluded, much slaughter of farmed fish is carried out inhumanely, causing considerable stress (Mood & Brooke 2012). As already noted, this will produce an inferior end product, so welfare and quality objectives coincide.

Despite this accumulating knowledge, the stream of European and UK legislation about minimising suffering in connection with animal slaughter has so far excluded fish. The 1993 directive simply ignored them. The current 2009 EU legislation specifically excludes fish but states that the issue should be investigated. A European Commission report followed which compared national practices around fish transport and slaughter in the relevant member states against the OIE standards (thus indicating how such global governance recommendations may be influential). It found that the standards are largely met for transport but only partially so in relation to slaughter, varying with the different species. A positive finding was that slaughter of salmon with percussive stunning in the UK did meet the standards. In its follow-up, the Commission resiled from the prospect of legislation, advising that improvements may be achieved by voluntary, private measures or by member state action. Such confidence in private governance has been sharply criticised by a European animal welfare group which works closely with the European Parliament. Its strongest concerns were expressed over slaughter methods used for sea bass and sea bream, fish which enter the UK supply chain; most of the farms concerned were GG certified which should mean that stunning was practised but this was not the case, raising questions about the effectiveness of this private standard.[25]

At this point, it should be noted that there is neither regulation nor public advice relating to the killing of capture fish nor any official recognition that there should be humane considerations involved although many customary fishing practices are likely to cause fear and pain (Braithwaite 2010; Mood 2010). Suggestions have been put forward for making ameliorative changes not only for targeted fish but also for those whose escape is facilitated by selective gear which may nevertheless result in damage entailing suffering and possible poor survival; as no regulation is anticipated such provisions could become part of an accredited scheme (Metcalfe 2009).

While public regulation does not deal with quality in relation to farmed fish and has been slow to establish welfare rules, there has been active private governance. The previous chapter considered the *Code of Good Practice for Scottish Finfish Aquaculture* (CoGPSFA) from the viewpoint of production for sustainability. Its primary purpose has been to establish Scottish salmon as a quality product. The industry began to establish standards early on with the certified Tartan Mark in place by the mid-1980s (Laird 1999). The 1990s saw the production of a series of codes of practice which from 2006 were compiled into the comprehensive CoGPSFA which with regular revisions remains the manual for salmon production and mandatory for members of the trade body, now the Scottish Salmon Producers' Organisation. The Code has third-party auditing. As noted in the previous chapter there is a similar Quality Trout scheme.

The Scottish salmon industry achieved a coup in 1992 when awarded the French Label Rouge quality mark, a notable accolade for a non-national product; it is separately audited and has been retained for more than a quarter century. European PGI (Protected Geographical Indication) status for Scottish farmed salmon was added in 2004. The Tartan Mark scheme ceased in 2008 but more recently, a high proportion of salmon production has been accredited under the welfare-focused RSPCA Freedom Food scheme. All these activities have been part of a successful campaign to position Scottish salmon as a premium product within the wider industry. As explained from the perspective of one of the major producing companies:

In Scotland, where we suffer is that we can't reach the cost of production in Chile or from Norway. So we need to find another route, a specialisation route, a high profile route, a high top tiering route.

> (Production manager, large aquaculture company)

Both food safety and fish welfare are aspects of quality and overlap with each other, positive fish health being more likely to produce a product good for human health. The CoGPSFA and GLOBALG.A.P (GG) each includes fish welfare as a basic principle; food safety is also a principle in the former while the latter refers to the safe production of food that delivers human health benefits. In addition, care has been taken to match CoGPSFA demands with those required by the Freedom Food scheme. By contrast, the ASC does not have such specific requirements, being focused on environmental and social sustainability, although arguing that expecting best practices in farming will mean that fish welfare and food safety are covered in practice.[26] Attention is given in the GG and CoGPSFA standards to welfare issues such as water quality and stocking density and a key expectation in both is that the farm will have a veterinary health plan (VHP) and the latter also specifies a separate biosecurity plan.[27] Both require anaesthesia before stripping (brood fish of eggs or milt) and preslaughter stunning by methods that produce instant unconsciousness.

The CoGPSFA standards are credited with having responded to advice in the 1996 FAWC report according to its successor (Farm Animal Welfare Committee 2014a) illustrating how soft governance by a public body may have some effects without legislation. Improvements in the welfare of farmed fish over the period between the two reports have been recognised (The Food Ethics Council & Pickett 2014). There does not seem to be any public regulation to protect the welfare of farmed fish on the horizon so the incorporation of such expert advice in private standards is all the more important. As with all rule systems their effectiveness, the extent to which they effect real improvements, is partly down to enforcement, in this case by the auditing bodies, and is difficult to assess from the outside. In any case, only part of the farmed seafood entering the domestic supply chain is accredited in the schemes described in this chapter.

Seafood distribution and processing

After dealing with the governance of safety and quality in the primary production of seafood, next to be considered is how they are achieved in the processing and distribution parts of the supply chain. This section first sets the scene by providing historical background, relevant because the distribution and processing of seafood has to a large extent remained separate from other food supply chains, though this has become more blurred in certain aspects in recent decades. Not only primary but also secondary processing of seafood is largely carried out by specialist seafood companies, not by the general food processing industry. Distribution also retains certain particularistic features.

The physical infrastructure that developed with the historic growth of fishing activities continues to be intrinsic to part of the seafood industry: the fishing harbours, auction halls and nearby premises housing the activities associated with servicing vessels and dealing with the catch. However, rather than the rail connections to the ports so important in the nineteenth and early twentieth centuries, transportation is now mainly by road. Much is still landed at UK ports by both domestic and non-British vessels but seafood wild and farmed also arrives overland and by air. While modern transportation means that functions can now more easily be geographically dispersed, processing is still particularly concentrated in two areas. Humberside, in eastern England, developed in the heyday of British trawling but despite losing its distant water fleet following the changes outlined in Chapter 3 has succeeded in maintaining its position as a centre of secondary processing. Grampian, containing the dominant port of Peterhead which takes by far the largest landings from UK vessels, has grown more recently to become the second largest processing area; this is linked to Scotland's position as the most important UK fishing region following the establishment of the new international regime (Carleton et al. 1999; Coull 1999; Symes & Haughton 1987).

While large companies source more widely, local auctions remain important for many local processors as well as local fishers of course. Fish auctions in England handle around 15,000 tonnes of fish annually (2009 data) (De Rozarieux 2011). In 2018, there were 11 functioning seafood auctions in England, two in Northern Ireland and six in Scotland but none in Wales.[28] For processors who source locally, changes affecting the supply of seafood explained in the previous chapter continue to have a potentially significant effect, varying with the port and fishing opportunities available to local fishers. They have to deal with the uncertainty of supply as well as at times its lack. The landing obligation (discard ban) in the 2013 CFP reform has the potential to increase the uncertainties at least in the short-term as there may be different sizes or species compared to the previous situation or supply overall might be increased or reduced and these impacts are likely to vary over time and in different locations (De Rozarieux 2015).

The distribution system as it had developed in the first half of the twentieth century was dominated by port and inland wholesalers; the former supplied some fryers and retailers direct but much fish was transported between them and sold on to fishmongers via the inland markets in major cities. These inland markets usefully mediated between demand and the non-standardised nature of supply (Taylor 1960). But, by the mid-1980s the role of the inland markets had greatly reduced, with strong competition from direct deliveries from ports, inland depots and independent wholesalers. There were 67 merchants in the largest one, Billingsgate (London) in 1987 compared to 150 in 1967; 17 in Birmingham down from 28; and 12 in Liverpool reduced from 25 at the earlier date (Rosson 1975; Symes 1988; Symes & Maddock 1989). Further details are available for Billingsgate: throughput of seafood at Billingsgate fell sharply between 1950 and the mid-1970s and roughly plateaued out during the 1980s; volumes then fell further by 15% during the 1990s (Denton 1991; Saphir 2002). More generally the period from the mid-1980s to mid-1990s was marked by noticeable increases in direct sales to supermarkets and caterers (Joseph & Findlater 1996). These trends have continued into the twenty-first century with particular impact from the decline of independent fishmongers who had previously been the mainstay of the inland markets' customer base. At 2018, the inland wholesale markets continue, albeit greatly reduced, the premier one at Billingsgate retaining its prestige and having 43 seafood traders. Numbers in the major wholesale markets elsewhere were down to five in Birmingham and seven each in Glasgow, Liverpool and Manchester.[29] But for the most part, wholesalers and processors supply each other and their supermarket and major foodservice customers through a variety of direct arrangements which may include contracts and have delivery arrangements included.

Moving from infrastructure and distribution to the seafood processing part of the supply chain, it consists of two types of activity, primary and secondary processing. Companies may specialise in either or carry out both. According to Seafish definitions, primary processing covers cutting, filleting, picking, peeling, shelling, washing, chilling, packing, freezing, heading and gutting of fish and shellfish; secondary processing means brining, smoking, cooking, freezing, canning, boning, breading, battering, vacuum and other controlled packaging or the production of ready-to-eat meals.

The products of secondary processing have changed considerably over recent decades. The traditional focus was on smoked items with cold smoking the predominant method in Britain. For the most part, this produced kippers and finnan haddocks which made up 90% of smoked production in the mid-1960s; other items included bloaters (ungutted to give a gamey flavour), smoked cod and haddock, smoked cod roe and the hot-smoked buckling (herring) and Arbroath smokies (haddock).[30] In addition to smoking, processing activity has included salt curing (producing pickled herrings) and some canning (of herrings, pilchards and sprats). Up to the 1960s, salmon was a small part of the smoking industry but the much greater availability produced by farming subsequently allowed this to greatly increase. Hot-smoked mackerel, not even mentioned in a 1965 manual, was becoming established by the mid-1980s (Connell 1987).

In considering fish processing, particularly smoking, the contribution of the public Torry Research Station, already noted in the previous chapter for its work on freezing fish at sea, should be recognised. The Torry mechanical kiln dating from 1939, variants of which are still in use, gave control of air temperature, the draft and humidity not possible previously with traditional chimneys. Another invention still in use is the Torry fat meter with which lipid content of oily fish can be measured, useful in scientific investigations. As well as the Research Station's inventions it produced extensive advice on aspects of seafood processing, publications valued sufficiently to be kept in the FAO's Corporate Document Repository.

Since the 1980s, the range of secondary processing has greatly extended with huge numbers of chilled and frozen easy-cook products and ready meals made for both the domestic and foodservice markets. Some of the technologies used such as modified atmosphere packaging require higher levels of capital investment, advantaging larger firms, but smoking and other types of preparation can still be done on a modest scale, so a range of size firms continued (Young 1987).

An overview of the seafood processing industry over the twentieth century based on the Census of Production has shown that fundamental changes took place in the quarter of a century starting in the late 1940s. Machinery to replace manual processes such as gutting became available while the Torry smoking kiln substituted technology and predictable results for the previous dependence on personal knowledge. Larger enterprises could benefit from economies of scale and take better advantage of such options and there was a decline of artisanal production although small firms have continued to be an important element of the sector (Reid & Robinson 2003). The financial impact of mechanisation costs could be considerable so investment must have been much less of a possibility for smaller companies (Flear 1973).

For the more recent period, the structure and economic state of the UK seafood processing sector has been charted in periodic surveys carried out by Seafish from 1986 onwards, the most recent one at the time of writing covering 2016 (Noble, Moran Quintana & Curtis 2017). Over this period the number of plants where seafood processing is carried out (the surveys count sites, not companies) fell from 988 to 376, a very considerable reduction. Employment in terms of full-time equivalents has also declined but much less reflecting an increase in jobs per site, from 19,359 to 17,999. There is currently great reliance on non-British workers and a recent survey found that about 42% of the labour employed by seafood processing companies came from other EU countries, varying regionally and with firm size (Curtis, Moran Quintana & Milliken 2017) but there is no information on how this dependence has developed over previous decades. Site reductions did not always mean that firms went out of business as they could have been rationalising premises or continuing with a different balance of activities that no longer met the survey criteria but many did cease to trade. The surveys, with their series of snapshots, have not analysed the departures, but they have pointed out various pressures which are particularly difficult for small enterprises. They have included shortage and uncertainty of supply, increasing costs including for energy and water and for meeting new hygiene and waste disposal requirements, the inability to pass on increased costs because of buyer power and perceived limits to what end customers will pay for seafood compared to other proteins and finally disadvantageous terms of trade in which processors typically receive less credit than they have to grant their customers, causing cash flow problems.

In the reports, the industry has been consistently characterised as consisting of a small number of large, multi-site companies and a large number of small,

single-site businesses.[31] Most recently as smaller enterprises have dispropor-
tionally declined, the difference in numbers between small and large companies has reduced (Banks 1988; Brown 2009; Curtis & Barr 2012; Curtis
2000; Curtis & White 2005; Garrett 2011; Joseph & Findlater 1996). The
twin structure of the processing industry has been modelled and larger companies assessed as more efficient (Harris & Robinson 2000) but the Seafish
surveys have shown the flexible way that companies respond to different customer groups and a study of costs and earnings in the sector found that
smaller companies can often achieve better profitability (Curtis & Bryson
2002). Another view based on the cod supply chain has identified a three-
way structure of the processor sector: large companies supplying national
retail and foodservice companies often by direct contract, next medium-size
ones sourcing for regional outlets by direct contract and from market purchasing and finally the small firms which rely on auctions and supply local
concerns (EUMOFA 2013); this goes beyond the simple large/small grouping
to understanding the functions of different processing enterprises.

Although only mentioned briefly in some of the surveys, an important
reason for reductions in the British industry must be the increasing amount of
processing carried out in China since the late 1990s. Typically, whitefish
captured in northern waters such as the Barents Sea is delivered frozen to
China where it is thawed, undergoes processing and is refrozen for export to
European markets. Low labour costs constitute the economic rationale for
this arrangement, but there has also been evidence of the system being used
to launder illegally caught fish into the supply chain, at least prior to the additional control measures brought in by the EU in 2010 (Album 2010; Clarke
2009). In that year, the second largest source of cod imports into Britain (after
Iceland) was China, reflecting this processing trade (Almond & Thomas
2011). Apart from whether the fish has been caught legally, there is the
environmental issue of the extensive extra mileage and concomitant green-
house gas emissions resulting from this arrangement. In more recent years,
China has been the top seafood importer by volume into the UK, the main
species involved being cod, pollack, haddock and salmon, all reflecting
processing activity.[32]

Food safety and quality in processing and distribution

Introduction

In the mid-twentieth century standards of fish handling on land could be
extremely poor as graphically described in a contemporary account (Taylor
1960, p. 93):

> Before the sales begin large fish are dragged over the dirty stone floors of
> the markets where seagulls wander, feet tramp and persons spit; after the
> sales, boxes piled up with fish have other boxes piled high upon them

squashing and bruising the fish beneath; and during the processing, water in the filleting troughs belonging to some merchants is allowed to become so dirty that it can only increase the rate of bacterial growth and spoilage of the fish.

The same source goes on to describe the returnable wooden boxes in which fish was sent from the ports to wholesalers and customers as 'a serious reflection on the trade's attitude towards hygiene' (p. 172) as they absorbed fish slime along with melting ice, stood around for days collecting dirt and micro-organisms, were rarely cleaned properly and eventually disintegrated during transport or upon arrival. A quarter century later, a report about one port noted that fish was held overnight inadequately iced in non-chilled premises, non-iced fish was left in the auction hall awaiting collection and there were poor standards of hygiene in merchants' premises and about the dock area generally 'The level of tidiness and cleanliness on an estate where food is being processed is clearly unacceptable' (Tower 1986, p. 31). Another account at this time recorded poor temperature control at all stages of the supply chain from vessel to retailer, resulting in tasteless fish (Mills 1987).

Further on in the chain, much of the filleting in port premises was carried out under poor conditions of hygiene. Fish smoking processes lacked quality control and a survey of kipper production in one centre found that only a quarter of the output could be classified as of good quality, some being rated as quite inedible (Burgess et al. 1965). Smoking stale fish was noted in this source as a major cause of poor quality, something echoed in the first inter-view quotation of this chapter about stale fish being smoked. Poor quality frozen fish was also noted.

From the perspective of the twenty-first century, it is good to know that the dire conditions outlined in the last few paragraphs no longer apply and that the situation has been totally transformed for the better. The change has been something that many working in the industry have experienced directly:

> I think that the major change I've seen is that we've got a consistently, got a much higher quality product that's going through the system.
>
> (Trade organisation representative 1)

This interview quote typifies general agreement from the research that quality and safety standards have improved markedly from the situations deplored by those writing about the early part of our period.

Public regulation for food safety

Various influences have been at work in producing the change but a central aspect has certainly been active public regulation. While it is European and linked British legislation that has had the most direct impact on the seafood processing industry, there is also a global governance element that should be acknowledged. The FAO has produced authoritative technical papers on various aspects of seafood safety and quality which are cited by agencies and consultants, constituting a discourse of expert knowledge which is bound to have affected policymaking.[33] In addition, the Codex Alimentarius Commission (CAC), under the joint aegis of the FAO and World Health Organization has produced its comprehensive *Code of Practice for Fish and Fishery Products* intended to assist in achieving 'safe and wholesome products that can be sold on national or international markets and meet the requirements of the Codex Standards' (Codex Alimentarius 2009a). More generally the CAC has been issuing successive versions of its massively comprehensive *International Code of Practice – General Principles of Food Hygiene* since 1969 (Codex Alimentarius 2009b). HACCP principles have been incorporated since 1993. European Member states are asked to refer to the CAC document when drawing up hygiene guidelines in 'European Directive 93/43/EEC On the hygiene of foodstuffs' which also includes a requirement for HACCP principles to be followed, surely not coincidental to its adoption by Codex in the same year. From another direction, the United Nations Environment Programme has published a guide for reducing the environmental impact of fish processing (COWI Consulting Engineers and Planners 2000).

Turning to European and British legislation, there are two strands relevant to seafood safety, one being general Food Law, the other a set of specific regulations for this sector. The latter started first in the 1980s with measures connected with establishing a common market for 'fisheries and aquaculture products' as part of the CFP. This required that standards should be established for seafood products which should only be marketed if in conformance with them, that is establishing a level trading field. Regulations duly followed setting out how these standards should be achieved. The next was about improving facilities and equipment for processing (in addition to items about marketing issues), required member states to produce national plans for achieving these improvements and set out conditions for related funding. Then, over 1991 and 1992, there were three Directives laying down in turn: hygiene standards on land and factory vessels; specific measures for dealing with live bivalves; and third, hygiene standards on fishing vessels more generally.[34] There were corresponding British regulations.[35]

An additional thread in pursuance of the common market in seafood products, and hence a level field, dealt with labelling and traceability. The labelling information required for seafood in the 2001 regulation was the commercial designation (that is the name in general use rather than the scientific version), the production method (whether caught at sea or in freshwater or farmed) and the catch area. Traceability was specified as ensuring that information about the designation, production method and catch area would be on identifiable at all stages of the supply chain.[36] Although not mentioned within this legislation, states had been asked to improve identification of the origins of traded species in the FAO *Code of Conduct for Responsible Fisheries* so there is also an element of global governance here (Deere 1999).

Subsequent European rules about seafood labelling were a 2009 requirement to identify previously-frozen fish and a 2011 enactment that the addition of water, even if less than 5%, must be identified and the term 'formed fish' applied when what looks like a whole piece is in reality made up of bits which have been combined by use of other ingredients, information which is clearly revealing and useful for consumers.[37] In the UK, labelling of fish had previously been included in 1996 general food labelling rules, but without either the production method or catch area being specified. The European legislation led to a series of British fish labelling regulations enacting the European requirements and making this information compulsory.[38]

In addition to the regulations in pursuance of the common market, another aspect of the CFP that had a significant impact on seafood processors and merchants was in connection with the control aspects of fisheries policy. The 2002 reform of the CFP regulation required that seafood should only be marketed by registered buyers or at registered auctions and that records should be available for checking. In the UK, this provision was implemented through a set of Registration of Fish Buyers and Sellers regulations dealing with the first sale of fish which made it an offence not only for someone unlicensed to sell it but (except for small amount for private consumption) for anyone unlicensed to purchase it. They also gave powers to enforcement officers to inspect records, premises and vehicles (as well as fishing vessels).[39] The most effective impact was that responsibility for fish being caught legally was passed up the supply chain instead of just being the province of fishers and that documentary proof was required. It is widely believed that these regulations were effective in severely curtailing illegal fishing, the new traceability in the system 'ruling out black fish or illegal landings, virtually a thing of the past now' (Industry advisor, trade organisation). As noted in Chapter 3, this is not entirely the case but there is agreement that it has become insignificant.

So there is a lot of regulation specifically about seafood bearing on those in the middle of the supply chain. In addition to this, the industry is impacted by general food safety legislation. This too started as part of common market equalisation of standards and it made the improvement of hygiene a European objective for the food processing industry from the early 1990s. A particularly important requirement in the 1993 directive entitled 'On the hygiene of foodstuffs' was that they should implement the Hazard Analysis of Critical Control Points (HACCP) system. The significance of this approach is that instead of simply requiring food businesses to provide safe food and not to provide unsafe food which was the traditional tactic in UK regulations, HACCP provides a prevention plan, a system for maximising the likelihood of safe food being produced.

There was of course already food hygiene legislation in Britain, most recently the 1990 Act, as explained in Chapter 1, and it included specific regulations over food hygiene in relation to market stalls and delivery vehicles which was very relevant to seafood because in the mid-1980s nearly a nearly a quarter of fresh fish sales were from stalls or mobile shops. However, the legislation prior to 1990 was considered imprecise and because of dependence on local authorities variably enforced and considered to have little impact on seafood quality (Seafish 1987).[40] Now with the EU lead, more forceful food safety legislation gradually came into place. The 1995 implementing UK food safety regulations for the European food hygiene directive set out detailed standards for premises and equipment, water quality, waste management and personal hygiene. They also introduced the principles of critical control points although without using the full HACCP terminology.[41]

Inadequate progress in implementing HACCP was picked up in the 1997 Pennington Report on the fatal 1996 Scotland *E. coli* outbreak. The report drew attention to the need for enforcement of food safety measures, including HACCP, and while it necessarily concentrated on meat contamination, the applicability of the recommendations to other foods was recognised (Sleator 1997). The inadequacy of implementation was highlighted again in a second 2009 Pennington Report on the 2005 *E. coli* outbreak in Wales in which a child died; it too recommended strengthening HACCP application (Pennington 2014).

These incidents had fed into the widespread public concern at the time over a series of food problems. The EU eventually reacted with a decisive change when it agreed the 2002 Food Law, which for the first time put food safety rather than the common market centre stage. It made traceability a major requirement for all food chains; as mentioned above, this had already been included in the seafood labelling regulation. A couple of years later, the Food Law legislation was followed by twin regulations with further details, one setting out the obligations of food business operators generally, including HACCP, the other dealing with additional issues when dealing with foods of animal origin. The latter included considerable detail relating to fishery products as a whole and to live bivalve molluscs in particular.[42]

A further 2002 European food safety regulation dealt with animal by-products designed to avoid health problems connected with transmissible spongiform encephalopathies like BSE plus other diseases and contaminants; this was later superseded by 2009 legislation. The previous Seafood Hygiene Directives just said that waste should be stored hygienically and regularly removed. The animal by-product legislation went into far greater detail, starting with definitions of three categories of risk, each with its own rules for handling, permitted uses and disposal methods, HACCP being required in all cases. The regulations exclude vessels at sea which, as already seen, have their own hygiene legislation except that when dealing with fish which when gutted are seen to be diseased, 'risk-proportionate' methods of disposal should be used. Shells from which all flesh has been totally removed are also excluded from the legislation. Nearly all other kinds of fish and shellfish by-products are in the lowest risk category 3; this still means care must be exercised in disposal, but it does permit processing for various uses including feed for farmed fish (except to the same species), pet food and biogas.[43]

Which is just as well because seafood processing generates a considerable amount of waste. Some years ago the quantity produced by the UK industry was estimated at about 300,000 tonnes annually, a third of the initial raw material (Archer, Watson & Denton 2001). A later estimate made on a different basis produced the much lower figure of 133,000 tonnes which is believed to reflect data collection issues rather than a big reduction in waste produced; in any case most of the waste is considered to be unavoidable, that is bones, shells and other uneatable matter, because fish and shellfish are too valuable for any edible part to be squandered (James et al. 2011). However, the 2013 CFP discard ban may produce a considerable addition to this processing waste in the form of fish below the minimum conservation reference size and therefore not allowed into the market for human consumption; it must still be landed and so is available for other uses as allowed by the animal by-products rules along with other unwanted catch. On the positive side, this may provide opportunities for those dealing with fishmeal and pet food (De Rozarieux 2015).

Dealing with seafood waste is impacted by UK and European general waste legislation as well as by the animal by-parts measures already discussed. Of particular relevance are the rules designed to reduce landfill which has been the main disposal route for many seafood processors. Key factors are that landfill taxes increase costs and therefore charges and that animal origin waste may only be placed in treated form and in specially licensed sites with the overall prospect of the landfill option becoming increasingly restricted (Archer et al. 2005).[44]

In principle, the ideal solution is for seafood waste to be recycled for other uses, environmentally beneficial and generating additional income as well as dealing with the disposal problem. There is no lack of potential applications including fishmeal and fish oil for aquaculture feed, compost, silage and severable extractable substances from shellfish waste such as chitin and chitosan which have varied industrial uses; shells also have potential uses in aggregates. Normal shellfish processing leaves some flesh remaining so that additional treatment, incurring higher costs, is needed to get fully clean shells which have a wider range of potential uses because of the animal by-product rules. One barrier to recycling is whether there are facilities to carry it out within a reasonable distance in terms of transport costs, another is whether there is commercial development of potential uses. There are just two fishmeal manufacturing plants in the UK, reduced from ten over the last 30 years, which are situated in Aberdeen and Grimsby. These do absorb a considerable share of processing waste but are distant from many fishing ports and seafood processors especially those in South and South West England. At the same time, Britain imports a high proportion of the fishmeal it uses, largely for aquaculture, though the level has been reducing in recent years.[45] For shellfish waste, the fishmeal option is in any case inappropriate and markets for other uses are not well-developed so that processors in this sector still mainly have recourse to landfill for disposal.

That meeting the standards of the two 1991 European Directives dealing with seafood hygiene on land would require considerable upgrading of facilities was recognised in an impact study based on the legislation when it was still in draft. The capital cost for the UK was estimated at £170 million (Myers & Wilson 1990). This indicates the scale of the gap between desirable standards and the actual situation at the time.

In subsequent years, considerable modernisation did take place, facilitated by CFP funding under the successive Financial Instrument for Fisheries Guidance (FIFG) and European Fisheries Fund (EFF) arrangements; in both programmes match finance had to be contributed. Projects included improved harbour and auction hall facilities while many processing companies obtained funding for new or enlarged buildings or for equipment. The first FIFG programme covering 1994–1999 allocated €123.6 million to the UK. A report on the outcomes of this programme for the British processing industry recorded that 154 processing and marketing companies received a total of €16.9 million with another €2.8 million granted for upgrading harbour and market facilities. It noted that 40% of British seafood companies benefited from the FIFG, notably by increased capacity and that in the EU generally there would have been very little processing investment without the fund (Nautilus Consultants 2003). For the second FIFG programme covering 2000–2006, a total of £73 million was allocated to Britain.[46] The EFF allocation to the UK over 2007–2013 was €130 million (£106 million) and by the end of 2014 most of this amount had been apportioned to 2,774 schemes. They included facilities for one enterprise to improve quality onboard with the installation of a freezer and cold storage area, equipment for other processing companies and harbour improvements (Marine Management Organisation et al. 2015). The UK share of the latest European Maritime and Fisheries Fund (EMFF) is €243 million (£190 million) over the period 2014–2020. It is questionable how much of these very necessary improvements in the inland infrastructure of the seafood industry would have been made without the CFP funding programmes. The usefulness of these funds is underlined by the British Ports Association's call for a successor fund to the EMFF to be established after Brexit.[47]

Public support of a different kind is provided by the European protected names scheme, which gives legal recognition to foods with special local or traditional characteristics. The system which started in 1992 with European legislation later updated in 2006 and most recently in 2012 initially had little uptake by British seafood producers. This has changed over time and by 2018 they had achieved 14 products with either Protected Designation of Origin or Protected Geographical Indication registration (none coming into the third Traditional Speciality Guaranteed category). They are shown in Table 4.1 in date order of the award being made. Though several of them are specialist products primarily serving niche markets and/or exports, Scottish farmed salmon covers the considerable total output of both conventional and organic production which is relevant to the domestic food chain. Legal protection of

Table 4.1 British seafood with protected names

Product	Year of award	Designation	Description
Whitstable oysters (Ostrea edulis and Crassostrea gigas)	1997	PGI	Oysters from beds in the vicinity of Whitstable, Kent.
Arbroath smokies	2004	PGI	Hot-smoked haddock produced within a defined geographical area by traditional methods using fish from designated Scottish fish markets.
Scottish farmed salmon	2008	PGI	Atlantic salmon conventionally and organically farmed on the west coast of Scotland, the Western Isles, Orkney and Shetland.
Cornish sardines	2009	PGI	Sardines caught within six miles off the Cornish coast, landed and processed within Cornwall.
Traditional Grimsby smoked fish	2009	PGI	Cod or haddock weighing between 200 g–700 g prepared and smoked in Grimsby, North East Lincolnshire, using a traditional method.
Lough Neagh eels	2011	PGI	Eels caught in Lough Neagh, Northern Ireland and the lower River Bann, using traditional methods; immature eels from 1 May to 8 January, mature ones from 1 June to 28 February.
Isle of Man queenies	2012	PDO	Queen scallops caught within the territorial waters of the Isle of Man.
Scottish wild salmon	2012	PGI	Atlantic salmon caught up to 1,500 metres from the coast of Scotland, using prescribed methods.
Fal oysters	2013	PDO	Oysters caught from 1 October to 31 March within the Truro Port Fishery using traditional vessels.
Conwy mussels (Mytilus edulis)	2016	PDO	Mussels harvested from the designated area of Conwy Estuary, North Wales using the traditional hand raking method from 1 September to 30 April.
London cure smoked salmon	2017	PGI	Superior grade Scottish salmon (farmed or wild), smoked using a traditional cure, in designated areas of East London.
West Wales coracle caught salmon	2017	PGI	Atlantic salmon caught in specific tidal areas of the Rivers Tywi, Taf and Teifi using traditional coracle fishing methods during the designated season for each river.
West Wales coracle caught sewin (sea trout – Salmo trutta)	2017	PGI	Sewin caught in specific tidal areas of the Rivers Tywi, Taf and Teifi using traditional coracle fishing methods during the designated season for each river.
Lough Neagh pollan (Coregonus pollan)	2018	PDO	Pollan harvested from Lough Neagh, Northern Ireland using traditional methods during the designated season.

Source: author.

Notes
PDO: Protected Denomination of Origin.

registered names against imitation or misuse is up to each EU member state; in the UK, there are no specific regulations on the subject but enforcement is by local trading standards officers using the *Food Safety Act 1990* or general legislation dealing with unfair trading and fraud.[48] Protected name status is believed to be economically beneficial to the companies concerned and British government thinking is that protected names will be replaced by a UK Geographical Indication system post-Brexit.

Governance in the seafood processing world for food safety and quality

Seafood processors and merchants thus have to operate with the impact of a very considerable level of public regulation and have also benefited from the public funds used to improve both public infrastructure and private facilities. The companies additionally experience private governance through standards and audit schemes. At the same time, processors themselves exercise governance over supplying companies within their supply chains. Through interview material these experiences of both being governed and exercising governance can be captured.

Generally, the rationale for food hygiene regulations was accepted in the seafood industry. Improvements could even be attributed directly to the legislation:

> The fish industry for many years was light years behind the meat industry, the dairy industry in terms of our controls because we knew we had a safe product. Why did somebody want to spend a fortune on doing up his factory when it didn't actually improve the product? But the regulations have now improved the hygiene side. We now have a good product but also produced in much, much better surroundings than we had in the past. That's certainly been a dramatic improvement.
>
> (Trade organisation representative 1)

There were some critical comments along the lines that 'It's a bit over the top, bit of overkill' (Director, medium company 2) and about the financial aspect: 'It's a lot of money on your working costs' (Managing director, small company 5). But generally companies of all sizes saw food safety regulation as beneficial:

> There is a reason for legal requirements and we're quite clear that we have to comply to that. Food safety laws, hygiene laws are there for definite reasons, to protect the consumer, the end consumer and I don't think it's a hindrance by any means. Of course, there are certain things that you wish it wasn't there but there is a reason for everything. The legality is there for reasons of protecting the final consumer. It's not only a commercial reality it's about protecting the final consumer, the final me and you.
>
> (Head of operations, large company)

They're perfectly reasonable in what they ask, and what they'll …, they'll do spot checks without telling you they're coming, in which they are perfectly correct, they keep you on your toes. As far as health and hygiene on the products that we produce, I haven't got any problems with that whatsoever.

(Director, medium company 1)

Respondents described various ways in which they acted to ensure that food hygiene standards were met. Examples were using the HACCP approach, maintaining temperature controls and microbiological testing:

Here is a hazard analysis: hazard risk, temperature, monitoring, what is the standard, what are you looking for, who's responsible, action if it's not right. Right through filleting, salting, washing, smoking, trimming, slicing, packing.

(Managing director, small company 5)

We are monitoring temperatures etc. all the time. If something goes out of spec we have got procedures in place to alter the environment or make a decision on the product.

(Director, medium-large company)

We send samples for analysis every week as well. This is one which just came back. These are what they're checking, *E. coli*, *Staph aureus*. Every week. Once a month we do a slightly different check, *Salmonella*, *Listeria*. That's what is required.

(Director, medium company 2)

Food safety is the objective where the enforcement of regulation is strongest and where companies have relationships with local environmental health departments (or in some cases, depending on location, with port health authorities). Although various weaknesses in local food control systems have been identified (Spears 2000) a general study of food safety regulation found that environmental health officers (EHOs) were particularly valued by small and medium-size companies as sources of information and advice (Hutter 2011).

Turning to another legal requirement, that of traceability, the respondents were clear about how this was satisfied. Typically they said that origins could be identified 'back to the boat' for capture fish:

We can trace it back to the boat and the day it's caught. On our packs, for example, we have, it's a serial number, every pack of fish that goes out, so we can trace it back to which boat we got it from, what day it was landed, so complete traceability.

(Director, medium company 1)

We can trace every item of shellfish back to the bed it was harvested from, we can trace every tuna loin back through the factories in Sri Lanka and the Maldives back to the boat from which it was fished.... Mussels and you can go all the way back, temperature of the vehicles and things like that. It's complete traceability.

(Group director, large company)

Traceability for farmed seafood could be even more detailed:

Theoretically, in most you can trace back an individual fish to the egg and you can almost map its life history. For example, if we want, on a farmed salmon we can go back and say when it's been inoculated, when it was in its original smolt format, where the eggs were from and trace the whole genetic history.

(Director, large company)

Such traceability to individual fish is very exceptional and generally it is at the level of batches. There are amalgamations at various levels: the output of different trawls on any boat and catches from different vessels combined by merchants, auction houses and beyond.

You won't know what's in that box, what came from each particular vessel once you've amalgamated it. It's almost ludicrous. This is why DEFRA, even they are not keen to enforce traceability to the *n*th degree because it's not practical at all.

(Partner, medium company)

Traceability is a big issue with raw materials coming out of China.... The primary processor might buy one to one and a half kilos fish from ten different boats for example which will then be consolidated into different containers and sent to China. The minute that that fish becomes consolidated from different vessels, how do you carry on, set about identifying through the process? By the time you have processed all those, you've lost that traceability back to an individual boat. What you might have is traceability back to five or six boats.

(Commercial manager, medium-large company)

The rules relating to batching have often been very imprecise as legal definitions relating generally to food have not readily been applicable to fish. Most recently the definition in a 2009 regulation recognises that fish of the same species caught by a single vessel or even by several ships operating in the same geographical area may be considered as a lot, the unit for which traceability must be in place; this marks acceptance of the scale at which batching occurs and hence the limits of traceability.[49]

Processing companies have detailed internal systems to maintain traceability and satisfy their own customers:

> As it arrives in our factory, we then trace it as we use it into the meals. We can trace it back when was it used, which day it was used, which line it was used on.
>
> (Head of operations, large company)

> We do an exercise every six months, take a couple of products on a particular day and say let's trace it back and see where it's all gone and make sure we can recall it if necessary.
>
> (Site manager, medium–large company)

The purpose of the traceability requirement when introduced in the 2002 European Food Law was in connection with food safety problems, giving a means to assess them accurately and enable targeted withdrawals. Having a recall system and being able to trace problems was certainly one reason mentioned by interviewees:

> Yes, we have product recalls probably a couple of times a year. It's normally to do with mussels.... Where we have had to recall we have been able to do it within a 2–3 hour period. We had a major recall of mussels last year, as did the retailers, when some frozen mussels entered the marketplace. We had everything back. We've got 14,000 customers. Every one of them who took from those batches of mussels, we had contacted, isolated the mussels in their premises and over the next few days, collected them. It is a major operation, but it is essential, and you need to be able to do it.
>
> (Group director, large company)

> If they [retailers] have an issue on a pack in store, they will ring us up if they're not happy with the quality or picked something up that they don't like, we need to go back in minutes not hours and days. Say, right we've done the traceability, it actually came from, the boat it came off, x, y and z.
>
> (Managing director, medium–large company)

An equally important objective of traceability has come to be about ensuring that fish has been caught legally, that is within quota; thus the 2009 regulation mentioned above in connection with the definition of the lot is about compliance with CFP rules. This was made clear by some interviewees for whom traceability was about ensuring that they had sourced legally caught or in some cases sustainably certified fish and could demonstrate this if necessary:

> That is what they are calling traceability. That is what they are satisfied with, having the knowledge that we have to prove to certain of our

customers like multinationals, like certain of our wholesalers, that have to prove that we are still holding sufficient quota for the fish.

(Partner, medium company)

As mentioned above in connection with the Registration of Buyers and Sellers Regulations this was indeed significant for enforcing fisheries management rules. But the overall limitations of the system were described by another respondent:

Under the European regulations, there is a traceability requirement … you have to be able to trace one up and one down which sounds brilliant but unfortunately the food chain is a lot longer than one up and one down. Somebody receiving a fish product in the UK, it may have gone through half a dozen hands before it got to us, so the traceability can be lost further down the chain which is what's happening with the IUU [Illegal, Unreported and Unregulated] fish where it was almost impossible to trace it because it was losing its identity in somewhere like Spain.

(Trade organisation representative 1)

The limitations of the traceability that is required legally and which is tailored to the industrial fishing system gives an incentive for schemes that deliver more direct provenance. One major distributor to the foodservice industry has an arrangement with selected vessels to allow advance ordering of certain species and chefs then receive information about the vessel, skipper and fishing conditions as explained in an interview. The South West [England] Handline Fishermen's Association operates tagging for each individual sea bass and pollack sold with which the purchaser can identify the fisher and boat responsible; the organisation emphasises its sustainable fishing methods and the quality produced. Another company also based in South West England is set up as a collective of fishers operating small boats plus a processing/distribution company; as well as again stressing quality and environmental benefits it aims to give fishers a greater share of the value of fish caught than is usually the case when reliant on auctions, through fixed prices.[50]

For the survey respondents in the mainstream, the rationale mentioned most often for maintaining traceability was to conform with buyer requirements. In other words, it is governance within the supply chain as much as public regulation which makes it so important for the seafood companies. British retailers prioritised traceability requirements as part of their reaction to both the 1990 *Food Safety Act* and the problems symbolised by the BSE outbreak so before the European food safety legislation (Hobbs, Fearne & Spriggs 2002). Subsequently, it has functioned to safeguard against both illegal and unsafe seafood:

Everyone has to have traceability now. Without traceability you can't, certainly, be involved in the UK retail business.

(Managing director, large company)

[Named major retailer] have to be absolutely scrupulous on the traceability of the product because if it was discovered that they got a product that's come from an unsustainable source or perhaps the ethics surrounding people catching the product or rearing the product, they would have serious repercussions on that.

(Trade organisation representative 1)

Retailers might exercise governance functions directly in their traceability requirements:

And it is because of our shall we say our major customer [a supermarket chain] that we developed the traceability just over a year ago where we can now trace back all batches of fish, all batches of cod and haddock that is at the moment, back to the catch area, the catch period, the trawler which goes into the port of first landing.

(Technical manager, medium company)

Traceability is paramount for us because we work with [named major retailer]. They will expect us to have full traceability backwards and forwards for all our processes.

(Head of operations, large company)

However, seafood companies serve a range of customers, some of whom are uninterested in traceability. Chef awareness was reported as 'very low' by one (Group director, large company), of fish fryer customers 'nobody's ever asked' said another (Managing director, small company 3) and generally in relation to foodservice it was 'not on traceability no, price is more the thing' (Manager, trade organisation 1), while from someone whose main sales were to fishmongers 'if they want it it's there but most of them don't give a damn' (Fish merchant, small company).

For many processing and trading companies, legal requirements for food safety and traceability were only part of their aims because quality was their top objective. In order to achieve it, they first aimed to exercise control over the raw materials they bought. Much of this was about relationships with suppliers in which they exercised their own governance functions within the supply chain:

The quality is not really, why is it not an issue? Because we work with suppliers we've known for a number of years or we work with new suppliers who we've inspected their facilities, we agree a specification with them.… We audit our suppliers four times a year, whether that be European suppliers or Asian suppliers.

(Commercial manager, medium-large company)

The business has been built on building, identifying first of all the right kind of suppliers that can give us not only the volume that we need at the price we need but also excellence in quality.... We also have a raw materials technical team which focus very heavily on the product we are buying. So we have a lot of supply based auditing that goes on. We get very involved with fishing fleets, helping them to improve quality through better handling methods. And also it's about having a very, very tight specification.

> (Managing director, medium-large company)

We also have quality systems and auditing that goes back into, down our supply chain. So, we will work with our suppliers, we visit them, they operate to quality standards, we educate them.... We sort of, almost train if you like our supplier's technical people into what we expect, what our standards are.

> (Director, large company)

These three quotes are from larger companies with fairly sophisticated arrangements. Here, firms were implementing their own systems of governance in relation to their suppliers. None referred to the Seafish Responsible Fishing Scheme for improving quality onboard mentioned earlier in this chapter but they may not have been sourcing from the UK.

Small companies did not refer to formal audit systems but were just the same making clear what kind of quality they expected and working with suppliers on a long-term basis:

> The suppliers that have come from historical usage and reputation, reputation means a lot.
>
> > (Depot manager, small company)

> Yes, the quality, they know what we need. If I don't get the quality, it just goes straight back. That's the way it works.
>
> > (Managing director, small company 3)

While most comments about quality referred to the raw material and sourcing, some companies had their own internal quality systems:

> We have a significant system of quality management actually in our factories.... Every intake, we would take of fish, whether it be fresh or frozen form or prawn, some sort of testing things like intrinsic quality, everything gets tasted, there's a sample taken from every batch that we take in is tasted so that an organoleptic assessment goes on everything that we do.
>
> > (Director, large company)

> I'm an independent checker of all the lines. I go to every line, as often as I can. Make sure that – today they're on chunky, cod. So first thing I do

is go to the raw material, make sure it is chunky cod. Look at the quality, visually, that's all you can do. Does it look OK? Colour OK? I need to check that all correct batter, crumbs, in place. We have to do checks on fish content all the time. Really important on frying line, that right amount of batter and crumb is on the product. Make sure it's all looking fine. I do taste panels every day, whatever is produced.

(Quality assurance assistant, medium company)

The companies, of course, responded to the quality requirements of their customers. These differed between sectors (supermarkets, fishmongers, foodservice) as well as between individual purchasers and were related to price. The differences illustrate the relativity of the idea of quality:

There are customers of ours at the lower end of the market, so they're wanting a cheap, a volume and low price, rather than a smaller volume and a high quality.

(Trader, medium–large company)

Our customers are all pretty good, fishmongers. Not like dealing with the supermarkets, the quality is secondary, it's price-driven. These guys we deal with don't mind paying for the fish. They understand better fish costs more on the market.

(Fish merchant, small company)

The restaurants we supply are the top, top restaurants, mostly Michelin star restaurants, we supply. Obviously, the head chefs are very demanding on the quality that they get.

(Director, small company)

Quality as the primary criterion for sourcing, followed by price, was a consistent finding in the series of Seafish processor surveys. But as noted in one of them it could be interpreted as processors seeking the level of quality relevant to their own business and customer base (Brown 2009).

Different definitions of quality could be relevant within the major supermarkets that each have a range of own-brands from the economising to the premium, but also between different chains targeting different points in the market. One interviewee whose company manufactured for a retailer at the higher end reflected certain expectations in the statement that the latter goes for quality 'so we ensure the material going into the meals is the best' (Technical manager, large company). However, another one whose company manufactured for a discount chain but said his opinions were based on what people who supplied other retailers told him, was of the view that:

… there isn't a huge amount of difference in quality, the quality required of all the major supermarkets, even down to [named discount chains] who people see as being cheaper so they expect to be low quality. In actual fact, often the opposite applies; you're getting a cheaper product at a quality that is sometimes much better than shall we say the standard supermarket product.

(Technical manager, medium company)

There are ways of bringing down the price by lowering quality which clearly are acceptable to some customers as described by some of the interviewees. Fillets of whitefish for breading may have been frozen in a block rather than the better result obtained by freezing them individually. Prawns sell more cheaply if glazed with water. Pangasius may be soaked in varying concentrations of phosphates which add weight meaning that 'It's selling you water really' (Managing director, large company).

Some companies were in a position to set their own quality standards even if they were suppliers to major retailers as was the case with both of the following:

We only make one type of kipper. We pride ourselves it's the best quality. It's not the cheapest. There's a lot cheaper ones going around.... So the quality aspect is, we maintain the quality, it's purely we drive our customers, we're not customer driven in that respect.

(Director, medium company 2)

Clearly, if we're doing our own brand, we would set our own quality level.

(Director, large company)

The second of these quotes makes the distinction between manufacturing supermarket own-label products and their own. But, for some firms the former was definitely dominant; in the words of one respondent 'We mainly live and breathe the brands of our customers' (Managing director, medium-large company). Major retailer customers set standards for their suppliers. Even the kipper producer just quoted had to make changes to conform: 'Then he came back up with a food hygienist who said we need to do this and need to do that', an example being the replacement of traditional wooden tenter sticks used to hang up the herring in the smoking kiln with ones made of stainless steel. Another referred more generally to the standards expected: 'Their demands in terms of the quality of the finished product are based on the fact that customers perceive they are buying the best products in the market' (Technical manager, large company).

In line with the picture in some of the literature outlined in Chapter 2 describing the way food producers can be controlled by the standards set by major buyers, this applies to many seafood processors especially those selling to the major retailers, the demand being for accreditation in the British Retail Consortium (BRC) scheme. The BRC Global Standard for Food Safety, introduced in 1998 as a British initiative and now used globally reached its seventh edition in 2015 with the eighth version of the standard appearing in 2018. The scheme, covering quality as well as food safety management, requires HACCP to be in place, sets standards for buildings, product control, process control and personnel and has third-party auditing. The Global Standard scheme which covers a range of products in addition to food was established in a company separate from the British Retail Consortium itself; this has been sold on and the programme is now operated by a service company, LGC.[51]

The BRC standards were considered by interviewees whose companies were in the scheme as having requirements markedly more stringent than legally needed. The expectation of standards beyond legal requirements has been explained as due to uncertainty as to how the 'due diligence' required in the 1990 *Food Safety Act* would be interpreted by the courts (Caswell & Henson 1998).

> A lot of companies that we would want to deal with, before you can deal with them, what is your BRC…. It is a worldwide food standard. So, anywhere in the world, if we want to produce for a supermarket chain in the United States, they would say to us what accreditation have you got, we've got grade A Global Food Standard, and they would know straight away what standard your factory is…. The majority of our customers now, in retail unless you've got BRC accreditation preferably at grade A, or grade B is acceptable, you're not going to manufacture in this day and age for a major supermarket or to some degree the major players in foodservice, particularly the pub groups…. You can't get even the grade B accreditation without having a much higher standard than the law actually requires.
>
> (Technical manager, medium company)

> All our depots have BRC A grade higher accreditation which gives peace of mind to our customers and ourselves, so that we can sleep at night.
>
> (Group director, large company)

While experiencing demand for accreditation from customers, processing companies might also be stipulating the same requirement from their suppliers, thus exerting governance within the supply chain as well as having to respond to it: 'All our suppliers must have BRC, must be BRC approved' (Commercial manager, medium-large company). Others explained further:

> So if a company has got BRC accreditation one knows that that company has got all the things like pest control and quality control in place…. Because we're doing raw materials for further manufacture, those companies insist on a supply chain that includes BRC accreditation all the way through.
>
> (Site manager, medium-large company)

We are increasingly asking our suppliers to also get accreditation against the Global Food Standard and that is right through to packaging, even distribution. There's a Global Food Standard for distribution of frozen foods. So we can use hauliers, which we know the hauliers then would all use clean wagons, they would have temperature control on the vehicles, they would have a policy if a lorry broke down of uplifting the frozen product without losing it and it would certainly satisfy us and give us some guarantees that the companies we were using are operating to a standard in their industry which is equivalent to our standard in our industry…. Increasingly the production factories we use in China are also getting the Global Food Standard accreditation.

(Technical manager, medium company)

In relation to the processing and distribution sector, Seafish again has been an active source of governance. The organisation has run two iterations of its Seafish Quality Processor Award from 1989 to 1999 and then from 2002 to 2008. Similarly its Quality Wholesaler Award was live from 1991 to 1999 and then between 2002 and 2008. With independent auditing, the schemes covered such topics as premises, equipment, hygiene standards and management controls. As re-assessments under the various schemes showed improvements in standards they can be seen as having achieved their purpose (Oehlenschläger & Harrison 2003).

The most recent Seafish award project is the establishment of a Responsible Fishing Ports scheme, starting in 2018, with those eligible being able to apply for certification. Initially it is for large ports, those providing auction or other selling facilities, but the intention is to further develop a standard appropriate for the smaller ports. As with the previous Seafish awards, the objective is to raise standards and the areas cover food safety and quality, traceability, safe working conditions and environmental care (waste management, emissions and carbon footprint). A Code of Practice has been produced setting out model standards and the scheme as usual specifies third-party auditing.[52]

Since ending its own processor quality scheme, Seafish has supported the generic award for small food producers, the Safe and Local Supplier Approval (SALSA) standard. SALSA, a non-profit organisation founded by the main food and hospitality trade associations, provides a more affordable certification option for smaller firms than the BRC route and also offers active support in the form of workshops, courses and mentoring. Food safety is the main objective of the standard and HACCP is required. As a national food safety award provider which at the same time provides recognition for small producers SALSA makes it easier for buyers, including those representing public bodies, to source locally. There are other food safety schemes available for producers among which the STS (Support, Training & Services Ltd) Public Sector one is particularly important for suppliers to the NHS and other public services.[53]

A final certification important for many processors and merchants is that for a chain of custody in relation to the MSC and ASC eco-labels. Collaboration between these two organisations means that there is a shared standard and that there can be a combined audit process. The purpose of the chain of custody is to ensure that those who deal in their environmentally certified seafood purchase it from certified producers or suppliers and that they keep it identifiable and segregated from non-certified items with all the record-keeping that can ensure traceability.[54] The chain of custody is also a feature of the GLOBALG.A.P aquaculture standard.

The Seafish 2008 processor survey found that nearly half the companies sampled were accredited, either to the BRC standard or to the Seafish Quality Processor Award then functioning. The large firms, with a single exception, were BRC certified and so were many of the medium-size concerns while small companies were less likely to be accredited and if they were, it was to the Seafish scheme (Brown 2009). A previous Seafish report had estimated that 60% of British seafood processors, based on trade volumes, were accredited to the BRC or another food safety standard which may be considered compatible with the survey findings when taking into account the size of the large companies (Archer & Denton 2002). The more recent Seafish surveys of processing companies have not recorded certifications but it is assumed that the proportion of seafood companies which have them will not be any smaller because of general supply chain expectations.

The range of public and private governance mechanisms affecting seafood companies is extensive and they are generally agreed to be producing high standards of food safety and quality. But every system of rules needs effective monitoring, the necessity for which is illustrated when failures come to light. One such was the case of a processing company where in 2008 environmental health personnel found the cold store to be rat-infested and to contain fish years out of date which had probably been defrosted and refrozen and which were in part covered with dead maggots. The firm had been producing ready meals and other products for several supermarket chains.[55]

In this world of private standards superimposed on regulations, where the former can be seen as more demanding than the latter there may be a risk that the importance of active regulatory monitoring may be lost. The appreciation by many small businesses of advice and information from EHOs has already been mentioned. However, since 2010 their numbers have sharply reduced because of financial pressures being experienced by local authorities due to the removal of central government funding. This double situation of extensive third-party auditing in the food system and reduced resources for public monitoring is the context in which the FSA has put forward its 'Regulating our Futures' (ROF) proposals. They would involve greater reliance on third-party assurance schemes with the regulatory function retained only for businesses not involved in such schemes; it would include a Primary Authority Scheme in which a company would relate to just one council for all its sites so that the local authorities where other branches were situated would lose their oversight role. The Agency argues that such a system would be more flexible (Food Standards Agency

2017). At an early stage of thinking about such changes a report which the FSA itself had commissioned pointed to various shortcomings of third-party schemes, questioning whether they had actually contributed to food safety; it mentioned that the schemes do not monitor general levels of standards, often do not provide advice on dealing with problems, do not necessarily have arrangements to communicate common problems to others in the industry, do not necessarily report serious public health problems requiring enforcement action and may have conflicts of interest due to the need to compete for business (Wright et al. 2013). Some of these points have been echoed in a strongly critical analysis of the ROF proposals (Millstone & Lang 2018). For Scotland, although the FSS has stated that it will consider using audit schemes to check food safety compliance and voluntary or co-regulation so moving along the ROF line, there is no plan for wholesale change equivalent to the FSA's proposals; interestingly, it has noted that sections of the food and drink industry do not welcome voluntary regulation, fearing that it could lead to erosion of standards (Food Standards Scotland 2017).

Ultimately the maintenance of standards depends on the people who work in the industry. The requirements of the 1991 Seafood Hygiene Directives imposed a previously unknown level of regulation which required a shift in attitudes and culture. A few years after their introduction, a study of four small/medium fish processing companies in Scotland using participant observation found that many employees were unconvinced about the necessity for such standards and needed constant surveillance to ensure that the rules were observed (Haugh 2000). Somewhat later in 2007 came the establishment of the Seafood Training Academy which since 2013 has been managed by Seafish. Working with educational institutions, trainers and industry partners it provides apprenticeships and qualifications for the onshore seafood industry and courses include food safety, HACCP, fish smoking and quality assessment. Seafish itself publishes educational material relevant to processing including one on HACCP in the seafood industry, some available from its own website, some from the Seafood Training Academy one. There does not seem to be an assessment of the overall effects of these programmes but they must have contributed to the achievement of higher standards in the seafood industry.

This chapter has reviewed a large number of regulatory requirements and private governance mechanisms primarily aiming at food safety and product quality which affect those dealing with seafood both onboard and on land. They are summarised in Table 4.2 in separate sections for vessels, aquaculture and processing and distribution; the protected names system is separately at the end because it cuts across all three of these production areas. The various Seafish schemes are categorised as private although the organisation is a state-mandated body because participation in them is entirely voluntary and there is no state enforcement, only the discipline of audit checks and supply chain reactions.

Table 4.2 Public and private governance for seafood safety and quality

Governance type	Detail	Governance source	Purpose	Status/dates
Vessels				
Public regulation	EU directives on hygiene rules and marketing seafood and UK fishery food safety regulations	EU and UK	Common market and food safety	Current
Public regulation	EU regulation on food safety and UK food hygiene regulations	EU and UK	Food safety	Current
Public funding	FIFG under the CFP	EU + match funding	Fisheries policies	1994–2006
Public funding	EFF under the CFP	EU + match funding	Fisheries policies	2007–2013
Public funding	EMFF under the CFP	EU + match funding	Fisheries policies	2014–2020
Private standards	Vessel Quality and Hygiene Scheme	Seafood Scotland	Quality	Ran in early 2000s
Private scheme	White Fish Quality Improvement Initiative	Shetland Seafood Quality Control	Quality	Current
Private standards	Responsible Fishing Scheme	Seafish	Food safety, quality and working conditions	Current
Private action	Various initiatives	Trade bodies and companies	Quality	Ad hoc

continued

Governance type	Detail	Governance source	Purpose	Status/dates
Aquaculture				
Public regulation	EU directives and UK regulations on feed and veterinary residues	EU and UK	Food safety	Current
Public regulation	EU directives and UK regulations on welfare, veterinary medicines and animal slaughter	EU and UK	Animal welfare	Current
Public regulation	EU and UK regulations on organic aquaculture	EU and UK	Organic standards	Current
Public regulation	Shellfish waters classification	EU and UK	Food safety	Current
Public advice	Guidance on reducing antibiotics	EU and UK	Human health	Current
Public advice	Welfare advice	Farm Animal Welfare Council/ Committee	Animal welfare	Current
Public advice	Welfare recommendations	ECPAFP and OIE★	Animal welfare	Current
Public funding	FIFG under the CFP	EU + match funding	Aquaculture development	1994–2006
Public funding	EFF under the CFP	EU + match funding	Aquaculture development	2007–2013
Public funding	EMFF under the CFP	EU + match funding	Sustainable aquaculture	2014–2020
Private advice	Guidelines on the use of veterinary medicines	RUMA	Animal and human health	Current
Standards scheme	Tartan Mark	Scottish Salmon Growers' Association	Quality and environmental protection	Mid-1980s–2008
Standards scheme	Code of Good Practice for Scottish Finfish Aquaculture	Scottish Salmon Producers' Organization	Quality, food safety, fish welfare and environmental protection	Current

Table 4.2 Continued

Governance type	Detail	Governance source	Purpose	Status
Standards scheme	Freedom Food	RSPCA	Animal welfare	Current
Standards scheme	Label Rouge	National Commission for Labels and Certification (France)	Quality and marketing	Current
Standards scheme	Quality Trout UK	Quality Trout UK	Quality, food safety, fish welfare and environmental protection	Current
Standards scheme	The Aquaculture Standard	GLOBALGAP	Quality, sustainability, safety	Current
Standards scheme	Best Aquaculture Practices, multi-species standards	Global Aquaculture Alliance/ Aquaculture Certification Council	Quality, food safety and environmental protection	Current
Standards scheme	ASC species specific standards	Aquaculture Stewardship Council	Environmental and social sustainability	Current
Standards scheme	Various standards	Organic Food Federation & Soil Association	Organic standards	Current
Processing/distribution				
Public regulation	EU directives on hygiene rules and marketing seafood and UK fishery food safety regulations	EU and UK	Common market and food safety	Current
Public regulation	EU regulation on food safety and UK food safety/hygiene legislation and regulations	EU and UK	Food safety and traceability	Current
Public regulation	EU regulations on seafood labelling and UK fish labelling regulations	EU and UK	Common market and consumer information	Current

Governance type	Detail	Governance source	Purpose	Status
Public regulation	EU and UK regulations on disposal of animal by-products and waste management	EU and UK	Food safety and environmental protection	Current
Public regulation	EU directives and UK regulations on imports from third countries	EU and UK	Food safety and animal health	Current
Public regulation	Regulation on registering fish buyers and sellers	UK	Fisheries management	Current
Guidance	Codes of practice for hygiene generally and for fish	Codex Alimentarius	Food safety and trading standards	Current
Public funding	FIFG under the CFP	EU + match funding	Promoting processing and marketing	1994–2006
Public funding	EFF under the CFP	EU + match funding	Promoting processing and marketing	2007–2013
Public funding	EMFF under the CFP	EU + match funding	Promoting marketing and processing	2014–2020
Training	Training/qualifications for food processors	Seafood Training Academy (public and private partners)	Quality and food safety, individual development	Current
Standards scheme	Global Standard for Food Safety	BRC Global Standards	Food safety and quality	Current

continued

Table 4.2 Continued

Governance type	Detail	Governance source	Purpose	Status
Audit	Company specific systems	Seafood Companies	Quality of raw materials	Current
Standards scheme 2002–2008	Quality Processor Award	Seafish	Quality and food safety	1989–1999
Standards scheme 2005–2008	Quality Wholesaler Award	Seafish	Quality and food safety	1991–1999
Standards scheme	Responsible Fishing Ports Scheme	Seafish	Food safety, quality, working conditions and environmental care	Under development
Standards scheme	Safe and Local Supplier Approval	SALSA	Food safety	Current
General				
Public regulation	EU Protected Food Name System	EU	Food authenticity and marketing	Current

Source: author.

Notes

⋆ ECPAFP is the European Convention for the Protection of Animals Kept for Farming Purposes, OIE is the World Organisation for Animal Health. 'Current' in relation to EU and UK legislation refers to the pre-Brexit situation and items may be subject to change. BRC Global Standards is within the LGC private company.

Some of these mechanisms are exerted from outside the supply chain, others within it. But before assessing the overall weight of these different types of governance there is one other crucial aspect to be considered, that is the nature of power relationships within seafood supply chains.

Power in seafood supply chain relationships

The major supermarket chains have for some time been recognised as the most powerful force in food chains as reviewed in Chapter 1. To what extent is this felt in the seafood sector?

The frankest comments about dealing with supermarkets in the interviews were from two respondents who were not speaking as their suppliers. One had, however, been in this position many years previously and had some unpleasant memories:

> We'd sit in their waiting room for an hour, too busy, can't see you. You get in there, all they want to do is squeeze price, all they wanted to do, and it was just whether we could just somehow get away with what we could manage and still keep the huge volumes that we wanted to supply them.... They came back, said they felt they'd been uncompetitive in the market, therefore, they were, what's the word, retrospectively, modifying their purchase price to the Christmas price. And that's what they're paying us and because they had paid us for some, could we send them a cheque for £80,000.
>
> (Trade organisation representative 3)

The other gave these reasons for choosing not to have commercial relations with supermarkets:

> I personally wouldn't touch them with a bargepole because we are too small to stand up to their corporate buying power and too small to make the investments that they need to see on site. We put our business in a position where we supply the suppliers to supermarkets.... We don't have the economic power, the bargaining power, the negotiating power to deal with the supermarkets direct. Not on any scale. I don't want to either.... If you don't watch it with supermarkets, they can make so many demands of you and your premises and your business criteria, they're telling you how much money you're going to make.
>
> (Managing director, small company 1)

The relative power positions of the major retailers in comparison to their seafood suppliers was described by one observer:

> I think that anybody who deals with supermarkets, it's an uneven playing field, which the supermarkets ultimately determine. Obviously, a

company as big as [named processing company], they would take advice from them. But ultimately the supermarkets do the determination of what they want on the counter, a lot of that is based on the bottom line profit. They're not interested in fish as an item, they're interested in fish as a profit.... They [supermarkets] do tend to call the tune with all their suppliers.

(Trade organisation representative 1)

Three other interviewees conveyed something of their current experiences of dealing with supermarkets:

It's a challenging environment, it's definitely a challenging thing dealing with the supermarkets. Because they're trying to get the best possible quality with all the integrity with all the great credentials. But they're in an extremely competitive environment where every customer is high value to them and wanting to get the best possible deal so therefore the whole package of that pressure comes together. ... To manage those relationships you need good people ... You need good people around you who can articulate their argument, people that are prepared to stand their ground.

(Managing director, medium-large company)

Our biggest customer at the moment will challenge us all the time. It almost becomes laughable, are you sure that's your best price, we want you to review this price, review that cost, look at this, look at that.

(Commercial manager, medium-large company)

It is a straightforward economic power issue. They're very, very difficult. ... I often say that when account managers have come out after a bit of a battering from one of the retailers, ... they may have the majority of the deck of cards but they don't have all of the cards actually. It's not an equal relationship, there's no doubt about that but there are things that we can do. And they're very, very tough. They're extremely tough and pretty sophisticated in the way they have developed it over the years.

(Director, large company)

In the view of the respondent who had avoided direct supply relations with retailers there was a saving grace in that the seafood industry was not entirely dependent on them:

Fortunately, in this country and in Europe, you have independent fish markets, which are like fish exchanges. Boats catch the fish, they tend to put it into a port and it tends to be free competition that applies to the buying of it. Where supermarkets get reviled is where they get an iron grip on supply and they can never quite get that iron grip on the fishing industry. They don't get the opportunity to really go overboard to the point of destroying their suppliers. I don't want to quote actually what I know about how they work. Suffice to say that the free market of auctions is a shield against the worst excesses that big buying groups could put on the industry if they were given a free run to do it. ... If the supermarkets don't play ball with the price they don't get much fish. So they have to. So there's a nice balance at the moment.

(Managing director, small company 1)

This balance of forces and the particular position of some companies could allow them to take a relatively independent stance in their dealings with supermarkets, positions that resulted from the choices made by such senior managers who might assess the value of business offered against other considerations:

Because we're a privately owned company and we're debt free, we're in a very lucky position that we can say no; lots of other people can't. And we're small enough to be able to restructure if we lost a chunk of business.

(Commercial manager, medium-large company)

We're trading now with [named supermarket chain]. I've built that business with [them] in the last five or six months. We've been talking to them for two years so we didn't just jump into bed with them. It's been a long steady dialogue. And we've stuck to our principles and really they've come to us now because they recognise that.

(Managing director, medium-large company)

You give them an equally hard time themselves. ... We've actually told in the past [named retailer] to bugger off, and they came back a few years later. Because, at the end of the day, if you're selling a quality product with all of the provenance that we can give it, then if they want to try and strangulate the business, the best thing to do is to tell them to bugger off. Because as the industry gets smaller, they need us probably more than we need them now. ... [Supermarkets are] a big part of our business, they are. But would we ever let them control us, no we wouldn't. There are other companies out there that have no choice, they have built businesses to serve multinationals.

(Partner, medium company)

These various interview excerpts confirm that supermarket power is an important factor in the seafood supply chain, as in the food system generally. But they also indicate that industry conditions, as well as the situation of specific firms and the reactions of those running them, can place limits on that power. Here, the model of four types of relationship put forward by Cox and his collaborators and discussed in Chapter 1, is relevant; these were dominant buyer, dominant supplier, independence or interdependence. Relationships between supermarkets and seafood suppliers may usually be characterised as cases of the dominant buyer, but they may sometimes be considered as closer to interdependence. One example was in a couple of the interview companies whose directors gave greater priority to certain standards above price. Another could be because of supplier size as with the large processors who have their own brands. The latter in turn may be in dominant supplier mode with some customers, for example, small retailers who only stock frozen seafood or when provisioning small operators in the foodservice market. Elsewhere in the supply chain, many relationships can probably be characterised as of either independence or interdependence between smaller processing companies and smaller retail and catering industry concerns.

A key criterion of supply chain relationships is relative levels of profit, highlighted in the Cox and collaborators' studies. There were some comments in the interviews related to profitability. One person who had referred to the financial pressures exerted by the supermarkets also said that business with them was still relatively profitable compared to supplying the catering sector because 'We would tend to compete against lots more small companies in the foodservice area whereas in retail it tends to be three or four big companies on the majority of items' (Director, large company). This indicates a certain balance of forces between the multiples and their main suppliers. On the other hand, echoing findings in the Seafish processor surveys in which companies indicated that they were unable to pass on higher costs because of buyer power, two interviewees talked about low margins:

> If you look at our accounts you will see that we're making a profit of just 1%, and that's in a good year, and that's before tax, 1%.
>
> (Chairman, medium wholesaler)

> So it's not a high margin industry. As a business, we've made 2% operating margin for the last three years. We had aspirations to be making 5 but even at 5 if you compare that with big branded manufacturers who own their own relationship with their customer, with their own customer which is the consumer. We don't have that luxury. ... I think commercially, the margins, the difference between making money and losing money in the industry are so fine, the margins are so fine. Really, the successful food companies in the UK are the people who manage to control every element of their business in the right way and the sum of all those small parts equals the profit.
>
> (Managing director, medium-large company)

However, the second of these two respondents also explained that fresh fish wholesaling, by contrast, could be profitable if carried out by small firms with very low overheads:

It's a lower margin business, you're selling in bulk. ... So some people might be happy to shift that fish on 5% if they've got an operating cost of 2%, they've got 3% profit margin. So £5 million worth of fish a year they quite happy with that that, a hundred and fifty grand, administration cost and they've made themselves a hundred grand. There are plenty of people happy to trade on that level.

(Managing director, medium-large company)

In another view, processors were still at an advantage compared to those doing the fishing:

If you are a processor, ... you may decrease your margins to accommodate some of those costs by reducing the price you pay for raw material and when you start doing that, that's when your fleet starts to have problems. Because they cannot pass on their increased diesel fuel costs, capital costs on to anyone. They are dependent on what market price they can get.

(Industry advisor, trade organisation)

These impressions can be compared with the British value chain analysis of three species outlined in Chapter 2 which found that processors often took a low proportion of the added value of their input but that they did make a higher percentage on some items like fish fingers and frozen coated scampi (Sandberg et al. 2004). It appeared from this source that except for the two specified products, processors were often at a disadvantage to both the retail and foodservice customers. It also showed that the fishing part of the supply chain was likely to get a low proportion of the final value, something which the fisher-distributor collective noted in the previous section aims to change. However, more recent estimates indicate that while the profits made with small boats, the kind involved in the collective just mentioned, are indeed very low and may be close to zero, the large-scale fleet makes as much as 19% (Carpenter 2017).

The previous section described supply chain relationships from the viewpoint of securing food safety and quality and noted the impact of requirements from large customers, particularly the major retailers. This one has focused on other aspects of relationships between the companies interviewed and the much larger and economically more powerful supermarkets. The power imbalance could make dealings difficult for the supplying companies but some nevertheless had the resources to maintain a level of independence and insist on certain conditions of their own.

Conclusions: the balance of public and private governance

This chapter like the previous one has been an account of extensive change in the seafood industry. Here, the topic has been the development of greatly improved standards of hygiene, food safety and quality of the product. The starting point was the documented poor quality midway through the twentieth century which continued into the 1980s. The impact of both public regulation and private governance systems is seen in the greatly improved situation from the last decade of the twentieth century onwards. The type of governance has varied for different sectors of the seafood industry.

The last chapter showed how primary production, both fishing and aquaculture, are heavily regulated for environmental protection and sustainability. In this one aquaculture is also seen to be regulated in some aspects bearing on food and public safety such as feed and veterinary medicines while seafood hygiene legislation applies to both production sectors. Other aspects such as the quality of the product and fish welfare have instead received attention through private governance. For fishing, the main effort in the UK has been by means of the Seafish Responsible Fishing Scheme but there has been much more development of aquaculture standards.

The aquaculture schemes fall into three categories. For the highly organised Scottish salmon farming industry, producers have through their trade organisations determined their own quality standards by self-producing codes of practice and for a period while the Tartan Mark was in operation even their own certification scheme. Trout farmers have followed suit with their own programme. The salmon farming industry has also chosen two other forms of certification, Freedom Food and Label Rouge. All these activities, though including provisions for some public interest and ethical aims such as environmental protection and animal welfare, are essentially marketing-driven and connected with the orientation of the Scottish industry to self-positioning as the provider of a premium product. A second group consists of general aquaculture schemes (in some cases containing species-specific standards) produced by bodies which are constituted as alliances of wider groups of stakeholders, involving not just primary producers but other seafood companies, retailers, food service and in the case of the ASC (Aquaculture Stewardship Council) also NGOs. Their schemes have a number of objectives covering quality, safety, sustainability and traceability but a fundamental purpose is to produce products that will suit the requirements of buyers, whether in retail or foodservice. A connected aim is to deflect criticism about environmental impacts. This second group has impacted the UK seafood supply chain via imports. Finally, the third group consists of organic standards, promoted and safeguarded by the relevant bodies within the relevant legislation. The FAO guidelines are most often mentioned in connection with the second group and possibly have affected the others as well. All these forms of private governance include adherence to legal requirements in whatever country they operate.

Turning to the processing and distribution sector the regulatory factor predominates in relation to food safety and traceability. Even for a big company supplying a major retailer the legal structures might seem pre-eminent: 'Our whole quality and processing framework is built round complying with the law and the various regulations that come with it' (Technical manager, large company). Quality, not specified legislatively, is generally more influenced by a range of informal and formal private governance arrangements. Though some depend on long-term business relationships and reputation, companies with major retailer and other large customers were more likely to use a formal system and particularly BRC accreditation with SALSA and other options also available which have at times included the Seafish processor and wholesaler awards. These private schemes stand on an extensive regulatory underpinning which at some level has taken into account the international Codex Alimentarius guidelines on food hygiene. In addition to specific schemes, many interviewees referred to a range of formal and informal auditing arrangements which they or their companies applied to ensure the quality of raw materials they wanted from their suppliers.

Public regulation, as well as being expressed by rules, may also be exerted by incentives. Funding provision to improve standards of vessels, infrastructure and equipment has made a significant difference across various parts of the seafood industry. Investment in the people who work in the seafood industry is also an important aspect of maintaining standards generally, to which the Seafood Training Academy has contributed, and this has been a mixed arrangement involving both public further education institutions and private partners.

A final governance incentive is provided by the EU protected names scheme which ranges across primary products and processed foods. Legislatively established and administered through national and EU systems, its objectives are largely about marketing and supporting small producers. For consumers, they also safeguard food authenticity, but this seems to be a lesser factor in the British supply chain in relation to the seafood items recognised.

The first thing shown by this analysis is the importance of state-led governance in the overall system; legislation for seafood safety, traceability and labelling has impacted greatly on the seafood industry. Second, it indicates that contrary to the trend of discussion in much of the literature on standards in food chains, they do not all have a simple function. In part there is indeed conformity with the buyer-driven model in the increasing demand for BRC certification, clearly representing the interests of retail buyers. Also in line with a common pattern, this is becoming more compulsory than voluntary for certain parts of the market, judging by some of the interview comments. The other schemes also satisfy buyer interests so that they can satisfy due diligence requirements and source legally caught fish. But the seafood-specific standards are industry driven, directly producer-led in the case of the salmon and trout farming, otherwise by the quango Seafish representing both industry and a public interest. They are about improving market position by meeting general demand for higher standards of quality and food safety rather than those of specific buyers and have not been created to satisfy specific purchaser requirements.

The research has also illustrated the differential impacts of public and private governance on different types of processing and distribution company. For smaller ones, legislation is the dominating factor along with market expectations but for bigger enterprises directly serving large downstream concerns, it is the private schemes that dominate. This is similar to findings elsewhere. Processing and distribution companies of all sizes must depend on the regulatory framework to ensure that general facilities such as auction halls and markets, although generally privately run, maintain food safety standards whether they use them routinely or only occasionally.

What has changed most is the increase of governance mechanisms overall. At the beginning of the period reviewed there was no regulation for food safety and quality in primary production which at the time consisted only of capture fishing except for requirements relating to bivalve molluscs and the hygiene rules then in operation were apparently making limited impact on processing and distribution practices. Now there is private and public regulation affecting production, both fishing and aquaculture, and a great deal that has changed the way processing and distribution companies carry out their activities. There has been an increase in and important impact of private governance but it has not replaced public rules. Rather, the latter deepened first and private schemes then built on and in various ways went beyond legislative requirements. The process has been one of change over time such as the increasing requirement for BRC accreditation, the development of other food safety schemes and the implementation, then cessation, of the Seafish schemes for wholesalers and processors while its Responsible Fishing Scheme has been strengthened and new standards for fishing ports are being progressed.

All this public and private governance is part of what in the scheme set out in Chapter 2 is categorised as external governance. To fully understand what drives change in supply chains, governance within them, involving power relationships must also be considered as illustrated in Figure 4.1.

The overlap between internal and external is the private governance exerted by buyers when they require particular accreditations. But some of the interviews also showed that other factors determine what occurs inside the central box which are best understood in terms of the Cox power model with its four possible structures: dominant buyer, dominant supplier, independence and interdependence. One feature of internal supply chain governance is the kind of long-term collaborative relationship posited by some of the other literature reviewed in Chapter 2 as was illustrated by several interviewee comments referring to such relations with suppliers; that could mean that they themselves were dominant buyers if large, but in other cases were more likely to be those of interdependence. It also includes other relationships in which the interview companies were on the receiving end of dominant buyers, notably supermarkets, which wielded power not so much by their demands for audited standards as argued by much supply chain governance theory, this having increasingly become a performance norm, but by the conditions, usually about pricing, that they set for business to be done. Even so, as one respondent commented, the buyers do not hold all the cards and individual companies were able to assert some level of independence by refusing certain terms even in relation to retailers hugely bigger than themselves.

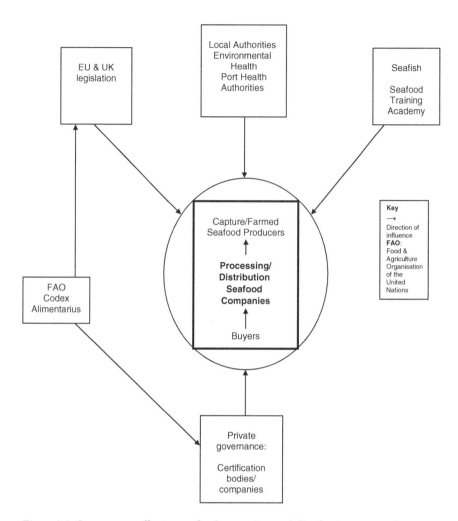

Figure 4.1 Governance affecting seafood processing and distribution companies.

But the account this far has not exhausted the governance factors in play. Supermarkets are themselves subject to some of these and the governance issues widen further when consumers are considered. These questions are picked up in the next two chapters which move on to the endpoints of the supply chain, that is retail, foodservice and consumption.

Notes

1 By contrast with the 3.4% and 5.2% GP consultations and hospital admissions respectively for seafood in this study the equivalent figures for beef and lamb were 10.7% and 4.4%, for eggs 9.1% and 32.1% and for the source of most problems,

poultry, they were 50.7% and 19.9%. Infection passed on by food handlers may be part of these problems rather than the products themselves always being the direct source.

2 The parasites will be killed by cooking or for fish to be eaten raw by freezing at a specified temperature and for a specified length of time; see Seafish 2012.

3 Information about FASFA is on their website at http://fasfa.co.uk.

4 General information about the Responsible Fishing Scheme is at www.seafish. org/rfs/. Seafish plans for the scheme to be separately managed by a not-for-profit organisation to facilitate international development were advanced when it signed a Memorandum of Understanding with GAA in April 2018 under which the scheme will migrate to a new programme it will set up over a two-year period.

5 The Seafood Scotland scheme was not formally wound up but ceased when it had 'served its purpose' having 'really delivered a better quality regime for whitefish' (personal communication, Jeremy Sparks, Seafood Scotland, 4 December 2012). Information about the White Fish Quality Improvement Initiative is on the SSQC website, www.ssqc.co.uk.

6 These documents have been variously titled Good Practice Guides, Good Manufacturing Guides and Good Manufacturing Practice Guides. There is a separate Good Practice Guide on dealing with live crustaceans.

7 Quotes taken from Seafish fact sheet *Seafood Freshness Quality*, 2011.

8 These regulations about hygiene onboard were '91/493/EEC Laying down the health conditions for the production and the placing on the market of fishery products' and '92/48/EEC Laying down the minimum hygiene rules applicable to fishery products caught on board certain vessels'.

9 Personal communication from the RFS Fleet Manager, Seafish (Mick Bacon) on 8 May 2018 who indicated that vessel inspections were infrequent.

10 Abusive conditions on some Scottish vessels have been reported in J Moulds 2017, 'Migrant workers used as forced labour on Scottish fishing fleet, charity claims', *Sunday Times*, 15 November 2017.

11 The first step in superseding 'The Merchant Shipping and Fishing Vessels (Health and Safety at Work) Regulations 1997' is 'The European Union (Definition of Treaties) (Work in Fishing Convention) Order 2018' which declares the ILO Convention to have the status of an EU treaty. The ILO Convention has wide provisions including social protection and standards of living and working conditions onboard.

12 The European legislation consisted of the successive Shellfish Waters Directives entitled 'On the quality required of shellfish waters', '79/923/EEC' and '2006/113/EC'. The former was transposed into UK legislation only in 1997 in the form of 'Surface Waters (Shellfish) (Classification) Regulations'. When in 2013 the 'Shellfish Waters Directive' was repealed by the 'Water Framework Directive (2000/60/EC)' it was considered that the existing 'Water Environment (Water Framework Directive) (England and Wales) Regulations 2003' already imposed most of the water quality standards and obligations required by the 'Shellfish Directive'; however, additional amendments were made in 'The Water Environment (Water Framework Directive) (England And Wales) (Amendment) Regulations 2016' to cover shellfish waters. For Scotland, the 'Water Framework Directive' was transposed into law in the *Water Environment and Water Services (Scotland) Act 2003* with secondary legislation including the 'Water Environment (Controlled Activities) (Scotland) Regulations 2011'; in response to the repeal of the 'Shellfish Waters Directive' the *Aquaculture and Fisheries (Scotland) Act 2013* included special provisions for protecting shellfish waters.

13 Early UK legislation was the 'Public Health (Shellfish) Regulations 1934'. The key European legislation detailing conditions relating to the relevant shellfish species is '91/492/EEC Laying down the health conditions for the production

and the placing on the market of live bivalve molluscs' implemented by the 'Food Safety (Live Bivalve Molluscs and Other Shellfish) Regulations 1992'.

14 This is 'Regulation (EC) 183/2005, Laying down requirements for feed hygiene'. There were separate implementing UK regulations entitled 'Feed (Hygiene and Enforcement) Regulations' for England, Northern Ireland, Scotland and Wales, also dated 2005.

15 Details of two decontamination reviews by the EFSA Panel on Contaminants are: 'Assessment of decontamination processes for dioxins and dioxin-like PCBs in fish oil by physical filtration with activated carbon', *EFSA Journal*, 2017, vol. 15, no. 12, p. 5081 and 'Assessment of a decontamination process for dioxins and PCBs from fish meal by replacement of fish oil', *EFSA Journal*, 2018, vol. 16, no. 2, p. 5174.

16 This is 'Regulation (EU) No 56/2013 Amending Annexes I and IV to Regulation (EC) No 999/2001 of the European Parliament and of the Council laying down rules for the prevention, control and eradication of certain transmissible spongiform encephalopathies'.

17 The most recent is 'Regulation (EU) No 37/2010 of 22 December 2009 on pharmacologically active substances and their classification regarding maximum residue limits in foodstuffs of animal origin' and there is a series of UK implementing regulations. The 'Animals and Animal Products (Examination for Residues and Maximum Residue Limits) Regulations 1997' seems to be the first of these to specifically include 'aquaculture animals'.

18 These are the separate 'The Products of Animal Origin (Third Country Imports) Regulations for England 2006' and for each of Northern Ireland, Scotland and Wales 2007 plus their various amending regulations corresponding to Directives '90/675/EEC' and '97/29/EC' dealing with veterinary checks on products entering from third countries.

19 An account of Norway's experience can be found on the WHO website under the title 'Vaccinating salmon: how Norway avoids antibiotics in fish farming', www.who.int/features/2015/antibiotics-norway, accessed 3 April 2018.

20 Commission Notice 2015/C299/04, *Guidelines for the Prudent Use Of Antimicrobials In Veterinary Medicine*. See also *The New EU One Health Action Plan Against Antimicrobial Resistance* 2017, 'one health' referring to the interconnection between human and animal health.

21 The terms of reference of the Farm Animal Welfare Council, an independent advisory body based in Tolworth, were

> to keep under review the welfare of farm animals on agricultural land, at animal gatherings, in transit and at the place of slaughter; and to advise the Government and devolved administrations of any legislative or other changes that may be necessary. The Council can investigate any topic falling within this remit; communicate freely with outside bodies, the European Commission and the public; and publish its advice independently.
>
> (FAWC 2009)

22 The relevant European legislation is 'Directive 98/58/EC of 20 July 1998 concerning the protection of animals kept for farming purposes'. Details in its Annex of what is to be considered adequate husbandry have been phrased with only terrestrial animals in mind. While the related UK and Scottish *Animal Welfare Acts* were produced in 2006, the equivalent *Welfare of Animals (Northern Ireland) Act* did not appear until 2011.

23 The acronym OIE comes from the original name of the organisation, Office International des Epizooties; when this changed to the World Organisation for Animal Health the original acronym was retained.

24 The Farm Animal Welfare *Council* (see note 16) was replaced in 2011 by the Farm Animal Welfare *Committee* which sits within DEFRA. The terms of reference of

the successor Committee (available at www.gov.uk) are similar to those of the previous body except that they no longer refer to communicating with outside bodies and the European Commission but it is interesting to note the change, albeit minor to a less delegated position, a reversal of the usual pattern described by analysts of the state.

25 'Directive 93/119 On the protection of animals at the time of slaughter or killing' did not include fish and so neither did the series of implementing UK 'Welfare of Animals (Slaughter or Killing) Regulations' from 1995 onwards. The updated 'Regulation (EC) No 1099/2009 of 24 September 2009 on the protection of animals at the time of killing' while again excluding fish noted that further investigation of the issue was needed resulting in a report (European Commission Directorate-General for Health and Food Safety 2017) and recommendations (European Commission 2018). The latter's conclusion that it would be better to rely on voluntary action or that it should be left to member states to take action would seem to be unusual for the European Commission but seems to reflect the differential impact a common regulation would have on large and small-scale enterprises and hence on the aquaculture industries of different EU countries. The decision not to regulate over fish slaughter has been sharply criticised in (Eurogroup for Animals 2018).

26 The ASC's view is set out by its Standards Director, Bas Geerts, in a blog 'The principles behind the ASC standards' dated 9 July 2015 at www.asc-aqua.org, accessed on 24 April 2018.

27 Biosecurity has been defined by the UK Forestry Commission as a 'set of precautions to prevent the introduction and spread of harmful organisms'; if there is not a separate biosecurity plan the issue should be covered within the VHP.

28 Ports in England with seafood auctions: Brixham, Fleetwood, Grimsby, Hull, Looe, Lowestoft, Newlyn, North Shields, Plymouth, Rye and Whitby; in Northern Ireland: Kilkeel and Portavogie; in Scotland: Fraserburgh, Kinlochbervie, Lerwick, Peterhead, Scalloway and Scrabster. The Register of Buyers and Sellers lists some other locations as auction sites but they do not have functioning auctions.

29 The numbers of fish traders have been taken from websites or provided by the markets concerned in response to email requests.

30 Cold smoking means the smoke temperature is up to 30°C while in hot-smoking it is in the range 70–80°C which cooks the fish. Hot-smoked products have been more popular in other parts of Europe than Britain except for Arbroath smokies. Prior to smoking, the fish is brined, or in some cases dry-salted, for specific periods of time. A full account of the various methods is in (Burgess et al. 1965).

31 The size criterion was in terms of full-time employees: small 1–25 FTEs; medium: 26–100 FTEs; and large 100+ FTEs.

32 The annual *UK Seafood Industry Overview* produced by Seafish and available on its website includes information on the top 20 import countries showing value and volume. The detail of top species imported from China is from the Seafish *China Profile* in its 'Focus on Ethical Issues in Seafood' series.

33 See Cato 1998; Huss 1995; Huss, Ababouch & Gram 2004; Sumner, Ross & Ababouch 2004. FAO work on seafood quality goes back decades, at least to an FAO Technical Conference on Fish Inspection & Quality Control held in 1969, reported in Burgess 1972.

34 The initial requirement for shared standards to facilitate a common market for seafood was in '(EEC) No 3796/81 On the common organization of the market in fishery products'. The other four were: '(EEC) No 4042/89 On the improvement of the conditions under which fishery and aquaculture products are processed and marketed'; '91/493/EEC Laying down the health conditions for the production and the placing on the market of fishery products' and '92/48/EEC of

16 June 1992 Laying down the minimum hygiene rules applicable to fishery products caught on board certain vessels in accordance with Article 3 (1) (a) (i) of Directive 91/493/EEC' (both already mentioned in the section on food safety on fishing vessels); and '91/492/EEC Laying down the health conditions for the production and the placing on the market of live bivalve molluscs'.

35 Initial domestic implementation of the standards aspects was by 'The Sea Fish Marketing Standards Regulations 1986' subsequently superseded for Scotland by 'The Sea Fish (Marketing Standards) (Scotland) Regulations 2004'. The main implementing legislation for the Directives about hygiene in processing consisted of the 'Food Safety (Fishery Products) Regulations 1992' and the 'Food Safety (Live Bivalve Molluscs and Other Shellfish) Regulations 1992' and subsequently 'The Food Safety (Fishery Products and Live Shellfish) (Hygiene) Regulations 1998'.

36 '(EC) No 2065/2001 Laying down detailed rules for the application of Council Regulation (EC) No 104/2000 as regards informing consumers about fishery and aquaculture products'.

37 The labelling requirements are in 'Regulation 1224/2009, Establishing a Community control system for ensuring compliance with the rules of the common fisheries policy' and 'Regulation (EU) No 1169/2011 On the provision of food information to consumers' which came into force in December 2014.

38 These were 'The Fish Labelling (England) Regulations 2003' later followed by 'The Fish Labelling (England) Regulations 2010' and 'The Fish Labelling Regulations 2013' following further EU measures. Each of these has equivalent measures in the devolved administrations, that is 2003, 2010 and 2013 separate Fish Labelling Regulations for Northern Ireland, Scotland and Wales.

39 The relevant CFP legislation is 'Regulation (EC) No 2371/2002 of 20 December 2002 On the conservation and sustainable exploitation of fisheries resources under the common fisheries policy' (article 22) and the UK regulations are 'The Registration of Fish Buyers and Sellers and Designation of Fish Auction Sites Regulations 2005' (applying to England only), 'The Registration of Fish Buyers and Sellers and Designation of Fish Auction Sites Regulations (Northern Ireland) 2005', 'The Registration of Fish Sellers and Buyers and Designation of Auction Sites (Scotland) Regulations 2005', and The Registration of Fish Buyers and Sellers and Designation of Fish Auction Sites (Wales) Regulations 2006'.

40 The *Food Safety Act 1990* replaced the *Food Act 1984* which consolidated various *Food and Drugs Acts* from 1955 to 1982. 'The Food Hygiene (Market Stalls and Delivery Vehicles) Regulations 1966' and 'The Food Hygiene (General) Regulations 1970' were made on the basis of powers in the *Food and Drugs Act 1955*.

41 Details are 'Directive 93/43/EEC On the hygiene of foodstuffs' and 'The Food Safety (General Food Hygiene) Regulations 1995'.

42 Details are 'Regulation (EC) No 178/2002 of 28 January 2002 Laying down the general principles and requirements of food law, establishing the European Food Safety Authority and laying down procedures in matters of food safety', 'Regulation (EC)No 852/2004 of 29 April 2004 On the hygiene of foodstuffs' and 'Regulation (EC)No 853/2004 of 29 April 2004 Laying down specific hygiene rules for food of animal origin'.

43 These were 'Regulation (EC) No 1774/2002 of 3 October 2002 Laying down health rules concerning animal by-products not intended for human consumption', subsequently superseded by 'Regulation (EC) No 1069/2009 of 21 October 2009 Laying down health rules as regards animal by-products and derived products not intended for human consumption'. There were enacting regulations for Scotland 2003, England 2005 and Wales 2003 & 2006. While most seafood waste falls into the lowest risk category 3, exceptions are shellfish containing excess levels of algal toxins which fall into the highest risk category 1 and live shellfish

which have died in transit which are in intermediate category 2 (Archer et al. 2005).

44 Licensing of landfills started with the *Environmental Protection Act 1990* and taxing them with 'The Landfill Tax Regulations 1996'. The main EU legislation is 'Directive 1999/31/EC of 26 April 1999 on the landfill of waste', transposed into UK legislation in 'The Landfill (England and Wales) Regulations 2002', 'The Landfill Regulations (Northern Ireland) 2003' and 'The Landfill (Scotland) Regulations 2003'.

45 The amount of fishmeal used in the UK halved between the mid-1990s and 2008 and over the same period the proportion imported reduced from over 80% during the late 1990s to below 70% (Seafish 2016). The figure for the former number of fishmeal plants in Britain is in (University of Newcastle-upon-Tyne & Poseidon Aquatic Resource Management 2004).

46 The first FIFG programme 1994–1997 was used in the following seven areas: vessel decommissioning, fleet modernisation, aquaculture, enclosed sea waters, fishing port facilities, processing and marketing and other measures (European Commission Directorate-General for Fisheries 1999) There were six areas of intervention through the second round of the FIFG, 2000–2006: fleet, aquaculture, fishing ports, processing and marketing, sector organisation and innovative measures (European Commission Directorate-General for Fisheries and Maritime Affairs 2010). The £73 million figure is in (Hough & Presland 2000). A considerable proportion of these funds was used for vessel decommissioning programmes as described in Chapter 3.

47 The BPA's research and conclusions are summarised in media release 'UK fishing ports call for bold vision from ministers ahead of New Year Fisheries Bill', 31 December 2017, available on its website www.britishports.org.uk.

48 The initial European legislation was 'Regulation (EEC) No 2082/92 of 14 July 1992 on certificates of specific character for agricultural products, followed by 'Regulation (EC) No 509/2006 of 20 March 2006 on agricultural products and foodstuffs as traditional specialities guaranteed' and 'Regulation (EC) No 510/2006 of 20 March 2006 on the protection of geographical indications and designations of origin for agricultural products and foodstuffs' and most recently 'Regulation (EU) No 1151/2012 of the European Parliament and of the Council of 21 November 2012 on quality schemes for agricultural products and foodstuffs'. While the schemes have always been open to all foods produced in the Community/EU it is only in the 2012 regulation that for the first time the fact that products may come from fisheries and aquaculture as well as agriculture was stated. Current information on British protected names is at www.gov.uk/ government/collections/protected-food-name-scheme-uk-registered-products.

49 The 1991 Directives on marketing fishery products and live molluscs defined a batch as 'the quantity of fishery products obtained under practically identical circumstances'. Other European food legislation has used the terminology of the 'lot' rather than the 'batch'. Most recently in relation to seafood the lot is defined in 'Regulation (EC) No 1224/2009 establishing a Community control system for ensuring compliance with the rules of the common fisheries policy', as 'a quantity of fisheries and aquaculture products of a given species of the same presentation and coming from the same relevant geographical area and the same fishing vessel, or group of fishing vessels, or the same aquaculture production unit'. It also specifies the lot as the unit for traceability, recognises that lots may be split or merged and states that when a lot consists of the catch of several vessels, records are to be kept for at least three years.

50 Information about the South West Handline Fishermen's Association is on www. linecaught.org. For information on the Sole of Discretion collective, set up in 2016, see their website http://soleofdiscretion.co.uk and interview with founder

Caroline Bennett 'How fishing got ethical, thanks to this Plymouth collective' 20 September 2017 at www.farmdrop.com.
51 LGC, the owner of the BRC Global Standard, is a London-based company which provides a range of scientific and consultancy services. Originally the UK Government Chemist and forensic service provider, it was privatised since when it has been successively owned by private equity firm LGV capital (2009), Bridgepoint private equity firm (2010) and since 2015 by a US-based investment company, KKR. Thus the most important food safety certification service in Britain, the BRC Global Standard, has become financialised.
52 Information about the Responsible Fishing Ports Scheme is on the Seafish website, www.seafish.org.
53 The four trade organisations which established SALSA are the British Retail Consortium, the Food and Drink Federation, the National Farmers Union and the British Hospitality Association. Information about SALSA is available on its website, www.salsafood.co.uk. STS produces a *Code of Practice and Technical Standard for Food Processors and Suppliers to the Public Sector*, its 8th issue dated 2013 (checked in 2018); information on its website www.sts-solutions.co.uk. Another standard which has been used by some seafood companies is EFSIS, originally the European Food Safety Inspection Service, now operated by service company SAI Global.
54 Information about the MSC/ASC chain of custody is on the MSC website, www. msc.org which also contains listings of certified suppliers at http://cert.msc.org/supplierdirectory.
55 The case is reported in two items on the BBC website, 'Rats and maggots found at Brookenby fish company', 29 September 2010 and 'Maggot fish factory boss given suspended sentence', 25 October 2010.

References

Alasalvar C, Garthwaite T & Öksüz A 2002, 'Practical evaluation of fish quality', in *Seafoods: Technology, Quality and Nutraceutical Applications*, Alasalvar C & Taylor T, eds., Springer Verlag, Berlin/Heidelberg/New York.

Album G 2010, *Survey of the Trade Flow in the Fisheries Sector in Asia: Analysis for the Norwegian Ministry of Fisheries and Coastal Affairs*, Friends of the Earth Norway/WWF Norway, Oslo.

Almond S & Thomas B, eds., 2011, *UK Sea Fisheries Statistics 2010*, National Statistics & Marine Management Organisation, Newport & London.

Aquatic Water Services Ltd 2015, *Summary Report: Review of Approaches for Establishing Exclusion Zones for Shellfish Harvesting Around Sewage Discharge Points*, www.food.gov, Wadebridge.

Archer M & Denton JW 2002, *Survey of Good Manufacturing Practice Standards in the UK Fish Industry*, Sea Fish Industry Authority, Edinburgh.

Archer M, Edmonds M & George M 2008, *Thawing Seafood*, Sea Fish Industry Authority, Edinburgh.

Archer M, Watson R & Denton JW 2001, *Fish Waste Production in the United Kingdom: The Quantities Produced and Opportunities for Better Utilisation*, Sea Fish Industry Authority, Edinburgh, Seafish Report Number SR537.

Archer M, Watson R, Garrett A & Large M 2005, *Strategic Framework for Seafood Waste Management*, Sea Fish Industry Authority, Grimsby, Report SR574.

Balcombe J 2016, *What a Fish Knows* Oneworld Publications, London.

Banks R 1988, *Fish Processing in the UK: An Economic Analysis*, Sea Fish Industry Authority, Edinburgh.

Bayliss P 1996, 'Chemistry in the kitchen: fish and fish products', *Nutrition & Food Science*, vol. 96, no. 1, pp. 41–43.

Braithwaite V 2010, *Do Fish Feel Pain?* Oxford University Press, Oxford.

Bremner HA 2002, 'Understanding the concepts of quality and freshness in fish', in *Safety and quality issues in fish processing*, Bremner HA, ed., CRC Press/Woodhead Publishing, Boca Raton/Cambridge.

Brown A 2009, *2008 Survey of the UK Seafood Processing Industry*, Sea Fish Industry Authority, Edinburgh.

Burgess G 1972, 'What price quality?', *Fish Industry Review*, vol. 2, no. 2, pp. 2–3.

Burgess GHO, Cutting C, Lovern JA & Waterman JJ 1965, *Fish Handling and Processing* HMSO, Edinburgh.

Cabello FC 2006, 'Heavy use of prophylactic antibiotics in aquaculture: a growing problem for human and animal health and for the environment', *Environmental Microbiology*, vol. 8, no. 7, pp. 1137–1144.

Campos CJA, Kershaw S, Morgan OC & Lees DN 2017, 'Risk factors for norovirus contamination of shellfish water catchments in England and Wales', *International Journal of Food Microbiology*, vol. 241, no. 16, January, pp. 318–324.

Carleton C, Cappell R, Graham I & Marshall D 1999, *Port Markets Strategy Study*, Nautilus Consultants and Sea Fish Industry Authority, Edinburgh, Seafish Report No SR528.

Carpenter G 2017, *Not in the Same Boat: The Economic Impact of Brexit across UK Fishing Fleets*, New Economics Foundation, London.

Caswell JA & Henson SJ 1998, 'Interaction of private and public food quality control systems in global markets', in *Globalisation of the Food Industry: Policy Implications*, Loader RJ, Henson SJ & Traill WB, eds., Centre for Food Economics Research, Department of Agriculture and Food Economics, University of Reading, Reading.

Cato JC 1998, *Seafood Safety: Economics of Hazard Analysis and Critical Control Point (HACCP) Programmes*, Food and Agriculture Organization of the United Nations, Rome, Fisheries Technical Paper 381.

Cefas 2011, *Investigation into the Levels of Norovirus in Influent and Treated Wastewater Samples from a Sewage Treatment Works*, Food Standards Agency, London.

Clarke S 2009, *Understanding China's Fish Trade and Traceability Systems, Hong Kong*, Traffic East Asia, Hong Kong.

Codex Alimentarius 2009a, *Code of Practice for Fish and Fishery Products*, World Health Organization and Food and Agriculture Organization of the United Nations, Rome.

Codex Alimentarius 2009b, *Food Hygiene (Basic Texts)*, 4th edn, Codex Alimentarius Commission Joint FAO/WHO Food Standards Programme, Rome.

Cole DW, Cole R, Gaydos SJ, Gray J, Hyland G, Jacques ML, Powell-Dunford N, Sawjney C & Au WW 2009, 'Aquaculture: environmental, toxicological and health issues', *International Journal of Hygiene and Environmental Health*, vol. 212, no. 4, pp. 369–377.

Compassion in World Farming 2009, *The Welfare of Farmed Fish*, CIWF, Godlaming.

Connell JJ 1987, 'New developments in the marketing of fish', *Food Marketing*, vol. 3, no. 1, pp. 118–129.

Coull J 1999, 'Changing balance of fish production in Scotland', *Marine Policy*, vol. 23, no. 4–5, pp. 347–358.

COWI Consulting Engineers and Planners 2000, *Cleaner Production Assessment in Fish Processing*, United Nations Environmental Programme (UNEP) and Danish Environmental Protection Agency, Paris/Copenhagen.

Curtis H & Barr R 2012, *2012 Survey of the UK Seafood Processing Industry*, Sea Fish Industry Authority, Edinburgh.

Curtis H, Moran Quintana M & Milliken K 2017, *UK Seafood Processing Sector Labour*, Sea Fish Industry Authority, Edinburgh.

Curtis HC 2000, *2000 Survey of the Fish Processing Industry*, Sea Fish Industry Authority, Edinburgh.

Curtis HC, Alva ML & Martin AA 2005, *Economics of Quality at Sea for Nephrops*, Sea Fish Industry Authority, Edinburgh.

Curtis HC & Bryson J 2002, *Costs and Earnings of the UK Sea Fish Processing Industry*, Sea Fish Industry Authority, Edinburgh.

Curtis HC & Martin AA 2003, *Economics of Quality at Sea*, Sea Fish Industry Authority, Edinburgh.

Curtis HC & White R 2005, *2004 Survey of the UK Fish Processing Industry*, Sea Fish Industry Authority, Edinburgh.

Cutting CL 1955, *Fish Saving: A History of Fish Processing* Leonard Hill, London.

Damsgård B 2008, 'Husbandry techniques and fish quality', in *Improving Farmed Fish Quality and Safety*, Lie Ø, ed., Woodhead Publishing & CRC Press, Great Abington & Boca Raton FL.

Davies SJ 2008, 'Colouration and flesh quality in farmed salmon and trout', in *Improving Farmed Fish Quality and Safety*, Lie Ø, ed., Woodhead Publishing & CRC Press, Great Abington & Boca Raton FL.

De Rozarieux N 2011, *A Review of English Fish Markets*, Department for Environment, Food and Rural Affairs, London, Fishing for the Markets Work Package 5.

De Rozarieux N 2015, *Potential Implications of the Landing Obligation on Onshore Seafood Supply Chains in the UK, Report Commissioned by Sea Fish Industry Authority*, Tegen Mor Fisheries Consultants, St Ives.

Deere C 1999, *Eco-labelling and Sustainable Fisheries*, IUCN and FAO, Washington and Rome.

Denton JW 1991, *Billingsgate Market Study Interim Report*, Sea Fish Industry Authority, Edinburgh, Consultancy Report No 31.

Denton W 2003, 'Fish quality labelling and monitoring: getting it right at the start', in *Quality of Fish from Catch to Consumer: Labelling, Monitoring and Traceability*, Luten JB, Oehlenschläger J & Ólafsdóttir G, eds., Wageningen Academic Publishers, Wagengingen.

Done HD, Venkatesan AK & Halden RU 2015, 'Does the recent growth of aquaculture create antibiotic resistance threats different from those associated with land animal production in agriculture?', *The AAPS Journal*, vol. 17, no. 3, pp. 513–524.

Doré B, Keaveney S, Flannery J & Rajko-Nenow P 2010, 'Management of health risks associated with oysters harvested from a norovirus contaminated area, Ireland, February-March 2010', *Eurosurveillance*, vol. 15, no. 19, May.

Eddie GC 1971, 'Fish inspection and quality control – are formal systems needed?', *Fish Industry Review*, vol. 1, no. 2, pp. 19–23.

EFSA 2005, 'Opinion of the Scientific Panel on contaminants in the food chain on a request from the European Parliament related to the safety assessment of wild and farmed fish', *The EFSA Journal*, vol. 236, pp. 1–118.

EFSA 2009, 'General approach to fish welfare and to the concept of sentience in fish: scientific opinion of the panel on animal health and welfare', *The EFSA Journal*, vol. 954, pp. 1–27.

EFSA 2012, 'Update of the monitoring of levels of dioxins and PCBs in food and feed', *EFSA Journal*, vol. 10, no. 7, p. 2832.

EFSA 2016, 'Technical specifications for a European baseline survey of norovirus in oysters', *EFSA Journal*, vol. 14, no. 3, p. 4414.

EFSA Panel on Biological Hazards (BIOHAZ) 2012, 'Scientific opinion on norovirus (NoV) in oysters: methods, limits and control options', *EFSA Journal*, vol. 10, no. 1, p. 2500.

EFSA Panel on Contaminants in the Food Chain (CONTAM) 2016, 'Statement on the presence of microplastics and nanoplastics in food, with particular focus on seafood', *EFSA Journal*, vol. 14, no. 6, p. 4501.

Engelhard GH 2008, 'One hundred and twenty years of change in fishing power of British North Sea trawlers', in *Advances in Fisheries Science 50 Years on from Beverton and Holt*, Payne A, Cotter J & Potter T, eds., Blackwell Publishing, Oxford.

Espe M 2008, 'Understanding factors affecting flesh quality in farmed fish', in *Improving Farmed Fish Quality and Safety*, Lie Ø, ed., Woodhead Publishing & CRC Press, Great Abington & Boca Raton FL.

EUMOFA 2013, *Price Structure in the Supply Chain for Fresh Cod in the United Kingdom*, European Market Observatory for Fisheries and Aquaculture Products, Brussels.

Eurogroup for Animals 2018, *Looking Beneath the Surface: Fish Welfare in European Aquaculture*, Eurogroup for Animals, Brussels.

European Commission 2018, *Report from the Commission to the European Parliament and the Council on the Possibility of Introducing Certain Requirements Regarding the Protection of Fish at the Time of Killing*, European Commission, Brussels.

European Commission Directorate-General for Fisheries 1999, *Memorandum Submitted by Directorate-General XIV (Fisheries) to House of Commons Agriculture Committee Enquiry into Sea Fishing*, HMSO, London.

European Commission Directorate-General for Fisheries and Maritime Affairs 2010, *Ex-post Evaluation of the Financial Instrument for Fisheries Guidance (FIFG) 2000–2006*, European Union, Luxembourg.

European Commission Directorate-General for Health and Food Safety 2017, *Welfare of Farmed Fish: Common Practices During Transport and Slaughter*, European Commission, Brussels.

Farm Animal Welfare Committee 2014a, *Opinion on the Welfare of Farmed Fish*, Department for Environment, Food and Rural Affairs, London.

Farm Animal Welfare Committee 2014b, *Opinion on the Welfare of Farmed Fish at the Time of Killing*, Department for Environment, Food and Rural Affairs, London.

Farm Animal Welfare Council 1996, *Report on the Welfare of Farmed Fish*, FAWC, Tolworth.

FAWC 2009, *Farm Animal Welfare in Great Britain: Past, Present and Future*, Farm Animal Welfare Council, London.

Flannery J, Keaveney S, Rajko-Nenow P, O'Flaherty V & Doré W 2012, 'Concentration of Norovirus during wastewater treatment and its impact on oyster contamination', *Applied and Environmental Microbiology*, vol. 78, no. 9, pp. 3400–3406.

Flannery J, Rajko-Nenow P, Winterbourn JB, Malham SK & Jones DL 2014, 'Effectiveness of cooking to reduce norovirus and infectious F-specific RNA bacteriophage concentrations in *Mytilus edulis*', *Journal of Applied Microbiology*, vol. 117, no. 2, pp. 564–571.

Flear F 1973, 'Production management', *Fish Industry Review*, vol. 3, no. 4, pp. 6–9.

Food Standards Agency 2017, *Regulating Our Future: Why Food Regulation Needs to Change and How We Are Going to Do It*, FSA, London.

Food Standards Scotland 2017, *Regulatory Strategy*, Food Standards Scotland, Aberdeen.

Fraser O & Sumar S 1998, 'Compositional changes and spoilage in fish: an introduction', *Nutrition and Food Science*, vol. 98, no. 5, pp. 275–279.

Garrett A 2011, *2010 Survey of the UK Seafood Processing Industry: Summary Report*, Sea Fish Industry Authority, Edinburgh.

Graham M 1943, *The Fish Gate* Faber and Faber, London.

GVA James Barr 2014, *The Crown Estate Shellfish Site Leases Rent Review*, GVA James Barr, Glasgow.

Harris R & Robinson C 2000, *Efficiency in the UK Fish Processing Sector 1974–1995*, Centre for the Economics and Management of Aquatic Resources, University of Portsmouth, Portsmouth, CEMARE Research Paper 146.

Hassard F, Sharp JH, Taft H, LeVay L, Harris JP, McDonald JE, Tuson K, Wilson J, Jones DL & Malham SK 2017, 'Critical review on the public health impact of norovirus contamination in shellfish and the environment: a UK perspective', *Food and Environment Virology*, vol. 9, no. 2, pp. 123–141.

Haugh H 2000, 'Modernisation in a traditional industry', *Journal of Small Business and Enterprise Development*, vol. 7, no. 3, pp. 220–227.

Hernández Serrano P 2005, *Responsible Use of Antibiotics in Aquaculture*, Food and Agriculture Organization of the United Nations, Rome, Fisheries Technical Paper 469.

Hill RG & Coutts JA 1986, *Fish Quality: A Survey of UK Ports*, Sea Fish Industry Authority, Hull, Internal Report No. 1293.

Hobbs JE, Fearne, A. & Spriggs, J 2002, 'Incentive structures for food safety and quality assurance: an international comparison', *Food Control*, vol. 13, no. 2, pp. 77–81.

Hopper AG, Batista I, Nunes ML, Abrantes J, Frismo E, Van Slooten P, Schelvis-Smit AAM, Dobosz E, Miguez Lopez E, Cibot C & Beveridge D 2003, 'Good manufacturing practice on European fishing vessels', in *Quality of Fish from Catch to Consumer: Labelling, Monitoring and Traceability*, Luten JB, Oehlenschläger J & Ólafsdóttir G, eds., Wageningen Academic Publishers, Wageningen.

Horne J 1971, *Some Notes on Fish Handling and Processing*, Torry Research Station, Aberdeen.

Hough J & Presland A 2000, *European Structural Funds*, House of Commons Library, London.

Huss HH 1995, *Quality and Quality Changes in Fresh Fish, FAO Fisheries Technical Paper 348*, Food and Agriculture Organization of the United Nations, Rome.

Huss HH, Ababouch L & Gram L 2004, *Assessment and Management of Seafood Safety and Quality*, Food and Agriculture Organization of the United Nations, Rome, 444.

Huss HH, Reilly A. & Ben Embarek PK 2000, 'Prevention and control of hazards in seafood', *Food Control*, vol. 11, no. 2, pp. 149–156.

Hutter BM 2011, *Managing Food Safety and Hygiene: Governance and Regulation as Risk Management* Edward Elgar, Cheltenham.

Jacobs M, Ferrario J & Byrne C 2002, 'Investigation of polychlorinated dibenzo-*p*-dioxins, debenzo-*p*-furans and selected coplanar biphenyls in Scottish farmed Atlantic salmon (*Salmo salar*)', *Chemosphere*, vol. 47, no. 2, pp. 183–191.

Jacobs MN, Covaci A & Schepens P 2002, 'Investigation of selected persistent organic pollutants in farmed Atlantic salmon (Salmo salar), salmon aquaculture feed, and fish oil components of the feed', *Environmental Science and Technology*, vol. 36, no. 13, pp. 2797–2805.

James R, Archer M, Henderson J & Garrett A 2011, *Resource Maps for Fish across Retail & Wholesale Supply Chains*, Waste & Resource Action Programme (WRAP), Banbury.

Joint FAO/NACA/WHO Study Group 1999, *Food Safety Issues Associated With Products From Aquaculture*, World Health Organization, Geneva, WHO Technical Report Series 883.

Joseph M & Findlater A 1996, *1995 Survey of the UK Sea Fish Processing Industry*, Sea Fish Industry Authority, Edinburgh.

Knowles TG, Farrington D & Kestin SC 2003, 'Mercury in UK imported fish and shellfish and UK-farmed fish and their products', *Food Additives and Contaminants*, vol. 20, no. 9, pp. 813–818.

Kose S 2011, '2011, "On-board fish processing"', in *Fish Processing: Sustainability and New Opportunities*, Hall G, ed., Wiley-Blackwell, Chichester.

Laird LM 1999, 'Impact of the quality movement on salmon farming in Scotland and the development of standards for organic aquaculture', in *Towards Predictable Quality: Abstracts of Contributions Presented at the International Conference Aquaculture Europe 99, Trondheim, Norway, August 7–10 1999*, Laird LM & Reinersten H, eds., European Aquaculture Society, Oostende.

Le Guyader FS, Bon F, DeMedici D, Parnaudeau S, Parnaudeau S, Bertone A, Crudeli S, Doyle A, Zidane M, Suffredini E, Kohli E, Maddalo F, Monini M, Gallay A, Pommepuy M, Pothier P & Ruggeri FM 2006, 'Detection of multiple noroviruses associated with an international gastroenteritis outbreak linked to oyster consumption', *Journal of Clinical Microbiology*, vol. 44, no. 11, pp. 3878–3882.

Little DC, Milwain GR & Price C 2008, 'Pesticide contamination in farmed fish: assessing risks and reducing contamination', in *Improving Farmed Fish Quality and Safety*, Lie Ø, ed., Woodhead Publishing & CRC Press, Great Abington & Boca Raton FL.

Lowther JA, Gustar NE, Powell AL, Hartnell RE & Lees DN 2012, 'Two-year systematic study to assess norovirus contamination in oysters from commercial harvesting areas in the United Kingdom', *Applied and Environmental Microbiology*, vol. 78, no. 16, pp. 5812–5817.

Lumley A, Piqué JJ & Reay GA 1929, *The Handling and Stowage of White Fish at Sea*, HMSO, London, DSIR Food Investigation Special Report No 37.

Lund V & Mejdell CM 2006, 'A warm heart for a cold fish: moral obligations and welfare considerations in fish farming', in *Ethics and the Politics of Food*, Kaiser M & Lien ME, eds., Wageningen Academic Publishers, Wageningen.

Mackie IM 1997, 'Methods of identifying species of raw and processed fish', in *Fish Processing Technology*, 2nd edn, Hall GM, ed., Blackie Academic and Professional, London.

MAIB 2018, *MAIB Annual Report 2017*, Marine Accident Investigation Branch, Southampton.

Mansfield B 2003, 'Fish, factory trawlers, and imitation crab: the nature of quality in the seafood industry', *Journal of Rural Studies*, vol. 19, no. 1, pp. 9–21.

Marine Management Organisation, DEFRA, Marine Scotland & Welsh Government 2015, *Review of the European Fisheries Fund in the UK 2014*, Department for Environment, Food and Rural Affairs, London.

Martinsdóttir E 2002, 'Quality management of stored fish', in *Safety and Quality Issues in Fish Processing*, Bremner HA, ed., CRC Press/Woodhead Publishing, Boca Raton/Cambridge.

Martinsohn JT, Geffen AJ, Maes GE, Nielsen EE, Ogden R, Waples RS & Carvalho GR 2011, 'Tracing fish and fish products from ocean to fork using advanced molecular technologies', in *Food Chain Integrity: A Holistic Approach to Food Traceability, Safety, Quality and Authenticity*, Hoorfar J, ed., Woodhead Publishing, Cambridge.

Mavromatis P & Quantick P 2002, 'Histamine toxicity and scombroid fish poisoning: a review', in *Seafoods: Technology, Quality and Nutraceutical Applications*, Alasalvar C & Taylor T, eds., Springer Verlag, Berlin/Heidelberg/New York.

Merritt JH 1969, *Refrigeration in Fishing Vessels* Fishing News Books, London.

Metcalfe JD 2009, 'Welfare in wild-capture marine fisheries', *Journal of Fish Biology*, vol. 75, no. 10, pp. 2855–2861.

Mills A 1987, *A Technical Study of Fish Processing in the UK*, Sea Fish Industry Authority, Hull, Technical Report 328.

Millstone E & Lang T 2018, *Weakening UK Food Law Enforcement: A Risky Tactic In Brexit*, Food Research Collaboration, London.

Mood A 2010, *Worse Things Happen at Sea*, Fishcount.

Mood A & Brooke P 2012, *Estimating the Number of Farmed Fish Killed in Global Aquaculture Each Year*, Fishcount, London.

Myers MA & Wilson P 1990, *Impact Study: EC Health and Hygiene Regulations*, Sea Fish Industry Authority, Edinburgh.

Nautilus Consultants 2001, *The Development of the Seafood Scotland Vessel Quality and Hygiene Scheme*, www.nautilus-consultants.co.uk, Edinburgh.

Nautilus Consultants 2003, *FIFG Processing Study: Study on the Impact of FIFG Measures on the Fish Processing Industry Summary Report*, http://ec.europa.eu/fisheries/publications/studies_reports, accessed 14 July 2009, Brussels.

Noble S, Moran Quintana M & Curtis H 2017, *Seafood Processing Industry Report*, Sea Fish Industry Authority, Edinburgh.

Oehlenschläger J & Harrison D 2003, 'Fish quality awards and labels in Germany and Great Britain', in *Quality of Fish from Catch to Consumer: Labelling, Monitoring and Traceability*, Luten JB, Oehlenschläger J & Ólafsdóttir G, eds., Wageningen Academic Publishers, Wageningen.

Pennington TH 2014, '*E. coli* 0157 outbreaks in the United Kingdom: past, present, and future', *Infection and Drug Resistance*, vol. 7, pp. 211–222.

Reid C & Robinson C 2003, 'Fish processing in the UK 1907–1990: Evidence from the Census of Production', in *Politics and People in the North Atlantic Fisheries Since 1485, Studia Atlantica 5*, Starkey D, ed., North Atlantic Fisheries History, Hull.

Rico A, Phu TM, Satapornvanit K, Min J, Shahabuddin AM, Henriksson PJG, Murray FJ, Little DC, Dalsgaard A & Van den Brink PV 2013, 'Use of veterinary medicines, feed additives and probiotics in four major internationally traded aquaculture species farmed in Asia', *Aquaculture*, vol. 412–413, no. 1, November, pp. 231–243.

Robb D 2002, 'The killing of quality: the impact of slaughter procedures on fish flesh', in *Seafoods: Technology, Quality and Nutraceutical Applications*, Alasalvar C, ed., Springer Verlag, Berlin/Heidelberg/New York.

Robinson R 1998, *Trawling: The Rise and Fall of the British Trawl Fishery* University of Exeter Press, Exeter.

Romero J, Feijoó CG & Navarrete P 2012, 'Antibiotics in aquaculture – use, abuse and alternatives', in *Health and Environment in Aquaculture*, Carvalho ED, David GS & Silva RJ, eds., In Tech, Rijeka, Croatia.

Rosson P 1975, 'Fish marketing in Britain: structural change and system perform-ance', *European Journal of Marketing*, vol. 9, no. 3, pp. 232–249.

Sandberg MG, Gjermundsen A, Hempel E, Olafsen T, Curtis HC & Martin A 2004, *Seafood Industry Value Chain Analysis: Cod, Haddock and Nephrops*, Seafish, Edin-burgh.

Saphir N 2002, *Review of London Wholesale Markets*, Department for Environment, Food and Rural Affairs, London.

Scoging AC 1991, 'Illness associated with seafood', *Communicable Disease Report*, vol. 1, no. 11, pp. R117–R122.

Seafish 1987, *Guidelines for the Handling of Fresh Fish by Retailers*, Sea Fish Industry Authority, Edinburgh.

Seafish 2004, *Enhancing the Value and Improving Sustainability of the Primary Catch Sector By Raising Product Quality*, Sea Fish Industry Authority, Edinburgh.

Seafish 2008, *Options to Improve Catch Quality on Inshore Vessels, Research and Develop-ment Fact Sheet*, Sea Fish Industry Authority, Grimsby.

Seafish 2012, *Parasites in Fish*, Sea Fish Industry Authority, Grimsby.

Seafish 2016, *Fishmeal and Fish Oil Facts and Figures*, Sea Fish Industry Authority, Edinburgh.

Shepherd CJ, Monroig O & Tocher DR 2015, *Production of High Quality, Healthy Farmed Salmon from a Changing Raw Material Base, With Special Reference To A Sus-tainable Scottish Industry*, Scottish Aquaculture Research Forum (SARF).

Shewan JM, Macintosh RG, Tucker CG & Ehrenberg ASC 2012, 'The development of a numerical scoring system for the sensory assessment of the spoilage of wet white fish stored in ice', *Journal of the Science of Food and Agriculture*, vol. 4, no. 6, pp. 283–298.

Sleator A 1997, *E. coli Foodborne Disease*, House of Commons Library, London, Research Paper 97/63.

Spears K 2000, *Official Control of Foodstuffs: Evaluation of Policy, Practice and Performance in the UK by Case Study*, South Bank University, London.

Stevenson P 2007, *Closed Waters: The Welfare of Farmed Atlantic Salmon, Rainbow Trout, Atlantic Cod and Atlantic Halibut*, Compassion in World Farming and World Society for the Protection of Animals, Godalming & London.

Sumner J, Ross T & Ababouch L 2004, *Application of Risk Assessment in the Fish Indus-try*, Food and Agriculture Organization of the United Nations, Rome.

Symes D 1988, *The Inland Wholesale Fish Markets: 3. The Distribution of Fresh Fish*, Sea Fish Industry Authority and University of Hull, Edinburgh & Hull, Technical Report 347.

Symes D & Maddock S 1989, 'The role of inland wholesale markets in the distribu-tion of fresh fish in the UK', *British Food Journal*, vol. 91, no. 5, pp. 7–12.

Symes DG & Haughton GF 1987, 'Decline and continuity in the Humber fish indus-try', *Geography*, vol. 72, no. 2, pp. 241–242.

Tam CC, Larose T & O'Brien SJ 2014, *Costed Extension to the Second Study of Infec-tious Intestinal Disease in the Community: Identifying the Proportion of Foodborne Disease in the UK and Attributing Foodborne Disease by Food Commodity*, University of Liver-pool, Liverpool.

Taylor RA 1960, *The Economics of White Fish Distribution in Great Britain* Duckworth, London.

The Food Ethics Council & Pickett H 2014, *Farm Animal Welfare: Past Present and Future*, RSPCA, London.

Tinarwo A 2006, 'The ethical slaughter of farmed fish', in *Ethics and the Politics of Food*, Kaiser M & Lien ME, eds., Wageningen Academic Publishers, Wageningen.

Tower J 1986, *Fleetwood Port Study Group: Working Paper on Fish Processing and Marketing*, Sea Fish Industry Authority, Industrial Development Unit, London, Internal Report No. 1300.

University of Newcastle-upon-Tyne & Poseidon Aquatic Resource Management 2004, *The Fish Meal and Fish Oil Industry: Its Role in the Common Fisheries Policy*, European Parliament, Luxembourg.

Waterman JJ 1987, *Freezing Fish at Sea: A History* HMSO, London.

Watterson A, Little D, Young JA, Boyd K, Azim E & Murray F 2008, 'Towards integration of environmental and health impact assessments for wild capture fishing and farmed fish with particular reference to public health and occupational health dimensions', *International Journal of Environmental Research and Public Health*, vol. 5, no. 4, pp. 259–277.

Westrell T, Dusch V, Ethelberg S, Harris J, Hjertqvist M, Jourdan-da Silva N, Koller A, Lenglet A, Lisby M & Vold L 2010, 'Norovirus outbreaks linked to oyster consumption in the United Kingdom, Norway, France, Sweden and Denmark, 2010', *Eurosurveillance*, vol. 15, no. 12.

Whittle KJ 1997, 'Opportunities for improving the quality of fisheries products', in *Seafood from Producer to Consumer: Integrated Approaches to Quality, Proceedings of the International Conference on the Occasion of the 25th Anniversary of the WEFTA, Held in Noordwijkerhout, The Netherlands, 13–16 November 1993*, Luten JB, Børresen T & Oehlenschlägen J, eds., Elsevier, Amsterdam.

Willoughby S 1999, *Manual of Salmonid Farming* Fishing News Books, Blackwell, Oxford.

Wright M, Palmer G, Shahriyer A, Williams R & Smith R 2013, *Assessment and Comparison of Third Party Assurance Schemes in the Food Sector: A Common Framework – Final Report for the Food Standards Agency*, Greenstreet Berman, London, CR2435 R2 V8.

Young JA 1987, 'Marketing in a dynamic environment: an overview of the UK fish processing industry', *Food Marketing*, vol. 3, no. 1, pp. 144–161.

5 Governing seafood consumption

Introduction

The governance of food consumption, as outlined in Chapter 2, consists of the complex interplay of delivery systems with various messages competing to influence what people take from them. The outcomes vary with the social capacities, values and experiences which consumers carry when making their food decisions. In this chapter the views of consumers about seafood are examined in the context of the health and ethical discourses around them.

As with the other stages of the supply chain, there have been great changes in the consumption end of the seafood supply chain during the six decades since the middle of the twentieth century. Along with the general retail transformation and changes in foodservice, a major new influencing factor from the middle of this period was the development of nutritional knowledge about the benefits of seafood and the resulting public health advice. Somewhat later, the environmental discourse on sustainability issues came into play.

The results in terms of both attitudes towards seafood and its consumption have been varied as reflected in the views of people in the industry. Some were upbeat about seafood being seen as a healthy food and about developing consumer interest in provenance:

> People are generally buying more fish, it's more popular than it was because of the health aspect, because people are made aware of the health aspects of eating fish.
>
> (Director, medium company 1)

> I don't say that the majority of people but there is a much larger group now, a growing group of people who actually care about where their food comes from. We see this now, there's a lot of pubs and restaurants actually showing the origin of their meat and we see it with fish as well.
>
> (Manager, trade organisation 2)

But negative perceptions were also reflected: 'there's an awful lot of people eating no fish' (Trade organisation representative 3) and that many customers 'were concerned about how to cook it and they didn't want to touch it an awful lot' (Category technologist, major retailer). Other views expressed about consumers included their desire for convenience, the impact of the recession and both conservatism and adventurousness in seafood choices.

These themes are picked up in the section on consumer attitudes. But first, the scene is set by an outline of seafood consumption patterns over the period. The chapter then shows how the public health message about seafood was developed before exploring the complexity of consumer thoughts on this subject and the approaches used by those aiming to affect them, that is to exercise a governance influence.

Seafood consumption trends

Changing consumption of seafood in Britain over the years is shown in Table 5.1 as the average per person for food eaten at home. It covers the period from 1945 to 2015 at five-year intervals with official statistics providing more details for the later decades.[1] In the immediate post-war period, there was high consumption, equivalent to an annual average of 13.5 kilograms per person each week at a time when fishing stocks that had recovered during the fighting yielded abundant supply while meat was still scarce. However, in the mid-1950s it started to fall with the increased availability of alternative proteins. The decline continued in the following decades to reach a very low point in the mid-1970s when it was at an annual average of 6.6 kilograms. Thereafter, consumption of seafood rose again to reach a relatively high point in the mid-2000s when it was up to 8.7 kilograms. It then fell back again in the late 2000s and at 2010 was at 7.9 kilograms per person. Subsequently, it stabilised during the mid-2010s at a level similar to that of the 1990s, around 7.5 kilograms per person for home consumption. However, the 2016/2017 figure has again reduced which may have been due to the impact of food price inflation after the fall in the value of sterling

More striking than the overall change in quantity is the variation in the type of seafood consumed over the decades illustrated in Figure 5.1. White-fish bought for cooking has steadily decreased and so has 'takeaway fish' presumably mainly white from fish and chip outlets. By contrast, there has been a big increase in the category of ready meals and other prepared fish products, possibly containing much whitefish. Consumption of oily fish has had a changing trajectory: at the beginning of the period much was sold fresh, probably consisting mainly of herring but this then declined and was at very low levels from the mid-1970s for a considerable time (which, probably not coincidentally, overlapped with the closure of the British herring fishery 1977–1983). Subsequently while purchase fresh, that is for home cooking has remained low, overall consumption of oily fish increased significantly over the 1990s and 2000s, reflecting the greater availability of salmon and, although not itemised in the data set, possibly also mackerel.[2] Another feature has been the rising trend of shellfish consumption over most of the period,

Table 5.1 Seafood consumption 1945–2015 (grams per person per week)

Year	Whitefish fresh	Whitefish total	Oily fish fresh	Oily fish total	Shellfish	Tinned/ bottled fish	Ready meals and other products	Take-away fish	Total fish and fish products
1945	NA	NA	NA	NA	NA	NA	NA	NA	261
1950	89	NA	16	NA	3	NA	NA	NA	188
1955	90	NA	11	NA	3	NA	NA	NA	169
1960	67	NA	9	NA	3	NA	NA	NA	166
1965	64	NA	7	NA	2	NA	NA	NA	164
1970	50	NA	6	NA	1	NA	NA	NA	152
1975	37	54	2	9	2	20	23	20	128
1980	32	54	3	11	3	19	27	22	137
1985	29	53	3	11	4	21	33	18	140
1990	24	48	3	12	5	30	33	18	147
1995	20	41	4	14	6	31	30	25	147
2000	15	37	4	18	6	33	28	21	143
2005/2006	19	29	7	26	12	38	49	13	167
2010	15	24	5	24	13	28	51	10	151
2015	12	21	4	26	10	26	52	11	146

Source: author based on National Food Survey for 1945–2000 (previously at www.defra.gov.uk/statistics/files/defra-stats-family-food-nfs-allfood.xls, now archived) and the Expenditure and Food Survey (EFS) from 2001 onwards with data from 1974 to 2011 (previously at www.defra.gov.uk/statistics/foodfarm/food/familyfood, now archived) which from 2008 became known as the Living Costs and Food module of the Integrated Household Survey.

Notes

NA: Not available.

'Total whitefish' covers fresh (including chilled), frozen, dried, salted and smoked fish.

'Fresh oily fish' refers to what in National Food Survey was called 'fresh fat fish', and is assumed to have the same meaning as 'herring and other blue fish, fresh or chilled' in the terminology of the later surveys. Total oily fish includes fresh, frozen, dried, salted and smoked 'blue' fish and also fresh and frozen salmon.

'Takeaway fish' combines the survey categories 'takeaway fish' and 'takeaway fish meals'.

'Total fish and fish products' is based on the sub-total columns 'whitefish total' and 'oily fish total' ignoring the preceding column in each case, plus the columns for shellfish onwards, for the years from 1975 onwards (they may differ from the sum of the preceding relevant columns because of rounding); it exceeds the sum of the previous columns for earlier years because it includes seafood categories for which separate information is not available.

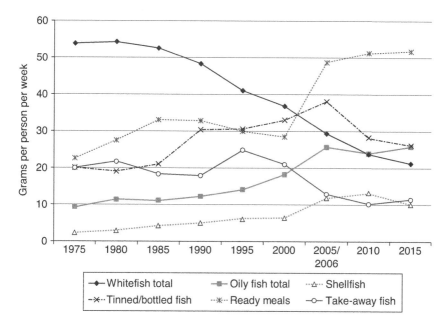

Figure 5.1 Type of seafood consumed 1975–2015.

Source: author based on National Food Survey for 1980–2000 and from 2001 the Expenditure and Food Survey (EFS) from 2008 known as the Living Costs and Food Survey.

but which has reversed since the late 2000s recession. Canned fish although with shifts over time has maintained its role and fits with the same convenience-seeking trend of ready meals that has been occurring across the food system. This has been associated with broad social changes, particularly the participation of all adults in the labour market (Fofana 2001).

Seafood eaten outside the home also needs to be taken into account. Official statistics for the period from 2000/2001 to 2015 show that it added an average of between 21 and 28 grams per person weekly, the most popular categories being fried fish and fish-based sandwiches. A different source deploying market research shows that in 2014 the largest species/categories of seafood eaten out were fish fingers and cod in that order, followed a long way down by haddock and then scampi (langoustines). Looking at this in conjunction with retail consumption, more than half the total intake of fish fingers was via foodservice as was one-third of cod, haddock and mussels and most – 80% – of the calamari (squid) consumed (Seafish 2016). Adding the average amount eaten outside to home consumption figures the amount per person was estimated at 161 grams per person in 2015 bringing the total annually to 8.2 kilograms.

Demand for fresh fish is relatively sensitive to price changes and income (DEFRA 2001; Fofana 2001). The early 1990s recession reduced the market for fish generally and has been specifically documented for salmon and trout (Seafish 1999; Shaw & Egan 1996). The reduction in the late 2000s and early 2010s can be related to the general economic downturn from 2008. Expenditure on fish as a proportion of spending on food gradually increased over the decade 2001 to 2011 from 4.3% to 5.2% while analysis of the impact of price rises between 2007 and 2012 showed that fish was one of the foods bought less and also traded down, that is cheaper types bought (DEFRA 2013; Elliott, Hargreaves & Pilgrim 2012). However, an analysis using an index incorporating a price element showed a converse picture in which to a certain extent volume decline represented the replacement of greater quantities of the least costly types of seafood, herrings and cheaper whitefish, by smaller quantities of higher value items (Reid 2003). In all of these shifts, one of the factors at work is that fish is always in competition with other sources of protein.

The consumption averages considered so far gloss over many social differences some of which can be seen from the more detailed data available for later periods. One factor is age: people in older age groups on average eat more seafood than younger ones although amounts vary from year to year and fall back somewhat in the oldest 75 plus group. This broad picture has held true over a long period as illustrated in Figure 5.1 (in two sections because the age groups used in the surveys changed).[3] Similar findings of higher seafood consumption by older people have been noted in other countries (Brunsø 2003).

Income is the second aspect examined and given the fact already noted that seafood consumption is sensitive to price it might be expected that there would be a relationship with how much is purchased. However, the interesting point to note from Figure 5.3 is that there is in fact no income gradient to overall consumption. Analysis of different types of seafood does show some impact such as greater consumption of ready meals by those in the lowest income band while in the highest there is most consumption of oily fish. But the extent of differences varies in each of the selected years and, in any case, there is considerable diversity within each seafood type with both more and less expensive options in most of them, for example, oily fish covers salmon at one end and herring and sardines at the other.

The third social variable examined is whether or not the household includes any children. Figure 5.4 demonstrates that children in the household were associated with much less seafood eating than occurred in adult-only households. Within seafood spending, households with children consumed a higher proportion in the form of ready meals and tinned fish while childless ones took more in forms which would need cooking from scratch, but the differences are not great.

What we learn from considering these social variables is that they affect seafood consumption in complex ways. They suggest that the quantity and type of seafood eaten might alter over the life course along with changes in age, income and whether there are children in the household. Further,

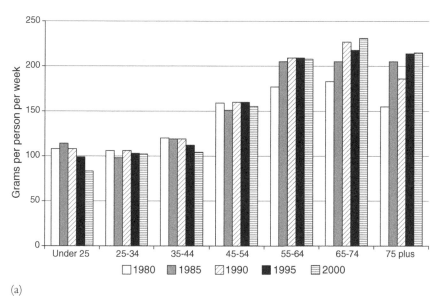

(a)

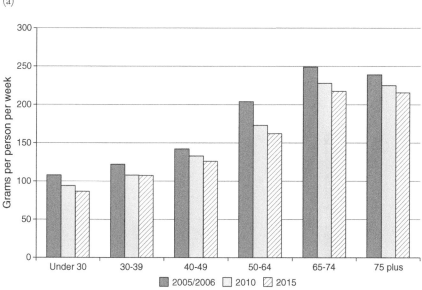

(b)

Figure 5.2 Seafood consumption by age: Figure 5.2a Seafood consumption by age 1980–2000 and Figure 5.2b Seafood consumption by age 2005/2006–2015.

Source: author based on National Food Survey for 1980-2000 and from 2001 the Expenditure and Food Survey (EFS) from 2008 known as the Living Costs and Food Survey.

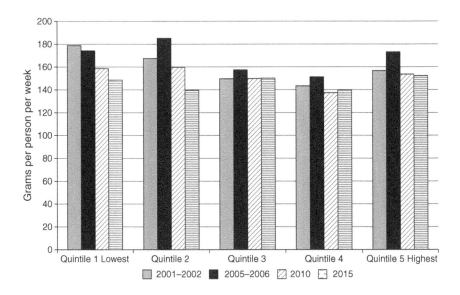

Figure 5.3 Seafood consumption by income quintile for selected years.

Source: author based on National Food Survey for 1980–2000 and from 2001 the Expenditure and Food Survey (EFS) from 2008 known as the Living Costs and Food Survey. 2001/2002 is the earliest year for which this income information is available.

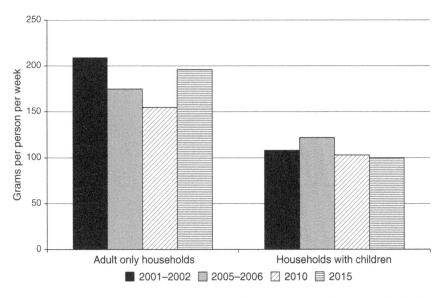

Figure 5.4 Seafood consumption in households with and without child(ren) for selected years.

Source: author based on National Food Survey for 1980–2000 and from 2001 the Expenditure and Food Survey (EFS) from 2008 known as the Living Costs and Food Survey. 2001/2002 is the earliest year for which this household composition information is available.

seafood is a category that covers a great range of species and many types of preparation which elicit different consumption preferences. These social factors then interact with any attempts to influence the consumption of seafood.

Continuing the examination of seafood consumption, the national statistics do not tell us about species apart from picking out salmon and the broad distinction between white, other oily fish and shellfish. They do not indicate which of them are in the tinned fish, takeaways and ready meals categories. The question of species is important from the supply and sustainability perspectives and equally for the public health implications of consumption.

Most of the fish eaten in Britain has for a long time consisted of a narrow range of species, strongly related to supply availability and initially based on what was caught by British fishers, predominantly whitefish and herring. But specifics have changed over time and also have a regional dimension. In the mid-1980s, the top three species sold in all the major inland wholesale markets in England were cod, plaice and haddock in that order but in Glasgow it was whiting, haddock and lemon sole (Symes D 1988). Research carried out in North East England in a similar timeframe confirmed that half of the consumption of the households involved consisted of cod, haddock and plaice (Gofton & Marshall 1991). An examination of species used in catering in the mid-1990s determined that fish and chip establishments mainly sold cod and haddock, hotels salmon, trout, herring and mackerel while restaurants were big on sole, prawns and trout (Maddock & Young 1995). Half of retail sales of fresh fish around this time were accounted for by cod, haddock and salmon (Carleton et al. 1999). By 2012, the most popular, the 'big five', had become tuna, cod, salmon, haddock and prawns (Future Foundation 2012; Seafish 2012). In 2015, salmon overtook tuna in the top spot (Seafish 2017). The whole period thus shows significant changes and an extension in the range.

There are some additional features of consumption which are not reflected in quantitatively-oriented sources. One is a long-established pattern of fish purchasing taking place mainly on Tuesdays and Fridays (Taylor 1960); more recently there has been a return to fish for Friday dinners (Future Foundation 2012). Overlaying such patterns is the response to seasons and weather, familiar to some of the research participants in the impact on demand:

> The market demand is asymmetric. You've got a big demand for certain products, salmon, getting towards Christmas, pick-up towards Easter, if it's sunny in the summer, you've got barbecues to deal with.
> (Production manager, large aquaculture company)

> It's the weather, it's all to do with the weather, to do with rain. If it could rain at tea time, they won't go to the chip shop.
> (Managing director, small company 3)

A picture of the seafood being eaten having been established, the rest of this chapter turns to possible influencing factors. There are clearly many economic, social and cultural dimensions in play in relation to consumption, so the impact of governance factors can only partially explain such a complex phenomenon. Nevertheless, from commercial, sustainability and public health perspectives efforts are ongoing to persuade and shape consumption and sometimes avoidance of seafood in its various forms.

The discourse of seafood and health

Development of a message – fish and health

The main governance intervention to impact on seafood consumption has been the development of a message about its health benefits. This section traces the basis for the public advice on the nutritional benefits provided by seafood, recounts which agencies were involved in promulgating it and shows how the initiative has been allowed to pass to the seafood industry.

The first interview quotation of this chapter states a commonplace of the seafood industry about the healthiness of fish, an opinion which is widely shared by the public. But the characterisation of fish as having specific health benefits and the official promulgation of this view is quite recent, particularly so in the case of shellfish. In the early period of the development of nutritional science, fish was seen mainly as a source of protein. To an advocate it was 'first class protein', the special merits of which were:

> its unequalled value for invalids, due to its digestibility; its value for sedentary workers, who need to nourish their nervous systems without providing too much muscular energy; and its value as a change, and as an easily digested high-grade supplement to an ordinary diet.
>
> (Graham 1943, p. 23)

In the early 1960s, the dietary value of fish was considered to be for protein, for calcium especially if the bones of tinned varieties were eaten, and in 'fat' (previous term for what is now described as 'oily') fish, for vitamins A and D (Pyke 1961; White Fish Authority 1959). Nearly two decades later, nutritional information about fish was much the same, protein, trace elements and certain vitamins (Yudkin 1977). It should be noted that none of these sources mentioned shellfish. Thus, while considered a valuable food, fish was seen as nutritionally comparable with other sources of protein with which it competed.

But starting in the mid-1980s, a transformation in thinking started with the publication of research showing that fish consumption could reduce the risks of heart disease (Burr et al. 1989; Kromhaut, Bosschieter & Coulander 1985). The operative factor was elucidated to be omega-3 polyunsaturated fatty acids (PUFAs) which are essential to human physiology and have to be obtained through diet; of their three forms, alpha-linolenic acid is available from plant sources but the other two, eicosapentaenoic acid and docosahexaenoic acid, are found only in marine animals. Although some studies have found no benefit from fish-eating in relation to cardiovascular disease (Ascherio et al. 1995; Kühn et al. 2013; Morris et al. 1995) the weight of evidence indicates that omega-3 PUFAs can play an important role in cardiovascular health, notably in reducing the risk of cardiac mortality, and that fish is the best means of consuming them (He et al. 2004; Mozaffarian & Wu 2011).

Following this lead, there have been many investigations into other possible links between fish consumption and a range of health issues. Fish-eating has been associated with reduced risks in relation to age-related macular disorder, a major cause of blindness (Chong et al. 2009; Christen et al. 2011) and of dementia or cognitive decline in older people (Albanese et al. 2009; Cederholm 2017; Kesse-Guyot et al. 2011; Morris et al. 2016). It has been shown to reduce the risk of depression in European countries (Li, Liu & Zhang 2016) although not in other parts of the world (Albanese et al. 2012) and among young Australian women but not men (Smith et al. 2014). Fish eaten during pregnancy has been associated with higher assessed intelligence in children subsequently (Hibbeln et al. 2007). Although earlier studies looking at various cancers had mixed results, more recent meta-reviews indicate that fish consumption lowers risks for breast, colorectal and liver cancers (Huang, Duan & Hu 2015; Wu et al. 2012; Zheng et al. 2013). The picture in relation to endometrial, prostate and other cancers that have been investigated is unclear with varied findings. Attention has also focused on omega-6 to omega-3 ratios and the argument that they are far too high in western diets and a major factor in the obesity problem, meaning that the former should be reduced and omega-3 intakes should be increased (Mukhopadhyay 2012; Simopoulos 2008; Simopoulos 2016). With so many demonstrated benefits, it is not surprising that fish has almost been elevated to a health food, indeed (in the form of salmon) a superfood (Pratt & Matthews 2004). There have been some dissenting views (Hooper et al. 2006; Jenkins et al. 2009) but the majority expert opinion is that fish-eating is beneficial to human health (De Roos, Sneddon & Macdonald 2012; Kris-Etherton, Harris & Appel 2002; Ruxton et al. 2007; Sanders 2012).

The evidence of benefits conferred by fish consumption and the link with omega-3 led to another seemingly much more numerous set of investigations in which marine oils derived from fish have been tested for preventive or therapeutic purposes in connection with a range of conditions. Such material, much more manageable than fish with its diversity of species and modes of preparation, could be treated in the same way as a drug, lending itself to the gold standard procedure of the randomised controlled trial (RCT) in which typically fish oil is administered in the form of capsules to an intervention group while control groups receive a vegetable oil placebo or another therapy. This ignores the fact that the impact of omega-3, a nutrient and not a drug, cannot be isolated from its interaction with the rest of the diet whether comparing individuals in a local area or trials in different countries (De Lorgeril & Salen 2002; James et al. 2018).

The results of these omega-3 trials have been mixed: some recorded benefits such as reducing mortality in people with known cardiovascular disease, ameliorating rheumatoid arthritis symptoms and reducing wheeze and asthma in children of women who received supplements during pregnancy (Akbar et al. 2017; Artham et al. 2008; Bisgaard, Stokholm & Chawes 2016; Siscovick et al. 2017); others showed little effect or were subsequently assessed as producing insufficient evidence due to study design issues. A recent large meta-analysis covering trials of omega-3 supplements on patients with diagnosed heart disease found that they delivered no significant benefit, contrary to previous positive conclusions (Aung et al. 2018) while another systematic review covering people both with and without prior disease concluded that taking omega-3 supplements did not reduce the risk of heart disease, stroke or death (some of the trials had included fish-eating not just supplements but their numbers were judged too low for conclusions to be reached) (Abdelhamid et al. 2018). In relation to dementia and cognitive impairment, an overview of systematic studies and meta-analyses involving administration of discrete nutrients (various individual vitamins or omega-3) concluded that there was insufficient evidence that any lowered risks of these problems but that fish consumption, where reported, did do so (SACN 2018). The National Institute for Health and Care Excellence (NICE) did in the past include a recommendation for some patients who had recently had a heart attack to be given omega-3 but this has now been superseded. In various clinical guidelines current at the time of writing recommendations are that patients be advised to eat fish regularly (twice weekly including oily fish) but that omega-3 supplements should not be routinely advised.[4] Thus the great weight of evidence is that taking omega-3 supplements is not beneficial.

Research directly comparing fish consumption with fish oil would be useful but has generally been lacking. However, a small study solved the control issue by supplying trout twice weekly to patients assigned to the relevant group while the others received omega-3 capsules; it found that while both interventions lowered total cholesterol, fresh fish resulted in a preferable lipid profile (Zibaeenezhad et al. 2017). A limitation of this study is that it just assessed a clinical marker and does not extend to whether there were any differences in eventual outcomes.

The general trend of advice coming from research has been to recommend fish-eating but to indicate that supplements are acceptable for people who do not wish to consume it or for whom it is desirable to further boost omega-3 levels. As with supplementation in general, a much better impact is obtained from foods containing the desired nutrients than from taking these in isolation. Fish in addition to omega-3 continues to be valuable for protein and is an important source of vitamins and minerals including selenium and iodine, varying with each species (Sheeshka & Murkin 2002; Simopoulos 1997).

Communicating messages about seafood and health

The material about the potential impacts of fish on health noted so far were in the academic and professional sphere so the next thing to consider is what kind of knowledge then percolated to the wider public and how it was disseminated. There have been two routes, one in the form of advice from public bodies, the other as commercial promotion.

The public-private body Seafish reflected the new research about fish and health at an early stage, in a document of the late-1980s. After listing the then conventional advantages of low-fat protein and the range of other nutrients in seafood, it stated: 'The regular consumption of fish can reduce the chances of heart disease' (Seafish 1987, para 3.7). However, this information was not yet in the general public arena.

Chapter 2 noted that after the end of wartime food policy, official advice about what to eat was slow to re-emerge but that expert bodies, the Committee on Medical Aspects of Food Policy (COMA) and then the Scientific Advisory Committee on Nutrition (SACN), provided nutrition information to the government. COMA had produced reports in 1974 on coronary heart disease and in 1984 on cardiovascular disease, neither of which mentioned fish. The first official advice about fish-eating came in the third COMA report on dealing with this disease area (Committee on Medical Aspects of Food Policy 1994), reflecting recent research at the time. It recommended an increase in the population average consumption of long chain omega-3 PUFA from about 0.1 grams/day to about 0.2 grams/day (1.5 g/week) and translated this into clear nutritional advice: 'We recommend that people eat at least two portions of fish, of which one should be oily fish, weekly' (para S.3.7.3). But as one element in what was a very technical report it received no special publicity and no effort was made at the time to convey the message more widely.

This changed as the Food Standards Agency (FSA), established in 2000 a few years after the publication of the 1994 COMA report, developed its nutritional role. Its website publicised the COMA recommendation, advising consumers to eat two portions of fish a week, one of them oily. This enabled Seafish and seafood companies to cite government advice to eat fish regularly whereas previously the COMA report existed as advice to the government rather than to the public.

A separate strand of official consideration regarding health aspects of fish consumption had meanwhile developed which concerned potential risks from contaminants. In the previous chapter, it was noted that contaminants may be present in both wild and farmed fish. The issue was first examined by the then Ministry of Agriculture, Fisheries and Food and the results published in a Food Surveillance Information Sheet in 1998; reassuringly, it stated that dietary intake of the elements examined were within safety limits and posed no risk to those eating even large amounts of seafood.

The FSA took up the issue and following research on imported seafood which found relatively high levels of mercury in certain species, issued interim advice to restrict marlin, shark and swordfish consumption in 2002. Next, after a risk assessment by the Committee on Toxicity (COT), came revised precautionary advice in 2003 for pregnant and breastfeeding women and those intending to conceive to limit tuna consumption; they and also children were still recommended to avoid the previously established mercury-risk species. A full risk/benefit review was then requested and jointly carried out by COT and the Scientific Advisory Committee on Nutrition (SACN) which had replaced COMA. The judgement was that the advantages of fish-eating outweighed the risks but that care should be taken by certain identified population groups (Scientific Advisory Committee on Nutrition and Committee on Toxicity 2004). The conclusion that the benefits of seafood are greater than the possible risks has subsequently been widely endorsed by others, including the World Health Organisation (FAO & WHO 2011; Mozaffarian & Rimm 2006; Santerre 2010).

Consequently in June 2004 the FSA issued a revised version of its advice, now combining the positive health and negative risk avoidance messages. This was a complicated script which said that pregnant and breastfeeding women plus girls and women of child-bearing age should eat one to two portions of oily fish weekly but that other women plus men, in general, could eat as many as four. Further, all children plus pregnant women were advised not to eat the higher risk three species at all; in addition, pregnant women only were told to limit tinned tuna consumption to four cans per weeks. This new complexity did not change the usual form in which fish consumption advice was generally promulgated being in the simplified 'two portions of fish a week, one of which should be oily' version.

The next issue to affect the advice on seafood consumption being given to the public was sustainability. Concerns about wild fish stocks at a time when the CFP was perceived as failing to protect them collided with the two portions a week advice. A notable input to the debate was a report which estimated that 33 million more portions of oily fish would be needed each week to increase consumption levels to the recommended amount for British adults, hugely adding to pressure on stocks (Royal Commission on Environmental Pollution 2004). Concern about additional strains on fishery resources, especially given their importance as a food source in poorer countries, surfaced along with doubts about the feasibility of increasing supply sustainably to fill the gap between current fish-eating and the levels that would match the advice (Brunner et al. 2009; Foster 2005; House of Commons EFRA Committee 2009; Jenkins et al. 2009). To put two portions a week in the context of current consumption levels, with a conventional serving taken as 140 g, the total quantity of seafood used would have to almost double compared to what it has been in recent years.

FSA documentation had referred to some informal contact with DEFRA about the implications of the consumption advice for fish stock sustainability saying the latter had provided reassurances as they formulated it, that is suggesting the issue had been taken into account. However, in response to environmentally motivated criticisms of the fish consumption advice, the Agency undertook a public consultation in 2009 in which the health benefits of eating fish were reiterated but views were invited on how this could be combined with sustainability considerations (Food Standards Agency 2009). As a result, the last version of the Agency's fish consumption advice was issued later that year; two portions a week, one oily, was still the recommendation (with the same safety provisos for certain population groups) but for the first time shellfish were included. There had been industry lobbying for the inclusion of shellfish and Seafish organised a review which compiled information about the omega-3 content of certain shellfish species. The advice was amplified by statements asking consumers to use sustainability criteria in their choices, including certification, and to eat a wider range of species but it did not address the general issue of the potential difficulties of assuring supply should the twice-a-week advice be universally adopted. The quandary, dealing with the potential contradiction of simultaneously pursuing a healthy diet and a healthy environment, remains and can only be solved by managing fisheries and aquaculture in ways that fully respect the needs of the environment as discussed in a previous chapter.

Before the seafood advice was formulated, fish consumption had featured very little in general government nutritional advice. Seafood was not mentioned in the 1978 general recommendations. The first public health strategy, *Health of the Nation*, was published in 1992; its dietary focus was on reducing saturated fat consumption. The next one, *Saving Lives: Our Healthier Nation*, included diet among the changes recommended for reducing the risk of developing coronary heart disease or stroke, calling for the 'increased consumption of such foods as fruit, vegetables, and oily fish' without any elaboration as to quantities (Department of Health 1999, para 6.12). Neither of the next two public health documents, a 2004 public health White Paper nor the 2010 public health strategy of a new government mentioned fish. So it was left to the FSA to promulgate the public health message to England and Wales that fish is a healthy food.

The situation was different elsewhere because following the outcome of a special enquiry (the James Report), a nutritional plan, *Eating for Health: A Diet Action Plan* for Scotland (known as the *Scottish Diet Action Plan*) was produced and this did have a seafood consumption target namely that oily fish should double to an average of 88 grams weekly with whitefish consumption continuing at the same level. The report also contained a number of statements about the need to increase fish consumption along with fruit, vegetables and cereals so giving it full prominence as part of a healthy diet (Scottish Office 1993; Scottish Office 1996). The next public health strategy for Scotland reaffirmed those same targets (Scottish Office 1999). Northern Ireland too had a food and nutrition strategy, and this included the two-a-week, one oily fish target (Food and Nutrition Strategy Group 1996). The difference between the approach or at least emphasis in the official documents produced for England and Wales compared to those for Scotland and Northern Ireland illustrates the way political or value choices may be intertwined with nutrition science.

Political choices were apparent again when the 2010 Coalition Government removed the FSA's public health nutrition responsibilities in England and Wales and returned them to the Department of Health (DH) in 2010. For these parts of the country food information moved to the DH and later to the Public Health England pages of the general government website but it was greatly reduced compared to the previous FSA coverage and without specific material about seafood. Public Health England (PHE) was a new executive agency of government created in a reorganisation of the National Health Service (NHS); it has stated its information mission as providing 'evidence-based advice to government, local government, the NHS, public health professionals and the public' (Public Health England 2016a, p. 6), an interesting order of priority in which the public comes last. The FSA by contrast had affirmed its purpose as putting the consumer first and being open and accessible and independent.

Conveying general nutritional advice started in 1994 with 'The Balance of Good Health', visualised as a plate divided into five unequally-sized wedges. One was 'meat, fish and other alternatives' and the commentary advised: 'Fish includes frozen and canned fish such as sardines and tuna, fish fingers and fish cakes. Aim to eat at least one portion of oily fish such as sardines and salmon each week'. This was the first form in which the 'eat fish' advice was placed in general nutritional guidelines and it presumably was based on what was in the COMA report of the same year but unlike the latter's twice a week was here rendered as at least once. The Balance of Good Health was not conceived as advice for the public but as 'information for educators and communicators' and it was with this statement that it was initially reproduced by the FSA.[5]

However, this was an interim measure and the FSA subsequently revised the advice and the infographic to produce the Eatwell Plate as information for the public. Fish was again included in the protein wedge. The Eatwell Plate incorporated very limited verbal material but, as described already in this chapter, the FSA then had specific and detailed seafood advice elsewhere on its website. It is unclear where responsibility for the Eatwell Plate rested immediately after the FSA's nutrition remit was removed but following further government changes, responsibility for it was transferred to Public Health England (PHE) in 2013.

As updating was needed, PHE undertook a thorough revision of the Eatwell Plate, relaunched in 2016 as the Eatwell Guide. It is still in the shape of a plate with wedges of different sizes representing food groups but with more text which in the case of proteins includes the phrase 'two portions of sustainably sourced fish per week, one of which is oily'. In the accompanying booklet, there is a little more detail: the portion size of 140 grams, the statement that most people should eat more fish but also an indication that limiting consumption of certain types of seafood is recommended and advice to seek more information on the NHS website (Public Health England 2016b). In the Live Well section of the NHS website, there is indeed the full information formerly provided by the FSA and then periodically reviewed. It sets out details of levels of omega-3 fatty acids in different species of fish and shellfish and recommendations about how much of each type it is advisable to eat, with specific guidance for pregnant and breastfeeding women; there is also a small section about sustainability issues. PHE had considered the question of sustainability in relation to the new dietary advice by commissioning a review from the Carbon Trust; this reported that the Eatwell Guide has a potentially 32% lower environmental impact than current British diets, but it did not deal with issues around the production of seafood (Carbon Trust 2016).

When Public Health England was given responsibility for the Eatwell guidelines this was for the whole of the UK; hence the booklet states that it has been produced 'in association with the Welsh Government, Food Standards Scotland and the Food Standards Agency in Northern Ireland' (front page footer). These different agency names reflect the diversity of how nutrition responsibilities have been allocated in the four constituent parts of Britain following the 2010 changes in the FSA's remit, something with implications for how fish-eating advice is conveyed to the public. In Northern Ireland, responsibility initially remained with the FSA but nutritional information was placed on the province's general government website, NI Direct. Subsequently, the information has returned to the FSA website for Northern Ireland only but it consists only of the bare Eatwell Guide information and there are no links to or advice about obtaining more information regarding fish.[6] At the same time, NI Direct as well as retaining the outdated Eatwell Plate at the time of writing had the fish-eating advice that was formerly on the FSA site but without certain additions about safety and sustainability that are included in the NHS source. Nutritional policy for Wales passed to the Welsh Government but its website only has links to the Eatwell Guide and no additional information about fish. The FSA in Scotland retained nutrition responsibilities in 2010 but a few years later this was superseded by a new body, Food Standards Scotland (FSS) created in the *Food (Scotland) Act 2015*. Prior to this legislation, the FSA in Scotland website retained the fish advice which the UK-wide FSA had produced before its nutritional remit was taken away. With the production of the revised Eatwell Guide, information about this is on the FSS website including a Scottish version of the accompanying booklet which has the same link to the NHS Live Well site for detailed information about fish consumption (Food Standards Scotland 2016). There is also some fish information in the 'Five Food Groups' section of the FSS website but not the full version. If this paragraph is confusing, it accurately represents the situation over advice to the public about seafood since responsibility for nutrition was removed from the FSA.

The upshot is that the consumer advice about seafood with all its complications such as which fish and shellfish contain high omega-3 levels, which have higher levels of pollutants and should be eaten less frequently and the special advice for pregnant women which was once provided from a single point, the Food Standards Agency, now has to be located by varied paths which must be inhibitory to access by most members of the public. Only for Scotland is nutritional advice found on a food website, that of the FSS, but it is not as full as it used to be. The detailed information about fish is on the NHS website, the main purpose of which for most users is probably as a guide to healthcare services and factual source about health problems and it may not be the place where most people would seek dietary advice; further, one has to be motivated to follow links from the 'Eat well' page to the 'Fish and shellfish' page and to locate more information about oily fish from a link on the 'Superfoods' page.

When the FSA still had a public health role it was in a position to be the authoritative source of nutritional advice to consumers. A general assessment of the FSA during that time found it to be consumer-focused and noted its investment in consumer education initiatives (Brooker & Taylor 2009) while from a business perspective the organisation was seen as providing expert advice on nutrition (Connect Research 2010). Since the reduction in the FSA's responsibilities there is no single obvious place for the public to seek nutritional advice. The Scientific Advisory Committee on Nutrition continues to function, providing guidance for government agencies, but it does not have a public face. Thus the mechanism for dealing with new information and giving consumers up-to-date health advice regarding seafood is unclear.

However, there is no vacuum because the seafood industry is ready with its own messages about the benefits of seafood. Seafish, as the industry promoter, appropriately spreads the word about seafood and health on its website which is oriented to its industry constituency as well as being a voice to the wider public. As already noted, the organisation referred to fish reducing the risk of heart disease as early as 1987 and has been swift to mention other potential health benefits on its changing pages. Its 'Eat 2 portions of seafood' page available in 2013, for example, began by stating that not only is seafood delicious, it is 'one of the healthiest things you can put on your plate', going on to list not just the range of nutrients and by then well-known heart disease prevention but many other areas where there had been some positive finding in the medical science literature, including for skin health, inflammatory bowel disease and depression.[7] The language is promotional, quite different from the way such topics are mentioned in the NHS fish advice. The same text was on the Seafish website in 2018, now entitled 'Health benefits' with the same sub-headings such as 'Your skin looks great' and 'boost your brainpower'. The 2013 page linked to a Norwegian-produced promotional document, still available, entitled *A Sea of Health: Nutritional Content and Health Benefits of Seafood*. Seafish has funded and again publishes on its website reports commissioned by the trade association the Shellfish Association of Great Britain about the nutritional benefits of shellfish, a formal one supplied with five pages of references and a less formal one more geared to lay members of the public and including traffic light ratings for nine species (Woolmer 2010a; Woolmer 2010b).

From 2014 to mid-2016, Seafish ran a campaign entitled 'Superfishoil', concentrating on the omega-3 health message and linking it with various promotional activities through social media and the national press. An undated document on the Seafish website available in 2018 headed 'Omega-3 as easy as ABC' presents three groups of species as 'superior', 'excellent' and 'good' sources of omega-3: the types of fish that figure in official advice such as herring and salmon are in the 'superior' group while at the lower end whitefish which are not normally recommended as omega-3 sources, though nutritious in other ways, are in the 'good' group; the quantity of omega-3 per 140 grams serving is given next to each type of fish in milligrams and while it is all factual information the numbers may distract the casual reader from appreciating that the sources listed as 'good' have very low levels of omega-3 and so failing to prioritise oily fish as recommended in public health sources.

In 2017, Seafish launched a new campaign called 'Fish 2 a Week' intended to increase seafood consumption by focusing on the official recommendation and the advantages to health it can bring. Information about this campaign is on the offshoot Seafish website, Fish is the Dish, which is directed to the public (and discussed later in this chapter) where there is an interesting piece called 'Now That's what I Call Omega-3' in which fish prepared in various ways is presented in a game show top-20 format with omega-3 quantities again in milligrams starting with the lowest, cod and sole, and culminating with mackerel at number one, an imaginative way of getting across positive messages about fish but again potentially confusing in relation to ensuring that one portion weekly should be oily. Thus the benefits of fish-eating have morphed from a public health message into a marketing tool.

Counter-messages?

Not all the news about fish is upbeat and certain problems have been raised from time to time. However, few of them have apparently made much impact on the public.

One longstanding issue was the cholesterol content of prawns which had routinely led dieticians to advise restricted consumption. However, research has shown that intake of the dietary cholesterol in cold-water prawns did not lead to elevated levels of cholesterol in the trial participants and it is now accepted that this is not a problem for people needing to control their cholesterol levels (Isherwood et al. 2010).

With the increase of aquaculture production, the question of whether there is a difference in nutritional benefit from farmed compared to wild fish has been raised, specifically, whether there is a lower proportion of polyunsaturated fatty acids than in wild equivalents (Denton & Lacey 1991). One factor is the deliberate substitution of vegetable oil for fish oil in feed in order to reduce reliance on wild fish and improve sustainability. Some comparative research has indeed found relatively lower omega-3 levels in the species examined (Fuentes et al. 2010; George & Bhopal 1995; Karapanagiotidis et al. 2006). Farmed salmon was found to have considerably lower levels of vitamin D than the wild form in one study (Lu et al. 2007). But other work has indicated that farmed fish can provide as much or even more of the beneficial fatty acids (Cahu, Salen & De Lorgeril 2004; Cole et al. 2009; Jensen et al. 2012; Nichols et al. 2014). None of this seems to have impinged on the consciousness of British consumers.

A specific aquaculture feed issue is the 2013 EU derogation which allows protein derived from pigs and poultry to be used in aquaculture as noted in Chapter 4. The FSA advice to ministers provided in advance of the negotiations leading to this change was that the UK should not support it on the grounds that a more precautionary approach was advisable and because of majority opposition to it from consumers canvassed in a specially commissioned study; it was also noted that the change could create difficulties for fish eaters who either do not eat meat or who avoid pork. From the documentation considered by the FSA, it appears that there was a difference of view between producer interests that favoured the relaxation (one reason being better sustainability if substituted for wild fish in feed) and consumer interests that opposed it. The UK government abstained when the issue was considered by the relevant EU Committee but the change was approved by a qualified majority vote and has come into effect.[8] As the previous chapter noted, the Scottish salmon industry has so far decided not to use feeds including pig or poultry meal, but it is unclear whether UK trout farmers following the same Code of Practice have followed suit. In any case, as allowed by the EU it is likely that imported farmed fish fed with such ingredients whether from EU countries or elsewhere have entered the UK food chain. Again, this has not become a public issue in Britain.

The existence of contaminants in fish has not been given much public attention in Britain either despite documented evidence about them indicated in the previous chapter. Indeed, official fish-eating advice includes warnings that pregnant and breastfeeding women should avoid certain types altogether and moderate amounts of certain others precisely because of the risk of contaminants. There is a contrast with public perceptions in the US where there is far greater concern over substances such as methylmercury in seafood. But there has been one notable exception when contaminants in fish did impinge on public consciousness in the UK. This was the publication of American research funded by the Pew Trust which stated that there were significantly higher levels of organochlorine contaminants, dioxins and PCBs, in farmed compared to wild salmon and that the problem was greater in European-reared fish, including from Scotland, than the products of either North or South America, so much so that it would be advisable not to eat it more often than once every two months (Hites et al. 2004). Furthermore, the article was not simply put out in a scientific journal, but rather the findings were deliberately publicised in an effective campaign that hit the headlines on both sides of the Atlantic. In response, the FSA stated on its website that the levels of contaminants shown in the study were within existing safety recommendations and that the benefits of eating salmon would outweigh the risks. As already noted, EFSA subsequently judged the difference between wild and farmed salmon insufficient to make a difference to human health (Luoma & Löfstedt 2007).

Whatever the negative effect on sales, as with most food scares, it was a temporary phenomenon. However, the impact on demand was sufficiently severe that several years later two of the research interviewees still felt very strongly about the article:

> Three years ago a ridiculous trust in America called the Pew Foundation came out with something totally, absolutely outrageous and decimated our industry for about six months.
>
> (Managing director, medium-large aquaculture company)

> Were the contaminants real, it would be a different case. But they weren't real, the whole thing was a pure fabrication. And it was about propaganda to attack an industry. The dishonesty of them.
>
> (Trader, medium-large company)[9]

In fact the Hites et al. study was not the first time that the issue of contaminants in farmed salmon had been raised in Britain and questions asked about the advice to consume it. A BBC 2 documentary in January 2001, *Warnings from the Wild: the Price of Salmon*, reported on some earlier research on the subject, indicating higher levels of contamination in farmed than wild salmon, associated with their feed.[10] However, this programme did not seem to make a particular public impact and no consequences seem to have followed.

The brief 2004 salmon crisis having passed, seafood was restored to its image of both health and safety. This does not seem to have been dented by an incident in which salmon was tainted by diesel and a wide recall actioned by the FSA in 2008 although the complexity of supply chains was such that salmon from one farm was implicated in 50 products sold by ten retail chains.[11] Neither did another incident in which a Michelin-starred restaurant was found to have been the site of one of the largest norovirus outbreaks ever recorded, affecting over 500 people and associated with contaminated shellfish (Health Protection Agency 2009). Two years later, an FSA-commissioned study reported that norovirus affected three-quarters of British-produced oysters, but neither the agency nor the NHS issued new advice for consumers who were simply expected to be aware of the risks in eating raw shellfish.[12] Neither of these official reports seems to have caused any particular anxiety for the public at large – most of whom do not of course habitually eat oysters or visit the country's top restaurants.

Impact of the seafood health message

The overall impact of the 'eat fish' health message on the British public is difficult to gauge due to limited research on the subject. Work carried out in 2001 gives an interesting perspective on consumer views about seafood and health at a time when the advice was relatively new. Those interviewed thought seafood to be a healthy choice compared to other proteins particularly because of its wild and natural associations. They linked health and food safety and many rated shellfish as unsafe because of food poisoning risks. The interviewees knew about and often mentioned omega-3 benefits but equally (rather in contradiction) low-fat qualities of seafood and they rated whitefish as the healthiest as well as the safest option (Gross 2001b). This suggests that the significance of the relationship between omega-3 fatty acids and oily fish had not yet been absorbed and that respondents were reflecting another aspect of nutritional guidance, namely emphasis on reducing fat intakes.

Some years later, research in Britain found that only 27% understood the two-a-week seafood message (compared to 77% for the five-a-day fruit and vegetable advice) with women and older people more aware than men and the young; however, nearly everyone knew that omega-3 fatty acids were beneficial and 61% identified them with oily fish (Future Foundation 2012). This indicates both a diffusion of the idea of health connected with seafood and the fact that what has been absorbed is not exactly in the official form and probably arises from various sources. More recent market research commissioned by Seafish reported that 28% of UK adults knew about the two-a-week advice, so the situation had not changed on that score, but it found that a bare quarter knew that eating fish would provide omega-3; this does not apparently mean that others did not know about omega-3, just that they did not necessarily connect it with consuming seafood.[13]

Knowledge about omega-3 without taking in the general seafood nutritional advice suggests that rather than being motivated by dietary recommendations relating to fish, people are responding to advertising about specific substances in the process that has been described as nutritionism, as discussed in Chapter 2; this in turn is linked to the supplements industry which markets various omega-3 products. A number of health claims related to omega-3 fatty acids have been made, some but not all of which have been upheld (EFSA 2011). The marketing of omega-3 supplements contradicts the message that we have seen coming from medical research which is that direct fish consumption is more beneficial than taking isolated nutrients.

The FSA role was pivotal in establishing the healthiness of fish-eating in the public mind because it stood as an objective source. But no active diffusion of the 'eat fish' health message was carried out by the FSA; for example it did not undertake an advertising campaign on this issue as it did in relation to salt reduction and its website, though designed at that time to be attractive to the public, may be presumed to have been used by only a minority of the population. Health and nutritional professionals may well have given the advice to their patients and clients, but this does not reach a mass audience. Rather, the seafood industry has been able to refer to the advice as coming from an authoritative body, the FSA, and absorb it into its promotional activity. Advice on marketing seafood proffered three decades ago, 'Nutrition is an aspect of quality that can distinguish a product from its competitors' (Nettleton 1985, p. 173) has been fully taken up by Seafish and the seafood industry, the competition being with other sources of protein, particularly meat.

The only British state exercise in promoting fish consumption has come from the Scottish Government which launched a campaign in 2009 and in the following year allocated £300,000 'to increase awareness of the health benefits of eating seafood and highlight the conservation credentials of Scotland's fishing fleet'. The money was allocated to Seafood Scotland, the industry-based organisation linked to Seafish, to be spent not only on promoting consumption but to developing market opportunities; thus the objective would seem to have been supporting producers at least as much as improving public health.[14]

This section has shown how the developing views of nutritionists and scientists, then policymakers and the seafood industry have created the widely accepted discourse of fish as a healthy food. Has this affected consumption? Some of the research interviewees thought so:

> The amount of fish has increased dramatically as people begin to realise the benefits of omega-3.
>
> > (Managing director, medium-large aquaculture company)

> Fish, seafood generally, up to the recession has enjoyed tremendous growth, as a protein source within the UK, fresh natural fish has enjoyed stronger growth than any other type of protein … [because] it ticks all the boxes of a healthy eating mindset.
>
> > (Industry advisor, trade organisation)

As noted in Chapter 2, there is some evidence that knowledge about healthy food recommendations positively influences consumption and that some campaigns have altered certain dietary behaviours (Wakefield, Loken & Hornik 2010; Wardle, Parmenter & Waller 2013) although no testing in relation to the 'eat fish' advice seems to have been done. Actual consumption is then affected by a range of social circumstances as shown by research in other European countries (Trondsen et al. 2003; Verbeke & Vackier 2005). The British population certainly has not adopted the two-a-week prescription en masse and successive results from the National Diet and Nutrition Survey have confirmed consumption to be well below this level (Bates et al. 2012, 2016; Roberts et al. 2018). An analysis focused on children showed that just under 5% ate fish and less than 2% consumed the full two-a-week (Kranz, Jones & Monsivais 2017). In a ten-year review of the Scottish Diet Action Plan, it was observed that consumption of oily fish had not increased despite the target to double it (failure was noted for most of the other dietary targets as well) (Lang, Dowler & Hunter 2006). A survey of children found that only 16–18% (depending on the age group) ate fish twice a week and similar proportions never ate it at all though over half of all in the 11 and over age groups knew about the fish-eating advice (British Nutrition Foundation 2013).

But if there were to be an effect it would be expected to develop gradually. The fish-eating advice was formalised in the mid-1990s and its dissemination has been gradual as it has not been the subject of a mass campaign. The National Food and Living Costs and Food Surveys show that average annual seafood consumption in each of the 1990s years ranged from 141 to 149 grams per person each week except for one exceptional year, 1995 when it was 158. Between 2001/2002 and 2009 the range was 170 with a peak from 2005/2006 to 2007 but after the turn of the decade it has reduced and from 2011 was back to the 1990s level. It is possible, therefore, that the message did have some effect and thus a governance outcome. It may, however, have been short-term, lacking in public reinforcements especially since the FSA's nutritional role ceased, and certainly overlaid by cost considerations once the economic downturn got underway. In any case, there are many other influences on seafood choices positive and negative than health advice and to these the next section turns.

Influences on consumer attitudes to seafood

Unlike the prescriptive nature of government agency advisories, an alternative approach aims to understand patterns of eating and non-eating of seafood by consumers in their own terms. In part an academic literature aiming to provide an analysis of attitudes and behaviour within the social sciences disciplines, there is also an agenda of producing information that will be useful for marketing purposes. Indeed, a variety of different approaches have been used in attempts to exercise governance upon consumption which are also examined in this section.

Research on attitudes and the dislike factor

One longstanding facet of the encounter with consumer views is recognition of a strand of strongly negative feeling about eating and/or cooking fish. Some of the research interviewees, as already indicated at the beginning of this chapter, mentioned such antipathies:

> … a lot of young people don't eat fish or are even prepared to try it.
> (Commercial manager, medium-large company)

> We're more comfortable going into a hotel restaurant, having somebody else cook it, not with taking it home and cooking it ourselves.
> (Trade organisation representative 1)

There is indeed a body of research that confirms these perceptions. It reflected and attempted to explain the long period of decline and low consumption of seafood in the 1970s and 1980s.

A study carried out in the late-1980s in North East England found that bones and 'offensive smell' were off-putting to many, that fish was thought to be troublesome to cook and the food most often rated as 'least enjoyed eating'. Equally important was showing how fish fitted into ideas about meal construction, as it was often considered to be less substantial or less suitable for main meals compared to meat while tinned fish was thought appropriate for sandwiches and light meals. Convenience was found to be particularly important to younger food decision-makers who liked frozen products. Fish was already thought of as a healthy food (this was a decade before 'eat seafood' advice began to be promulgated) but that did not override its lesser role and status in the food system. (Gofton & Marshall 1991; Marshall 1988, 1993).

Other research carried out in a similar time frame concentrated on pelagic fish. One found a generally negative attitude to these oily fish, another that herring was less liked than haddock because of its bones and cooking smell though found palatable either cooked or smoked, while very little mackerel was eaten at all (Baird, Bennett & Hamilton 1988; Marshall & Currall 1992). The interplay between positive and negative ideas about fish and the differential uses of fresh, frozen and canned types were echoed in research about a decade later (Leek, Maddock & Foxall 2000). Alternatively, the decline in fish-eating was attributed in a commercial analysis to the shift towards convenience foods, something that was relatively slow to develop with seafood (Mintel 2004). It seems to have remained the case that there are polarised tastes in relation to fish, reflected by one market research categorisation into three types of consumers: fish rejecters 20%; fish tolerators 70% and fish lovers only 10% (Porritt & Goodman 2005).

One factor not mentioned in these studies, but which can be added on the basis of evidence noted in the previous chapter, is the impact of variable quality before major improvements took place late in the twentieth century. Given that fresh, smoked and frozen fish were all negatively affected, many indifferent if not worse fish-eating experiences must have resulted, contributing to the lack of enthusiasm among many consumers and affecting knowledge and eating habits in succeeding generations. Poor quality may also have been a cause of smells that some people so dislike which are not experienced with adequately fresh fish.

All the same, fish has had a continual role in British eating patterns albeit as already noted a lesser one, implicitly in comparison with meat as the dominant protein of choice. The choice of species eaten, as seen earlier in the chapter, has varied over time and been obviously related to supply, from the domestic fishing industry, from its main processing output in forms of smoked fish and after canning technology had been mastered from the ready availability of tinned fish. But choices have also reflected cultural preferences and the reigning 'big 5' comprise two strands: the whitefish cod and haddock centrally associated with fish and chips (discussed in the next chapter) and three others, salmon, tuna and prawns, which have in common dense texture and pink-to-red flesh colour, qualities which position them as satisfactory alternatives to meat in the meal structure system. The prestige value of fresh salmon, a luxury item before farming brought availability and price within everyday reach, and the familiarity with canned salmon and tuna must also have played a part. Thus changes in consumption have resulted from the conjunction of supply and distribution factors with the social and cultural ideas of consumers.

Issues that have elicited more recent research on consumer preferences have been connected to certain categories of fish affected by new regulations. Thus a Seafish-commissioned survey at the beginning of the 2000s in preparation for the seafood labelling regulations showed that participants had a negative image of farmed fish (Gross 2001a). Another found poor perceptions of frozen compared to fresh fish although many people with this view nevertheless bought frozen seafood regularly (Nevin 2003). In the mid-2000s a study of English consumers focused on attitudes to previously-frozen then thawed fish prior to the introduction of further labelling rules which mandated the inclusion of such information. These attitudes were found to be negative: fillets labelled as thawed got lower ratings compared with the identical product assessed without such attribution (the survey also registered generally positive feelings about healthy seafood but costs and dislike of bones as the top reasons for non-consumption) (Altintzoglou et al. 2012). Another line of enquiry has been about consumer attitudes to organically farmed fish. EU-funded research in five countries including Britain found much scepticism about the concept because those questioned tended to think that 'organic' referred to a natural situation and therefore wild fish (Aarset et al. 2004). These snapshots, isolated pieces of information collected for different purposes, mainly commercial in nature, can only provide hints about what most people think about seafood.

Encouragement

The lack of enthusiasm for fish identified and noted as a barrier to consumption may be of concern for either commercial or public health reasons. Facing these attitudes, attempts to woo consumers into eating more seafood have taken various forms. Advertising was noted in the early 1990s as playing a small part, with a low overall ratio of advertising spend to sales but one which was greater than for the other fresh items (meat, fruit and vegetables) and with most of it promoting frozen products (LeGrand 1992).

Regardless of formal advertising, the use of various media in relation to food generally has become significant (Rousseau 2012). Celebrity chefs were credited by a couple of the research interviewees with a positive impact on consumption:

I think these TV chefs and BBC chefs have helped to some extent. I think that people are more aware of what to do with things, how to get the best of certain types of fish, how to put certain fish together to come out with a nice combination of things.

(Director, medium company 1)

… there's a definite Rick Stein effect…. For instance, if he spends ten minutes talking about Cornish sardines, the next day the fish shop down the road here, the fish man right up to the retailer would all say the next day, there are people definitely looking to try that fish, because they saw it on telly, they'll say, well I'll give that a go.

(Manager, trade organisation)

The credibility of other restaurateurs and television presenters was endorsed by restaurant customers according to research which quotes a fishmonger saying 'Delia [Smith] only had to mention monkfish and the very next day everyone was asking for some' and from a fishing agent: 'There was a massive upsurge in demand for dab as a result of Fish Fight and Jamie Oliver' (Fishing for the Markets 2011; Revill Nation Ltd 2011) while this same programme resulted in a sustained increase in demand for various minor species according to one major retailer (Sainsbury's 2013).[15] Celebrity chefs have had a growing influence, some linked to branded restaurants and other commercial products. Their television cooking programmes, while primarily used as entertainment, may also have an impact on broadening tastes and skills for at least a section of viewers (Caraher, Lang & Dixon 2000; Henderson 2011; Randall 1999; Rowe, Prestage & Cook 1999; Wood 2000). Market research has credited TV chef programmes as the biggest single influence on cooking fish (mother was well down the list, below experiences abroad and cookbooks) (Future Foundation 2012). The credibility of some chef personalities was expressed in the phrase 'Jamie says' (with reference to celebrity chef Jamie Oliver) attributed to focus group participants in some research about attitudes to seafood meaning that he was a trusted source of information, unlike the case with commercial interests or what participants might consider sensationalising media reports.[16]

Nevertheless, despite the anecdotal evidence of celebrity chefs' immediate influence, it seems unlikely that any individual programme would have a long-term effect; rather each adds to a generally positive perception of seafood, adding awareness of a greater range of species and confidence about cooking fish. The influence of TV is increasingly being shared with or may even come to be superseded by YouTube food channels, some involving the same big-name chefs, and food bloggers and the ability to keep returning to them, especially the latter, may make their impact longer-lasting.[17]

There are a very large number of seafood cookery books available, some linked with celebrity chefs, and the provision of seafood recipes is a common aspect of promotional strategy found on the websites of seafood suppliers who sell online. It is a sound approach because lack of recipe knowledge was identified as a barrier to fish consumption by a third of those questioned in one piece of research (Future Foundation 2012). Recipe display is a key method used by Seafish for promoting seafood consumption. From 2011 it has run the initiative 'Fish is the Dish' with its own website oriented to consumers, featuring recipes, competitions and items about seafood-related activities. At one time the site provided links to selected seafood suppliers but no longer does so. The project makes full use of social media in its mission to break down barriers of perceived difficulty and to showcase ways of cooking fish that will fit into busy lives. It has generated its own booklet consisting entirely of fish recipes produced by participant bloggers and arranged special events headed by celebrity chefs.[18] As already noted, Seafish material emphasises the health aspect and Fish is the Dish includes various pieces oriented to health issues including about omega-3 benefits but there is also much emphasis on the incentive of taste and provision of straight-forward recipes.

Another significant promotional effort run by Seafish is an annual Seafood Week each autumn, working with supermarket and foodservice partners for special promotions and using celebrity chefs to gain publicity. It ran from 2001 to 2008 (in the last year it was a Seafood Fortnight) and has resumed again from 2015. The activity is publicised on the Fish is the Dish website, reinforcing the impact. When in 2017 Seafish began its Fish 2 a Week campaign which aimed to increase consumption to meet the official nutritional advice it again used Fish is the Dish. An example of combining the Seafish promotional tools was provided by the 2017 Fish is the Dish Feed Your Mind campaign during that year's Seafood Week.

Fish is the Dish includes promotion directed at children. The educational programmes contain lesson plans and related material for primary schools geared separately to England, Northern Ireland, Scotland and Wales curricula. Seafish also facilitates contacts between seafood industry representatives and schools. This is not the only effort directed at children; the Marine Stewardship Council (MSC) runs a Fish and Kids programme in Britain, also geared to primary schools, offering classroom material and themed assemblies with the possibility of school certification; here the emphasis is on sustainability, fishing and the marine environment rather than on health.[19]

The promotional work undertaken by Seafish's predecessor, the White Fish Authority (WFA) decades earlier was of a different nature. The WFA worked with processing companies and commissioned market research on a number of fronts, the motivation being to increase domestic consumption of the products of the fishing industry; this was before the research that is the basis of the current health message had started. Under its aegis blue whiting fish fingers, canned products, frozen and composite fillets were variously tri-alled by housewives, fish fryers, hospitals and schools (David Elliott and Associates 1976, 1979; White Fish Authority 1978c, 1980; White 1977). New shellfish products were developed (Urch 1976; White Fish Authority 1977) and extensive market research and promotional effort into mackerel use commissioned (David Elliott and Associates 1977; White Fish Authority 1978a, 1978b). Two other projects were the development of dishes suitable for cook-freezing and the production of fish recipes for schools (English 1978; White Fish Authority 1974). This form of intervention largely ceased under the successor quango, Seafish which has had a greater focus on marketing and promotion. But Seafish did organise a competition in 1999 to support the development of new products by fish processing companies specifically for mid-price restaurants. Twenty-five companies entered and, at the time of the evaluation, the placing of some new products with minor (but not major) caterers as well as with retailers had resulted (Fossey 2000). This exercise seems to have been a one-off which was not repeated. The Torry Research Station had been an occasional collaborator with WFA projects but also carried out its own development work on new products using pelagic fish (Marshall, Boyd & Gofton 1992; Mills & Teepsoo 1992). Such industrial activity is no longer thought appropriate for state or publicly funded action and has for some time been left to market agents.

There does not seem to have been much direct impact on consumption attributable to this development work. Although apparently well-received when tried during the research, nothing further seems to have come of the blue whiting trials, the shellfish developments were less successful and 'deboned retextured mackerel', the product of another exercise, has unsurprisingly not re-appeared. However, there was one worthwhile achievement because hot-smoked mackerel and pâté based upon it, the subject of one exercise, have certainly found a place in subsequent British fish-eating.

A specific impact on seafood consumption whether of promotional efforts by organisations or inspiration from cookery books, celebrity chefs and bloggers can never be isolated because each has joined many other sources of influence in interacting with the social and supply chain factors affecting all patterns of food eating. But they have played some part in the shifts outlined earlier in this chapter in the type of seafood eaten just as the health message has probably been a factor in the amounts of fish consumed. At the same time, there has been interaction with another key factor considered earlier in the chapter, that of price. Those working in the seafood industry reflected the resulting different motivations affecting the consumer base:

> People starting to travel trying more, what were perceived to be more exotic fish and people going on holiday and eating fresh tuna or mahi-mahi or swordfish so capitalised on that trend…. It's obvious that trends in consumption have altered massively as people have been less able to get less cod and haddock locally, price of white fish as well has done that. People have been more open to trying, to new species. Farmed fish, farmed salmon has exploded in that time.
>
> (Managing director, medium–large company)

When it comes down to it, consumers aren't, there's a few purists that possibly are, but they want quality but don't want the price, they want quality but buy on price.

(Managing director, large company)

Sustainability and consumer attitudes

The influences discussed so far in this section have been positive towards consumption with the exception of the price issue but there is also a significant constraining factor in play, the question of sustainability. Some of the industry interviewees were conscious of public awareness and how it could affect purchasing decisions:

All of our customers ask because you get a lot of customers, their own customers coming in saying, I thought that wasn't sustainable, thought that was endangered.

(Depot manager, small company)

The general public in the restaurants are very much into the whole provenance and want to know where comes from, that it's sustainably caught.

(Manager, trade organisation 1)

Environmental NGOs have worked to make the public aware of environmental issues affecting seafood and to persuade consumers to make more sustainable purchases, activities which are part of the general ethical consumption movement (Harrison 2005). WWF, in developing the MSC and ASC eco-labelling schemes as described in earlier chapters, saw them as about facilitating informed decisions about fish because 'consumers also have the power to effect change' (Gubbay & Searle 2001, p. 5). The Marine Conservation Society (MCS) produces a *Good Fish Guide* and detailed website information to assist consumers in making informed choices because 'you can play a key role in securing the future of our seas and marine wildlife by making more environmentally responsible choices when buying seafood' as it states. The MCS information, kept updated, is available in various formats including an app for easy reference when making a purchase or foodservice choice. Traffic light ratings are given for each species which may be separately identified according to the area of capture or country where farmed and whether it has MSC or ASC certification; dark red indicates 'fish to avoid' while at the other end of the five-point scale dark green means the most sustainably caught or farmed fish. Greenpeace also has sustainable consumption advice on its website and its campaigning has raised awareness about fishing methods, particularly from its criticisms of bottom trawling. These can be looked at as potential double governance attempts, first by the organisations in relation to consumers and second when those consumers influence seafood sourcing through their buying power (Oosterveer & Spaargaren 2011).[20]

The NGOs have been credited with effectiveness at least as far as public consciousness is concerned in one industry view:

> Raising awareness by NGOs etc. in the public domain raises in turn consumer awareness, making consumers more aware and switched on to these issues.
>
> (Industry advisor, trade organisation)

Both MCS and Greenpeace have produced supermarket sustainable sourcing league tables which they publicised. The next chapter on retailing of seafood gives more details, but here it is relevant to note that at least in part the ratings have an impact because the multiples believe that they could influence purchasing behaviour. In practice, this may be as much about choosing a supermarket with a better image as about selecting sustainably sourced seafood but is still a way that consumers can be influenced to select retailers with more sustainable sourcing policies.

The potential effectiveness of the MCS listings has not gone unchallenged and can become politicised. When the organisation removed mackerel from its 'fish to eat' list early in 2013, there were objections from politicians; subsequent discussions resulted in some mackerel caught by UK vessels – specifically the South West England handline fishery – being restored to the highest category while that caught elsewhere was placed in the intermediate 'eat with caution' band (the downgrading had been precipitated by the mackerel quota dispute noted in Chapter 3).

Later in 2013, Seafish issued a media release contesting the MCS's continued placement of North Sea cod on its 'fish to avoid' list, disputing the assessment but giving recognition to its impact.[21] The MCS cod assessment was again attacked, this time by the Scottish Fishermen's Federation, in the following year when at the end of a BBC MasterChef show viewers were referred to the MCS site for information about sustainable fish.[22] Again, the vehemence of condemnation over the MCS avoidance rating was a tribute to its potential impact and paradoxically these public disagreements probably contributed to greater public awareness of the sustainability issue over cod.

In comparison with NGO efforts little has been done by public authorities to promote sustainable choices by consumers. The DEFRA Fishing for Markets project noted in Chapter 3 was intended to make use of oft-discarded fish species and one proposal was to set up a 'Seafood Missionaries' programme to promote them to consumers but no such action seems to have been taken. The European Commission runs the Inseparable Eat, Buy and Sell Sustainable Fish website to promote sustainable seafood consumption; with its individual country listings this is a potential resource for the motivated but does not seem to have been publicised and it seems unlikely that many members of the public are aware of its existence.[23]

Seafish, for its part, provides a lot of 'Responsible sourcing' information on its main website geared to professional buyers. On its promotional consumer site, Fish is the Dish, sustainability information is much less prominent and has only gradually been incorporated. It is there for anyone who searches for it, but the content is low key and stops short of attempting to be persuasive. In mid-2018, the 'Buying sustainably' page suggested substitution of less utilised species for the usual popular ones 'under considerably more strain', a sustainability statement which is also a means of encouraging consumption; in addition, there were links to the MCS database and the Marine Stewardship Council (MSC) as well as to Seafish's own Risk Assessment Tool, a sophisticated system for rating fisheries in relation to the state of stocks, management, bycatch, and habitat more relevant to professionals than to average members of the public. At the same time, a separate 'Guide to labels' page listed some of the best known including the MSC, RSPCA Freedom Food and Global Aquaculture Alliance. These two pages mark a considerable advance on the early 2014 'Sustainability and labels' page which said that Fish is the Dish does not endorse any labels (and none were mentioned) but recommended eating a variety of seafood and choosing seasonally; it also gave specific reassurance about the sustainability of haddock (as MSC-certified despite there being no general endorsement or other mention of this certification on the site at the time) and of cod (on the basis that 95% came from well-managed fisheries). This too was an advance because when the site was visited in early 2013 there was no sustainability information at all. Seafish would seem to be balancing sustainability advice against its broader remit of simply encouraging more seafood consumption.

The impact on consumers of campaigning for and information about sustainable purchasing has been unclear. One study of intentions did indicate that consumers would respond positively to certified seafood products (Jaffry et al. 2004). However, in a similar time frame, Seafish-sponsored research found the sustainability of seafood to be a peripheral issue to the majority of purchasers, one which had little impact on their decisions (Seafish 2005). In a more telling test, when Unilever in pursuance of its sustainability goals substituted the then recently MSC-certified hoki for cod, partly as fish fingers, sales fell and the innovation was eventually discontinued (Porritt & Goodman 2005). When asked about purchasing certified fish in general research about sustainability only the most committed were interested and this was assessed as 'a niche aspiration' contrasting with other aims more readily adopted like minimising waste (Owen, Seaman & Prince 2007). A Waitrose-commissioned survey in 2009 concluded that there was 'widespread ignorance of the issues around sustainable fishing' with 78% of those questioned making no effort to purchase sustainable seafood.[24] Yet, not much later Asda research based on a panel of its customers found that over half, across all three income bands, said that sustainable fish was an issue they cared about (Asda 2011). These surveys cover a fairly short timeframe and it may be that the most recent of them, the Asda findings, show that sustainability messages gradually reach more people; an alternative explanation is that they reflect a period when coverage of overfishing and quota problems had been more prominent in the media.

Turning to consumer knowledge about MSC eco-labelling some UK research found familiarity with the MSC logo to be relatively low at 30% but when asked to choose between special offer cod and more expensive but eco-labelled hake, about half did choose the latter (Potts et al. 2011). In MSC-sponsored research in six countries, including Britain, its label recognition averaged at 23%.[25] In another piece of research which looked at various criteria of sustainable and healthy food, 'sustainably sourced fish' was rated as an important issue by 70% of respondents but only 38% said they actively sought MSC items (Department for Environment 2011).

Survey responses are of course not necessarily an accurate guide to what people will actually purchase but the best-targeted messages can affect a positive motivation towards buying sustainable seafood (Honkanen & Young 2015). The film about the need for marine conservation, *The End of the Line*, released in mid-2009, seems to have had a longer-term impact because research showed an interest in seafood sustainability being retained after a year (Channel 4 Britdoc Foundation 2011). Another positive indication is the premium attached to whitefish described as more environmentally favourable 'line-caught' or carrying an MSC label in British supermarkets, in other words, people are willing to pay extra for an assurance of sustainability (Sogn-Grundvåg, Larsen & Young 2013). So is the survey finding that the proportion who felt they could make a positive difference to sustainable fishing through their purchasing decisions more than doubled between 2009 and 2013 although when actually shopping for fresh fish, respondents gave less priority to future availability than to nutritional factors (Arnold & Pickard 2013). Given this range of variable evidence, it seems that a shifting but sizeable minority of consumers may be motivated to make more sustainable choices when eco-labelled seafood is offered.

Some scepticism about the extent of consumer interest in sustainability was felt by those working in the seafood industry:

> I think there is a growing consumer pull [on sustainability]. I think the part which is disappointing is that I don't believe that consumers are actually prepared to pay more for it. I think that everyone talks, people talk about what they will do but when it comes to actually translating that into action, I don't believe there is compelling evidence.
>
> (Managing director, medium-large company)

And the low label recognition found in the surveys was echoed by a retailer respondent:

> The MSC logo which is used on packs, we had to take it off the packs because the customers weren't associating anything with it … don't actually know what it means.
>
> (Buyer, major retailer)

Nevertheless, a commercial view has been that even if consumers do not show much interest it would be better to take a proactive stance for the future (Mintel 2004). Product image could be seen to be harmed if seen as connected with environmental problems (this was stated in relation to farmed fish) (Shaw & Egan 1996). As another research interviewee put it:

> The phrase that I think I've heard, and I think sums up where I'd be, is 'People want better value for their values'.... If you move away from the sustainability agenda, you do so at your peril. And I think the more mature businesses, in whatever sector they are, all see that. It may not be the highest profile topic among consumers or among customers, retailers or distributors or whoever you deal with, but it's still there and I think that the market will be very unforgiving if business actually moves away from the sustainability agenda completely and I think that's the same in fish.
>
> (Director, large company)

There is also some agreement that consumers expect brands and supermarkets to be responsible for sustainable or at least responsible sourcing (Arnold & Pickard 2013; Mintel 2010; Washington & Ababouch 2011). In British research asking about responsibility for ensuring sustainable fisheries, 55% said it was the supermarkets; to put this in context, the identical proportion said fishermen while the government got the biggest vote at 63% (Sainsbury's 2013). Supermarkets can enable more sustainable decisions through 'choice editing' of what is available to buy (Jones, Hillier & Comfort 2011; Owen, Seaman & Prince 2007; Sustainable Consumption Roundtable 2006). There was considerable, but not majority, public support for more of this to be done on ethical grounds generally although much less backing if health is the motive (Arnold & Pickard 2013).[26] This is at variance with some findings in nudge literature of support for such health-related measures (Reisch, Sunstein & Gwozdz 2017) but perhaps given the different starting points of the enquiries it is not surprising that they produced different conclusions.

In the seafood context, choice editing is a sustainability nudge which many consumers seem likely to approve. A senior manager of one of the major retailers has been reported as saying that sustainability issues are 'too complex' for consumers to understand and should be sorted out for them by business.[27] Indeed, ethical decision-making is difficult because of the range of possible motives and concerns of the individual shopper, added to which is the complexity of information about seafood (Barclay & Miller 2017). Hence the conclusions of analysts that achieving more sustainable consumption of seafood needs to be done through the operation of the supply chain and/or by retailers in particular (Iles 2007; Tetley 2016). Those commenting in the seafood industry research concurred, their views supporting the idea that choice editing is a more productive route than expecting individual consumers to make sustainable choices:

They have so many other things to worry about and they just assume [named supermarket] is doing the right thing. And I think they assume every retailer is doing the right thing and they wouldn't be stocking anything if was unsustainable or would kill you or whatever.

(Buyer, major retailer)

When you really look in depth at the surveys, what they're really saying is: we know there's an issue out there with seafood sustainability, we don't really understand it, it's very, very complex, we get all these confusing messages, actually we just want it dealt with. Now, we want it dealt with either by you Mr Supermarket or you Mr Brand-owner.

(Director, large company)

NGO environmental campaigning together with media coverage of the fishing industry in the period characterised by reports of overfishing and low quotas, before positive effects of the CFP emerged, were felt to give the seafood industry a poor public image and raised particular anxieties about cod. Seafish included enhancing the industry's reputation in its 2012 high-level objectives because it considered that public perceptions were of 'severe shortages of fish' and 'extreme environmental impacts'.[28] Similar thoughts had been expressed in some interviews:

There are certain misconceptions because obviously everybody reads about the shortage of cod and how levels are near collapse. But this is a North Sea problem, not a Cornish problem. So we have to try and educate the customers as best we can through the retailers that we haven't got a cod problem down here. Not everyone's convinced by that and a lot of people that are told there's no problem with Cornish cod will not buy it because of the general feeling about it.

(Director, medium company 1)

I think also we have to work on the consumer perception that this is an industry in crisis, and it's not. There are elements that are continuing to struggle. But there's still is a reputational challenge to be got over with consumers around the world.

(Director, large company)

The Seafish 2018–2021 Corporate Plan, as well as highlighting the sourcing of sustainable seafood as a key challenge, mentions the 'shifting industry image' affected by media and NGOs (Seafish 2018, p. 7) and includes the intention to be proactive in putting forward positive messages and countering negative ones. This still leaves consumers needing to make sense of contrasting messages about fish as a source of health on the one side and problems connected with overfishing and fish farming on the other.

Trust and risk in consumer attitudes to seafood

There is one other potentially important factor that may affect consumer attitudes to seafood, that of trust and risk. In previous sections, we have seen that although there have been some safety issues connected with fish, consumers seem to have accepted that either they were one-off problems satisfactorily dealt with or in the case of contaminants that the risks are much lower than the benefits of consumption. But a further issue is that of food authenticity: is it what it says on the label?

The answer for seafood is 'not always'. This seems not to be a surprise to the public as a survey carried out for the FSA showed respondents to be aware of a number of food misdescription issues, fish along with meat and dairy products being considered the most risky both in relation to causing illness (if not what they were supposed to be) and to cheating (COI Communications & Define Solutions 2003). In addition to these issues, deceit in relation to seafood may be a way of laundering illegally caught fish through the supply chain.

When research in Ireland found as many as 39% of fish samples wrongly labelled, there was widespread media coverage including in Britain which raised questions about what might be happening elsewhere (Miller & Mariani 2010). Subsequently, a survey carried out by the Food Safety Authority of Ireland (FSAI) also showed a considerable minority of fish products to be mislabelled. Many such frauds have been documented further afield and indeed are considered to be a problem in the global fish supply chain (Jacquet & Pauly 2008; Pardo, Jiménez & Pérez-Villarreal 2016; Reilly 2018).

Problems over the authenticity of seafood in Britain were spotlighted in a 2011 newspaper report which stated: 'Customers are not getting what they pay for as DNA testing reveals that shops sell millions of wrongly-identified fish products'. The investigation jointly commissioned from Bangor University by the Sunday Times and Greenpeace had found a relatively modest 6% of samples with wrongly declared fish such as pangasius in a pollack product and Pacific cod declared as Atlantic cod, the implicated samples having been obtained from six major retailers including the four leaders.[29] Earlier the same year, a Channel 4 Dispatches programme dealing with several issues over seafood revealed that the largest supermarket in Britain, Tesco, had been selling what was claimed to be sustainable Pacific cod, a fifth of which turned out to be Atlantic cod at a time when the latter was subject to low quotas due to stock levels, the implication being that it had been caught illegally, though the retailer claimed that it sourced both Atlantic and Pacific cod from responsibly managed fisheries.[30]

In fact this was not the first time analysis had demonstrated such deceptions in the UK, but the issue had not previously been so publicised. An FSA investigation had found that up to 15% of salmon and 10% of sea bass and sea bream labelled as wild were actually the product of farming which would normally fetch a lower price (FSA 2007). In a survey of fish in catering establishments co-ordinated by the FSA and carried out in 52 local authorities, 10% of the fish was wrongly described, most often haddock being substituted for the more expensive cod and a high proportion of the 'misdescriptions' were from fish and chip shops (FSA 2008).

However, further research seems to show that the rate of mislabelling in Britain is not that great though it can be pointed out that even a relatively low rate will amount to a considerable volume. One study found that less than 1.5% of fish fingers tested were other than the species claimed (Huxley-Jones et al. 2012). Two-country research which demonstrated 7% mislabelled products in the UK (similar to the above Bangor University results) found a much higher rate of falsification in the samples from Ireland, 28%; intriguingly while the Irish ones were cheaper whitefish labelled as more expensive cod, the British ones included several in which Atlantic cod was presented as the cheaper and more sustainable Pacific cod; this could have been related to greater environmental awareness in Britain or alternatively might have been a disguise for illegal fishing (Miller, Jessel & Mariani 2012). But a subsequent supermarket investigation confined to the UK, with a similar overall finding that 6% of samples were mislabelled, noted that they were generally substitution of cheaper for more pricey fish such as Pacific cod for Atlantic cod, or haddock for cod; an interesting feature of this study was that no simple fillets were mislabelled, and the problem was generally in more-highly processed dishes in which deception would be easier to hide (Helyar et al. 2014). Ease of deception also increases risk in the foodservice sector: in a Which? investigation of fish and chip shops, one in six pieces of fish was of a different species to what was ostensibly purchased[31] and a study of English sushi restaurants found a 10% level of substitution (Vandamme et al. 2016).

A prosecution provided another type of evidence when a trader was convicted of substituting cheaper Japanese sea bass (*Lateolabrax japonicus*) for European sea bass (*Dicentrarchus labrax*) supplied to seafood processors who then turned them into an own-brand product for the Iceland supermarket chain. In a period of three years over 400,000 mislabelled packs were in the food chain. The fraud was identified by a trading standards officer visiting an Iceland store, illustrating the importance of such public monitoring of labelling regulations.[32]

Trans-country DNA testing has been commissioned by MSC to validate certified products as the entire basis of eco-labelling is that it is a credence attribute based on trust. Reassuringly, such trust has proved to be justified as very low mislabelling rates of less than 1% have been found. Almost three in ten of the samples in one exercise had been obtained in the UK, 28% in another the first two surveys, 11% in the one carried out in 2015 (Anderson 2016; Marine Stewardship Council 2012; Marine Stewardship Council 2013). It should be noted, however, that DNA testing has had some limitations, different species in canned tuna being particularly difficult to identify; this led to its omission from the 2015 set of tests but research has been underway to find a solution that will enable tinned tuna to be restored to the programme.

The European Commission too has carried out research into fish fraud. It organised an extensive investigation of whitefish, broadly defined, which took place in every member state (plus those in the European Free Trade Association) in the summer of 2015. This produced 3,900 samples, both unprocessed and processed from retail, foodservice and point of import sources and they represented as many as 150 different species. The overall mislabel rate was a low 6%; the UK result was below this at 4% but many countries had lower rates still; at the other end of the range there were a few countries with high rates (European Commission 2015). In the meantime, further cross-European research was in train in six countries and it too found a low rate averaging just under 5% (just 3.3% in Britain) which the analysts assessed as marking a real reduction compared to the situation a few years previously; the fall was attributed to European regulation and active governance, especially over labelling and traceability requirements (Mariani et al. 2015). The low European rates were compared in this last item to the North American situation where high mislabelling rates continued, a conclusion in which the authors of a US report concurred, suggesting that the European model would be worth following (Warner et al. 2016).

What do consumers in Britain think about the mislabelling of seafood now that information about the problem has entered the public domain? It is instructive to compare the impact of the Bangor University research, published as it was in a national newspaper, with the 2013 furore over 'beef' products found to contain horse and pig meat. Unlike the 'horsemeat scandal', the fish issue was successfully entitled a labelling failure; it seems not to have been widely reported nor to have aroused public emotion. By contrast, the attempt to regard the meat products findings as purely a labelling issue did not seem to convince the public and the substitutions were widely discussed as a betrayal of trust, causing some major players to make significant changes in their supply chains. Thus general confidence in fish as a food apparently is not affected by such incidents and fish seems to be altogether a less sensitive area than meat. However, this is an assessment of what has taken place in the public arena and individuals will have their own particular views and responses on questions about trust in seafood.

This section has looked at research on consumer attitudes to fish and at various attempts to affect seafood consumption, whether to increase it on the grounds of health benefits or to shape it in the cause of sustainability. Much of what ensues in actual consumption decisions depends on what and how seafood is delivered through both retail and foodservice channels and these are considered in the next chapter.

Conclusions: governance of seafood consumption

The types of governance exerted on consumers are summarised in Table 5.2. Nutritional advice from different sources deliver somewhat dissimilar messages; some have the simple goal of improving health, others are about

Table 5.2 Governance relevant to seafood consumption

Governance type	Detail	Governance source	Purpose
Nutritional advice	2 × week, 1 oily; exceptions: vulnerable groups, certain species	FSA → Dept Health → Public Health England and NHS	Public health
Nutritional advice	2 × week, 1 oily	Seafish, seafood company websites	Promoting seafood consumption
Nutritional advice re fish and chips	Fish and chips does not have particularly high fat levels	Seafish	Promoting seafood consumption
Nutritional advice	Omega-3/fish oil health claims	Supplements companies	Promoting supplements
Cooking information	TV programmes, celebrity chefs, cookery books, food blogs	Media, chef activity, publishing, individuals	Communication, information, entertainment
Cooking information	Fish is the Dish website, recipes	Seafish, seafood company websites	Promoting seafood consumption
Nutritional advice and cooking for children	Seafood school programmes	Seafish, MSC	Promoting (certified) seafood to children
Seafood availability	Choice of seafood sold (affected by supply issues)	Retail and foodservice	Promoting seafood consumption
Underutilised species promotion	Fishing for Markets programme, promotions	DEFRA, supermarkets	Sustainable consumption, commercial
Commercial new product development	Continuous developments	Supermarkets, foodservice	Promoting seafood consumption
Promotions, advertising	Supermarket promotions, Seafood Week	Supermarkets, Seafish	Promoting seafood consumption
Sustainability advice	Eco-labels, advice lists, Inseparable website	MCS (Good Fish Guide), MSC, EU	Sustainable purchasing and consumption
Availability	Sustainable seafood products/options	Retail and foodservice	Promoting sustainable consumption

Source: author.

increasing consumption for commercial benefit. There are many sources of cooking guidance and encouragement, sometimes about trying unfamiliar types of fish. On the other hand, consumers are warned off other fish and asked to take environmental considerations into account in what they select. These considerations may or may not enter minds when choices are made from what stores and restaurants present.

From the public health viewpoint there has been some limited action aiming to change the products and choices available in a preferred direction by decreasing fat and salt levels in fish and chips. However, the main effort has been in the form of nutritional guidelines relating to seafood, intended to influence individual behaviour. Since the reversion of nutrition responsibilities to the Department of Health, the fish-eating advice formulated by the FSA has been transferred to the websites of various agencies and, as a result, the content is likely to reach fewer people, leaving a gap instead of an obvious place to go for complete and up-to-date recommendations.

Thus although the message is still formally promulgated in the official discourse, dissemination has been left to private interests. Seafish, quite appropriately given its remit, as well as individual companies now use all promotional and advertising possibilities to spread the fish and health connection. It is particularly striking that Seafish has been developing programmes for schools, sometimes with commercial partners. Seafish in describing itself as 'the authority on seafood' has self-positioned as the trustworthy presenter of information to the public. However, its nutritional advice is largely provided with the primary objective of promoting seafood purchasing and hence the seafood industry rather than for a public health purpose. There does not seem to be an easily available objective source of consumer advice about the nutritional impact of fish and chips despite its significance in the national diet.

In many ways it may not matter that fish-eating is promoted by those with most to gain economically if the end result is still beneficial. This could be regarded as the case for seafood to quite a considerable extent, but such an approach has its limits. The FSA advice in its final form, now on the NHS website, is fairly complicated with special provisions for different demographic groups and in relation to certain fish species considered to pose some health risks. These nuances tend to be underplayed if not totally forgotten in commercial messages. Health gains are obtained particularly from oily fish and certain shellfish species, but this aspect is underemphasised as it would imply a lesser benefit from other types of seafood. Finally, the form in which fish is probably eaten the most, fried whitefish, is the least likely to deliver health gains but this fact is not presented to the public. A further point is the transmogrification of the dietary advice to promote not fish-eating but omega-3 supplements (by certain commercial interests but not by Seafish) these, in reality, providing little benefit.

Retail and foodservice establishments in their governance by availability do not prioritise health. They do not particularly promote oily fish or refrain from the extensive provision of coated (battered or crumbed) fish options in the case of supermarkets or fried fish in many foodservice outlets. They cannot indeed be expected to go against the habitual preferences of their customers which these stocking choices reflect.

Thus there is a dissonance between governance with a public health objective and governance whether by availability or by health messages where the objective is really sales and commercial success. The organs of the state marshalled and publicised scientifically valid information to improve the health of the population, but the upshot seems to be that the state gave an imprimatur to certain constructions about fish and health for private industry to use in its own interests.

Notes

1 The term consumption is used conventionally as in the statistical series from which data has been taken which record purchasing; actual consumption would need to take into account factors such as cooking practices and wastage.
2 Processed oily fish such as kippers are not separately identified in the dataset.
3 The age is that of the 'household reference person' taken to represent the household for British official statistical purposes since 2001/2002, based on financial responsibility for the accommodation, income and age. A clear definition can be found in the Office for National Statistics paper *Survey Methodology: Appendix B* which relates to the Living Costs and Food Survey.
4 The NICE clinical guidelines referring to fish and omega-3 supplementation are: NICE 2008, 2013a;, 2014 which deal with familial hypercholesterolaemia, rehabilitation after myocardial infarction and cardiovascular disease risk assessment/ reduction respectively. The organisation has also produced an evidence summary of trials of omega-3 medicines used for people with schizophrenia concluding that these were either ineffective or had limited impact (NICE 2013b).
5 The Balance of Health can be viewed at http://docplayer.net/26164565-The-balance-of-good-health.htm and at the end contains the FSA's statement of purpose mentioned in the previous paragraph.
6 This has led to the curious situation at the time of writing that the FSA website section listing various activities in which it has a role under the heading 'How to stay safe' ends with a section headed 'Nutrition (Northern Ireland only)' under which there is a link to the Eatwell Guide which applies to the whole of the UK.
7 'Eat 2 portions a week' was accessed from www.seafish.org on 1 January 2013, 'Health benefits' on 18 June 2018.
8 The Agency's Director of Food Safety had recommended support for the relaxation (Gleadle A 2011, 'Proposal to relax certain provisions of the current feed ban', Report to FSA Board meeting, 7 September 2011) but the Board did not agree. This report was sent with the formal letter of advice reflecting the Board decision to oppose the change from the Chair Jeff Rooker to DEFRA Minister Jim Paice on 15 September 2011 along with an expression of support for the change from the Deputy Chief Veterinary Officer and arguments against it from the Chief Medical Officer and the Which Chief Policy Advisor (all these documents were obtained from the FSA website). When the issue was considered by the EU's Standing Committee on the Food Chain and Animal Health the UK representative made a short statement and abstained; the proposal was then approved by a qualified majority vote (the Summary Report of the 18 July 2012 meeting was obtained from http://ec.europa.eu). DEFRA's reasons for abstaining are set out more fully in an Explanatory Memorandum provided to the House of

Commons European Scrutiny Committee for its 17 July 2012 meeting, the record of which is available from www.publications.parliament.uk; it shows that the FSA's arguments against the change were accepted but that the decision was taken to abstain rather than to oppose the proposal because of the then UK government's general deregulatory stance.

9 Some reporting indicated that supermarket sales of salmon held well in the immediate aftermath of the study's publication (see Lawrence F 2004, 'Salmon warning fails to deter shoppers', *Guardian*, 13 January 2004 and Lyst C 2004, 'Salmon sales defy health warnings', *The Scotsman*, 13 January 2004) but the quoted interviewees spoke about a big reduction in demand for six and one month respectively; they were in completely different businesses and might well have had different experiences or they may have had different memory recall. The information sheet published by Seafish in March 2004, *Seafood in Retail: Snapshot* showed a drop in purchase of fresh salmon in the month after the Hites et al. article was published but a speedy recovery almost immediately. Speculatively, it may be the reassurance provided by the FSA that limited anti-salmon reaction by consumers.

10 An article describing the programme under the heading 'Farmed salmon "contaminated"', 3 January 2001, came from the BBC News website, http://news.bbc.co.uk.

11 See Topping A, 'Supermarkets recall salmon over contamination, 16 February 2008, *Guardian* and Gammell C, Borland S and Cramb A 2008, 'Salmon products tainted by diesel recalled', *Daily Telegraph*, 26 February 2008,

12 For a news item on the restaurant incidents see Wallop H 2009, 'Fat Duck: sewage-infested oysters to blame for illness says official report', *Daily Telegraph*, 10 September 2009. For a summary of the norovirus survey see Ghosh P 2011, 'Winter vomiting virus: British oysters contain bug', BBC News, 29 November 2011. The full 2011 report *Investigation into the Prevalence, Distribution and Levels of Norovirus Titre in Oyster Harvesting Areas in the UK* is on the FSA website. An NHS review, 'Winter vomiting virus found in most oysters', 29 November 2011 is at www.nhs.uk.

13 The figures cited from Seafish-commissioned research are at www.seafish.org/eating-seafood/seafood-for-health, accessed on 28 June 2018.

14 News releases on what was then the Scottish Government website, www.scotland.co.uk, were headed 'Eat more fish, Scots urged' of 15 May 2009 and 'Eat more fish campaign' dated 28 April 2010.

15 The Channel 4 series *Hugh's Fish Fight* which ran in January 2011 was fronted by celebrity chef Hugh Fearnley-Whittingstall and in tandem there was a series of demonstrations by Jamie Oliver of recipes using less well-known species under the heading 'The Big Fish Fight'.

16 This research was reported in the presentation by Maureen Reynier, 'Understanding the seafood consumer' given at the Seafish Conference on Seafood and the Consumer held on 9 October 2012 in Birmingham.

17 See McDonald L 2013, 'Are YouTube food channels killing TV chefs?', *The Independent*, 21 March 2013.

18 The website is at www.fishisthedish.co.uk/. The recipe booklet is *Fish is the Dish by Seafish*.

19 There is a separate MSC website for the Fish and Kids programme, https://fishandkids.msc.org.

20 The first edition of the MCS *Good Fish Guide* was published in 2002. MCS advice was on a separate website www.fishonline.org from 2004 to 2018 when it was renamed 'goodfishguide' and moved to the main MCS website where it is most easily accessed at www.goodfishguide.org.uk. Greenpeace consumption advice is at www.greenpeace.org.uk/what-we-do/oceans/better-buys-what-fish-can-i-eat/.

21 Political reaction to the MCS's mackerel downgrading decision was reported in 'Politicians condemn mackerel move', 23 January 2013 on www.fishnewseu.com. The partial reversal was announced in the MCS press release of 16 May 2013, 'Political stand-off reflected in fresh sustainability ratings for the nation's favourite fish: only mackerel caught by the best method is given revised "fish to eat" rating by the Marine Conservation Society' and according to a Seafish release of the same date, 'Seafish comment: mackerel back on the Fish to Eat list' came after 'the MCS has consulted extensively with UK industry'. The cod statement dated 14 November 2013 is 'Seafish advises consumers to continue buying cod with a clear conscience' on its website www.seafish.org.

22 Reported in Sheridan D 2014, 'That's codswallop, trawlermen claim, as BBC show points to North Sea blacklist', *The Times*, 29 April 2014.

23 The Inseparable website is at http://ec.europa.eu/fisheries/inseparable/en.

24 Information about the YouGov survey sponsored by Waitrose is in the 2 June 2009 press release 'Waitrose calls for a sea change on the issue of sustainable fishing as new research reveals: 72% are unaware that some fish are as close to extinction as the white rhino' at www.waitrose.presscentre.com.

25 The research carried out by AMR Marketing Research is reported on the MSC website www.msc.org, dated 4 October 2010.

26 As the Sustainable Consumption Roundtable ceased in 20111 and its archive site is not maintained the report is now kept at https://research-repository.st-andrews.ac.uk.

27 The manager responsible for sustainability and ethical sourcing was quoted with this view in Smith L 2012, 'Fisheries sustainability "too complex" for consumers says Waitrose', 16 October 2012, www.fish2fork.com.

28 These phrases were used in a presentation by Jon Harman, 'Seafood and the consumer: fish is food' given at the Seafish Conference on Seafood and the Consumer held on 9 October 2012 in Birmingham.

29 The FSAI survey was reported in '19 pc of fish mislabelled: survey', 31 March 2011 on the Fish Information & Services website, http://fis.com and *The Sunday Times* report was by Leake J and Dowling K 2011, 'Fishy labels: what's really in that pack of haddock?' published on 24 April 2011.

30 The Tesco mislabelling problem is covered in Thompson A 2011, 'Dispatches: Britain's fish unwrapped', 14 January 2011 at www.channel4.com and Boucher P 2011, 'There's something fishy going on: how mislabelled cod is slipping through the net', *The Independent*, 4 January 2011.

31 The finding of the Which? Fish and chip shop investigation is in Lawrence F, 'A fishy tale as chip shops are caught selling cheaper species', *Guardian*, 13 September 2014.

32 For an account of the case in which the trader was jailed and the company fined see 'Former Royal Navy chef jailed over £1m "fake" sea bass scam', *Telegraph*, 30 January 2015 (no author given). The £1m of the title refers to the value of sales of the fish to Iceland; the company of the convicted supplier earned £19,686 from the arrangement.

References

Aarset B, Beckmann S, Bigne E, Beveridge M, Bjorndal T, Bunting J, McDonagh P, Mariojouls C, Muir J, Prothero A, Reisch L, Smith A, Tveteras R & Young J 2004, 'The European consumers' understanding and perceptions of the "organic" food regime: the case of aquaculture', *British Food Journal*, vol. 106, no. 2, pp. 93–105.

Abdelhamid AS, Brown TJ, Brainard JS, Biswas P, Thorpe GC, Moore HJ, Deane KHO, AlAbdulghafoor FK, Summerbell CD, Worthington HV, Song F & Hooper L 2018, 'Omega 3 fatty acids for the primary and secondary prevention of cardiovascular disease', *Cochrane Database of Systematic Reviews*, vol. 7, p. CD003177.

Akbar U, Yang M, Kurian D & Mohan C 2017, 'Omega-3 fatty acids in rheumatic disease: a critical review', *Journal of Clinical Rheumatology*, vol. 23, no. 6, pp. 330–339.

Albanese E, Dangour AD, Uauy R, Acosta D, Guerra M, Gallarda Guerra SS, Huang Y, Jacob KS, Llibre de Rodriguez J, Hernandex Noriega L, Salas A, Sosa AL, Sousa RM, Williams J, Ferri CP & Prince MJ 2009, 'Dietary fish and meat intake and dementia in Latin America, China and India: a 10/66 Dementia Research Group population-based study', *American Journal of Clinical Nutrition*, vol. 90, no. 2, pp. 392–400.

Albanese E, Lombardo FL, Dangour AD, Guerra M, Acosta D, Huang Y, Jacob KS, Llibre Rodriguez JJ, Salas A, Schönborn C, Sosa AL, Williams J, Prince MJ & Ferri CP 2012, 'No association between fish intake and depression in over 15,000 older adults from seven low and middle income countries – the 10/66 study', *PLOS One*, vol. 7, no. 6, p. e38879.

Altintzoglou T, Nøstvold BH, Carlehög M, Heide M, Ødtli J & Egeness F-A 2012, 'The influence of labelling on consumers' evaluation of fresh and thawed cod fillets in England', *British Food Journal*, vol. 114, no. 11, pp. 1558–1570.

Anderson L 2016, *From Ocean to Plate: How DNA Testing Helps to Ensure Traceable, Sustainable Seafood*, Marine Stewardship Council, London.

Arnold H & Pickard T 2013, *Sustainable Diets: Helping Shoppers*, Institute of Grocery Distribution, Watford.

Artham SM, Lavie CJ, Milani RV, Anand RG, O'Keefe JH & Ventura HO 2008, 'Fish oil in primary and secondary cardiovascular prevention', *The Ochsner Journal*, vol. 8, no. 2, pp. 49–60.

Ascherio A, Rimm EB, Stampfer MJ, Giovannucci EL & Willett WC 1995, 'Dietary intake of marine n-3 fatty acids, fish intake, and the risk of coronary disease among men', *New England Journal of Medicine*, vol. 332, no. 15, pp. 977–983.

Asda 2011, *Green is Normal: Asda Sustainability Study*, Asda, Leeds.

Aung T, Halsey J, Kromhout D, Gerstein HC, Marchioli R, Tavazzi L, Geleijnse JM, Rauch B, Ness A, Galan P, Chew EY, Bosch J, Collins R, Lewington S, Armitage J & Clarke R 2018, 'Associations of omega-3 fatty acid supplement use with cardiovascular disease risks: meta-analysis of 10 trials involving 77,917 individuals', *JAMA Cardiology*, vol. 3, no. 3, pp. 225–234.

Baird PB, Bennett R & Hamilton M 1988, 'The consumer acceptability of some underutilised fish species', in *Food Acceptability*, Thomson DMH, ed., Elsevier Applied Science, London & New York.

Barclay K & Miller A 2017, 'The sustainable seafood movement is a governance concert, with the audience playing a key role', *Sustainability*, vol. 10, no. 1, p. 180.

Bates B, Cox L, Nicholson S, Page P, Prentice A, Steer T & Swan G, eds. 2016, *National Diet and Nutrition Survey: Results from Years 5 and 6 (Combined) of the Rolling Programme (2012/2013–2013/2014)*, Public Health England and Food Standards Agency, London.

Bates B, Lennox A, Prentice A, Bates C & Swan G, eds. 2012, *National Diet and Nutrition Survey: Headline Results from Years 1, 2 and 3 (Combined) of the Rolling Programme (2008/2009–2010/2011)*, Department of Health and Food Standards Agency, London.

Bisgaard H, Stokholm J & Chawes BL 2016, 'Fish oil-derived fatty acids in pregnancy and wheeze and asthma in offspring', *The New England Journal of Medicine*, vol. 375, no. 26, pp. 2530–2539.

British Nutrition Foundation 2013, *National Pupil Survey 2013: UK Survey Results*, BNF, London.

Brunner EJ, Jones PJS, Friel S & Bartley M 2009, 'Fish, human health and marine ecosystem health: policies in collision', *International Journal of Epidemiology*, vol. 38, no. 1, pp. 93–100.

Brunsø K 2003, 'Consumer research on fish in Europe', in *Quality of Fish from Catch to Consumer: Labelling, Monitoring and Traceability*, Luten JB, Oehlenschläger J & Ólafsdóttir G, eds., Wageningen Academic Publishers, Wageningen.

Burr ML, Fehily AM, Gilbert JF, Rogers S, Holliday RM, Sweetnam PM, Elwood PC & Deadman NM 1989, 'Effects of changes in fat, fish and fibre intakes on death and myocardial infarction: diet and reinfarction trial (DART)', *The Lancet*, vol. 2 (8666), no. 30, September, pp. 757–761.

Cahu C, Salen P & De Lorgeril M 2004, 'Farmed and wild fish in the prevention of cardiovascular diseases: assessing possible differences in lipid nutritional values', *Nutrition Metabolism and Cardiovascular Diseases*, vol. 14, no. 1, pp. 34–41.

Caraher M, Lang T & Dixon P 2000, 'The influence of TV and celebrity chefs on public attitudes and behaviour among the English public', *Association for the Study of Food in Society Journal*, vol. 4, no. 1, pp. 27–46.

Carbon Trust 2016, *The Eatwell Guide: A More Sustainable Diet, Methodology and Results Summary*, Carbon Trust, London.

Carleton C, Cappell R, Graham I & Marshall D 1999, *Port Markets Strategy Study*, Nautilus Consultants and Sea Fish Industry Authority, Edinburgh, Seafish Report No SR528.

Cederholm T 2017, 'Fish consumption and omega-3 fatty acid supplementation for prevention or treatment of cognitive decline, dementia or Alzheimer's disease in older adults – any news?', *Current Opinion in Clinical Nutrition & Metabolic Care*, vol. 20, no. 2, pp. 104–109.

Channel 4 Britdoc Foundation 2011, *The End of the Line*, Channel 4 Britdoc Foundation, London.

Chong E, Robman L, Simpson J, Hodge A, Aung K, Dolphin T, English D, Giles G & R Guymer 2009, 'Fat consumption and its association with age-related macular degeneration', *Archives of Ophthalmology*, vol. 127, no. 5, pp. 674–680.

Christen WG, Schaumberg DA, Robert RG & Buring JE 2011, 'Dietary ω-3 fatty acid and fish intake and incident age-related macular degeneration in women', *Archives of Ophthalmology*, vol. 129, no. 7, pp. 921–929.

COI Communications & Define Solutions 2003, *Consumer Attitudes to Food Misdescription: Qualitative Research Report of Findings*, Food Standards Agence, London.

Cole DW, Cole R, Gaydos SJ, Gray J, Hyland G, Jacques ML, Powell-Dunford N, Sawjney C & Au WW 2009, 'Aquaculture: environmental, toxicological and health issues', *International Journal of Hygiene and Environmental Health*, vol. 212, no. 4, pp. 369–377.

David Elliott and Associates 1976, *Blue Whiting Fish Frier and Customer Interviews*, White Fish Authority, Epsom and Edinburgh, Technical Report 146.

David Elliott and Associates 1977, *Mackerel Research: Fishmongers*, White Fish Authority, Epsom and Edinburgh, Technical Report 154.

David Elliott and Associates 1979, *Blue Whiting Research: Group Discussions on Canned Fillets*, White Fish Authority, Epsom and Edinburgh, Technical Report 169.

De Lorgeril M & Salen P 2002, 'Fish and N-3 fatty acids for the prevention and treatment of coronary heart disease: nutrition is not pharmacology', *The American Journal of Medicine*, vol. 112, no. 4, pp. 316–319.

De Roos B, Sneddon A & Macdonald H 2012, *Fish as a Dietary Source of healthy Long Chain n-3 Polyunsaturated Fatty Acids (LC n-3 PUFA) and Vitamin D: A Review of the Current Literature*, Food & Health Innovation Service, Aberdeen.

DEFRA 2001, *Report of the National Food Survey Committee 2000/01*, Department for Environment, Food and Rural Affairs, London.

DEFRA 2013, *Family Food 2012*, Department for Environment, Food and Rural Affairs, London.

Denton M & Lacey R 1991, 'Intensive farming and food processing: implications for polyunsaturated fats', *Journal of Nutritional Medicine*, vol. 2, no. 2, pp. 179–190.

Department for Environment 2011, *Attitudes and Behaviours around Sustainable Food Purchasing*, DEFRA, London, Report SERP 1011/10.

Department of Health 1999, *Saving Lives: Our Healthier Nation*, The Stationery Office, London.

EFSA 2011, 'Scientific Opinion on the substantiation of health claims related to docosahexaenoic acid (DHA), eicosapentaenoic acid (EPA) and brain, eye and nerve development (ID 501, 513, 540), maintenance of normal brain function (ID 497, 501, 510, 513, 519, 521, 534, 540, 688, 1323, 1360, 4294), maintenance of normal vision (ID 508, 510, 513, 519, 529, 540, 688, 2905, 4294), maintenance of normal cardiac function (ID 510, 688, 1360), "maternal health; pregnancy and nursing" (ID 514), "to fulfil increased omega-3 fatty acids need during pregnancy" (ID 539), "skin and digestive tract epithelial cells maintenance" (ID 525), enhancement of mood (ID 536), "membranes cell structure" (ID 4295), "anti-inflammatory action" (ID 4688) and maintenance of normal blood LDL-cholesterol concentrations (ID 4719) pursuant to Article 13(1) of Regulation (EC) No 1924/2006', *EFSA Journal*, vol. 9, no. 4.

Elliott M, Hargreaves J & Pilgrim S, eds., 2012, *UK Sea Fisheries Statistics 2011*, National Statistics & Marine Management Organisation, Newport & London.

English HR 1978, *Testing of Fish Recipes to be Incorporated into a New Recipe Book for Use in the School Meal Service*, White Fish Authority, Epsom & Edinburgh, Technical Report 158.

European Commission 2015, *Fish Substitution/Test Results/Fish Substitution Questions and Answers*, EC, Brussels.

FAO & WHO 2011, *Report of the Joint Expert Consultation on the Risks and Benefits of Fish Consumption*, Food and Agriculture Organization of the United Nations, Rome, FAO Fishery and Aquaculture Report No. 978.

Fishing for the Markets 2011, *Social Research: Fish Restaurateurs and their Customers*, Department for Environment, Food and Rural Affairs, London, Work Package 4.

Fofana A 2001, 'Socio-economics of Fish Consumption in the United Kingdom', in *XIIIth EAFE Conference, Salerno 18–20 April 2001*.

Food and Nutrition Strategy Group 1996, *Eating and Health: A Food and Nutrition Strategy for Northern Ireland*, Health Promotion Agency for Northern Ireland, Belfast.

Food Standards Agency 2009, *Review of Agency's Advice on Fish Consumption, Public Written Consultation*, FSA, London.

Food Standards Scotland 2016, *The Eatwell Guide: Helping You Eat a Healthy, Balanced Diet*, Food Standards Scotland, Aberdeen.

Fossey E 2000, *The Seafish Challenge Reviewed*, Sea Fish Industry Authority, Edinburgh.

Foster C 2005, *Fish Consumption and Production: The Sustainability Challenge*, National Consumer Council, London.

FSA 2007, *Survey on the Production Method and Geographic Origin of Fish: Part 1 – Information at Retail Sale, and Part 2 – Verification of 'Wild' Fish*, Food Standards Agency, London.

FSA 2008, *Survey on Fish Species in the Catering Sector*, Food Standards Agency, London, Food Survey Information Sheet 007/08.

Fuentes A, Fernandez-Segovia I, Serra JA & Barat JM 2010, 'Comparison of wild and cultured sea bass (*Dicentrarchus labrax*) quality', *Food Chemistry*, vol. 119, no. 4, pp. 1514–1518.

Future Foundation 2012, *Our Future with Fish: Investigating Customer Attitudes, Behaviour and Motivations*, Sainsbury's, London.

George R & Bhopal R 1995, 'Fat composition of free living and farmed sea species: implications for human diet and sea-farming techniques', *British Food Journal*, vol. 97, no. 6, pp. 19–22.

Gofton L & Marshall D 1991, *Fish: Consumer Attitudes and Preferences: A Marketing Opportunity*, Horton Publishing, Bradford.

Graham M 1943, *The Fish Gate*, Faber and Faber, London.

Gross T 2001a, *Consumer Attitudes Towards Farmed Seafood*, Seafish Research and Information, Edinburgh.

Gross T 2001b, *Consumer Attitudes Towards Health and Food Safety*, Sea Fish Industry Authority, Edinburgh.

Gubbay S & Searle A 2001, *Fish of the Day: Can Consumers Help Save UK Fisheries?*, WWF, Godalming.

Harrison R 2005, 'Pressure groups, campaigns and consumers', in *The Ethical Consumer*, Harrison R, Newholm T & Shaw D, eds., Sage Publications, London.

He K, Song Y, Daviglus ML, Liu K, Van Horn L, Dyer AR & Greenland P 2004, 'Accumulated evidence on fish consumption and coronary heart disease mortality: a meta-analysis of cohort studies', *Circulation*, vol. 109, no. 22, pp. 2705–2711.

Health Protection Agency 2009, *Foodborne Illness at The Fat Duck Restaurant: Report of an Investigation of a Foodborne Outbreak of Norovirus among Diners at The Fat Duck Restaurant, Bray, Berkshire in January and February 2009*, Health Protection Agency, London.

Helyar SJ, Lloyd HaD, de Bruyn M, Leake J, Bennett N & Carvalho GR 2014, 'Fish product mislabelling: failings of traceability in the production chain and implications for illegal, unreported and unregulated (IUU) fishing', *PLOS One*, vol. 9, no. 6, p. e98691.

Henderson JC 2011, 'Celebrity chefs: expanding empires', *British Food Journal*, vol. 113, no. 5, pp. 613–624.

Hibbeln JR, Davis JM, Steer C, Emmett P, Rogers I, Rogers I & Golding J 2007, 'Maternal seafood consumption in pregnancy and neurodevelopmental outcomes in childhood (ALSPAC study): an observational cohort study', *Lancet*, vol. 369, no. 9561, pp. 578–585.

Hites RA, Foran JA, Carpenter DO, Hamilton Mc, Knuth BA & Schwager SJ 2004, 'Global assessment of organic contaminants in farmed salmon', *Science*, vol. 303, no. 5655, pp. 226–229.

Honkanen P & Young J 2015, 'What determines British consumers' motivation to buy sustainable seafood?', *British Food Journal*, vol. 117, no. 4, pp. 1289–1302.

Hooper L, Thompson RL, Harrison RA, Summerbell CD, Ness AR, Moore HJ, Worthington HV, Durrngton PN, Higgins JPT, Capps NE, Riemersma RA, Ebrahim SBJ & Smith GD 2006, 'Risks and benefits of omega-3 fats for mortality, cardiovascular disease and cancer: a systematic review', *BMJ*, vol. 332, no. 7544, pp. 753–760.

House of Commons Environment, Food and Rural Affairs Committee 2009, *Securing Food Supplies up to 2050: The Challenges Faced by the UK*, The Stationery Office, London, Fourth Report of Session 2008–2009.

Huang R-X, Duan Y-D & Hu J-A 2015, 'Fish intake and risk of liver cancer: a meta-analysis', *PLOS One*, vol. 10, no. 1, p. e0096102.

Huxley-Jones E, Shaw JIA, Fletcher C, Parnell J & Watts PC 2012, 'Use of DNA barcoding to reveal species composition of convenience seafood', *Conservation Biology*, vol. 26, no. 2, pp. 367–371.

Iles A 2007, 'Making the seafood industry more sustainable: creating production chain transparency and accountability', *Journal of Cleaner Production*, vol. 15, no. 6, pp. 577–569.

Isherwood C, Wong M, Jones WS, Davies IG, & Griffin BA 2010, 'Lack of effect of cold water prawns on plasma cholesterol and lipoproteins in normo-lipidaemic men', *Cellular and Molecular Biology*, vol. 56, no. 1, pp. 52–58.

Jacquet JL & Pauly D 2008, 'Trade secrets: renaming and mislabelling of seafood', *Marine Policy*, vol. 32, no. 3, pp. 309–318.

Jaffry S, Pickering H, Ghulam Y, Whitmarsh D & Wattage P 2004, 'Consumer choices for quality and sustainability labelled seafood products in the UK', *Food Policy*, vol. 29, no. 3, pp. 215–228.

James MJ, Sullivan TR, Metcalf RG & Cleland LG 2018, 'Pitfalls in the use of randomised controlled trials for fish oil studies with cardiac patients', *British Journal of Nutrition*, vol. 112, no. 5, pp. 812–820.

Jenkins DJA, Sievenpiper JL, Pauly D, Sumaila UR, Kendall CWC & Mowat FM 2009, 'Are dietary recommendations for fish oils sustainable?', *Canadian Medical Association Journal*, vol. 180, no. 6, pp. 633–637.

Jensen IJ, Maehre H K, Tommeras S, Eilertsen KE, Olsen RL & Elvevoll EO 2012, 'Farmed Atlantic salmon (*Salmo salar* L.) is a good source of long chain omega-3 fatty acids', *Nutrition Bulletin*, vol. 37, no. 1, pp. 25–29.

Jones P, Hillier D & Comfort D 2011, 'Shopping for tomorrow: promoting sustainable consumption within food stores', *British Food Journal*, vol. 113, no. 7, pp. 935–948.

Karapanagiotidis IT, Bell MV, Little DC, Yakupitiyage A & Rakshit SK 2006, 'Polyunsaturated fatty acid content of wild and farmed tilapias in Thailand: effect of aquaculture practices and implications for human nutrition', *Journal of Agricultural & Food Chemistry*, vol. 54, no. 12, pp. 304–310.

Kesse-Guyot E, Péneau S, Ferry M, Jeandel C, Hercberg S, Galan P & the SU.VI.Max 2 Research Group 2011, 'Thirteen-year prospective study between fish consumption, long-chain N-3 fatty acids intakes and cognitive function', *The Journal of Nutrition, Health & Aging*, vol. 15, no. 2, pp. 115–120.

Kranz S, Jones NRV & Monsivais P 2017, 'Intake levels of fish in the UK paediatric population', *Nutrients*, vol. 9, no. 292.

Kris-Etherton PM, Harris WS & Appel LJ 2002, 'Fish consumption, fish oil, omega-3 fatty acids, and cardiovascular disease', *Circulation*, vol. 106, pp. 2747–2757.

Kromhaut D, Bosschieter EB & Coulander C de L 1985, 'The inverse relation between fish consumption and 20-year mortality from coronary heart disease', *The New England Journal of Medicine*, vol. 312, no. 19, pp. 1205–1209.

Kühn T, Teucher B, Kaaks R, Boeing H, Weikert C & Buijsse B 2013, 'Fish consumption and the risk of myocardial infarction and stroke in the German arm of the European Prospective Investigation into Cancer and Nutrition (EPIC-Germany)', *British Journal of Nutrition*, vol. 110, no. 6, pp. 1118–1125.

Lang T, Dowler E & Hunter DJ 2006, *Review of the Scottish Diet Action Plan*, Health Scotland, Edinburgh.

Leek S, Maddock S & Foxall G 2000, 'Situational determinants of fish consumption', *British Food Journal*, vol. 102, no. 1, pp. 18–39.

LeGrand L 1992, 'Fish products: a summary of trends in the UK', *British Food Journal*, vol. 94, no. 9, pp. 31–36.

Li F, Liu X & Zhang D 2016, 'Fish consumption and risk of depression: a meta-analysis', *Journal of Epidemiology and Community Health*, vol. 70, no. 3.

Lu Z, Chen TC, Zhang A, Persons KS, Kohn N, Berkowitz R, Martinello S & Holick MF 2007, 'An evaluation of the vitamin D3 content in fish: is the vitamin D content adequate to satisfy the dietary requirement for Vitamin D?', *The Journal of Steroid Biochemistry and Molecular Biology*, vol. 103, no. 3–5, pp. 642–644.

Luoma SN & Löfstedt RE 2007, 'Contaminated salmon and the public's trust', *Environmental Science and Technology*, vol. 41, no. 6, pp. 1811–1814.

Maddock S & Young JA 1995, 'Catering for the fish consumer – a UK perspective', *British Food Journal*, vol. 97, no. 11, pp. 21–25.

Mariani S, Griffiths AM, Velasco A, Kappel K, Jérôme M, Perez-Martin RI, Schröder U, Verrez-Bagnis V, Silva H, Vandamme SG, Boufana, B., Mendes R, Shorten M, Smith C, Hankard E, Hook SA, Weymer AS, Gunning D & Sotelo CG 2015, 'Low mislabeling rates indicate marked improvements in European seafood market operations', *Frontiers in Ecology and the Environment*, vol. 13, no. 10, pp. 536–540.

Marine Stewardship Council 2012, *DNA Testing of MSC-Labelled Products*, MSC, London.

Marine Stewardship Council 2013, *DNA Testing Report 2013*, MSC, London.

Marshall D 1988, 'Behavioural variables influencing the consumption of fish and fish products', in *Food Acceptability*, Thomson DMH, ed., Elsevier Applied Science, London & New York.

Marshall D 1993, 'Appropriate meal occasions: understanding conventions and exploring situational influences on food choice', *International Review of Retail, Distribution and Consumer Research*, vol. 3, no. 3, pp. 278–301.

Marshall DW, Boyd NJ & Gofton LR 1992, 'Taking new product evaluation beyond the "sensorial"', in *Pelagic Fish: The Resource and its Exploitation*, Burt JR, Hardy R & Whittle KJ, eds., Fishing News Books, Blackwells, Oxford.

Marshall DW & Currall J 1992, 'Consumer attitudes towards pelagic fish', in *Pelagic Fish: The Resource and its Exploitation*, Burt JR, Hardy R & Whittle KJ, eds., Fishing News Books, Blackwells, Oxford.

Miller D, Jessel A & Mariani S 2012, 'Seafood mislabelling: comparisons of two western European case studies assist in defining influencing factors, mechanisms and motives', *Fish and Fisheries*, vol. 13, no. 3, pp. 345–358.

Miller DD & Mariani S 2010, 'Smoke, mirrors, and mislabeled cod: poor transparency in the European seafood industry', *Frontiers in Ecology and the Environment*, vol. 8, no. 10, pp. 517–521.

Mills A & Teepsoo H 1992, 'Utilisation of deboned retextured mackerel flesh', in *Pelagic Fish: the Resource and its Exploitation*, Burt JR, Hardy R & Whittle KJ, eds., Fishing News Books, Blackwells, Oxford.

Mintel 2004, *Fish UK September 2004*, Mintel, London.

Mintel 2010, *Fish and Shellfish UK September 2010*, Mintel, London.

Morris MC, Brockman J, Schneider JA, Wang Y, Bennett DA, Tangney CC & van de Rest O 2016, 'Association of seafood consumption, brain mercury level, and APOEâ4 status with brain neuropathology in older adults', *JAMA*, vol. 315, no. 5, pp. 489–497.

Morris MC, Manson JE, Rosner B, Buring JE, Willett WC & Hennekens CH 1995, 'Fish consumption and cardiovascular disease in the physicians' health study: a prospective study', *American Journal of Epidemiology*, vol. 142, no. 2, pp. 166–175.

Mozaffarian D & Rimm EB 2006, 'Fish intake, contaminants and human health: evaluating the risks and benefits', *Journal of the American Medical Association*, vol. 298, no. 15, pp. 1885–1899.

Mozaffarian D & Wu JHY 2011, 'Omega-3 fatty acids and cardiovascular disease: effects on risk factors, molecular pathways, and clinical events', *Journal of the American College of Cardiology*, vol. 58, no. 20, pp. 2047–2067.

Mukhopadhyay R 2012, 'An essential debate: a controversy over a dietary recommendation for omega-6 fatty acids shows no signs of resolving itself', *ASBMB Today*, December.

Nettleton JA 1985, *Seafood Nutrition: Facts, Issues and Marketing of Nutrition in Fish & Shellfish* Osprey Books, Huntington NY.

Nevin C 2003, *Consumers' Perceptions of Frozen and Chilled Seafood*, Sea Fish Industry Authority, Edinburgh.

NICE 2008, *Familial Hypercholesterolaemia: Identification and Management: Clinical Guideline*, National Institute for Health and Care Excellence, London.

NICE 2013a, *Myocardial Infarction: Cardiac Rehabilitation and Prevention of Further Cardiovascular Disease: Clinical Guideline*, National Institute for Health and Care Excellence, London.

NICE 2013b, *Schizophrenia: Omega-3 Fatty Acid Medicines: Evidence Summary*, National Institute for Health and Care Excellence, London.

NICE 2014, *Cardiovascular Disease: Risk Assessment and Reduction, including Lipid Modification: Clinical Guideline*, National Institute for Health and Care Excellence, London.

Nichols PD, Glencross B, Petrie R & Singh SP 2014, 'Readily available sources of long-chain omega-3 oils: is farmed Australian seafood a better source of the good oil than wild-caught seafood?', *Nutrients*, vol. 6, no. 3, pp. 1063–1079.

Oosterveer P & Spaargaren G 2011, 'Organising consumer involvement in the greening of global food flows: the role of environmental NGOs in the case of marine fish', *Environmental Politics*, vol. 20, no. 1, pp. 97–114.

Owen L, Seaman H & Prince S 2007, *Public Understanding of Sustainable Consumption of Food: A Report to the Department for Environment, Food and Rural Affairs*, DEFRA, London.

Pardo MÁ, Jiménez E & Pérez-Villarreal B 2016, 'Misdescription incidents in seafood sector', *Food Control*, vol. 62, April, pp. 277–283.

Porritt J & Goodman J 2005, *Fishing for Good*, Forum for the Future, London.

Potts T, Brennan R, Pita C & Lowrie G 2011, *Sustainable Seafood and Eco-labelling: The Marine Stewardship Council, UK Consumers and Fishing Industry Perspectives*, Scottish Association for Marine Science, Oban, SAMS Report 270–11.

Pratt S & Matthews K 2004, *SuperFoods: Fourteen Foods that Will Change Your Life* Bantam Books, London.

Public Health England 2016a, *From Plate to Guide: What, Why and How for the Eatwell Model*, Public Health England, London.

Public Health England 2016b, *The Eatwelll Guide: Helping You Eat a Healthy, Balanced Diet*, Public Health England, London.

Pyke M 1961, *Nutrition*, The English Universities Press Ltd, London.

Randall S 1999, 'Television representation of food: a case study of "Rick Stein's Taste of the Sea"', *International Tourism and Hospitality Research Journal: the Surrey Quarterly Review*, vol. 1, no. 1, pp. 41–54.

Reid C 2003, '"A common delicacy": UK fish consumption in the twentieth century', in *Politics and People in the North Atlantic Fisheries Since 1485*, Starkey D, eds., North Atlantic Fisheries History Association, Hull.

Reilly A 2018, *Overview of Fraud in the Fisheries Sector*, Food and Agriculture Organization of the United Nations, Rome.

Reisch LA, Sunstein CR & Gwozdz 2017, 'Beyond carrots and sticks: Europeans support health nudges', *Food Policy*, vol. 69, May, pp. 1–10.

Revill Nation Ltd 2011, *Customer and Market Intelligence*, Department for Environment, Food and Rural Affairs, London, Fishing for the Markets Work Package 3.

Roberts C, Steer T, Mablethorpe N, Cox L, Meadows S, Nicholson S, Page P & Swan G 2018, *National Diet and Nutrition Survey: Results from Years 7 and 8 (Combined) of the Rolling Programme (2014/2015–2015/2016)*, Public Health England and Food Standards Agency, London.

Rousseau S 2012, *Food Media: Celebrity Chefs and the Politics of Everyday Interference*, Bloomsbury, London.

Rowe M, Prestage M & Cook E 1999, 'TV chefs and their seafoodie fans rescue Britain's fishermen', *Independent on Sunday*, 15 August, p. 7.

Royal Commission on Environmental Pollution 2004, *Turning the Tide: Addressing the Impact of Fisheries on the Marine Environment* London, Cm 6392.

Ruxton CHS, Reed SC, Simpson MJA & Millington KJ 2007, 'The health benefits of omega-3 polyunsaturated fatty acids: a review of the evidence', *Journal of Human Nutrition and Dietetics*, vol. 20, no. 3, pp. 275–285.

SACN 2018, *SACN Statement on Diet, Cognitive Impairment and Dementia*, Scientific Advisory Committee on Nutrition, London.

Sainsbury's 2013, *Switch the Fish: Facts, Choices, Action – A Micro Report on the Sustainable Fishing Debate*, Sainsbury's, London.

Sanders T 'Why do fish consumption studies come to different conclusions in terms of heart disease?', in *Heart Research and Seafish Conference: The Mediterranean Diet Revisited, 2 November 2012 at Fishmongers' Hall*, London.

Santerre CR 2010, 'The risks and benefits of farmed fish', *Journal of the World Aquaculture Society*, vol. 41, no. 2, pp. 250–257.

Scientific Advisory Committee on Nutrition and Committee on Toxicity 2004, *Advice on Fish Consumption: Benefits and Risks*, The Stationery Office, London.

Scottish Office 1993, *Scotland's Health a Challenge to Us All: The Scottish Diet*, Scottish Office, Edinburgh, The James Report.

Scottish Office 1996, *Eating for Health: A Diet Action Plan for Scotland*, Scottish Office, Edinburgh.

Scottish Office 1999, *Towards a Healthier Scotland: A White Paper on Health*, The Stationery Office, Edinburgh.

Seafish 1987, *Guidelines for the Handling of Fresh Fish by Retailers*, Sea Fish Industry Authority, Edinburgh.

Seafish 1999, *United Kingdom Fish Catering Sector Handbook*, Sea Fish Industry Authority, Edinburgh.

Seafish 2005, *Consumer Attitudes to the Environment and Seafood*, Sea Fish Industry Authority, Edinburgh.

Seafish 2012, *Seafood Industry Factsheet*, Sea Fish Industry Authority, Edinburgh.

Seafish 2016, *Seafood: Consumption (2016 Update)*, Sea Fish Industry Authority, Grimsby.

Seafish 2017, *Seafood Consumption (2017 Update)*, Sea Fish Industry Authority, Grimsby, Seafood Industry Factsheet.

Seafish 2018, *Corporate Plan 2018–2021*, Sea Fish Industry Authority, Edinburgh.

Shaw SA & Egan DN 1996, 'Marketing', in *Developments in Aquaculture and Fisheries Science*, Pennnell W & Barton BA, eds., Elsevier, Amsterdam.

Sheeshka J & Murkin E 2002, 'Nutritional aspects of fish compared with other protein sources', *Comments on Toxicology*, vol. 8, no. 4–6, pp. 375–397.

Simopoulos AP 1997, 'Nutritional aspects of fish', in *Seafood from Producer to Consumer: Integrated Approaches to Quality, Proceedings of the International Conference on the occasion of the 25th anniversary of the WEFTA, held in Noordwijkerhout, The Netherlands, 13–16 November 1993*, Luten JB, Børresen T & Oehlenschlägen J, eds., Elsevier, Amsterdam.

Simopoulos AP 2008, 'The importance of the omega-6/omega-3 fatty acid ratio in cardiovascular disease and other chronic diseases', *Experimental Biology and Medicine*, vol. 233, no. 6, pp. 674–688.

Simopoulos AP 2016, 'An increase in the omega-6/omega-3 fatty acid ratio increases the risk for obesity', *Nutrients*, vol. 8, no. 3, p. 128.

Siscovick DS, Barringer TA, Fretts AM, Wu JHY, Lichtenstein AH, Costello RB, Kris-Etherton PM, Jacobson TA, Engler MB, Alger HM, Appel LJ & Mozaffarian D 2017, 'Omega-3 polyunsaturated fatty acid (fish oil) supplementation and the prevention of clinical cardiovascular disease: a science advisory from the American Heart Association', *Circulation*, vol. 135, no. 15, p. e867-e884.

Smith KJ, Sanderson K, McNaughton SA, Gall SL, Dwyer T & Venn AJ 2014, 'Longitudinal associations between fish consumption and depression in young adults', *American Journal of Epidemiology*, vol. 179, no. 10, pp. 1228–1235.

Sogn-Grundvåg G, Larsen TA & Young JA 2013, 'The value of line-caught and other attributes: An explanation of price premiums for chilled fish in British supermarkets', *Marine Policy*, vol. 38, March, pp. 41–44.

Sustainable Consumption Roundtable 2006, *I Will If You Will: Towards Sustainable Consumption*, Sustainable Development Commission.

Symes D 1988, *The Inland Wholesale Fish Markets: 1. The Inland Markets Survey*, Sea Fish Industry Authority and University of Hull, Edinburgh and Hull, Technical Report 345.

Taylor RA 1960, *The Economics of White Fish Distribution in Great Britain* Duckworth, London.

Tetley S 2016, *Why the Big 5? Understanding UK Seafood Consumer Behaviour*, PhD, Kent Business School, University of Kent.

Trondsen T, Scholderer J, Lund E & Eggen AE 2003, 'Perceived barriers to consumption of fish among Norwegian women', *Appetite*, vol. 41, no. 3, pp. 301–314.

Urch M 1976, *Recipe Development of Six Cockle and Mussel Dishes*, White Fish Authority, Epsom and Edinburgh, Technical Report 133.

Vandamme SG, Griffiths AM, Taylor S, Di Muri C, Hankard EA, Towne JA, Watson M & Mariani S 2016, 'Sushi barcoding in the UK: another kettle of fish', *PeerJ*, vol. 4, p. e1891.

Verbeke W & Vackier I 2005, 'Individual determinants of fish consumption: application of the theory of planned behaviour', *Appetite*, vol. 44, no. 1, pp. 67–82.

Wakefield M, Loken B & Hornik RC 2010, 'Use of mass media campaigns to change health behaviour', *The Lancet*, vol. 376, no. 9, October, pp. 1261–1271.

Wardle J, Parmenter K & Waller J 2013, 'Nutrition knowledge and food intake', *Appetite*, vol. 34, no. 3, pp. 269–275.

Warner K, Mustain P, Lowell B, Geren S & Talmage S 2016, *Deceptive Dishes: Seafood Swaps Found Worldwide*, Oceana, Washington.

Washington S & Ababouch L 2011, *Private Standards and Certification in Fisheries and Aquaculture: Current Practice and Emerging Issues*, Food and Agriculture Organization of the United Nations, Rome.

White Fish Authority 1959, *The White Fish Industry*, White Fish Authority, London.

White Fish Authority 1974, *Fish in the Cook/Freeze System of Catering*, White Fish Authority, Epsom and Edinburgh, Technical Report 102.

White Fish Authority 1977, *Development of a Breaded Seafood Product: Seafood Platter*, White Fish Authority, Epsom and Edinburgh, Technical Report 147.

White Fish Authority 1978a, *Mackerel Promotion Exercise Conducted in 6 Supermarkets in the London Area*, White Fish Authority, Epsom, Technical Report 161.

White Fish Authority 1978b, *Summary of Market Research Carried Out to Determine the Market Potential and Market Opportunities for Fresh Mackerel in the UK*, White Fish Authority, Epsom and Edinburgh, Technical Report 156.

White Fish Authority 1978c, *The Assessment of Blue Whiting Acceptability in Institutions*, White Fish Authority, Epsom and Edinburgh, Technical Report 160.

White Fish Authority 1980, *Opportunities for Composite Fillet Portions of Blue Whiting in Institutional Catering*, White Fish Authority, Epsom and Edinburgh.

White T 1977, *Blue Whiting Processing Trials Stornaway 1977*, White Fish Authority, Edinburgh, Technical Report 153.

Wood RC 2000, 'Why are there so many celebrity chefs and cooks (and do we need them)? Culinary cultism and crassness on television and beyond', in *Strategic Questions in Food and Beverage Management*, Wood RC, ed., Butterworth-Heineman, Oxford & Woburn MA.

Woolmer A 2010a, *Shellfish: The Natural Choice for Healthy Diet*, Shellfish Association of Great Britain and Sea Fish Industry Authority, London & Edinburgh.

Woolmer A 2010b, *The Nutritional Benefits of Shellfish Part 1 and Part 2*, Shellfish Association of Great Britain and Sea Fish Industry Authority, London & Edinburgh.

Wu S, Feng B, Li K, Zhu X, Liang S, Liu X, Han S, Wang B, Wu K, Miao D, Liang J & Fan D 2012, 'Fish consumption and colorectal cancer risk in humans: a systematic review and meta-analysis', *The American Journal of Medicine*, vol. 125, no. 6, pp. 551–559.

Yudkin J 1977, *Nutrition* Hodder and Stoughton, Sevenoaks.

Zheng J-S, Hu X-J, Zhao Y-M, Yang J & Li D 2013, 'Intake of fish and marine n-3 polyunsaturated fatty acids and risk of breast cancer: meta-analysis of data from 21 independent prospective cohort studies', *BMJ*, vol. 346, no. 27, June 2013, p. f3706.

Zibaeenezhad MJ, Ghavipisheh M, Attar A & Aslani A 2017, 'Comparison of the effect of omega-3 supplements and fresh fish on lipid profile: a randomized, open-labeled trial', *Nutrition and Diabetes*, vol. 7, no. 1, December.

6 Governance at the end of the supply chain

Seafood retailing and foodservice

Retail and the governance of consumer supply

Fishmongers and supermarkets

Although seafood has been the subject of similar retail changes to those affecting fresh foods in general in the last six decades it involves some special features. These have been subject to certain governance influences as well as having governance impacts on consumers.

At the end of the 1950s, there were about 15,000 fishmongers and 17,000 fish and chip shops in the UK with some overlap between them (White Fish Authority 1959). The second item of information encapsulates a very particular aspect of seafood consumption, the extent to which it has consisted of fish cooked outside the home and purchased in takeaway form (and is considered in detail later in this chapter). Fish selling was not infrequently combined with either poultry or other foods but was sufficiently distinctive to be described as deploying craft skills and to be considered by those involved as 'a career with a thrill in it' (National Federation of Fishmongers 1955). Although most fishmongers are assumed to have been solo enterprises, many high streets featured one of the MacFisheries chain of shops of which there were 420 by 1956, part of a vertically integrated company which included fishing trawlers and a wholesale fish business. At the same time, the development of frozen fish had extended the retail options for fish which could now be stocked by general grocery stores (Chaloner 1971). MacFisheries developed into a general supermarket chain during the 1960s and 1970s but failed to compete successfully and after it was sold off at the end of the latter decade its remaining wet fish shops were all closed.[1]

Seafood was the last category of fresh foods to be absorbed by the supermarkets. Initial attempts in the 1960s were unsuccessful because factors like short shelf life could not be overcome at that stage but efforts restarted in some larger stores in the late 1970s with the innovation of modified atmosphere packaging (MAP) (Goulding 1985). This made it possible to treat fish more like other foods in the supermarket system rather than it needing special arrangements but there was a quality penalty. The implications of changing from the use of a wholesale market to a supermarket's own distribution network, using MAP, was described by one of the research interviewees:

> Historically, [named supermarket] used to get a lot of supply from Billingsgate to supply all their London stores. But then they decided they want to go to central distribution and again that was all about cost saving. But of course, one of the problems with fish if you want to keep it really well you need to keep it on ice, one of the problems with ice is that ice melts. Difficult to put on a lorry taking cheese and god knows what else to the store, ice melting all over the floor. So [they] made a decision, and that's been followed by quite a few of the other supermarkets now, they will move away from the old traditional way of distributing fish and they would now distribute it with a thing called MAP packaging, modified atmosphere packaging. When they decided, [they were] the first people to do it and when they went across to MAP packaging, of course, we didn't have the facility to do it at Billingsgate, so they took the order away. [*After the interviewee wrote a critical piece about this for a trade paper the retailer complained.*] What they were unhappy about was that I was letting the cat out of the bag, that their supposed fresh fish was no longer fresh fish, it was actually MAP packaged fish.
>
> (Trade organisation representative 1.)

Fishmongers had sharply reduced to 4,800 by 1971 (Rosson 1975). Nevertheless, 1991 market analysis indicated that fishmongers still sold 42% of fresh fish and the supermarkets only 28% (the 27% listed as 'other' is assumed to have been sold through mobile vans and by stalls); however, the supermarkets dealt with most tinned and frozen fish (LeGrand 1992). By 1995, supermarket fresh fish sales were up to 61% (Murray & Fofana 2002). In 2005, there were just under 1,300 fishmonger outlets all told, including mobile fish vans and market stalls, with 85% of chilled and frozen seafood being sold by supermarkets (James 2006; Seafish 2005). Supermarkets had finally become the main, in very many places the only, source for buying fish.

However, shopping arrangements have not been static and general developments have provided some additional options for purchasing seafood. Direct selling by producers to the public has been one direction of change which some companies have adopted. In a database of seafood processing and distribution companies compiled during 2009/2010, more than a tenth of the total had a retail shop and/or online service. Some of these concerns had their own fishing boats, one was a shellfish farmer, many primarily carried out primary processing and distribution while others produced smoked fish (Greenwood 2015). These primarily represent short supply chains between consumers and processors or merchants.

Community Supported Fisheries (CSF) constitute another short supply chain alternative, this time linking consumers with fishers, directly or via a wholesaler. Scheme members pay in advance for a share of the catch and receive a box of seafood at specified intervals in return. The arrangement is intended to provide a consistent income for fishers and to make better use of the full range of fish actually caught, thus supporting sustainable production. An initial project, Catchbox, was set up in 2013 as an action-based research project with a co-operative governance structure and was funded by DEFRA. It ran pilots for several months in two successive years serving initially two, then three coastal towns in southern England. They were assessed as successful having brought economic benefits to participating fishers and enlarged the knowledge and seafood tastes of participating consumers (Giorgi et al. 2016). Following this pilot, at the time of writing two CSF schemes were in existence, each serving a particular part of London.[2] These short chains with their benefits in terms of very fresh fish and support for sustainable fishing may develop further but with their small output seem unlikely ever to play anything but a minor role in retail arrangements.

Achieving seafood safety and quality in retail

Achieving quality and the correct handling of fish have been issues at the retail end just as has been tracked in all the preceding stages of the supply chain. A mid-1960s account said that many fish shops were dirty, unhygienic and in disrepair, categorising the fish sold in them as ranging from good to poor in quality (Burgess et al. 1965). Two Seafish surveys in 1983, which involved analysis of hundreds of samples, found low standards of freshness with a fifth falling below acceptability levels. Although too few in number for statistical significance, the best results were achieved by mobile traders, attributed to faster turnover from their active sales techniques. On the negative side, particular concerns were noted about the low scores for MAP pre-packed fish sold by supermarkets despite sell-by dates being observed. The ratings for cleanliness and general appearance were in reverse to the quality of products with supermarkets scoring highly and mobile sellers poorly (Myers 1983).[3]

Seafish functioning, as we have seen at other points in the supply chain in the role of quality promoter, subsequently issued guidelines for retailers emphasising the need for better temperature control and proper use of ice; the document linked the decline of fish-eating in the previous quarter century to the poor quality of so much sold, the only source that has been found to make this surely well-justified observation (Seafish 1987). In addition, it appears that Seafish developed a specific Code of Practice for producing and handling MAP fish as this is mentioned in the 1983 report. In later years, Seafish was involved in a further quality activity geared to retail which was the development together with the Billingsgate Seafood Training School of a fishmongery course could then be offered by all the teaching institutions involved in the Seafood Training Academy; this has become a VRQ (vocationally related qualification) in Fishmonger Skills.

Standards of independent shops had evidently improved greatly by the time of the Seafish-commissioned research in the mid-2000s because those questioned thought that fishmongers provided better quality than the supermarkets. Consumers gave a higher valuation to good hygiene than fishmongers appeared to do and also credited choice and the expertise and advice of personnel in these outlets (Seafish 2005). It seems from this work that there might be a long-term place for independents to continue in tandem with supermarket supply, fishmongers competing on quality, stalls and vans on price. Some shops supplied restaurants in addition to selling directly to the public, strengthening their viability.

However, as supermarkets are now the main source of seafood for most shoppers, the key question is how well they perform in relation to both food safety requirements and quality. There is no up-to-date survey comparable to the work done by Seafish in the 1980s that can provide a direct comparison. There have been several investigations in which supermarket fish has been sampled, but, as related in Chapter 5, they have generally been to check on the authenticity of their labels not, with very limited exceptions, to assess their quality.

Failing such evaluations we can at least start with the subjective evaluations of people in the trade on what they think of overall standards of the seafood sold in supermarkets. Some did indeed think that supermarkets deserved credit for improving quality:

> The way that the retail markets have driven the supply chain down that continuous improvement route has meant that quality management controls generally, food safety and traceability standards, have increased tremendously because of the demands that the retailers have put on in terms of factory standards and going for things like BRC accreditation which is pretty much the norm for anyone who wants to supply the retail market and big wholesalers as well.
>
> (Industry advisor, trade organisation)

> What the retailers are doing is raising the bar all the time, fighting the consumers' cause because again they don't want to be on [named television programme] next week. It's the power of the consumer, power of the press. The supermarkets' own label being as popular as it is, and supermarkets putting their name to it, they don't want to make anyone ill, they want to make a good product. So all the time raising the bar with suppliers in terms of standards that we must adhere to.
>
> (Commercial manager, medium-large company)

> I tell you where we shop, at [named retailers] and so on. Because you get the quality, they insist on the quality. They've made a major contribution to the quality standards in this country.
>
> (Managing director, small company 1)

On the other side of the scale, the opposite view was held by others, the second quotation expressing the reaction of someone with personal standards based on daily access to very-recently landed fish:

> In terms of quality supply the retailers, depending on who they are, different aspirations, all say we want higher quality, our customers demand the highest possible quality and we want to be the highest possible quality. In actual fact they don't really care. They do set certain parameters which the supplier is obliged to meet, and they are quite stringent and quite strict. Albeit they don't really care because profit and market share control what they do and if they find they are losing either of those … they will modify their purchasing strategies accordingly and they will cut corners for the commercial results they are seeking to achieve…. Their customers haven't got a clue what they're buying. It's a total con.
>
> (Trade representative 3)

> It's like when you go to the supermarkets, I've seen what the fish is like. It's all off, you see it, it's all off and it's not right, they sell that 'cos it's the right temperature but it's all rubbish what you see on the supermarkets … It's not fresh. They put it in the packages but it's not fresh. It lies in own juices there, not good for it.
>
> (Managing director, small company 3)

A rare test of quality was provided by a 2013 piece of investigative journalism in which Torry ratings were applied to samples of cod, plaice and salmon purchased from the largest four supermarkets. The majority were found to be just at or below the level considered acceptable for consumption while comparator samples from a single fishmonger had noticeably higher scores. However, this was a very small survey of 12 samples from supermarkets and three from the fishmonger, not a scientific study, so it simply tells us that the quality of fish from supermarkets is not always high and cannot indicate how typical the findings are of standards as a whole.[4] It does suggest that more considered research into the quality of fish sold in retail establishments would be useful and one subject that could be examined is whether there is a difference in quality between what is sold on wet fish counters and ready-packaged uncooked seafood. It is notable that there has been so little research into the quality and food safety of seafood as sold which would require qualitative human assessment whether using the Torry or an alternative scale compared to the number of investigations of authenticity using cutting-edge DNA testing and other new technological tools. Both are equally needed.

While opinions from interviewees about quality provided by supermarkets were mixed, we saw in Chapter 4 unanimous views from different sources that the quality of seafood produced by the industry as a whole was very good and much better than it had been in the past. We also saw that there were extensive systems in place to maintain high standards and that for many suppliers supermarkets are the driving force in the maintenance of such standards. It is of course possible for excellent quality seafood to leave the processing factory but to be in a less good condition when it is actually sold depending on conditions in the distribution system and the level of care taken along the way, but the retailers have every incentive to run systems that will maintain food safety and quality standards.

In the first place, they are of course bound by public regulation. The *Food Safety Act 1990* with its 'due diligence' principle forced supermarkets to ensure that they sold products that met high standards, as previously noted, and they are equally affected by subsequent regulations, both those specifying hygiene standards for seafood and general food safety legislation. As with other food businesses, larger companies are expected to self-regulate and local monitoring and enforcement concentrates on smaller concerns (Hutter 2011). However, prosecutions against the major retailers brought by local authorities demonstrate that supermarkets continue to be subject to active regulatory monitoring which remains a necessary backstop to private and self-governance as shown by various prosecutions against all the majors for selling out-of-date items (this was not specifically about seafood which has not been singled out in reporting of these cases).[5] Most, though not all, of the incidents found occurred several years in the past; if the prosecutions incentivised greater efficiency in preventing sale of out-of-date products which could have been a food safety hazard they certainly served their purpose.

The fines imposed were unlikely to have mattered financially to the companies, rather it was the damage to their reputations when the cases were reported that must have hurt. Such potential damage creates pressures to prioritise food safety as both a retailer respondent and a supplier made explicit:

> In food, as you know, there's been more and more scares. So again, us and the supermarkets are trying to foresee some of these, what are the issues of the future, what can we do to put things in place to deal with those. At the end of the day, it's making our food safer,
>
> (Commercial manager, medium-large company)

> And it's more the case that if there is some kind of scare in the industry, we want to make sure whatever it is, we are absolutely 100% whiter than white.
>
> (Buyer, major retailer)

Hence there is a drive for supermarket suppliers to have BRC food safety accreditation. The multiples need to respond to any safety issue and an example is the FSA investigation of mercury in imported fish and shellfish mentioned in the previous chapter. The report of the investigation appended statements from four of the major retailers, all of them emphasising that their suppliers routinely monitor mercury levels.[6]

Apart from safety and quality, the role of supermarkets has been significant in enlarging the range of seafood products available to consumers. The readiness of some consumers to eat a wider range of seafood was noted in the previous section; hypothetically, there must have been a series of symbiotic moves in which retailers with their suppliers have trialled new options and consumers have, at least some of the time, responded favourably. Fresh salmon, fresh tuna and warm-water prawns, now top sellers, have only become generally available in recent decades. The supply factors discussed in Chapter 3 have been responsible for such availability but the supermarkets' distribution systems have made mass market purchasing possible. In addition, a great number of seafood prepared meals and other types of ready-to-eat dishes in both chilled and frozen form have been made available by the multiples.

Retailer information is one route to influencing choices and specific promotions can be effective; one supermarket has carried out Switch the Fish events in which it gave away fish from certain less often eaten species; sales of these varieties increased in subsequent months (Future Foundation 2012). Another has explained the greater ease of promotions with farmed fish which can be better planned in advance (Tesco 1999). Demonstrating the impact of marketing, another retailer was credited by a processor in the research with changing the fortunes of one species; a 1990 report on a once huge pilchard fishery, noting it had reduced to less than 600 tonnes a year for human consumption, much of it exported, listed 12 constraints which would make development of the market difficult (Eurographic Ltd 1990) but a few years later when re-branded as 'Cornish sardines' fish sales took off:

> [named supermarket] have done all the scientific research, good enough for me. Since they done that, the Cornish sardine fishery is quite big. ... We sell 100 kilo a day whereas we couldn't sell 100 kilo a year previously.
>
> (Managing director, small company 7.[7])

In addition, convenience of presentation has been a factor in extending the attractiveness of these options. As one of the respondents said:

> Fish was in the old days presented with lots of bones; the majority of fish is now presented either skinless and boneless or certainly boneless. It is also presented in a form that people of a culinary bent can still cook it so it's more convenient now than it ever was, and I think that's why it's increased.
>
> (Managing director, medium-large aquaculture company)

This echoed statements by two leading supermarkets presented as evidence to a Parliamentary enquiry. One reported rapid growth in sales of packaged fish, particularly of prepared cuts where bones and skin have been removed (Tesco 1999). The other noted increasing preference among its customers for convenience products like coated and smoked fish, overtaking sales of the raw form (Asda 1999).

A general driver in the food market has been a constant emphasis on new products and innovation. Very different from the public sector efforts at product development outlined in the previous chapter, an account by one of the research participants, describes a process of interchange between the seafood processor and a major retailer customer in which the former does most of the work:

> We have people dedicated to new product development all the time. Whether they come up with new sauces or new impact formats. ... With [named supermarket] for example, we will send down maybe 20 or 30 new products for them to look at. And they will come back and say they would like to progress on two or three. And we go through a proper review with them of what it will be, what it will look like, what the selling price will be. And you go through all that and then they will say yeah, we'll try that or don't like that.
>
> (Director, medium-large company)

The supermarkets have thus been exercising the governance of availability as people can only buy what is on sale but at the same time they cannot determine what will sell successfully so there is a relationship of interdependence with their customers. As far as food safety is concerned the retailers are both the subjects of regulation and drivers of governance mechanisms within their supply chains to fulfil the legal requirements. On quality, however, which is not legislated, each supermarket is a driver of governance, using its buying power to obtain products that fit their overall brand image and commercial strategy (and of course to obtain favourable prices).

The struggle for supermarket sustainable sourcing

However, there is another area where other agents, namely environmental NGOs, have been exercising governance over the supermarkets and that is in relation to sustainable seafood sourcing. Various tactics have been used with differing impacts.

Greenpeace launched its operation in 2005 with a report critically reviewing the sourcing policies of the top nine seafood retailers (Greenpeace 2005). Its 2006 stunt to put pressure on one supermarket chain made a deep impression including the fact that it did result in a sourcing change as reflected in one (albeit critical) interview comment:

> Greenpeace sitting on the roof of Asda's building, that's unacceptable behaviour as well. Yes it gets the headlines, gets Asda to say it will stop buying North Sea cod. It's like the plastic bag issue in supermarkets, it's over-simplified by the media. So that's all people can take in.
>
> (Commercial manager, medium-large company)

Just one year later, the NGO was able to report considerable change: all the retailers had produced sustainable procurement policies and progress was being made towards removing unsustainably fished species from their shelves (Greenpeace 2006). The league tables rated the multiples on sustainable sourcing which Greenpeace included in its two reports. Having proved to be an effective tool of governance, the idea was picked up by other organisations

MCS has produced three such rankings on a survey basis.[8] The quango National Consumer Council and successor body Consumer Focus produced retailer rankings on 'sustainable fish' as part of a general assessment of performance on environmental criteria in three reports (Allder & Yates 2009; Dibb 2006; Yates 2007). Farmed fish welfare is a factor in the Compassion in World Farming (CIWF) periodic Most Compassionate Supermarket assessments.[9] All the ratings recognise the long-term efforts that some of the supermarkets have made in their sourcing practices and may motivate others to do more, thus exercising a governance impact upon them. At the same time, they assist retailers who are competing on quality because it gives their claims validation from publicly trusted sources. Thus while NGO campaigning has been effective, to some extent they were beating on doors that if not open were at least ajar.

Both of the supermarkets represented in the interviews referred to the MCS ranking but neither to the CIWF one. One of them mentioned the need to take note of where it stood in the MCS ranking, illustrating the importance attached to this assessment and hence acknowledging its governance impact:

> The MCS do a league chart, the ranking thing, now that will go to the press. We came out quite well in it, we were quite pleased with it. … We need to be doing the work behind the scenes so if anything does come up then we know we're fine with everything.
>
> (Buyer, major retailer)

However, other retailers when they have a choice may resist the governance implicit in such NGO rankings. For the MCS 2013 survey, the same number of supermarkets declined to take part in the survey as completed the questionnaire, including two of the top four. Predictably the chains that had performed worst in the past were the least likely to co-operate in the exercise, indicating limitations to an NGO's ability to affect them. At the time of writing, there had not been a further MCS supermarket survey after 2013 and there were no plans for another one.[10] It may be that the rankings had served their purpose and that there would be diminishing returns from simply routinising them.

Greenpeace started a new campaign in 2008 focusing on tuna (Greenpeace 2008). It had previously noted a problem with retailers' sustainable sourcing policies applying only to their own-label ranges and not to branded canned fish (Greenpeace 2006). Public awareness over tuna (and other seafood sustainability issues) was also raised by a television film, *The End of the Line*, which its producers used as a tool in extensive lobbying activity (Channel 4 Britdoc Foundation 2011). In a follow-up report, Greenpeace recorded that three of the multiples sourced all their own-brand tuna from more sustainable pole-and-line operations (Greenpeace 2011). During that year the campaign was supported by the inclusion of tuna issues in the Channel 4 programme *Hugh's Fish Fight*. The 2012 report, *Changing Tuna: How the Global Tuna Industry is in Transition to Sustainable Supply*, reported not only that the remaining major UK retailers had committed to switching to pole-and-line tuna by specific dates but further that the companies producing the two main brands sold in Britain (Princes and John West) had also committed to this change (Greenpeace 2012). This has been a striking achievement and Greenpeace, the Fish Fight campaign and *The End of the Line* film may all share some credit for a successful exercise in governance with a considerable impact on improving the sustainability of sourcing by British retailers. That did not mean that the battle was won: the 2017 tuna league table while commending several supermarket chains for own-brand sustainable tuna also reported that the John West brand (owned by Thai Union) which had promised 100% sustainability by 2016 had achieved just 2% while Princes (owned by Mitsubishi) was at a better but still very inadequate 25%. Brands thus proving harder to crack, Greenpeace turned to putting pressure on supermarkets to stop stocking unsustainable ones; its campaign generated a reported 40,000 emails to Waitrose on the subject within a few days after which the retailer gave an ultimatum to the John West company; another campaign directed at Sainsbury's did not, however, result in any apparent change as far as stocking this brand was concerned and they continued to do so. Nevertheless, Greenpeace was able to announce in 2017 that its global campaigning had resulted in Thai Union undertaking various significant changes towards sustainable tuna as well as in tackling labour abuses.[11]

Back in the UK, MCS's traffic light sustainability classification which aims to produce change via consumers has instead had a more direct impact on retailer sourcing. A particularly effective aspect seems to be that sale of items classified as 'fish to avoid' (category 5 in one version) has been a key factor in lowering position in both Greenpeace and MCS rankings:

> So really it's about working with the best, avoiding the worst and that is primarily we would say avoid anything on our banned list and avoid any that are on the MCS fish to avoid list.
>
> (Category technologist, major retailer)

> There's all the sustainability matrix that we go through with the supplier before we even agree to list anything. ... So for example, on a fresh fish line, the first thing to decide would be what grade MCS says, Marine Conservation Society. So anything grade 5 we do not stock.
>
> (Buyer, major retailer)

The MSC certification scheme is also central to supermarket seafood sourcing. In fact, the multiples have been described as dominating discussions in the formative stage of the programme with an 'overwhelming desire for this sort of labelling' (MacMullen 1998, p. 36) and similarly were among those who urged WWF to set up what became the ASC as noted in Chapter 3. The retailer interviewees referred to their confidence in the MSC:

> We do believe firmly in the MSC and that centres around the original formation of the MSC, being a multi-stakeholder group, and there was plenty of opportunity for everyone to almost feed into the development of those standards. We do think it's a fair standard and we don't currently see any other standard that would be deemed as an equivalent.
>
> (Category technologist, major retailer)

> The MSC, their accreditation system that we consider to be the gold standard of sustainability.
>
> (Buyer, major retailer)

They also mentioned a range of approaches taken as part of their sustainable sourcing policies:

> And then we look at catch method, there are certain catch methods that we exclude, beam trawling, cyanide, that kind of thing. So, some catch methods we'll exclude straightaway.
>
> (Buyer, major retailer)

> From a responsibility point of view, we are looking to increase the amount of lesser-known species that we sell.... We are also looking to increase in the amount of aquaculture that we take from but on that front, we do need to be careful from a feed point of view, on the feed that is used for aquaculture, making sure that there is ... sustainability concerned with feed.
>
> (Category technologist, major retailer)

Another variant is the published scheme of another British supermarket which has its own traffic light rating developed through interchange with environmentalists as well as with the seafood industry. MSC-certified seafood is preferred but if that is not available the ratings are applied (Washington & Ababouch 2011, p. 44).

Such attention to environmental criteria has not always been evident and one interviewee had a disillusioned story to tell about the clash between sustainability and price for one supermarket chain which changed from pole-and-line caught to cheaper purse-seine capture tuna in the mid-1980s (however, in a more recent period this same retailer has changed back to the more sustainable option for own-brand supplies). So there was a critical perspective about the supermarkets' sustainability efforts on the part of some of the (non-retailer) research participants:

> Certainly, the buyers don't want to be seen to be sourcing fish that isn't squeaky clean. Because it's a PR disaster waiting to happen. You have got that because the movement has gathered real momentum. They wouldn't want to be the one to be seen to step out of line, the PR effect would be quite damaging.
>
> (Managing director, medium-large company)

> With the credit crunch, 18 months ago, at the beginning of that, the retailers, sustainability went out of the window and economics became the prime mover. All of the retailers moved from cod to haddock and that was not a sustainability issue, that was purely and simply an economic issue. And now that the price of haddock has gone up they're all back to cod.
>
> (Site manager, medium-large company)

With the varying motives involved, an overall judgement was perhaps best delivered by this mixed reflection from another interview:

> The UK retailers … are very, very interested in sustainability but in all honesty some of that is about their own general environmental credentials as opposed to passionate commitment to the sustainability of fisheries per se.… The UK retailer I've found is among the most committed around the world. The UK has led the sort of pole side of sustainability from the marketplace more than anywhere else.
>
> (Director, large company)

For retailers who wish to source sustainably, there is another source of advice other than the MCS guide as there have been contributions on 'responsible sourcing' from Seafish over a long period which have developed over the years. Starting in 2007 the organisation produced both general information and individual species-based 'responsible sourcing guides', kept updated; at one time there were 34 for capture species and four dealing with farmed seafood. These have more recently been replaced by an online tool, the Risk Assessment for Sourcing Seafood (RASS) together with a more extensive series of documents on specific topics such as IUU fishing, DNA testing and microplastics. RASS contains details of fisheries for each species, which are given risk ratings on four criteria: stock status, management, bycatch and habitat. There is also a set of aquaculture profiles for the farmed species most relevant to the British supply chain, each of which contains comprehensive information including cultivation methods and locations, governance aspects and potential hotspot issues like feed, nutrient pollution and escapes.[12]

The year 2011 saw the founding of a new initiative which could assist the supermarkets, the Sustainable Seafood Coalition (SSC). Instigated by the NGO ClientEarth, which provides its secretariat, the membership consists mainly of seafood companies and major retailers with some foodservice and trade body involvement so the organisation represents the entire UK supply chain downstream of (but not including) primary producers. The campaigning Fish Fight (now ended) was also a founding member but no additional NGO seems to have been involved. With a vision that 'all seafood sold in the UK is from sustainable sources' its mechanisms are two voluntary codes of conduct, on labelling and on sourcing, which lay down the steps that justify a claim of sustainable or responsible sourcing. Starting with risk assessments against stated minimum criteria, in relation to fisheries sustainability claims should rest on certification or other third-party checks while responsibility claims may be made in relation to low-risk fisheries or medium risk ones where agreed improvements are taking place; for farmed products, they should depend on audited standards and appropriate action being taken if the result is unsatisfactory (Sustainable Seafood Coalition 2018). The codes are intended as a corrective to misleading or unverifiable claims of sustainable or responsible sourcing that were identified in the investigation that preceded and incentivised the establishment of the SSC (ClientEarth 2011).[13] A report by Which? had also criticised several supermarkets for making unsupported claims about the sustainability of the fish they sold and for failing to provide essential information.[14] The codes are voluntary so there is no third-party auditing but the SSC commissioned a report two years after the codes were agreed from an independent consultant. This found that of products with claims examined (most stating responsible sourcing rather than sustainability) 83% met the labelling code requirements (compared to 68% in the 2011 investigation) and 89% those of the sourcing code. This seems to show that the codes are having some effect though the report did recommend more information both on packs and online (Pazderka 2017).

The supermarkets also have the option of working with another organisation that supports seafood sustainability, the Sustainable Fisheries Partnership (SFP) which was encountered in Chapter 3 in relation to the review of industrial fisheries' sustainability. Under its aegis there was an innovation in transparency from the retailer Asda when in 2014 they jointly published the *Asda Wild Fisheries Annual Review 2013* giving a list of fisheries from which each capture species was sourced, its sustainability category and a brief summary of connected environmental issues, presented as a global first. The SFP's Ocean Disclosure Project was then launched in 2015 with the participation of three UK retailers (including Asda) plus two aquaculture feed companies and similar information about the fisheries from which these companies source is now available in online format for all of them, remaining an unusual exercise in transparency and a potential source of information-sharing by other companies.[15]

Comparing the SSC and SFP approaches, the Sustainable Seafood Coalition depends on an internal assessment by retailers and rests on codes without third-party auditing but has the advantages of incorporating active work to improve fisheries and also of covering farmed seafood. With the SFP Ocean Disclosure arrangement which only deals with capture fish, an organisation separate from retailers, namely the Sustainable Fisheries Partnership, rates the fisheries; this is a more objective approach but it is unclear how the ratings themselves in which the lowest level is 'needs improvement' compare with assessments by other organisation which use terms like 'poor'. These are not of course mutually exclusive routes to responsible sourcing and indeed there are retailers involved in both initiatives. The basic situation is that the demand for seafood that the retailers seek to fulfil far exceeds the volume of certified product available, so they need systems which help them make better choices.

Some of the multiples had worked for many years on sustainable sourcing while others appear to have been motivated more recently by environmental NGO campaigning. Either way, they have complex rationales for such policies apart from what may well be a sincere desire to support sustainability. As with Unilever when it jointly set up the MSC, retailers have a sensible commercial interest in working to ensure future supplies of fish. Promoting less well-known species to reduce discards of those same fish and relieve cod may also be a mechanism for selling more seafood and getting ahead of competitors in what is offered to shoppers. The supermarkets are in part responding to the environmental NGOs and a concern about green issues among a section of consumers and in part working on their image as socially responsible organisations, important in maintaining the trust of customers.

This section has provided an account of changing patterns of seafood retailing which, as in the rest of the food system, has eventuated in supermarket domination. The multiples have been key players in both improving quality and increasing the range of seafood sold, whether of diversified species or in terms of various convenience formats. In this way, they have changed seafood consumption; from a health point of view increasing seafood purchasing by making it easier and more convenient has been valuable but the type of seafood sold has not necessarily been the oily fish most beneficial except for the major increase in salmon availability thanks to the success of aquaculture.

As with all food operators, supermarkets are publicly regulated but as the most downstream party in the supply chain, not privately governed. However, they have been the object of environmentalist campaigning which has had some successes in producing change over a short period of time. As a result, seafood sustainability has been increasingly incorporated into retailers' business objectives. This then changes consumption through choice editing. Such commitments may be expected to intensify pressure on the rest of the supply chain which is likely to manifest in increased demand for certifications for both capture and farmed seafood.

Foodservice and the governance of consumer supply

There is agreement that consumption outside the home is relatively more important for seafood than the other forms of protein, but it is not easy to establish the proportions that apply. A source from the mid-1980s reported that the domestic and catering markets for seafood were the same size (Goulding 1985) and one from the mid-1990s had a similar assessment (Backman 1996). Market research from the early 2000s stated that of all forms of protein, seafood was the most likely to be eaten outside of the home (Seafish 2003). These three indications do not match the consumption statistics from food surveys discussed earlier in this chapter which showed that only 7–8% of seafood consumption was outside the home, or if takeaways are included 13–16%, over the period the years 2000 to 2015. These inconsistencies are no doubt due to different definitions of both the seafood base (the assessments of larger proportions outside the home possibly examined only fresh and frozen fish) and of what counts as eating out; fish and chips seem to occupy a special space between home and outside eating. But regardless of the exact figures it still seems to be the case that a relatively high proportion of fish and shellfish eaten has been cooked outside the home and this accords with the evidence discussed in the previous chapter about unease over dealing with raw fish felt by many consumers.

The fish and chips channel

While seafood may be offered in all forms of foodservice, it is unusual in having its own specialised product and delivery system, 'fish and chips' with what is to a considerable extent a distinct supply chain. There are also a small number of specialist seafood restaurants. An analysis of the top five seafood species consumed outside the home in 1999 showed that as much as 30% was delivered via fish and chip shops (Seafish 1999).

Fish and chips developed in the late nineteenth and early twentieth centuries along with the new mass availability of trawler-produced whitefish plus railway transport for distribution, becoming a permanent feature of the working-class urban diet. So while seafood generally is recognised as a relatively expensive protein and sensitive to prices, in the form of fish and chips it has had a long association with poorer sections of society; this may account in part for the lack of income gradient in seafood consumption. The popularity of fish and chips has been so great that it has evolved into a recognised national dish and symbol of Britishness, having left behind its original connection with poverty and immigrants – fried fish was Jewish in origin, fried potatoes Belgian or French (Panayi 2014; Walton 1992).

In the mid-2000s, fish and chip shops were still the most patronised of all eating-out options, accounting for a third of seafood dispensed in the profit (non-institutional) foodservice sector followed by restaurants with a quarter and then pubs and hotels) (Mintel 2004; Seafish 2003). As the economic recession at the end of the decade took hold, there was a decline of fish and chip eating in all types of outlet but this has reversed from the mid-2100s and fish and chip shops continued to be the largest single source (Seafish 2017).

Discrete elements of supply, distribution and delivery to the consumer make up the fish and chip supply chain. Most of the fish, primarily cod and haddock, is supplied to the shops in frozen form, whether as frozen-at-sea fillets or fish that is just headed and gutted at sea before being frozen and shipped to China where it is defrosted, processed further and refrozen. Although a minority of fryers do use fresh fish, frozen is the norm. From the early development of the trade, a great proportion of fish for frying came from Icelandic and Faroese waters and with the major addition of the Barents Sea as a source this is still the case to a considerable extent but now the fishing takes place from non-British boats, for reasons explained in Chapter 3. The exception is that haddock from the North Sea supplies much of the Scottish market. A standardised product is delivered to a set of trade sizes and the whole system shows considerable industrialisation of the wild fish base.[16]

The second element of the system consists of specialist wholesalers who provide a one-stop service. In addition to fish, they can supply not just the frying medium and batter mix but also drinks, a range of other fast food items which are increasingly offered by fish and chip shops (such as sausages, pies, burgers and pizza), cleaning materials, packaging and even catering equipment. There are a few seafood processing companies which focus on selling fish to fryers and they may prepare it to order, but the dedicated wholesalers supply fish only in frozen form and do not carry out any form of processing.

Fish and chip shops provide the third component of the structure. In the mid-1980s, there were about 10,000 of them (Marketpower 1984), by the second half of the 1990s, the number had gone down to between 8,630 and 8,750 (Backman 1996; Seafish 1999). According to mid-2000s market research, there were 4,600 such establishments (Mintel 2004) but their trade organisation, the National Federation of Fish Friers (NFFF), has for some time been indicating the number as 10,500, a number also used by Seafish. NFFF membership is around 8,500 and while of course fish and chip establishments are not necessarily all Federation members, this figure may be closer to the situation. In any case, even the lowest estimate in this paragraph is a number vastly greater than the branches of a major rival fast food option, McDonald's, as the NFFF likes to point out on its website.[17]

The great majority of fish and chip establishments are single owner operations and, of the chains that have formed, most have just a few branches. The exception is Harry Ramsden's which has been thriving with 24 restaurants nationally in 2013 and 34 in 2018 (a chain which has had a series of different corporate owners). The range of owners allows for great diversity in the sector as one interviewee explained:

> The one thing they all have in common is they sell fish and chips. But after that point, that's it, there's nothing else they have in common.

Different ranges, different fats, different batters, different fish, different potatoes, different ways of doing things, different temperatures, different people serve, different packaging.

(Director, trade organisation)

Accompanying these differences and the small scale of most enterprises is considerable quality differentiation. Whether they source their fish on quality varies and was judged differently by different companies. One specialist supplier in the research felt that only 18–20% put quality above price. But another was able to say that 90% bought on quality while a fish wholesaler thought:

Without exception they tend to buy the top end of quality and the best quality fish produced is frozen-at-sea fillets.

(Managing director, large company)

However, there seems to be a belief in the industry that consumers do not favour frozen fish and so this is not made clear to them:

If you went to a fish and chip shop and say where do you get your fish, they will all say fresh, always, without exception. They're all frozen but they will never admit it.

(Managing director, large company)

Historically, there have been quality issues connected with fish and chip shops and they were the subject of specific legislation in the early part of the twentieth century. There was controversy about the quality of ingredients and issues over standardisation of portion size and price (Harvey, McMeekin & Warde 2004).

On the quality of what is currently delivered by fish and chip outfits the judgement made by two of the interviewees was harsh:

In my experience, there would be maybe 25% of fish and chip shops make a genuine effort to produce a decent quality product.

(Managing director, large wholesaler)

I put that now at and I still say we've got more than our fair share, between 35 and 40%, or even slightly over 40% of our customer base who really are good for the trade. Turn that round, of course, the majority of the people in the trade don't deserve to be in it.

(Chairman, medium wholesaler)

A more optimistic view held that things were improving:

If you went back ten years you would definitely be looking at less than 10%, quite definitely. I would think now you have got to be nudging up towards 50%, I would say it's higher than that, that are at an acceptable standard or above.

(Director, trade organisation)

The incentive to improve may be lessened by the fact that fish and chip businesses appear to be very profitable already, according to some of the interviewees, and the figures mentioned in the following quote contrast markedly with the very low margins mentioned Chapter 4 in relation to other seafood companies:

> You should, a good chip shop, the very best, on the top of the game, should be getting slightly above 60% gross profit. A poor one, that would be one that would buy-in either part-fried or frozen chips, probably even buying the fish in either IQF [Individually Quick Frozen] or even worse probably pre-battered or pre-breaded, you'd be looking down at the 50 mark.... I would say that an average of 55 ... would certainly be achievable.

(Director, trade organisation)

> If you want to get rich buy a fish shop, if you don't mind unsocial hours and smelling like a piece of fish.
> (Managing Director, large company (which supplies fish and chip shops))

Nevertheless, the quality situation was seen to be improving and two types of action by external agencies were seen as relevant. The input of environmental health services in raising standards was highlighted in one comment which refers to an increase in regulation compared to the past:

> If you go back 20 years, there was either no training at all and the EHOs were more like black cats, the place had to have rats running through it for the EHO to come in. Whereas now there is an inspection maximum 18 months, and in most cases it's once a year.... Where ourselves, Seafish and most of the EHOs now, it's not a case of going in and condemning right left and centre, it's more a case of working at it.

(Director, trade organisation)

A snapshot view of the standard of food hygiene in the fish and chip establishments of one city has been provided by an exercise carried out by Norwich City's Environmental Health Department. Of the 38 businesses, 28 (74%) were rated as good or very good, three newly registered shops were in need of urgent improvement and another three also needed to improve.[18] This suggests that standards are much higher than the more pessimistic comments have suggested.

The other approach is a series of incentives. Seafish oversees the Fish and Chip Quality Awards which have been running since 1988 with the involvement of the trade body, the National Federation of Fish Friers (NFFF). It includes a great number of awards which have developed over the years with categories that start with Fish and Chip Shop of the Year and Fish and Chip Restaurant of the Year going on to Young Fish Frier of the Year, the Good Catch Award for responsible sourcing, the Staff Training and Development Award and others. Various private companies with an interest in supplying the trade sponsor these awards which incentivise attention to quality standards. Another factor is that Seafish and the NFFF are jointly responsible for training courses and there is a Fish Frying Certificate qualification which as well as frying skills also covers food hygiene and health and safety. These activities were seen as raising standards:

> Seafish's competition for the Fish Frier of the Year which is great because that has driven standards in all these shops. Some of the shops that I could take you to, they are state of the art, they are absolutely wonderful places.
>
> (Chairman, medium wholesaler)

One aspect of the competitions is the inclusion of sustainability criteria for sourcing the fish as shown by the Good Catch Award mentioned. However, one of the interviewees took a cynical view of what this meant:

> They had to build in sustainability, food safety and all these other things to win the prize. Whether they believe it or not I don't know but they do preach it.
>
> (Managing director, large company)

The difficulties preventing small businesses generally in the 'casual eating' sector from actively sourcing sustainably have been recognised (Sharpe 2010). The interviewees connected with the fish and chip trade agreed that the greater part of it was neither interested in nor knowledgeable about sustainability or traceability with a few exceptions:

> I think, in general, they see it as, 'if you catch it, we're going to sell it'. So therefore, if it's there, why go on to us about sustainability.
>
> (Director, trade organisation)

> We've got posters proclaiming that ocean-wild fish is from sustainable resources. We've got some very far-thinking customers and they've got in their shops brochures telling the story of where the fish comes from, even to the names of the vessels.
>
> (Chairman, medium wholesaler)

The wholesalers supplying frozen fish relied on the Icelandic reputation for successful fisheries management when asked about sustainability on the basis that: 'The Icelanders have a very strong sustainability because if they don't, they don't have an economy' (Managing director, large wholesaler).

Fish and chips, once constituting the only fast food available, now have considerable competition. One fish supplier interviewed thought young people 'don't want fish and chips, they want kebabs, they want a pizza' (Managing director, small company 3). Sales of fish and chips seem to have reduced in the late 1990s, a situation investigated in Seafish research which found a difference of perception: while fryers thought this was due to the price being too high because the cost of fish had risen, consumers were more concerned about health issues (Seafish 2000).

Subsequently, Seafish organised trials to measure fat levels in fish and chip portions and these produced a figure lower than the proportion for a burger or doner kebab, using standard nutritional tables (Watson 2006). Having recognised that some consumers do not think that fish and chips constitute healthy food, the emphasis was on showing that its fat content compares well with other fast food options. More realistically, the general view of fish and chip operators as found by one piece of research was that fish and chips are not a healthy choice but eaten as a treat; as one quoted owner said: 'You're not going to go into a fish and chip shop if you want to eat healthily. Everything's cooked in fat' (Connect Research 2010, p. 12).

Some years later Seafish returned to the question of nutrition in relation to fish and chips from different but complementary angles in a large research project sponsored jointly with the Agriculture and Horticulture Development Board (Seafish & AHDB Potatoes 2016). One strand was a 'mystery shopper' exercise in which portions were purchased from hundreds of fish and chip establishments throughout Britain and then weighed, another was an online consumer survey while in a third, samples were analysed for nutritional content after using different cooking methods. The first exercise found a staggering variation in portion size so that the range for a 'medium' portion of cod was 93 to 562 grams, for 'medium' chips from 100 to 797 grams; prices also varied greatly. In the second, feedback was that consumers would like nutritional information, lower fat levels and a larger choice. This last point meant more small portions, particularly of chips (since many people currently throw some away) and a wider range of fish species. The third part of the project tested cooking methods and recommended a light batter and frying in monounsaturated rapeseed oil to achieve the lowest levels of saturates, transfats and fats in total. The resulting message to fish and chip proprietors was that standardised portions and more choice of small ones, different frying oil and provision of nutritional information would deliver larger profits while better satisfying customers (reduced waste would also be a benefit). A dedicated trade website under the heading 'Enjoy Fish and Chips' has been set up by Seafish to disseminate these messages and generally support the sector.[19] One exercise being pursued is to produce recommendations for standard portion sizes which among other things would facilitate provision of nutritional information The status of the messages to what are quite independent businesses is of course purely advisory and the long-term impact on the fish and chip offer to the public remains to be seen but there is every likelihood that the initiative will prove to be another example of the Seafish governance impact on fish and chip businesses.

Nevertheless, concerns about fried fish and indeed fried foods generally from the viewpoint of cardiovascular health are real (Gadiraju et al. 2015). The American Heart Association Nutrition Committee has counselled avoidance of commercially prepared fried fish (and other convenience fish dishes) on the grounds that they are low in omega-3 and high in trans-fats (Kris-Etherton, Harris & Appel 2002). Increased risk of heart failure has been found connected with a higher intake of fried fish while greater consumption of baked or grilled fish was associated with reduced incidence (Belin et al. 2011).

A key factor is the amount and type of oil consumed in fish and chips. There is limited evidence about actual levels produced by shops which are likely to vary due to the heterogeneity of the sector including the choice of frying medium and the extent of usage before each batch is replaced. Some local authority environmental health departments have undertaken sample surveys and found high levels of saturated fat and in some cases of trans-fats and often also of salt (Antrim Borough Council 2009). A joint study by six South West London councils found that some fish and chip meals contained more than double the recommended daily allowance of saturated fats though there was a large variation between establishments.[20] A survey of takeaway outlets in an East London borough with particular emphasis on use by children found high levels of overall and saturated fat as well as the presence of trans-fats in both the fish and the chip portions tested (Lloyd, Caraher & Madelin 2010). Though lower than for Chinese takeaways or pizza, high levels of salt have been found in fish and chips (Jaworowska et al. 2012). Some councils have had projects to help their fish and chip shops produce healthier versions of their products. The FSA ran a campaign in 2009 and 2010 addressed to fish and chip outlets with a particular focus on reducing chip oil absorption.[21] These were worthwhile but not sustained efforts so the Seafish 'Enjoy fish and chips' which has some overlapping aims may have a more long-term effect.

Thus while the great majority of fish and chip shops as small businesses are operating predominantly in a market environment, they experience certain governance influences to varying degrees. As well as food hygiene regulations monitored by environmental health officers, there have been some efforts by local government and the national FSA to improve the healthiness of the products while Seafish and the dedicated trade body use incentives to improve quality generally and more recently also nutritional values and to urge sustainable sourcing.

Governance in the foodservice sector

The wider foodservice arena includes a very great number of other small and large restaurants, pubs and hotels which may serve seafood (sometimes in the form of fish and chips). The main governance in place is public regulation; the European General Food Law and various UK enacting regulations apply as in other food businesses.

An added governance mechanism is provided by the FSA's Food Hygiene Rating Scheme covering England, Northern Ireland and Wales and the Scottish Food Hygiene Information Scheme. The FSA scheme began in 2010 and was rolled out to local authorities on a voluntary basis till by 2016 all had joined; a similar process took place in Scotland over 2009 to 2014. Both schemes encompass all establishments where food is sold covering restaurants, takeaway businesses (including fish and chip establishments), hotels, hospitals, schools and care homes as well as food shops including supermarkets. Their hygiene practices are inspected by local authority staff and a rating is awarded. In the FSA scheme, there is a six-point scale from zero meaning urgent improvement is needed to five marking very good standards. In the Scottish scheme, the establishment is either awarded a pass or marked 'improvement required', but in addition the Eat Safe award is given to those exceeding legal requirements. In Northern Ireland and Wales, it is a legal requirement that establishments display a sticker with their rating in a reasonably prominent place; this is voluntary in England and Scotland. However, each scheme has its database, enabling all ratings to be checked online.[22]

A precursor 'scores on the doors' scheme in one English city found it to be an effective method of improving compliance with food safety rules once comparative information was published on its website, attributed to competitive reactions by operators rather than to pressure from the public (Stanton, Burton & Gooding 2008). The FSA has commissioned various enquiries to see what effect its own scheme is having on businesses and consumers. These have found increasing public awareness over time though this has been lower in England than in Wales and Northern Ireland. Significant proportions of people questioned have stated that they would use the scores to decide whether or not to patronise any establishment though actual choices were not necessarily tested and in practice could not be readily made where stickers are not displayed. A large majority of the public think that ratings display should be compulsory.[23]

Research on businesses has shown that sticker display in England lags far behind the other two areas and there, unsurprisingly, establishments with higher scores are more likely to display. But, even in England, a considerable majority supported mandatory display. Generally, those allocated lower scores were working on improvements, indicating that the scheme provides positive incentives for better standards (BMG Research 2018). Indeed, standards have risen since the FSA scheme started so that two-thirds of businesses had achieved the top, very good, grade by 2017 and it has been estimated that the underlying hygiene improvements will have reduced risks of foodborne disease for consumers (Poppy 2017). In Scotland, the impact both on consumer awareness and on business motivation for improvement seems to be less than elsewhere (Vegeris 2015). The FSA and other national bodies support the extension of the mandatory display of ratings which in relation to England and Scotland would require legislation.

While food safety thus has statutory regulation plus the two rating schemes, foodservice otherwise is mainly driven by market forces. There does not seem to be a source of data by which changes in seafood dishes offered may be tracked over time, but a personal observation is that restaurants in recent years offer much more seafood on their menus and a greater variety of species than in the past. However, businesses are likely to vary their approaches to quality and sustainability according to the market segment in which they compete:

> The genuine chefs as opposed to the cooks are very keen to have and always have been, keen to have top quality and would inspect and have always checked, that one is not quite as fresh as that one, I'll have that one.… The chap who is working for a fast food outlet, he wants a bag of prawns, ready-made, as long as the sell-by date is on the packet.
>
> (Managing director, small company 5)

However, restaurant chains, pub groups and institutional catering organisations are increasingly experiencing similar pressures to those felt by the major retailers in relation to issues over quality and sustainability and responding in a similar way (Taylor 2000). This was familiar to some of the research interviewees:

> Increasingly the foodservice sector is looking for the same levels of traceability and quality assurance as the retail trade has had.
>
> (Managing director, large company)

> Bear in mind that a lot of the foodservice companies also have big businesses with people like local authorities, health, education, health authorities etc. It's an important business, and it's a relatively stable business in recession So there's an agenda from them as well about the ethical nature of their purchasing. And that includes the sustainability of seafood. So that they're getting that sort of pressure. It's come later in the foodservice area than it has in the retail area, I think that's fair, but I certainly see that as being very important.
>
> (Director, large company)

These influences have not been the stuff of headlines in the same way as seen in some campaigns addressed to the supermarkets, but have operated more subtly. One line of approach is reflected in the above quotation with its reference to the public sector as there has been an increasing interest in sustainability criteria in public procurement (Amann et al. 2014). In the UK, a formal framework started with the launch of the Public Sector Food Procurement Initiative in 2003 under the Strategy for Sustainable Farming and Food. In this context, it did not address seafood specifically, but an evaluative review of the programme noted that nine government departments, as well as the NHS, obtained more than 80% of their fish from 'managed sources' – the term is not explained but it at least indicates thought being given towards sustainability considerations (Deloitte 2009). There were, however, specific seafood requirements in the 2011 Government Buying Standards for food and catering services which stated that fish must be sustainably sourced and in addition served on the basis of the 'twice a week, one oily' nutritional guidelines; these applied not only to government departments but to their executive agencies including the military and the prison service.[24] The Government Buying Standards were revised in 2014 and the fish requirements strengthened.[25]

Most food in these public services has come to be provided by contract caterers so it is their procurement policies that need to be addressed. Research in one geographical area showed that such companies welcomed involvement in the Public Sector Food Procurement Initiative which fitted with their corporate responsibility policies. It led to joint work and the production of a guide containing a set of principles with suggested indicators, two of which addressed sustainable fish sourcing (Rimmington, Carlton Smith & Hawkins 2006). The guide is available to catering companies.

Since then the NGO Sustain (The Alliance for Better Food and Farming) has been a significant actor in providing momentum towards more sustainable fish sourcing by contract caterers and the foodservice sector in general. Initially, it established the Sustainable Fish City project which signed up both public and private organisations as part of the 2012 London Olympics and Paralympics events and legacy commitment. The campaign continued in London after the Games, tracking the progression of each London Borough in using certified fish (Compton 2013; Sustain 2012) and in 2014 extended to a nationwide campaign, now Sustainable Fish Cities in the plural. At the time of writing 15 cities, one county and some major contract caterers, restaurant chains and public bodies had signed the pledge to pursue sustainable fish sourcing. As with other NGOs, it has on occasion been able to muster public support: a 2015 campaign to get two restaurant chains and a pub chain to produce seafood sourcing policies elicited so many emails to the companies concerned that after just one week each had produced a sustainable fish policy and the action could be called off.[26]

Sustain adopted the league table device when it turned up the pressure on contract caterers in a new report (Sustain 2017). Based like the MCS supermarket surveys on questionnaires completed (or in one case not) by the companies, one of which was a ready meal supplier rather than a contract caterer, the sustainable fish catering league is based on seven criteria including a public fish policy and the central sourcing triumvirate of: avoid the worst, promote the best and improve the rest. Interestingly, the majority of the contract caterers in the table are signatories to the Sustainable Fish Cities pledge but they were distributed equally in the high and low-scoring sections; this is a reminder that the pledge is about commitment and intent not necessarily that sustainable sourcing has been achieved.

The restaurant sector has its own sustainability governance organiser in the form of the Sustainable Restaurant Association (SRA). From 30 founding members in 2010, it grew to nearly 300 by 2018, meaning that thousands of establishments were covered, as a business body dedicated to assisting restaurants in being sustainability oriented. Star ratings, awarded on the basis of self-completion questionnaires, may be used by restaurants to advertise their credentials and there are annual Food Made Good Awards. Sourcing fish responsibly is one of the ten sustainability focus areas; members are encouraged to use the MCS *Good Fish Guide* as a basis for removing red-scoring species from menus and to substitute less used but more sustainable fish for the 'big five'. Although a trade organisation, SRA has a consumer-oriented offshoot website called One Planet Plate which features enticing pictures of individual dishes, each with its sustainability claim (which may be 'sources fish sustainably') a recipe for it and details of the restaurant concerned.[27]

Another governance initiative which from the outset was oriented to consumers, fish2fork was established in 2009 to promote sustainable seafood sourcing by restaurants. Its philosophy was similar to that originally motivating certification, providing information to consumers to enable them to choose sustainable options, thus sending market signals which would reward or penalise according to performance and stimulate change. Each restaurant or branch was rated on a ten-point scale based on a self-completed questionnaire or, if the establishment declined, on its own website information. Members of the public were invited to contribute reviews. Two years after the scheme was established a comparison of recent ratings with those allocated initially noted that as many as 45% of the restaurants had improved their position, though another 20% had slipped down to a worse level. This would appear to show that at a still early stage the rating system functioned as a motivator for improved sustainability albeit imperfectly. An assessment a few years later found that there were still many big-name chains with extremely poor ratings, findings that did get some media publicity and a little over a year later some of those criticised had greatly improved, possibly as a result. To what extent restaurant goers visited the website to check out ratings is unknown as is whether the sustainability assessments affected choices of where to eat. The project provided information for well-motivated consumers but its more important impact has been to incentivise the restaurants directly so that, as with the supermarkets, users would increasingly be offered only the relatively more sustainable options. In the same vein, chefs supportive of fish2fork wanted seafood suppliers also to be rated on sustainability to make environmentally positive decision-making easier. However, at the time of writing the project was not functioning and it is not clear whether this particular governance tool will be available in the future.[28]

This overview of governance in the foodservice sector has had two contrasting themes. Food safety is strongly regulated, not only by legislation but by the hygiene ratings schemes operated by the FSA and FSS, based as they are on an inspection regime. Participation in these was voluntary for local authorities at the outset – now all have joined – but in any case, has not been so for food establishments which all receive a rating willy-nilly. The only voluntary element remaining is that businesses in England and Scotland do not have to display their ratings which nevertheless are available to the public online. Concerns in Northern Ireland and in Wales are legally required to make their scores visible and as both the public and professionals want to see this in England too it seems likely that legislation will eventually follow; the public in Scotland do not seem to have been asked but legislation would be expected to follow that in the rest of the UK on such a public health matter.

On the other key attributes, quality and sustainability, until recently there were no governance mechanisms except for guides which mainly apply to high-end restaurants and, for quality, this is still largely the case for foodservice in general. The exception is the specialist fish and chips shops which have been the subject of efforts by Seafish and their own trade association for quality improvements which have been of the incentive kind and entirely voluntary but have had a positive impact according to some views gathered in the research.

Finally, action in favour of sustainability while also voluntary has come under more governance pressure in the recent period when, not coincidentally, there has been increasing public awareness about overfishing problems. For caterers supplying the public sector, sourcing fish sustainably is contractually required by government procurement standards so compulsory. For other companies, it remains voluntary but they may experience either positive or negative pressures to take it seriously and therefore change their practices. Such pressures have the greatest impact on larger companies and chains while possibly not touching the mass of small operators. This includes fish and chip shops but fortunately most fish used for frying is in fact from sustainable fisheries.

The outstanding question which so far has received limited attention is the need for monitoring of the sustainability policies which companies put in place. Sustain research found that catering companies supplying the Ministry of Defence did not meet the Government Buying Standards for fish despite their contractual obligations (Westcott 2018). Outside the public sector, sustainability policies are entirely voluntary and unaudited which raises questions about how they can be verified.

Conclusions about governance at the end of the chain

As summarised in Table 6.1, retail and foodservice concerns are the object of a range of governance efforts in relation to the seafood they sell. Consumers are not listed because they do not exert governance with intent but governance activity relating to consumers and the retail and foodservice businesses that provision them are interconnected as depicted in Figure 6.1.

Table 6.1 Governance relevant to seafood retail and foodservice

Retail

Governance type	Detail	Governance source	Purpose
Legislation	EU and UK food safety/hygiene legislation	EU and UK	Food safety and traceability
Legislation	EU regulations on seafood labelling and UK fish labelling regulations	EU and UK	Single market and consumer information
Regulatory oversight	Food Hygiene Rating/ Information Schemes	FSA and FSS	Higher food safety standards
Regulatory monitoring	Environmental health and trading standards	Local authorities	Adherence to food safety and labelling regulation
Authenticity testing	DNA and other tests	FSA, academic institutions, MSC	Checking for mislabelling and fraud
Training (skills and food safety)	Training/qualifications for retailers/ fishmongers	Seafood Training Academy	Quality and food safety, employee development
Campaigning	Reports, supermarket rating tables, direct action, mass tweets/ emails	Greenpeace, MCS, CIWF, Fish Fight, EJF	Sustainable sourcing, animal welfare, labour rights
Collaborative persuasion	Sustainable sourcing tools	Seafish	Sustainable sourcing
Collaborative persuasion	Advice lists especially re fish to avoid	MCS	Sustainable sourcing
Collaborative persuasion	Eco-labelled seafood availability	MSC, ASC et al.	Sustainable sourcing
Collaborative persuasion	Responsible sourcing codes	Sustainable Seafood Coalition/ ClientEarth	Sustainable sourcing
Collaborative persuasion	Ocean Disclosure Project	Sustainable Fisheries Partnership	Sustainable sourcing

Foodservice

Governance type	Detail	Governance source	Purpose
Legislation	EU and UK food safety/hygiene legislation	EU and UK	Food safety and traceability
Regulatory oversight and consumer choice	Food Hygiene Rating/ Information Schemes	FSA and FSS	Higher food safety standards
Regulatory monitoring	Environmental health and trading standards	Local authorities	Food safety
Authenticity testing	DNA and other tests	Academic institutions, MSC	Checking for mislabelling and fraud
Advice	Campaigns to decrease fat and salt in fish and chips	FSA and certain local authorities	Public health
Standards scheme	Fish and Chip Quality Awards	Seafish and NFFF	Quality, food safety, sustainable sourcing
Advice	Enjoy fish and chips website	Seafish	Better nutrition, more portion sizes, greater profits
Training	Training/qualifications for foodservice	Seafood Training Academy and NFFF	Food safety, quality, employee development
Public procurement	Government Buying Standards	UK government	Sustainable sourcing and public health
Collaborative persuasion	Sustainable sourcing pledge	Sustain/Sustainable Fish Cities	Sustainable sourcing
Collaborative persuasion	Sustainable sourcing guides	Seafish	Sustainable sourcing
Collaborative persuasion	Ratings, awards, assistance	Sustainable Restaurant Association	Sustainable sourcing
Collaborative persuasion	Restaurant sustainability ratings website	fish2fork	Sustainable sourcing

Source: author.

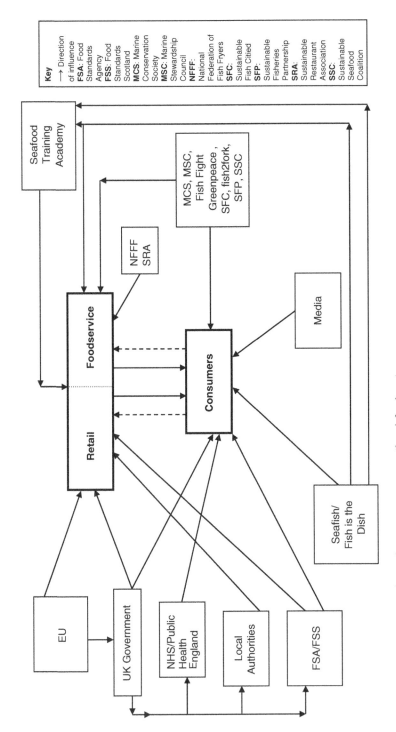

Key
→ Direction of influence
FSA: Food Standards Agency
FSS: Food Standards Scotland
MCS: Marine Conservation Society
MSC: Marine Stewardship Council
NFFF: National Federation of Fish Fryers
SFC: Sustainable Fish Citied
SFP: Sustainable Fisheries Partnership
SRA: Sustainable Restaurant Association
SSC: Sustainable Seafood Coalition

Figure 6.1 Governance relationships: consumers, retail and foodservice.

There are two foci in Figure 6.1. The retail and food service double box indicates that most of the sources of governance for the two sectors are identical or very similar. It is linked to the consumer box below by two sets of arrows, two because the relationships of consumers with retail and foodservice providers can be different due to variable patterns of usage. Each set has a straight line arrow down indicating the governance these food providers exert over consumers as the controllers of what is available but a dotted line going the other way because purchasing patterns do influence food providers but more weakly than implied by a governance impact. Providers cannot determine what people will buy but consumers can only purchase what is available; it is not an equal relationship. In any case, buying decisions usually involve many other considerations even when they include awareness about issues such as food safety or sustainability.

Retail and foodservice share with each other and the rest of the food chain the need to conform with the EU–UK food safety regulatory regime; in addition, the retail sector is particularly affected by seafood labelling legislation. They share too the monitoring of legislation by local authorities through environmental health and trading standards departments. The FSA and FSS provide advice and information for both sectors, may investigate seafood authenticity and could impact on them by recalls. The FSA and FSS food hygiene schemes include both sectors in the same system. All of these are exercises of state regulation. In relation to monitoring food authenticity, the important input of academic investigators is not shown in the diagram for lack of space, not part of the regulatory apparatus but a public contribution to the food system which has a governance impact by bringing to light facts that may require action by others.

Seafish has arrows in several directions, reflecting its varied roles. It has undertaken limited activity in relation to seafood retailing in its work on fishmongers but has had more continuous input to the fish and chip sector and supports both through the Seafood Training Academy, which involves public and private organisations. Through its Fish is the Dish website Seafish also has a direct line to influencing consumers. In this range of activities, Seafish is fulfilling its publicly mandated role of supporting the seafood industry, using its position to improve seafood retailing quality and the fish and chip sector in particular but in relation to consumers acting more on behalf of commercial, private interests in promoting sales. The assortment reflects the position of Seafish as a combination public-private governance actor.

Governance activity from civil society organisations is listed within another box. Retailers have been addressed by Greenpeace, Fish Fight and the MCS with considerable impact on their sourcing policies while catering companies and restaurants have been targeted by Sustainable Fish Cities and the fish2fork initiative. As well as the environmental NGOs, the box contains a motley collection of groups some of which cross the boundaries of civil society and private interests. Although the Marine Stewardship Council (MSC) has environmental NGO involvement, notably of WWF, it is a service for private interests, the fishing industry at one end of the supply chain, retail and food-service at the other, as well as for consumers (other certification bodies have not been included because they have little visibility in the British context). The Sustainable Seafood Coalition (SSC) though led by an NGO, ClientEarth, has mainly worked with retailers who need defensible 'respons-ible sourcing' policies. The Sustainable Fisheries Partnership (SFP) aims to be a bridge linking the fishing industry with environmental organisations. However, the National Federation of Fish Friers and the Sustainable Res-taurant Association are in a separate box, as trade bodies separate from environmental organisations. Hard and fast distinctions may be difficult to apply but what is more important is to recognise that diverse strands of gov-ernance are being exercised.

While some NGO campaigning has involved a hostile stance, at least ini-tially, there has also been much of what may be termed 'collaborative persua-sion', a joint effort for a shared objective as retailers have good reason to support seafood sustainability. In this regard, the Marine Conservation Society (MCS) has been particularly significant with its assessments of what is sustainable and what should be avoided having become widely accepted across retail and food-service despite some early opposition to certain judgements (affecting mackerel and cod). The sustainability cause has been embraced by large retailers and many foodservice businesses and they have been ready to work with supportive organisations whether in determining objective criteria for 'responsible sourc-ing' with the Sustainable Seafood Coalition, being transparent about fishery sources with the Ocean Disclosure Project, getting support from the Sustain-able Restaurant Association or taking the pledge with Sustainable Fish Cities.

The environmental NGOs' governance activity in relation to retail and foodservice rests on public trust based on open membership and participation by citizens. It is as citizens that they have from time to time called upon sup-porters to take part in such action as mass emails or tweets. Fish Fight, although its initial focus on ending discards at sea was about exerting political pressure for changes in the CFP, also inspired action from citizens directed at the supermarkets in relation to the prawn and tuna supply chains. But when giving advice about seafood choices, NGOs aim to influence those same people as consumers.

Considering all this governance activity chronologically, the regulatory basis started in the early 1990s with both UK and EU legislation which was strengthened in the early 2000s and always involved local authority imple-mentation. The Seafish annual fish and chip competition began in the late 1980s but training for retail personnel seems to have been initiated only in the mid-2000s. On sustainability, general government procurement standards began in 2003 but specific fish requirements only in 2011. The NGO activity also got going from the early 2000s, starting with the first MCS guide in 2002. So to summarise the chronological development, legislation was the first development in the 1990s and other governance activities generally intensified from the turn of the twenty-first century.

Turning to the purposes of governance activity, food safety, traceability and accurate information for consumers have been the object of public regulation. An important aspect has been the monitoring which local environmental health and trading standards staff undertake and three examples where prosecutions took place have been pointed out: supermarket sales of out-of-date foods and the fish mislabelling fraud perpetrated on customers of the Iceland chain in this chapter and the fish store with maggots and rats in Chapter 4. These cases came to light thanks to proactive surveillance so it is disturbing to know that due to heavy reductions in local authority budgets since 2010 following withdrawals of central government funding, these groups of staff and therefore capacity to carry out such work has greatly reduced (Auditor General for Wales 2014; Local Government Association 2016).[29] It is also worth noting research showing that 'food inspectors' are the most trusted group to make sure food is safe; double as many as trusted them as had confidence in either supermarkets or the government (Roberts, Draper & Dowler 2018) (figures in the Appendix).

Quality in the fish and chip sector has been progressed by Seafish and the trade organisation NFFF. Otherwise there is no external governance of quality in either retail and foodservice and these attributes depend on business motivations and market forces. By contrast, sustainability has been the objective with the greatest number of different governance efforts, including one important public one in the form of the government procurement standards but mainly coming from NGOs with or without private interest involvement. With many retailers and foodservice providers embracing the goal of sustainable sourcing, their choice editing is increasingly providing more ethically sound seafood to consumers.

Notes

1 Information about MacFisheries was accessed from www.macfisheries.co.uk/ on 11 October 2012 but by July 2018 the site had been archived at https://web.archive.org/web/20161019054149/www.macfisheries.co.uk/index.htm.

2 The two Community Supported Fisheries projects are Faircatch serving South West London (http://faircatch.co.uk) and SoleShare covering an area in East London (www.soleshare.net).

3 The terminology used in this report is 'controlled atmosphere packaging' (CAP) rather than MAP.

4 See Prince R 2013, 'How your supermarket "fresh" fish can be THREE [upper case in the original] weeks old: seafood bought from the big four was only two days away from rotting', *Daily Mail*, 17 November 2013.

5 See the following stories relating to out-of-date food on sale by major supermarkets: 'Asda fined £36,000 for selling out-of-date food' (in Staffordshire), 30 September 2008, www.birminghammail.co.uk and 'Asda store fined £75,000 for selling out of date food', 10 November 2016, www.itv.com; Walker W 2016, 'Supermarket giant fined for stocking out-of-date food', *Newbury Today*, 25 August 2016, www.newburytoday.co.uk; 'Store fined over out-of-date food' (Morrisons, in Eccles), 15 February 2007, www.manchestereveningnews.co.uk and 'Halifax supermarket fined over 17-days out-of-date food for sale' (Morrisons), 27 July 2007, www.halifaxcourier.

co.uk; 'Sainsbury's branches fined over out-of-date food' (in London), 10 January 2008, www.thisislocallondon.co.uk and 'Sainsbury's fined for selling out-of-date food' (in West Sussex), 14 May 2009, www.wscountytimes.co.uk; 'Tesco fined over out-of-date food' (in South Wales), BBC News, 23 January 2008, and 'Tesco fined for sale of out-of-date goods' (in Bracknell), 14 May 2011, www.thegrocer.co.uk.

6 The statements were from Asda, Morrisons, Sainsbury's and Waitrose, reproduced in FSA Food Survey Information Sheet 40, *Mercury in Imported Fish and Shellfish, UK Farmed Fish and their Products*, 2003.

7 The story of the change from pilchards to Cornish sardines is told in Stummer R 2003, 'Who are you calling pilchard? It's "Cornish sardine" to you', *The Independent*, 17 August 2003 and in a report on the BBC Inside Out South West programme 'Pilchards' on 30 January 2006. In these accounts, credit for the transformation is attributed differently, to a local processor; regardless of the exact circumstances, which have not been fully established, it is certainly interesting that the quoted individual gave all the credit to the named supermarket. The transformation of the Cornish sardine has subsequently been sealed by the fishery and product achieving MSC certification and Protected Geographical Indication designation respectively.

8 The MCS Supermarket Seafood Surveys 2006, 2011 and 2013 can be accessed on their website, www.mcsuk.org. Marks & Spencer and Sainsbury's were the highest rated in the most recent survey.

9 For the CIWF supermarket ratings which were produced for 2003/2004, 2005/2006 and 2010 (see Pickett 2006; Pickett & Burgess 2003; and 'Farm animals are winners in UK supermarket awards', 27 July 2010 on its website www.ciwf.org). In 2017 Tesco was awarded the CIWF Best Retailer Innovation Award for working collaboratively with Turkish farmers and processors to develop a humane slaughter system for their sea bass and sea bream.

10 The information that there was no plan in 'the foreseeable future' for another supermarket survey was in a personal communication from the MCS Enquiries Officer.

11 The three in 2011 were Marks & Spencer, Sainsbury's and Waitrose. The commitments reported in 2012 were Tesco (aim 2012), Morrisons (aim 2013) and Asda (aim 2014); Mitsubishi, owners of the Princes brand, made the commitment for 2014 and Thai Union, owner of John West, for 2016. Princes agreed to remove claims from its cans that it used fish caught sustainably after this was featured critically in a *Hugh's Fish Fight* programme and Greenpeace referred the company to the Office of Fair Trading: see Hickman M 2011, 'Fresh triumph for ethical tuna fishing campaign', *The Independent*, 12 April 2011, which pays tribute to 'one of the most successful campaigns in years'. However, it subsequently appeared that some of these commitments might not be kept and the Greenpeace 2014 ratings include criticisms as well as plaudits: see Densham A 2014, 'From win to bin: our 2014 tuna league table', 28 February 2014, and Densham A 2015, 'The winners and losers: tinned tuna league table kicks off new campaign to end destructive fishing', 2 October 2015, both at www.greeenpeace.org.uk. The most recent Greenpeace tuna league table and criteria used were accessed from www.greenpeace.org.uk/what-we-do/oceans/tuna/league-table and www.greenpeace.org.uk/wp-content/uploads/2017/07/tuna-scoring.pdf on 15 July 2018 as was Nicholls F 2016, 'Sainsbury's tell us to "taste the difference" – now people are telling them to #stoptheindifference', also on the Greenpeace website. The campaign for Waitrose to ban John West is reported by Sustainable Brands, 'Waitrose joins Tesco in threatening to can John West over broken sustainability pledge' 10 May 2016 on www.sustainablebrands.com. King S 2017, 'Winning on the world's largest tuna company and what it means for the oceans', 11 July 2017, www.greenpeace.org.uk, argues that Greenpeace campaigning has caused Thai Union

to commit to the desirable changes while Seaman T 2017, 'Will Thai Union, Greenpeace agreement cause higher prices?', 28 July 2017, www.undercurrent news.com, acknowledging in the title that there was an agreement between 'the world's largest tuna canner' and the NGO (in itself a remarkable event), discusses other factors in play including rising prices which are attributed to lower catches but without drawing the conclusion that lower catches might have convinced the company that sustainability action was necessary.

12 The RASS is at www.seafish.org/rass and the aquaculture profiles at http://seafish.org/aquacultureprofiles/index.

13 The SSC codes are the *Voluntary Code of Conduct on Environmental Claims* (the *Labelling Code*) and the *Voluntary Code of Conduct on Environmentally Responsible Fish and Seafood Sourcing* (the *Sourcing Code*).

14 The Which? Report findings are covered in Hall J 2012, 'Supermarket claims about fish are misleading, Which? says', *The Telegraph*, 19 July 2012.

15 The other two UK retailers participating in the Ocean Disclosure Project are Morrisons and Co-op Food and the information is published on https://ocean disclosureproject.org. The companies submit a list of fisheries from which they source and SFP uses public information from the FishSource database to obtain further information such as the type of gear and whether certified, determines whether the fishery is rated 'well-managed', 'managed' or 'needs improvement' and adds notes on relevant environmental issues. FishSource is itself an STP off-shoot established in 2007, information on www.fishsource.org.

16 There are a set of accepted sizes for cod and haddock fillets in the trade: 3 to 5, 5 to 8, 8 to 16, 16 to 32 and 32 plus and these are in ounces, a testimony to the longstanding British market. More recently, 'tight grades' have been produced by some companies: 4 to 6, 6 to 8, 8 to 10, 10 to 12. In addition, the specification can be skin on or skinless, pin bone in or boneless.

17 The number of fish and chip establishments comes from the National Federation of Fish Friers' website, www.federationoffishfriers.co.uk. The 8,500 membership figure is from Wikipedia. In Wallop H 2014, '15 fascinating facts about McDonald's in UK', *The Telegraph*, 12 November 2014, the number of McDonald's branches in the UK is stated as 1,249.

18 Information taken from www.norwich.gov.uk, undated but accessed on 19 February 2013.

19 The website is https://enjoyfishandchips.co.uk.

20 The South West London study was reported on the Kingston Borough Council under the heading 'Health promotion in fish and chip shops' (undated) on www. kingston.gov.uk/information/news_and_events/news/news_archive.htm?id+80352 and accessed 10 February 2013 but in July 2018 the page was no longer available.

21 Examples have been the Antrim BC Healthier Takeaways Project (see Antrim Borough Council 2009), the LB Wandsworth frying courses reported in Kasprzak E 2012, 'Oil and obesity: frying lessons for fast food workers', 5 May 2012, on the BBC News website and Wigan Council's Healthy Business Awards, reported under 'Frying tonight?' www.wigan.gov.uk, accessed 10 February 2013 but no longer available in July 2018. The FSA advice was produced as 'Tips on chips: Help businesses serve healthier food' and found to be helpful in the evaluation of pilot usage (Connect Research 2010).

22 Information about the Food Hygiene Rating and Food Hygiene Information Schemes is on the respective websites of the FSA www.food.gov.uk and the FSS www.foodstandards.gov.scot. The legal requirement to display ratings has been in force from 2013 in Wales and 2016 in Northern Ireland.

23 A series of tracker surveys of consumers in connection with the Food Hygiene Ratings Scheme is available on the FSA website.

24 The standards were publicised in a DEFRA press release of 16 June 2011, 'Let them eat hake, government takes lead in buying sustainable fish'.
25 In the Environment section, the revised standard is:

> All fish★ are demonstrably sustainable with all wild-caught fish meeting the FAO Code of Conduct for Responsible Fisheries (includes Marine Steward-ship Council certification and Marine Conservation Society 'fish to eat', or equivalent). No 'red list' or endangered species of farmed or wild fish shall be used (Marine Conservation Society 'fish to avoid'). ★Fish includes all fish including where it is an ingredient in a composite product.

> Under Nutrition, it states: 'If caterers serve lunch and an evening meal, fish is pro-vided twice a week, one of which is oily. If caterers only serve lunch or an evening meal, an oily fish is available at least once every three weeks' (Public Health England 2017), or at https://assets.publishing.service.gov.uk.

26 Information about Sustainable Fish Cities is at www.sustainweb.org/sustainable-fishcity. The campaign effective in one week is reported in 'Point the fish finger' campaign – a new update', 21 December 2015.
27 The SRA website is https://thesra.org and individual dishes are showcased on www.oneplanetplate.org.
28 Information was taken from the website www.fish2fork.com and the two articles mentioned are Smith L 2011, 'Huge leap towards sustainable seafood revealed by restaurant survey', 27 November 2011 and Smith L 2012, 'Restaurants call for seafood suppliers to be rated on standards', 14 March 2012; however, at the time of writing the website was not functioning and it was unclear whether it would be reinstated, making these items no longer accessible. The article naming various chains with low sustainability ratings is Smithers R 2015, 'More than half of UK's family restaurant chains serving unsustainable seafood', *The Guardian,* 18 November 2015, but on 24 January 2017 the article reporting better results entitled 'MCS, fish2fork comes out with seafood sustainability rankings' was on the website https://qsrmedia.co.uk.
29 Also see Garside J 2016, 'Trading standards institute: consumers are no longer pro-tected', *The Guardian,* 7 August 2016, and Gibson P 2017, 'Health inspectors used to be proactive: now all we do is react once disaster hits', *The Guardian,* 24 June 2017.

References

Allder J & Yates L 2009, *Green to the Core? How Supermarkets Can Help Make Green Shopping Easier,* Consumer Focus, London.

Amann M, Roehrich JK, Essig M & Harland C 2014, 'Driving sustainable supply chain management in the public sector: the importance of public procurement in the European Union', *Supply Chain Management: An International Journal,* vol. 19, no. 3, pp. 351–366.

Antrim Borough Council 2009, *Evaluation of the 'Healthier Takeaways Project',* Antrim Borough Council, Antrim, Environmental Health Department and Health and Wellbeing Team.

Asda 1999, *Memorandum Submitted by Asda Stores Ltd (J55),* The Stationery Office, London, House of Commons Agriculture Committee, *Sea Fishing,* Eighth Report of the Agricultural Committee, Session 1998/1999.

Auditor General for Wales 2014, *Delivering with Less: The Impact on Environmental Health Services and Citizens,* Welsh Audit Office, Cardiff.

Backman P 1996, 'Catering for the masses', *Seafood International,* September , pp. 60–65.

Belin RJ, Greenland P, Martin L, Oberman A, Tinker L, Robinson J, Larson J, Van Horn L & Lloyd-Jones D 2011, 'Fish intake and the risk of incident heart failure: the Women's Health Initiative', *Circulation Heart Failure*, vol. 4, pp. 404–413.

BMG Research 2018, *Display of Food Hygiene Ratings in England, Northern Ireland and Wales*, Food Standards Agency, London.

Burgess GHO, Cutting C, Lovern JA & Waterman JJ 1965, *Fish Handling and Processing*, HMSO, Edinburgh.

Chaloner WH 1971, 'Trends in fish consumption in Great Britain from about 1900 to the present day', in *Fish in Britain: Trends in Supply, Distribution and Consumption During the Past Two Centuries*, Barker TC & Yudkin J, eds., Department of Nutrition, Queen Elizabeth College, University of London, London Occasional Paper No. 2.

Channel 4 Britdoc Foundation 2011, *The End of the Line*, Channel 4 Britdoc Foundation, London.

ClientEarth 2011, *Environmental Claims on Supermarket Seafood*, ClientEarth, London.

Compton R 2013, *Good Food for London 2013: How London Boroughs Can Help Secure a Healthy and Sustainable Food Future*, Sustain, London.

Connect Research 2010, *Evaluation of the 'Tips on Chips' Pilot Advice Provided to Fish and Chips Shops*, Food Standards Agency, London.

Deloitte 2009, *Public Sector Food Procurement Initiative: An Evaluation*, Department for Environment, Food and Rural Affairs, London.

Dibb S 2006, *Greening Supermarkets: How Supermarkets Can Help Make Greener Shopping Easier*, National Consumer Council, London.

Eurographic Ltd 1990, *A Short Study of the Marketing of Pilchards in the United Kingdom*, Sea Fish Industry Authority, Edinburgh.

Future Foundation 2012, *Our Future with Fish: Investigating Customer Attitudes, Behaviour and Motivations*, Sainsbury's, London.

Gadiraju TV, Patel Y, Gaziano JM & Djoussé L 2015, 'Fried food consumption and cardiovascular health: a review of current evidence', *Nutrients*, vol. 7, no. 10, pp. 8424–8430.

Giorgi S, Herren S, King G & (Brook Lyndhurst) 2016, *Community Supported Fisheries (CSFs): Exploring the Potential of CSFs through Catchbox. A Report for DEFRA*, Department for Environment and Rural Affairs, London.

Goulding I 1985, 'Fish marketing in the UK', *Food Marketing*, vol. 1, no. 1, pp. 35–56.

Greenpeace 2005, *A Recipe for Disaster: Supermarkets' Insatiable Appetite for Seafood*, Greenpeace, London.

Greenpeace 2006, *A Recipe for Change: Supermarkets Respond to the Challenge of Sourcing Sustainable Seafood*, Greenpeace, London.

Greenpeace 2008, *Taking Tuna Out of the Can: Retailers' Roles in Rescuing the World's Favourite Fish*, Greenpeace, London.

Greenpeace 2011, *Tinned Tuna's Secret Catch*, Greenpeace, London.

Greenpeace 2012, *Changing Tuna: How the Global Tuna Industry is in Transition to Sustainable Supply*, Greenpeace, London.

Greenwood M 2015, *Governance and Change in the British Seafood Supply Chain 1950 to 2013*, Thesis submitted for the degree of Doctor of Philosophy, City University London.

Harvey M, McMeekin A & Warde A 2004, 'Conclusion: quality and processes of qualification', in *Qualities of Food*, Harvey M, McMeekin A & Warde A, eds., Manchester University Press, Manchester.

Hutter BM 2011, *Managing Food Safety and Hygiene: Governance and Regulation as Risk Management* Edward Elgar, Cheltenham.

James E, ed., 2006, *UK Sea Fisheries Statistics 2005*, National Statistics & DEFRA, Newport & London.

Jaworowska A, Blackham T, Stevenson L & Davies IG 2012, 'Determination of salt content in hot takeaway meals in the United Kingdom', *Appetite*, vol. 59, no. 2, pp. 517–522.

Kris-Etherton PM, Harris WS & Appel LJ 2002, 'Fish consumption, fish oil, omega-3 fatty acids, and cardiovascular disease', *Circulation*, vol. 106, pp. 2747–2757.

LeGrand L 1992, 'Fish products: a summary of trends in the UK', *British Food Journal*, vol. 94, no. 9, pp. 31–36.

Lloyd S, Caraher M & Madelin T 2010, *Fish and Chips with a Side Order of Trans Fat – The Nutrition Implications of Eating from Fast-Food Outlets: A Report on Eating Out in East London*, Centre for Food Policy, City University, London.

Local Government Association 2016, *LGA Trading Standards Review: Summary Report*, LGA, London.

MacMullen P 1998, *A Report to the Fish Industry Forum on the Marine Stewardship Council and Related Topics*, Sea Fish Industry Authority, Edinburgh, Technical Report No CR 152.

Marketpower 1984, *Catering: the Demands of Diversity*, Marketpower and Institute of Grocery Distribution, London and Watford.

Mintel 2004, *Premium vs Budget Eating Out*, Mintel, London.

Murray AD & Fofana A 2002, 'The changing nature of UK fish retailing', *Marine Resource Economics*, vol. 17, no. 4, pp. 335–339.

Myers M 1983, *Quality Evaluation of Fresh Fish at Retail Level*, Sea Fish Industry Authority, Edinburgh.

National Federation of Fishmongers 1955, *A Career with a Thrill in It*, National Federation of Fishmongers & White Fish Authority, London.

Panayi P 2014, *Fish & Chips: A History* Reaktion Books, London.

Pazderka C 2017, *Sustainable Seafood Coalition Report: Assessment of SSC Labelling and Sourcing Codes*, ClientEarth, London.

Pickett H 2006, *Supermarkets and Farm Animal Welfare 'Raising the Standard': Compassion in World Farming Trust Supermarket Survey 2005–2006*, Compassion in World Farming Trust, Petersfield.

Pickett H & Burgess K 2003, *Supermarkets and Farm Animal Welfare 'Raising the Standard': Survey of Supermarket Farm Animal Welfare Standards*, Compassion in World Farming Trust, Petersfield.

Poppy G 2017, *The Food Hygiene Rating Scheme: Chief Scientific Advisor's Report*, Food Standards Agency, London.

Public Health England 2017, *Government Buying Standards for Food and Catering Services (GBSF) Checklist*, PHE, London.

Rimmington M, Carlton Smith J & Hawkins R 2006, 'Corporate social responsibility and sustainable food procurement', *British Food Journal*, vol. 108, no. 10/11, pp. 824–837.

Roberts C, Draper A & Dowler E 2018, *Food: Views on the Food Supply Chain*, NatCen Social Research, London, British Social Attitudes 33.

Rosson P 1975, 'Fish marketing in Britain: structural change and system performance', *European Journal of Marketing*, vol. 9, no. 3, pp. 232–249.

Seafish 1987, *Guidelines for the Handling of Fresh Fish by Retailers*, Sea Fish Industry Authority, Edinburgh.

Seafish 1999, *United Kingdom Fish Catering Sector Handbook*, Sea Fish Industry Authority, Edinburgh.

Seafish 2000, *A Study of the Performance of the Fish and Chips Trade*, Sea Fish Industry Authority, Edinburgh.

Seafish 2003, *Focus on Foodservice*, Sea Fish Industry Authority, Edinburgh.

Seafish 2005, *Independent Fishmongers Study*, Sea Fish Industry Authority, Edinburgh, Market Insight Key Features.

Seafish 2017, *Fish & Chips in Foodservice: 2017 Update*, Sea Fish Industry Authority, Grimsby, Market Insight Factsheet.

Seafish & AHDB Potatoes 2016, *Does Size Matter? It Does to Your Customers*, Sea Fish Industry Authority, Edinburgh.

Sharpe R 2010, *An Inconvenient Sandwich: The Throwaway Economics of Takeaway Food*, New Economics Foundation, London.

Stanton J, Burton Y & Gooding C 2008, 'An assessment of the effectiveness of a five-star "Scores on the Door" scheme for improving food hygiene compliance among Norwich catering businesses', *Journal of Environmental Health Research*, vol. 7, no. 1.

Sustain 2012, *Sustainable Fish Legacy 2012*, Sustain, London.

Sustain 2017, *Fishy Business: How Well are the UK's Top Contract Caterers Supporting Ocean Conservation through their Sustainable Fish Buying Policies and Practices?*, Sustain, London.

Sustainable Seafood Coalition 2018, *Codes of Conduct*, Sustainable Seafood Coalition, London.

Taylor S 2000, 'Is McDonaldization inevitable? Standardization & differentiation in food and beverage organizations', in *Strategic Questions in Food and Beverage Management*, Wood RC, ed., Butterworth-Heinemann, Oxford and Woburn MA.

Tesco 1999, *Memorandum Submitted by Tesco Stores Ltd (J63)*, The Stationery Office, London, House of Commons Agriculture Committee, *Sea Fishing*, Eighth Report of the Agricultural Committee, Session 1998/1999.

Vegeris S 2015, *The Food Hygiene Rating Scheme and the Food Hygiene Information Scheme: Evaluation findings 2011–2014*, Policy Studies Institute, University of Westminster, London.

Walton JK 1992, *Fish & Chips and the British Working Class 1870–1940*, Leicester University Press, Leicester and New York.

Washington S & Ababouch L 2011, *Private Standards and Certification in Fisheries and Aquaculture: Current Practice and Emerging Issues*, Food and Agriculture Organization of the United Nations, Rome.

Watson R 2006, *Trials to Determine the Fat Content of Fish and Chips*, Sea Fish Industry Authority, Edinburgh, Seafish Technology and Training SR584.

Westcott R 2018, *Written Evidence Submitted by Sustainable Fish Cities, Part of Sustain, The Alliance for Better Food and Farming to the Environmental Audit Committee Inquiry on Sustainable Seas*, Sustain, London.

White Fish Authority 1959, *The White Fish Industry*, White Fish Authority, London.

Yates L 2007, *Green Grocers? How Supermarkets Can Help Make Greener Shopping Easier*, National Consumer Council, London.

7 Conclusions

Governance and power in the seafood supply chain

Impacts of governance changes

Over the seven decades from the end of World War II to the present, many economic and technological changes have changed food systems. For seafood, they include both the specific production developments in fishing and aquaculture and the widely shared advances in refrigeration and freezing, in transportation and logistics, and in global trade. But these have not been the only factors that have altered the arrangements which bring food to the table. All kinds of governance decisions which have been described in previous chapters have also made a significant contribution. The key difference is that these have not been processes that developed as a result of economic decisions by individuals and companies but have for the most part been made by those in positions of power whether in political systems or the world of industry, with or without wider public input whether from civil society groups or citizens through democratic processes. They are identifiable, were in some cases contested and, with exceptions, are capable of being reversed. It is all the more important to recognise and assess the value or otherwise of these governance moves when it is appreciated that they are open to change.

The governance instruments used to pursue sustainability, food safety and quality as well as those aiming to influence consumption in Britain have been detailed in previous chapters. The impacts of the most important ones are summarised in Table 7.1.

The first issue is supply from fishing and its sustainability. The major global governance change, one which is surely permanent, was the territorialisation of waters adjoining coastal states by means of the 200-mile Exclusive Economic Zones. From the British viewpoint, at the time it dealt a fatal blow to the then important distant waters fleet, but it enabled Iceland to establish fishery management policies which have ensured healthy stocks of cod for the UK supply chain via imports ever since. Elsewhere, supply from domestic fishing had been increased easily after World War II by the restoration of fishing and government financial support but after an interval, the pre-war phenomenon of too much fishing power chasing declining numbers of fish

Table 7.1 Impacts of main governance mechanisms on seafood supply and sustainability, safety, quality and consumption in Britain

Supply and sustainability – fishing

Governance mechanism	Governance source	Impacts
Financial incentives to modernise and expand capacity of fishing fleet	UK government	Short-term increases in supply of fish. Fleet capacity increased beyond fish resource
UNCLOS and 200 mile EEZs	United Nations	British distant water fishing for whitefish ended. Change to high proportion of whitefish being imported
Code of Conduct for Responsible Fisheries and eco-labelling guidelines	FAO 1995 and 2009	Global standards for fisheries established
Fishery management by quotas, licensing, multi-annual management plans, landing obligation	European Common Fisheries Policy (1983, 1992, 2002 and 2013)	On fishers: fishing restrictions with deleterious impacts on livelihoods. On fish stocks: no positive impact for many years but eventually recovery of some stocks
Fishing vessel decommissioning	European Common Fisheries Policy and UK government	Initially smaller fleet with similar capacity, eventually reduced capacity better matched with fish resource
Fishing quota distribution to sectors and regions	UK government delegated to POs and MMO	Uneven distribution; greater share to most industrialised sector, very small share to inshore fleet
Fixed quota allocations to licence holders, trading allowed	UK and devolved governments/ administration	Semi-privatisation of right to fish, benefitting a cohort of fishers at a point in time; longer-term problems
Strengthened enforcement of fisheries management rules	Sea Fisheries Inspectorates	Reduction of illegal fishing
Environmental campaigning over CFP	Various NGOs and Fish Fight	Strengthening of sustainability provisions in 2013 CFP reform
Certification – eco-labelling	Marine Stewardship Council	Incentive for improved fisheries management Several British fisheries certified Impact on stocks/ecosystems unclear

continued

Table 7.1 Continued

Supply and sustainability – aquaculture

Governance mechanism	Governance source	Impacts
Planning permission for all farms on land and marine farms in Scotland with environmental impact assessments	Local planning authorities	Local control of developments and environmental impacts
Authorisation of water use	Environment Agency/Scottish Environment Protection Agency	Control of water abstraction and pollution
Legislation dealing with fish disease (bio-security, movement control, record-keeping)	EU and UK regulations	Prevention of fish disease and its spread
Industry standards schemes including environmental protection (Code of Good Practice for salmon and trout farming; Shellfish Code of Good Practice)	Scottish Salmon Producers' Organisation/ Quality Trout UK, Association of Scottish Shellfish Growers	Farming standards established
Co-operative salmon farming arrangements (single generation, fallowing)	Aquaculture companies/then Scottish government legislation	More effective measures against parasites and disease
Certification v sustainability	ASC, GAA, GLOBALG.A.P., Friend of the Sea	Higher sustainability standards for a proportion of imported species
Certification – organic production	Organic Food Federation and Soil Association	Organic standards established
Legislation on organic aquaculture	EU and UK regulations	Organic standards regulated (unlike other private schemes)
Technical Guidelines on Aquaculture Certification	FAO 2011	Global standards established

Supply and sustainability – fishing and aquaculture

Governance mechanism	Governance source	Impacts
Tools for Ethical Seafood Sourcing (TESS)	Seafish	Not known but as the resource was a response to industry concerns it is presumed to be used and therefore to assist ethical sourcing
NGO campaigns and collaborative persuasion for more sustainable sourcing (league tables/ratings, advice lists)	Greenpeace, MCS, Sustainable Fish Cities, fish2fork	Shifts in retail and foodservice purchasing policies to sourcing from more sustainable, preferably certified fisheries; choice editing for consumers
Industry advice on sustainable sourcing for retail and foodservice	Seafish, NFFF, Sustainable Restaurant Association	Not known how these resources used but likely to have resulted in some shifts in purchasing policies
Purchasing power	Retailers and large foodservice suppliers and chains	Sustainable sourcing policies and wish for certified seafood has created a significant incentive for fisheries to become certified

Food safety and quality

Governance mechanism	Governance source	Impacts
Legislation on food hygiene of seafood and food safety generally	EU and UK regulations	Reduced risks to human health
Legislation on aquaculture feed, veterinary medicines and residues	EU and UK regulations	Reduced risks to human health
Water classification system and purification requirements for shellfish	EU and UK regulation, administered by FSA and FSS	Reduced risks to human health
Legislation on seafood traceability and labelling	EU and UK regulations	Consumers have better information. Fraud and laundering illegal fishing is more difficult

continued

Table 7.1 Continued

Farmed fish welfare guidelines	ECPAFP and OIE	European and global standards established
Farmed fish welfare guidelines	Farm Animal Welfare Council/Committee	Improved industry practice for fish welfare
Funding for vessel safety, aquaculture development, seafood processing and marketing under CFP (FIFG, EFF and EMFF)	EU with UK match funding	Industry development and higher standards
Voluntary fishing standards schemes (Responsible Fishing Scheme, Vessel Quality and Hygiene Scheme, White Fish Quality Improvement Initiative)	Seafish, Seafood Scotland and Shetland Seafood Quality Control	Improved catch quality and fisher safety
Industry standards schemes including welfare (Tartan Mark, Code of Good Practice for salmon and trout farming; Shellfish Code of Good Practice)	Scottish Salmon Producers' Organisation/ Quality Trout UK	
Association of Scottish Shellfish Growers	Farming standards established. Scottish salmon established as premium product	
Certification – quality and welfare	GAA, GLOBALG.A.P RSPCA (Freedom Food)	Incentive for higher welfare standards
Codes of practice for food hygiene generally and for fish	Codex Alimentarius	Global standards established
Food Hygiene Rating Scheme/Food Hygiene Information Scheme and regulatory monitoring	FSA and FSS	Higher food safety standards
Food safety certification	BRC Global Standards, SALSA, STS Public Sector	Higher food safety standards
Award schemes (Quality Processor Award, Quality Wholesaler Award)	Seafish	Higher food safety and quality standards
Fish and Chips Awards	Seafish and NFFF	Higher food safety and quality standards
Training/qualifications for food processors and fish retailer	Seafood Training Academy	Improved industry practice

Consumption

Governance mechanism	Governance source	Impacts
Public nutritional advice about seafood consumption	FSA then Public Health England, NHS and FSS	Not known but likely to have increased consumption by those making other healthy lifestyle choices
Public procurement	UK government	Contracts specify nutritional seafood guidelines-based provision and sustainable sourcing
Availability of greater range and convenience of seafood options	Retail and foodservice outlets	Greater range consumed
Seafood promotion	Fish is the Dish, TV programmes, books, retail	Not known but likely to have increased consumption range
Persuading consumers to sustainable choices	MSC, ASC, MCS, fish2fork by certified products, advice lists and supermarket ratings	Not known but sales of certified products indicate support for certification

returned, something which became apparent when the herring fishery had to be closed in the late 1970s.

The time was ripe for fisheries governance which had never been in place before and because the UK was now in the European Economic Community this came under the umbrella of the Common Fisheries Policy. The way it developed has been described in Chapter 3. Why did it take such a long time, three decades, for the CFP to produce positive results for fisheries? There were four main reasons. First of all the CFP was not designed at the outset to be a tool for sustainable management but rather for sharing resources and promoting the common market. Only gradually did it develop the range of mechanisms and arrangements needed for effective fishery management. This was in response to criticisms and campaigning from various sources together with the unavoidable recognition of stock declines. Second, the European fisheries needing to be managed are very complicated in the variety of species, ecologies, types of fishing practised and the history of fishing in these waters by different nations; never before had fisheries management of such a complex situation been attempted. Third, for the CFP to work, fishers and the fishing industry as a whole needed to accept the conservation case and support the management mechanisms. Finally, it required politicians to make quota decisions in line with scientific evidence and to implement other key policies such as decommissioning and enforcement in a constructive way. The second factor continues to be the case and while no-one now doubts the necessity for fishery management, the change in sentiment among fishers and politicians sits side by side with the desire to get the best deal each year. The impact of CFP policies and legislation eventually was a positive one in relation to the Northern waters of most interest to Britain, but it is a conditional positivity. It can never be a done deal because without continuation of management policies in line with scientific advice and their ongoing enforcement the situation could deteriorate again.

The distribution of national quotas decided under the CFP has involved another set of governance decisions, these being under UK control. The way that quotas have been shared out between fishing sectors has resulted in one part, the inshore fleet of under 10 metre boats, being severely disadvantaged. Changing the balance should be done as a matter of basic fairness and to support the social and economic sustainability of the coastal communities to which these fishers belong; the smaller vessels also employ more sustainable fishing methods. In the section of the fleet that has the lion's share of quota, a significant proportion is held by non-British owners, thanks to quota privatisation. Taking all these factors into account, the present distribution of the British share of quota within the fleet is not in the overall public interest.

Neither is the outcome of the series of quota decisions which have resulted in the greater part of it being semi-privatised. The beneficiaries were those fishing at the time when quota shares, which subsequently morphed into fixed quota allocations, were distributed and the companies who over time could afford to buy them out; the losers are individuals who now face much greater financial barriers to entering the fishing industry on an independent basis and the public at large which receives no benefit from the use of this public resource. This could be changed if the right to fish were to be treated like other coastal resources (as with Crown Estate leases) and rents charged for set time periods. The quota distribution issues bear on the economic and social sustainability of the fishing industry while a fairer share for the small-scale sector would also support environmental sustainability.

MSC certification of course has its raison d'être in improving the sustainability of fish stocks. As has been seen, there is disagreement as to whether all its certified fisheries are in fact sustainably managed and about what if any contributions the scheme has made to ecosystem improvements. Nevertheless, the general impact has undoubtedly been improved fisheries management as the scheme is built on the idea that improvements are not only made in order to obtain certification but also as a condition for maintaining it. The limitation is that it only covers a minority of global fisheries but MSC-certified fisheries do make a worthwhile contribution to the UK supply chain though there do not seem to be any figures for exactly what proportion it represents. The original theory behind certification was that consumers would be the engine of governance through buying choices, but it has turned out to be supermarkets and large foodservice chains that are playing this role. Their demand for certified seafood indicates that non-certified products will be at a growing disadvantage in profitable markets such as the UK. The MSC scheme as far as its principles and requirements are concerned has also been affected by global governance in the form of the FAO's Code of Conduct for Responsible Fisheries and eco-labelling guidelines. The MSC while being an agent of governance from the fishery perspective is dependent on the governance provided by state management (individually or in co-operation) in regulating and enforcing fisheries management rules.

Governance applied to domestic aquaculture has a bedrock of legislation but also more widespread governance inputs from other sources. The impact of the legislation is to set boundaries which can resist environmental damage, to safeguard water usage and to prevent the spread of fish diseases. Industry-led governance in the form of codes of practice has established species and farming specific standards for salmon, trout and shellfish. Certification from various bodies raises standards and is relevant to some imports. Such certification has also had the global governance input of FAO guidelines. The only privately-originating standards to be regulated are those for organic production, strengthening these specific rules with legal backing.

As mentioned in relation to MSC certification, governance for greater sustainability of fisheries has come from major supermarkets and large foodservice companies meaning that they have incentivised improved fisheries management. The same impetus has been relevant to the general aquaculture certifications. While for some of these companies environmental policies were self-generated, others were woken to the issue by various forms of NGO campaigning. They proved to be quite effective not only in relation to the companies concerned but in generating wider public awareness of sustainability issues. Seafish and trade bodies have also played a governance role with advice about sourcing sustainably. The combination of all these types of governance with state regulation has surely contributed to the eventual (partial) success of CFP fisheries management in which, as noted, key factors have been the fishing industry and political motivation.

One other significant issue affecting supply is forced labour which, as well as being a question of human rights and social sustainability, is associated with illegal fishing and therefore environmental sustainability. Awareness of this problem in seafood supply chains whether by companies or the general public is recent, and in addition it is much harder to tackle so time will tell whether the governance being exerted can be successful.

Food safety and quality encompass several dimensions which have attracted various modes of governance. There is a fairly comprehensive body of EU and UK legislation directed to food safety and it is presumed that this has safeguarded human health. An underlying element of global governance is provided by successive editions of the relevant elements of Codex Alimentarius. Legislative requirements such as those relating to cleanliness and cold storage have also contributed to better quality which it may be recalled was often poor before these rules came into effect. Active monitoring of land premises (though not of most vessels) has been an indispensable aspect of the effectiveness of such legislation. The modernisation of infrastructure and of processors' buildings and equipment has made a massive positive difference to the quality of seafood for which EU funding under the CFP was crucial; UK governments had never previously given any attention to these key parts of food chains.

An impressive body of private governance initiatives has also provided significant inputs to improved safety and quality. They have related to care of wild catch, farming methods and standards to be applied during processing and distribution. Seafish has made a special contribution to improved quality with its certification and award schemes relating to fishing, processing, distribution and the fish and chips sector; the latest initiative for fishing ports will no doubt also be an incentive to better standards. The Seafood Training Academy, another Seafish enterprise jointly with various partners, has been another pole of the structure that has contributed to greatly improved quality standards throughout the chain.

Welfare standards for fish were also examined under the quality heading and here the judgement must be more equivocal. While farmed fish has been brought under general legislation dealing with the welfare of kept animals there has so far been a failure to legislate for their specific situation. The disparity has been most conspicuous in the omission of fish from legal provisions relating to humane slaughter. The gap has been partly filled by the welfare provisions of aquaculture certification schemes and by Farm Animal Welfare Council/Committee guidelines but of course these are not compulsory. They do, however, have a background of global and European governance provided by the World

Organisation for Animal Health (OIE) and under the European Convention for the Protection of Animals Kept for Farming Purposes (ECPAFP).

Finally, governance of consumption has been considered, recognising that this is an area where there can only be influencing activities, the impact of which will depend on how they interact with many social factors. Here the state activity has been to publish nutritional guidelines founded on best evidence but not to actively promulgate them with one positive exception in that they are incorporated into public procurement guidance. Spreading the word then falls to commercial interests with the likelihood that the message is altered in transmission. Retail and foodservice providers have greatly extended the choice of seafood but consumption has continued to fall well below the recommendations especially for the most health-relevant oily fish element. Whether consumption is greater than it would have been without the public nutritional message is not known, but it is likely that people who generally follow healthy living advice are including oily fish in their diet so the message is probably benefiting at least a section of the population.

In summary, the governance mechanisms have achieved important public benefits particularly in two areas: the first has been moves to more sustainable fishing and aquaculture practice, countering to a significant extent the environmental damage of unfettered economic and technological developments, the second, improvements in the quality and range of seafood that can now be enjoyed. In both of these, the major governance contribution has been public from the British state together with the EU. For sustainability global governance has also provided important markers, starting with UNCLOS and continuing with various FAO contributions. Private interests have made noteworthy contributions, with certification supporting more sustainable fishing and a host of schemes facilitating improved practices in aquaculture, handling the catch and throughout the processing and distribution sections of the supply chain. Civil society, mainly in the form of environmental NGOs, has also played a helpful part in raising general awareness of sustainability issues and in motivating retailers and other companies to use their purchasing power to progress them.

However, there are also limitations to what these governance activities have accomplished. Sustainable fishing has only been realised in a section of European waters and needs continuing vigilance while it has not been achieved at all in much of the rest of the oceans including areas from which certain species are imported. There are also sustainability issues over certain farmed imports. In terms of UK implementation, there are distributional issues over the share-out of fishing quotas which need to be addressed. Legislative gaps regarding farmed fish welfare have been noted and there are no guidelines about reducing the suffering involved in the deaths of captured fish. In relation to food safety, the scientific knowledge needed to deal with norovirus is still being acquired while action to deal with the broader health issue of antibiotics in farming has been slow in coming but is now on the way. As with other sectors, food security has been ignored and with it the case for state action to advance aquaculture in Britain. Finally, along with other problematic aspects of the nation's diet, the benefits of oily fish are not being experienced by much of the population so the nutritional guidelines are not having the desired effect.

Brexit and the governance of the seafood supply chain

Given the achievements and also the limitations of governance in the seafood supply chain, the potential impact of Britain's planned departure from the EU, Brexit, can be considered. The two key areas are fishing and food safety regulation and issues connected with them such as traceability and labelling. What interlinks with all of them is the issue of trade, the nature of future arrangements between the UK and the EU and the extent of tariffs and non-tariff barriers that will be in place.

After Brexit and any transitional period, the UK will be an independent coastal state under UNCLOS (United Nations Convention on the Law of the Sea) and the country's EEZ (Exclusive Economic Zone) will no longer be part of EU waters. But waters and fish are not the same and obviously the latter are not governed by human-made boundaries. Nearly all commercially fished stocks in the British EEZ are shared with neighbours and so need to be managed jointly. As noted previously, UNCLOS lays down responsibilities as well as rights of coastal states, high among them being conservation and ensuring that fish are not exploited beyond MSY (Maximum Sustainable Yield) level. This means that in practice the demands of sustainable fisheries management limit the extent to which states can exercise sovereignty and act unilaterally (Ntona 2016).

The British share of quota in the CFP, as explained in Chapter 3, had a basis in historic catch records, a customary method at the time, which was then embodied in the relative stability principle. However, zonal attachment has subsequently been in use (in the EU-Norway agreement) and presents a more sophisticated approach. This is based on the distribution of each stock over time in different parts of the sea during fish life stages, taking into account that spawning, the juvenile phase and feeding may be in different waters to where stocks become fishable and are caught. Applying the concept is not straightforward and will be challenging given the complex mix of stocks in the UK's EEZ. Scientific analysis, which is ongoing and incomplete, so far on the basis just of adult populations, indicates a shift generally in Britain's favour, for some stocks to a large extent. This reflects the current situation but once adopted zonal attachment might have unforeseen consequences if, as predicted, climate change results in significant fish movements such as cod going north. The UK government has indicated that it will use zonal attachment principles for future international quota sharing (DEFRA 2018). For its part, the European Commission has proposed the maintenance of the existing sharing arrangements over fishing, specifically linking them with general trade concessions.[1]

If the total amount fished is not to change and to be maintained within sustainability objectives, any gains by Britain must be to the detriment of other countries whose nationals have been fishing these seas legitimately for decades, even centuries in some cases. Some EU countries obtain as much as half of what they fish (by volume or value) in the UK EEZ (Le Gallic, Mardle & Metz 2017) so have a lot at stake. There are indeed legal questions about the extent to which they might have historic fishing rights and while some analysis has concluded that such claims will not be upheld there are indications that they will be asserted nevertheless (Churchill 2016; Syreglou et al. 2017).[2] On the British side, an important factor is that Irish and French waters accessed through the CFP are valuable to English fishers though unimportant to Scottish ones so there are different UK interests (Lebrecht 2016). Hence negotiations about the allocation of quota in the UK EEZ will be very difficult. The worst outcome would be a failure to reach an agreement and the UK and the EU separately setting their own quotas resulting in an excessive overall total, overfishing and a potential reversal of the hard-won gains in stock recovery (Carpenter 2017; House of Lords European Union Committee 2016). The mackerel dispute and consequent overfishing noted in Chapter 3 stands as a warning about the risks of parties setting quotas independently when they have failed to achieve a shared arrangement.

Modelling the effect of zonal attachment in combination with different scenarios for future trade relationships has shown that additional quota could produce sizeable gains for some sections of the British fishing industry which would outweigh possible disbenefits arising from the imposition of tariffs. However, for the large number of small-scale fishers holding little or no quota, any gains would be outweighed by losses. This is because most concentrate on non-quota shellfish for which the EU is the largest market and their customer base would be damaged by tariffs plus other barriers that result in time-consuming and freshness-destroying border checks. (ABPmer et al. 2018; Carpenter 2017). Thus it has been estimated that nearly all elements of the seafood industry in Wales would be net losers of expected Brexit changes because it consists mainly of small boats taking shellfish (Carpenter, Williams & Walmsley 2018). Trade restrictions would also have negative effects on other sectors of the seafood industry namely aquaculture and processing and here too there would be no offsetting gains.[3]

A key role of the state is to balance competing interests and claims in order to optimise public benefit. At stake are the public gains from protecting fish resources and the marine environment generally for the future, gains for fishing interests from possible increased quota, continuing access to EU waters for fishing interests that depend on it and the trading arrangements that will be best for all sectors of the seafood industry as well as the economy as a whole. Compromises and concessions are to be expected and should be welcomed, not criticised, especially as trade with the lowest possible tariffs and fewest non-tariff barriers is the overriding need of a great part of the seafood sector. In addition, under UNCLOS there is a responsibility to minimise economic impacts on those from other countries accustomed to fishing in a nation's EEZ. So, even considering just the seafood sector, let alone the rest of the British economy, it would not, as some would have it, be a 'betrayal' to agree fishing rights in the UK EEZ to other EU countries in return for better trade conditions as well as complementary fishing access but a sensible maximisation of benefits for a wide range of interests.[4] Moreover, the overwhelming priority, sustainable management of fish stocks, requires co-operation and the maintenance of good relationships between states which can be facilitated by give-and-take over fishing access (Phillipson & Symes 2018).

The share-out of national quota is another issue where the state's role of balancing benefits to different groups is at issue. This has always been the UK's responsibility but Brexit provides an opportunity to revisit the arrangements. Disappointingly, the government has indicated an intention to leave untouched the existing system of semi-privatised FQAs (fixed quota allocations). Neither has it suggested any action in relation to foreign ownership of quota other than to strengthen Economic Link requirements. Proposals to use new criteria for allocating expected additional quota as a result of moving to zonal attachment that may benefit the small-scale sector are welcome but insufficient to rectify the situation affecting small boat fishers. The campaigning group, Fishing for Leave, has urged the replacement of TACs, associated as they are with the CFP, by effort management in the form of days at sea; in response the government proposes to carry out a limited trial of this approach in low-impact fisheries but it is clear that quota will continue to be the basic currency in which the right to fish is expressed and controlled (DEFRA 2018; Fishing for Leave 2017).

Brexit impacts on the supply of seafood for the domestic market will depend on eventual changes affecting both fishing and trade. Additional quota for whitefish, especially cod and haddock, would allow the British fleet to contribute a greater share of what is required for domestic consumption than it has done in recent years. However, nothing suggests that the UK would stop needing to import sizeable quantities of these species as presently supplied by Iceland and Norway. The option of Britain re-entering the European Free Trade Association to which these countries belong having been discounted, individual trade agreements will be needed with each and it seems likely that they will enable tariff-free whitefish imports to continue but there may be a gap before permanent arrangements are concluded (Daðason 2018).[5] As Britain imports a range of other seafood, fished and farmed, from many other countries some time will elapse before trading relations with all of them are put on the new basis; any impact on prices and availability is unpredictable in advance.

The other section of the seafood supply chain where EU regulation has been of fundamental importance is that of food safety and connected requirements such as traceability and labelling. Unlike the case with fisheries, when it comes to food standards there have not been calls for Brexit to bring major change. On the contrary, the sentiments expressed have been about safeguarding the standards achieved through this legislation, strengthening some of them and not allowing them to be weakened (Davies 2016; Leedham & Wareing 2017). Thus in terms of acceptability EU food regulations, including the specifications noted in this book relating to all aspects of production, have been a resounding success and must have prevented a considerable amount of illness.[6]

Under the *European Union (Withdrawal) Act 2018* EU food laws and implementing legislation will become part of the domestic system in the new category of 'retained EU law' on exit but will be open to subsequent alteration. Concerns over standards declining in relation to future trade agreements have been expressed in relation to meat and dairy products and not so far seafood but this could arise in the future. However, the importance of exports to continental Europe of shellfish, farmed salmon and other seafood products which will have to adhere to EU standards should be a safeguard for retaining these rules. In addition, the voluntary codes and certification systems used in the processing part of the seafood chain are all founded on the bedrock of existing UK and therefore EU law and it seems very unlikely that they would be made less stringent.

In addition to the major themes of fishing and food safety, there are some other Brexit issues that impinge on the seafood supply chain. In relation to the production end, aquaculture and inshore fisheries benefit from European environmental legislation which has among other things improved water quality in rivers and along the coasts. It seems likely that leaving the EU will lead to the weakening of environmental protections with unpredictable impacts on fish and shellfish (Baldock et al. 2016). Moving on to the middle part of the chain two prominent Brexit themes have been delays in the distribution system due to new border controls and labour issues. In relation to seafood, the former seems more likely to be relevant to exports than to imports for domestic consumptions as the most important come from two countries outside the EU, Iceland and Norway, and are landed in a different port from the main entry point from continental Europe. However, the dependence of the seafood processing sector on workers from EU countries is just as great as in rest of the food industry and may be expected to involve similar solutions in due course. Finally, near the consumer end of the chain, the important contributions to food safety made through European arrangements, including by EFSA, over risk assessment, risk management and the provision of warning systems for food safety and food crime will need to be replaced, requiring additional resources and possibly new powers for the FSA and FSS (Ainsworth 2017; Hawes 2018).

The seafood chain and governance theories

This book, pointing to tremendous changes in the seafood system, began by outlining two strands of theories relevant to understanding the rules that have affected them. Having now examined the seafood chain in detail we can ask how well theories about the state and about supply chains fit this particular case, what is the role of civil society and what are the implications for serving public interests.

Themes in academic accounts of the changing role of states have included a reducing, more distant but possibly more strategic function, the 'regulatory state' which controls at a distance through a series of specialised agencies and changes in governance processes particularly highlighting participatory networks. Some contributions have advocated a reduced role for states. However, what has been demonstrated in relation to seafood has been a hugely increased role for state regulation in relation to two major areas, fisheries management and food safety. For the UK this has been exercised at both European and national levels with significant global governance in the background. Another important area of new state action has been over aquaculture which is more nationally based.

Despite the pain of the long-drawn-out process before the CFP delivered benefits, it is hard to see how any other type of mechanism would have been more effective. This is not to deny that it could have been better designed from the start, been better supported and therefore delivered results sooner. However, fishing mortality had to be drastically curtailed so that stocks could recover and only state-level authority and legitimacy could impose and enforce the massive restrictions required. Equally, given the complexity of the Atlantic fisheries and the history of fishing within them, inter-state co-operation was essential and indeed remains so. It should also be remembered that the MSC certification scheme depends on state organised fisheries management to be in place.

However, the successive reforms of the CFP have increased pluralism in its operation, validating to some extent theories that emphasise widening participation in governance. First of all this has applied to the most recent reform process in which the European Parliament was a co-decision-maker, not only massively enlarging democratic input but also a conduit for outside representations which came from environmental NGOs as well as fishing interests. Second, one particular aspect of the 2002 reform has brought greater pluralism into the CFP with the creation of the RACs, subsequently ACs and the more recent ideas about focusing management on sea basins. The CFP remains very centralised with direction from the European Commission and crucial quota decisions by the Council, that is politicians from member states, but the future could see more being delegated to ACs. To the extent that this happens, it is likely that there will be better decision-making from those with more direct knowledge of the fish stocks in question, but the framework and legislation will still come from the EU centrally so this is not an area of reducing state action.

Within the UK the basic fact of the imposition of fisheries management is strong state action, nationally enforced. However, internal management of the policy displays various examples of state delegation. This has included devolution to Northern Ireland, Scotland and Wales, the delegation of much quota distribution and management to the POs (Producers' Organisations) and local management of coastal fisheries and other marine activities. For England, much of the state's marine responsibilities including for fisheries have been passed to the quango MMO (Marine Management Organisation), an executive non-departmental public body, that is not under direct ministerial control. However, the equivalent Marine Scotland after being set up on a similar basis was subsequently taken back into the Scottish Government. In Wales, Inshore Fishery Groups were established to locally manage marine affairs but at the time of writing have been suspended and the functions taken back into the Welsh Government. These examples illustrate that agencification is not a simple one-way process; in fact, developments following devolution have generally shown that there is not a single process at work but that variable decisions may be taken on the basis of different political views.

Aquaculture regulation has developed from scratch in Britain in response to the development of the industry, its purposes ranging across environmental protection, animal health and food safety. Rather than delegation, there has been an irregular growth of governance mechanisms with additional responsibilities assumed by existing agencies.

Parallel to the MMO in some ways, as another quango, Seafish occupies a more ambiguous position in relation to the way governance responsibilities for the seafood industry have been delegated. With the greater part of its funding coming from an industry levy, albeit one that is imposed by the state, its orientation is primarily to those who pay it, rather than the public at large, something which was emphasised after the Cleasby review when the future of the organisation was in question, but it was able to demonstrate sufficient support to ensure continuation. Hence it has been characterised in this book as a combination public-private agency. Seafish has done valuable work in promoting sustainable sourcing and awareness of labour exploitation and has undertaken various initiatives to improve the quality of seafood. These have all been of public benefit but the motivation has always been to promote the prosperity of the industry. Likewise, the organisation does address consumers, particularly through the Fish is the Dish website and its associated activities, providing useful information but the fundamental purpose is to promote seafood purchasing rather than public health or sustainable consumption. The role of Seafish can also be contrasted to that of the MMO; the latter implements regulation while Seafish carries out additional promotional activity. It is therefore the more surprising that DEFRA seems to have delegated responsibilities for future planning of seafood supply and the promotion of aquaculture development to Seafish. By contrast, although Seafish is an organisation serving the whole of the UK, it is the Scottish Government that has produced the Scottish Aquaculture Strategy.

Food safety is another field where there has been a striking growth in state governance, resulting in the present EU–UK regulatory system. Rather than a case of command-and-control being replaced by decentralised arrangements the history of food safety regulation in Britain generally shows that it has sometimes been lax in the past but has become more tightly controlled in recent decades. This has been in reaction to food crises and more generally to cope with the complexity of modern food chains. Another key factor in the strengthening of food safety legislation has been trade. The original rationale for the much of the early European regulation was to facilitate the common, then the single, market and food safety rules will be a key aspect of any future trade agreements which Britain makes with other countries. But while the regulatory structure, largely based on EU rules has greatly strengthened, the local monitoring and enforcement capabilities have in recent years been weakened as a result of budget cuts.

Private governance has been very noticeable in the pursuit of food safety and quality more generally as described in Chapter 4 and has certainly contributed to overall improvements. But the chronology of governance developments indicates that public action has generally led and private governance followed, possibly then developing further in various directions. Market mechanisms work best within a framework of state regulation which establishes both standards and a level playing field that prevents competition driving them downwards. Private standards schemes do have monitoring systems which include sanctions, but it should also not be neglected that the enforcement of food safety standards has ultimately rested with local authorities.

State governance theory has little or nothing to say about consumption which has rarely been the object of direct regulation, although the sugar tax does mark a shift in this direction. In relation to consumption of seafood, state governance activity has been in the form of nutritional guidelines, the fish two-a-week advice which had the convoluted trajectory recounted in Chapter 5. This was bound up with the history of the FSA. Its establishment with responsibilities previously administered directly by government departments was another instance of the delegationary trend, this time as a non-ministerial government department meaning one notch less independence than the quangos MMO and Seafish. However, the removal of its nutritional remit which was transferred to the Department of Health for England and the Welsh Assembly Government was a reversal of delegation at least for England. The Scottish Government retained this role in its FSA office, later transferred to the new Food Standards Scotland. The FSS is independent of ministers, directly reporting to the Scottish Parliament so there is more independence for the nutritional responsibility in Scotland than in England. Public Health England which has assumed responsibility for national nutritional guidelines is an executive agency of the Department of Health so the delegation there has not gone very far. All of this again shows that agencification is not a simple process and subject to political choices. The diminution of the FSA's role had nothing to do with better governance and it has not served the public well as reflected by the complications of locating the seafood advice.

The FSA's controversial plans for changes to food safety monitoring are an example of a different form of delegation. As described in Chapter 4, they would incorporate the outputs of private audit assessments into the regulatory system for implementing legislative food safety requirements, apparently diminishing the role of local authorities, though that is denied. The proposals might be considered an example of New Public Management thinking and a partial privatising of certain state responsibilities. They have been put forward in the context of severe cutbacks in the monitoring capacities of local authorities and it is hard to see what public benefits will ensue.

The private standards and audit schemes which the FSA proposes to use are a key aspect of how many supply or commodity chain theories consider governance to be exerted and the next question is how far these apply to seafood. They do, in part, but the picture is much more diverse than usually portrayed.

First, it is worth emphasising that some schemes are producer-led and concerned with improved market positioning, something which is rarely mentioned in the literature. This applies to the Code of Good Practice for Scottish Finfish Aquaculture and related Quality Trout schemes; Scottish shellfish farmers also have a Code of Practice. Related to these are the various Seafish quality schemes and awards which have involved Seafish setting standards in conjunction with industry representatives. These have not been put into operation to meet specific buyer requirements, rather to generally raise the level of standards for the greater commercial success of participating companies.

Second, the MSC and various aquaculture certification schemes have a double aspect. They certainly are in parts of the seafood chain used in the way many accounts describe: as a tool for buyer-driven control, an exercise of market power to ensure that the end products will meet the criteria set which as well as safety and eating quality may include sustainability and labour conditions. But there has also been considerable self-organisation by sections of the British fishing industry to obtain MSC certification or at least carry out pre-assessment exercises because these activities are seen to both improve the viability of fisheries and to strengthen the market position of those fishing them. The Global Salmon Initiative is of a similar nature with member companies committing to obtaining ASC certification. So these schemes may be as useful to producers as to buyers.

The third point relates to the spread of BRC and SALSA food safety schemes. The impression given by those working in processing companies who were interviewed was that such certifications were a prerequisite for operating in the market, and particularly if supplying supermarkets. However, this did not seem to be experienced as a particular burden and might be something they would expect from their own suppliers. Unlike the case when standards are imposed on producers in other countries, they are easier to accept as they have a starting point in domestic legislation and are determined within a common culture. So although these certifications are required by large buyers, they do not seem to be experienced as a form of onerous control.

The final issue is that supermarkets are not able to dominate the whole of the seafood industry and impose their own rules in the way they do with certain other products. Capture fish is inherently less amenable to manipulation in terms of availability and characteristics than other foods so while considerable standardisation of products has occurred, especially with farmed output, the retailers cannot control what is available. Further, as well as ensuring the safety and traceability of supplies, as with all food, they need to satisfy themselves that capture fish has been caught legally and that products conform to their sustainable sourcing policies. These factors together with the diversity and complexity of sourcing that is required militate against detailed retailer control. Instead, the stores need to have considerable reliance on the knowledge and capabilities of their seafood industry suppliers. This is the sort of situation in which supermarkets need a partnership, even if not one of equals. A combination of such factors, together with individual choices as exemplified by a small number of the research interviewees, has allowed some companies, as these respondents stated, to see themselves as standing up to the supermarkets and sometimes refusing business with them on terms they disliked. The supermarkets are also less able to control overall prices. Although much reduced compared to the historic situation, a fair proportion of first sale seafood in Britain still goes through the auction system at market prices which, therefore, cannot be forced down in the way they have been known to do in relation to some other foods by oligopolistic purchasing. Not only does a non-supermarket retail sector continue, which is also the case for other fresh foods, but the relatively large size of the foodservice market for seafood compared to the retail one is suggested as another factor in limiting supermarket control. In addition, a manufacturer brand presence acts as a counterweight, especially for frozen items. So while the retail chains do have considerable buying power, which they no doubt use to reduce the prices they pay, it has its limits.

Supermarkets do not drive the seafood chain but neither does any other section of it. It is much too diverse to be vertically co-ordinated. In the past, there has been some attempt at vertical co-ordination such as that of Mac-Fisheries in its heyday when the company supplied its shops from its own trawlers and wholesale business, as noted in Chapter 6, but this did not last. The aquaculture sector is the one most amenable to control; large Scottish salmon producers do have their own primary processing plants and one is co-ordinating upstream by establishing its own feed plant but these activities are limited to one sector.

Thus governance of supply chains has contingent aspects rather than being simply predictable as a function of the dominance of the most powerful companies within it, something not much considered in the agri-food and supply chain literature. This is why the Cox power model has been employed in Chapter 4. It provides scope for different relationships within any supply chain based on what parties need from and are able to offer each other, grouped into the four possible types. Buyer dominance, not only by the major retailers but also by large foodservice companies may indeed be the position which some seafood processing and distribution companies experience. However, there is also scope for certain levels of interdependence due to the various complexities attached to sourcing seafood which have been mentioned. If a given company has a range of customers, it may have more than one type of relationship with various of them and could in some of them even be in a dominant position itself. Smaller companies may be more likely to have relationships of independence or interdependence with small or medium enterprise buyers. Even within this framework, choices are not simply a reflection of structural relationships but are made as a result of assessments by individuals as was evident in the statements of some of the research interviewees.

Given all these factors and the variability found even among the small number of interviewed companies that had dealings with supermarkets, the idea of generalising a buyer-driven chain or other single characterisation is quite inappropriate. Only a minority of seafood companies serve the major retailers directly or even indirectly through supplying those that do so. The use of the 'buyer-driven' concept in the literature has generally been to characterise export chains, typically moving products from poorer producer countries to richer purchasing destinations as set out in the discussion of global commodity/value chains in Chapter 2. The model may indeed apply to certain imports of farmed seafood into the British supply chain but certainly not to all of it. Much imported seafood into the UK is from other rich countries which have comparable domestic standards and whose producers have other potential customers. While the major retailers do exert the power of their purchasing heft this is used to achieve lower prices while at the same time they need collaboration with their seafood suppliers to obtain the range and quality of products they seek. Verified standards are useful to both parties, buyer and supplier as part of this collaboration. This will include standards and systems that enable buyers to meet their sustainable sourcing policies if relevant.

If standards do not provide a single governance thread, the question is: how are seafood chains governed. Part of the answer is that with so many variables – different species, domestic fishing and farming, farmed and wild imports, large and very small processing companies – there is no single governance system. What does apply to British primary producers and processors and European producers exporting into the UK has been a unifying regulatory system. The role of state regulation is often mentioned in the agri-food literature but so often, after such an acknowledgement, most attention has been given to private forms of governance and NGOs. The importance of state regulation has rarely been given the attention it merits, something which has been redressed in this book.

In addition, the most widely used certification schemes provide a certain unity of shared expectations about acceptable methods. In some chains, such standards may be a dominating governance factor, particularly those involving imports from countries where state regulatory systems are less developed or enforced. In others, they are an aspect of collaboration and mutually useful as no company wants to be caught out for putting unsafe or illegally produced food in the market.

Many supply chain analysts have given special attention to the governance roles of NGOs. Their influence in relation to seafood has taken various forms which vary according to how far the orientation of each organisation is to work with companies in supply chains, as WWF did when instigating both the MSC and ASC schemes, or to (possibly hostile) campaigning from the outside like Greenpeace. The MCS fills an intermediate place, publishing its judgements and advice on what fish to eat or avoid from the outside but these are sufficiently authoritative for acceptance by at least some retail and food-service buyers. Greenpeace has pursued action in the fishing part of the chain on various fronts including over the use of FADs to catch tuna, against deep-sea trawling in general and for a higher share of quota to go to the lower impact section of the British fleet, with mixed results to date. Several NGOs, including Greenpeace, have targeted the other end of the chain, the retail and foodservice sectors. Here they have been more successful and achieved change to more sustainable seafood sourcing policies by several key players. However, their interventions have not always succeeded as when several supermarkets refused to complete the MCS questionnaire in its most recent survey or when Sainsbury's continued to stock a tuna brand despite a campaign for this to cease. Embracing sustainability goals fits the quality-oriented marketing strategies of some supermarkets and enhances their brand so this has been a relatively easy achievement for NGOs. Changing fishing practices is much harder.

Environmental NGOs have increased public awareness of sustainability issues relating to seafood and have caused some major commercial buyers to change their practices. In turn, sustainable sourcing policies and consequent interest in purchasing certified seafood have had impacts through the rest of the supply chain and incentivised take-up of the MSC scheme. In addition to this supply chain activity, some NGOs have pursued objectives in the public, state sphere as when lobbying European parliamentarians over the reform of the CFP which probably influenced the outcome. However, their impact should not be over-stated as has occurred in some analysis. The dominant forces impacting on actors in the seafood supply chain are states and regulation from the outside and the more powerful companies within. NGOs can be effective when they influence either of these forces to make changes, but they have neither the political power nor economic resources to achieve change directly.

This returns us to the governance model of the seafood chain put forward in Chapter 2 and drawn in Figure 2.2. Both external and internal sources were posited and both have been demonstrated at work through the stages of the chain as analysed. The strongest have been those external to the supply chain. The dominant impact has been shown to come from the EU–UK regulation imposed on fishing, aquaculture and food processing. Other important actors external to the supply chain are Seafish and certification bodies, the governance they have exerted being mainly supportive in nature. Within supply chains, private governance is applied through standards schemes, which may be available via Producer Organisations or from independent certification bodies and which may be NGO-influenced. The extent of adherence to these forms of private governance required of any company depends on dyadic relationships with suppliers and customers. In many cases the key is power relations within those dyads and which of the parties is dominant.

The second aspect of the model is about governance brought to bear on consumers, as drawn in Figure 2.3. Here, the state element in the form of nutritional guidelines is just one of many and likely to be less important for most than availability with its choice editing, the seafood actually supplied by food producers, retailers and the food service sector. Along with the other three factors at the bottom of the diagram, that is civil society campaigns and advice, the assurance provided by certification and information from various sources, nutritional guidelines play some part in influencing the choices that consumers make.

Governance in food chains has many purposes which in this book have been drawn out for seafood. The most important issue about them is whether their impact is in the public interest or not. For this to be the case, public forms instituted by the state are the key but do not always fulfil this objective. Private forms of governance should also be judged by the same criterion. Civil society can provide input to both types but perhaps the most important contribution it can make is to ensure that the question of what is in the public interest continues to be asked.

Notes

1 See Oliver T 2018, 'EU UK wide apart on fisheries Brexit', *Fishing News*, 15 March 2018.
2 See Barnes R and Rosello M 2016, 'Does Brexit mean plain sailing for UK fishermen ... or stormy waters?', http://theconversation.com, Boffey D 2017, 'UK Fishermen may not win waters back after Brexit, EU memo reveals', *Guardian*, 15 Feb 2017 and Boffey D 2017, 'Denmark to contest UK efforts to "take back control" of fisheries', *Guardian*, 18 Apr 2017.
3 Processed e.g. smoked salmon could in future have a 13% tariff applied by the EU as is currently the case with such products from Norway as explained in Ramsden, N 2018, 'Why Brexit could be a "nightmare" for UK's salmon smokers', *Undercurrent News*, 30 January 2018, accessed 30 August 2018.
4 A statement issued following a meeting of fisher organisations and POs in support of Brexit concluded by referring to political punishment for 'betrayal' if the outcome is not what they want as reported in Hjul J 2018, 'UK fishing groups unite on Brexit stand', *FishUpdate*, 30 April 2018, www.fishupdate.com. Barrie Deas, Chief Executive of the NFFO is quoted as talking about a 'sense of betrayal' over possible concessions in O'Caroll L 2018, 'Fishermen warn against carve-up of UK waters in Brexit deal', *The Guardian*, 13 June 2018.
5 Navarro L 2018, 'For UK and Norway, a smooth Brexit is crucial', *Intrafish*, 30 January 2018, www.intrafish.com reports on a Norway-UK Seafood Summit held

by the Norwegian Seafood Council at which representatives of both countries expressed the desire for existing seafood flows to continue after Brexit.

6 To demonstrate the relative protection given by UK-EU food safety law, Sue Davies, Strategic Policy Adviser for Which?, noted in evidence to a Parliamentary enquiry that the incidence of food poisoning in the US was one in six (16.7%) compared to just one in sixty-six (1.5%) in the UK (House of Commons EFRA Committee 2018). A UK figure of one in 60 is quoted in (HM Government 2013), the US one is from the Center for Disease Control and Prevention, www.cdc.gov/foodborneburden/2011-foodborne-estimates.html, accessed 10 September 2018.

References

ABPmer, InterAnalysis & Vivid Economics 2018, *Seafood Trade Modelling Research Project: Assessing the Impact of Alternative Fish Trade Agreements Post EU-Exit*, Marine Scotland, Edinburgh.

Ainsworth R 2017, *The Food Standards Agency's Preparations for the UK's Exit from the European Union*, Food Standards Agency, London, Report to Board Meeting 20 September 2017.

Baldock D, Buckwell A, Colsa-Perez A, Farmer A, Nesbit M & Pantzar M 2016, *The Potential Policy and Environmental Consequences for the UK of a Departure from the European Union*, Institute for European Environmental Policy, London.

Carpenter G 2017, *Not in the Same Boat: The Economic Impact of Brexit across UK Fishing Fleets*, New Economics Foundation, London.

Carpenter G, Williams C & Walmsley S 2018, *Implications of Brexit for Fishing Opportunities in Wales*, Public Policy Institute for Wales, Cardiff, New Economics Foundation and ABPmer.

Churchill R 2016, *Possible EU Fishery Rights in UK Waters and Possible UK Fishery Rights in EU Waters Post-Brexit: An Opinion Prepared for the Scottish Fishermen's Federation*.

Daðason V 2018, *Iceland, UK and Brexit: How Can Iceland and the UK Make a Better Trade Deal in Lieu of Brexit?*, BSc in Business Administration, Reykjavik University.

Davies S 2016, *Brexit: Risks and Opportunities for Food Policy and Regulation*, Food Research Publication, London.

DEFRA 2018, *Sustainable Fisheries for Future Generations*, Department for Environment, Food and Rural Affairs, London, Cmnd 9660.

Fishing for Leave 2017, *The Brexit Textbook on Fisheries*, Fishing for Leave, Glasgow.

Hawes E 2018, *Leaving the EU: Food Safety*, House of Lords, London, Library Briefing.

HM Government, 2013, *Review of the Balance of Competences between the United Kingdom and the European Union: Animal Health and Welfare and Food Safety Report*, https://assets.publishing.service.gov.uk/government/uploads/system/uploads/attachment_data/file/227367/DEF-PB13979-BalOfComp-HMG-WEB.PDF, accessed 11 October 2018, London.

House of Commons Environment, Food and Rural Affairs Committee 2017, *Brexit: Trade in Food Oral Evidence*, London, HC 348, 6 December 2017.

House of Commons Environment, Food and Rural Affairs Committee 2018, *Brexit: Trade in Food*, London, House of Commons, Third Report of Session 2017–2019, HC 348.

House of Lords European Union Committee 2016, *Brexit: Fisheries*, London, 8th Report of Session 2016–2017, HL Paper 78.

Le Gallic B, Mardle S & Metz, S. 2017, *Research for PECH Committee – Common Fisheries Policy and BREXIT – Trade and Economic Related Issues*, European Parliament, Brussels, Policy Department for Structural and Cohesion Policies.

Lebrecht A 2016, 'Better deal for UK fishermen will be hard to catch', *In Facts*, vol. 2, November.

Leedham O & Wareing P 2017, *Brexit: A Regulatory and Food Safety Perspective*, Leatherhead Food Research, Epsom.

Ntona M 2016, *A Legal Perspective on the Value of Scotland's EU Membership for Sustainable Fisheries*, Strathclyde Centre for Environmental Law & Governance, University of Strathclyde, Glasgow, Policy Brief No 5.

Phillipson J & Symes D 2018, '"A sea of troubles": Brexit and the fisheries question', *Marine Policy*, vol. 90, April, pp. 168–173.

Syreglou S, Baatz Y, Coles R, Hudson D, Quinn S, Serdy A, Tsimplis M, Veal R & Zhang J 2017, *The UK Maritime Sectors Beyond Brexit*, Institute of Maritime Law, University of Southampton, Southampton.

Index

Page numbers in **bold** denote tables, those in *italics* denote figures.

For Product Safety Concerns and Information please contact our EU
representative GPSR@taylorandfrancis.com Taylor & Francis Verlag GmbH,
Kaufingerstraße 24, 80331 München, Germany

Printed and bound by CPI Group (UK) Ltd, Croydon, CR0 4YY
01/05/2025
01858434-0003